STUDY GUIDE

Annette Kujawski Taylor
University of San Diego

Psychology: From Inquiry to Understanding

Second Edition

Scott O. Lilienfeld
Emory University

Steven Jay Lynn
Binghamton University

Laura L. Namy
Emory University

Nancy J. Woolf
University of California at Los Angeles

Allyn & Bacon

Boston Columbus Indianapolis New York San Francisco Upper Saddle River
Amsterdam Cape Town Dubai London Madrid Milan Munich Paris Montreal Toronto
Delhi Mexico City Sao Paulo Sydney Hong Kong Seoul Singapore Taipei Tokyo

10 9 8 7 6 5 4 3 2 1   14 13 12 11 10

Allyn & Bacon
is an imprint of

www.pearsonhighered.com

ISBN-10: 0-205-83883-9
ISBN-13: 978-0-205-83883-7

Table of Contents

CHAPTER 1

1.1   Explain why psychology is more than just common sense
1.2   Explain the importance of science as a set of safeguards against biases
1.3   Describe psychological pseudoscience and distinguish it from psychological science
1.4   Identify reasons we are drawn to pseudoscience
1.5   Identify the key features of scientific skepticism
1.6   Identify and explain six key principles of scientific thinking that will be used throughout the text
1.7   Identify the major theoretical frameworks of psychology
1.8   Describe different types of psychologists and identify what each of them does
1.9   Describe the two great debates that have shaped the field of psychology
1.10   Describe how psychological research affects our daily lives

CHAPTER 2

2.1   Identify heuristics and biases that prevent us from thinking clearly about psychology
2.2   Describe the advantages and disadvantages of using naturalistic observation, case studies, and surveys
2.3   Describe the role of correlational designs and distinguish correlation from causation
2.4   Identify the components of an experiment and the potential pitfalls that can lead to faulty conclusions
2.5   Explain the ethical obligations of researchers toward their research participants
2.6   Describe both sides of the debate on the use of animals as research subjects
2.7   Identify uses of various measures of central tendency and dispersion
2.8   Explain how inferential statistics can help us to determine whether we can generalize from our sample to the full population
2.9   Show how statistics can be misused for purposes of persuasion
2.10   Identify flaws in research design
2.11   Identify skills for evaluating psychological claims in the popular media

CHAPTER 3

3.1   Distinguish the parts of neurons and what they do
3.2   Describe electrical responses of neurons and what makes them possible
3.3   Explain how neurons use neurotransmitters to communicate with each other
3.4   Describe how the brain changes as a result of development, learning, and injury
3.5   Identify what roles different parts of the central nervous system play in behavior
3.6   Clarify how the somatic and autonomic nervous systems work in emergency and everyday situations
3.7   Describe what hormones are and how they affect behavior
3.8   Identify different brain-stimulating, -recording, and -imaging techniques
3.9   Evaluate results demonstrating the brain's localization of function
3.10   Describe genes and how they influence psychological traits
3.11   Explain the concept of heritability and the misconceptions surrounding it

CHAPTER 4

As you begin this course, you probably believe you already know a lot about psychology. You might also believe you know how to study in order to do well in this course. As a check of your knowledge, answer the following questions True or False:

T or F Psychology is primarily interested in abnormal behavior and its treatment.
T or F If you want to learn in college you should focus on your grades.
T or F If you want to remember something you should repeat it over and over.

How well do you think you did? If you are like most students, you answered "True" to each of these questions. Actually, the correct answer to each of the questions is "False." Don't feel bad if you answered these questions incorrectly. They were designed to challenge common misconceptions you might have about both psychology and the tools needed to achieve academic success.

Misconceptions exist in most subjects (e.g., ostriches don't really stick their heads in the ground), but especially in psychology. Throughout the text and this Study Guide you will learn about many misconceptions people hold. For example, the answer to the question "Psychology is primarily about abnormal behavior," is false. Many people think of psychology as the study of abnormal behavior. It is true that some psychologists study behavior that deviates from what is typical and other psychologists study and apply psychological knowledge to aid individuals demonstrating problematic behavior. However, psychology is much broader than the study of abnormal behavior. Most of psychology deals with the normal processes involved in thinking and behaving and many of the applications of psychology are of value to the ordinary individual. For example, among the many things psychologists study is how we learn—something that should be of particular practical interest to you as a college student. Your psychology course, therefore, will help you learn to differentiate claims that are unlikely to make accurate predictions, show you how common beliefs are not really supported by objective evidence, and teach you how to learn in college. Although you will learn more about what cognitive psychologists say about learning in the next section of this Study Guide , here are a few study tips related to common misconceptions.

MISCONCEPTION: MEMORIZING INFORMATION IS THE BEST WAY TO LEARN

Many introductory psychology students are just beginning their college careers. They often believe that the same study strategies that worked for them in high school will be good enough for college. Many of these techniques involve attempts to memorize information through rehearsal. Although such strategies may have helped students get by in high school, they are neither effective nor efficient methods of study at college. Students often spend much more time and effort studying than they need to and are surprised when their efforts don't pay off. Why don't their efforts pay off? Their efforts don't pay off because their study strategies do not involve an effort to *understand* the material.

I'm going to try to demonstrate this point with an exercise. DO NOT READ AHEAD!
Take 20 seconds to memorize the words below. Ready, Go.

I spoon eating a got bowl haven't of I'm oatmeal a but

WITHOUT LOOKING BACK, close your eyes and repeat the words. How did you do?

Now try this second example, the same way:

I'm eating a bowl of oatmeal but I haven't got a spoon.

Now repeat the words. How did you do?

These two examples contained EXACTLY the same words. Why was the second sample easier to remember? Because it was meaningful. The words made sense. Even if it is silly, they at least made a sentence. There is overwhelming evidence (as you will see in Chapter 7 on Memory and in the next section of this Study Guide) that it's easier and more efficient when we try to remember something that's meaningful, compared to trying to memorize something that's meaningless. Therefore, the prerequisite for studying for a test is to first understand the material. Before you try to commit material to memory in a way that will enable you to perform well on an exam, you must first complete the process of understanding. This process does not occur during the last minutes before an exam. Rather it's an ongoing process requiring your actively thinking about the material throughout the semester. This Study Guide includes the kinds of activities that will help you learn how to think about the material at a meaningful level. By reading the text, completing the Study Guide activities, and reviewing your class notes regularly, you will be developing your understanding of the material.

MISCONCEPTION: YOU WILL LEARN BEST IF YOU FOCUS ON GRADES

Not only do students believe that rehearsal is an effective learning strategy, students also believe that they will learn in college by focusing on grades. Grades *are* valuable as reflections of what you have learned and may be used by potential graduate programs and employers as indicators of your knowledge. Thinking about being evaluated can help you focus, prioritize, and avoid distractions when necessary. However, a focus on grades as a reason for studying is not enough to motivate you to *learn* the material. Research shows that when students are focused on a goal that is extrinsic to the task of learning (grades, awards, money), they tend to use superficial strategies and shortcuts to reach their goal—the grade (Nolen, 1996). They are also more likely to be negatively affected by anxiety and more likely to give up when confronted with obstacles. In contrast, when students focus on the task of learning itself, they use strategies that engage them in the process of learning, seek challenges, and show better retention (Dweck & Leggett, 1988: Elliot & McGregor, 1999). By being motivated to learn the material, students are more likely to engage in strategies that result in meaningful, enduring forms of learning and students are more likely to enjoy the process of learning.

Wanting to learn will make little difference if you cannot motivate yourself to exert the effort necessary to engage in effective learning strategies. Most of the students we have met in our 50 (combined) years of teaching say they want to learn and many do know some of the more effective strategies for learning. The majority, however, meet their doom in their lack of self-regulation. Self-regulation involves something called "metacognition" or what you know about what you know, and the motivational and problem-solving skills you put to work in monitoring and improving you knowledge. Self-regulation requires identifying goals and engaging in behaviors that lead to accomplishing your goals (Schunk & Zimmerman, 2001). For example, should your goal be to understand the material in class, self-regulation would involve your monitoring your understanding, figuring out what you need to do if you do not understand, and motivating yourself to actually do what it is you need to do. That is, it involves thought, motivation, and behavior. Monitoring your understanding of the material, therefore, is critical. Self-regulation involves stopping to think about whether you really understand the material and if not, doing something about it.

This Study Guide provides opportunities for you to monitor your learning. Before the practice tests we have included opportunities for you to stop and reflect on how well you know the material before you attempt the test. After taking and scoring the test, you can use your actual score as feedback on both whether you understand the material and whether you are accurately judging your understanding of the material. Finding out that you do not really know the material as well as you think should indicate the need to do something to improve your understanding.

Another critical component of self-regulation is actually motivating yourself to engage in the behaviors that are necessary to improve your learning. Not only should you check your understanding by reviewing your notes regularly, but you must review them far enough before an exam that if they do not make sense, you can get clarification before you start to study. Figuring out what kind of help you need and how to get it will take some thinking. Perhaps you will need to review the material, ask the teacher, or do some additional research. The important thing is to know when you need help understanding the material and to get help when you need it. You cannot and will not do well in college unless you take some responsibility for motivating yourself to do the things you need to do in order to learn. Learning and the good grades that reflect that you've learned involve some effort, some engagement, and some self-regulation.

SOME FINAL MISCONCEPTIONS ON TEST-TAKING AND ESSAY-WRITING

Students hold many misconceptions about test-taking. For example, students believe that cramming the night before the test keeps the information fresh, you shouldn't change your answer, and you should study differently for different types of tests. All of these beliefs have been challenged when looked at objectively. Cramming is ineffective (the next section will elaborate), when you study for any type of test as if it were an essay test you are more likely to study for understanding, and reflection can contribute to your changing a wrong answer to a right answer. In fact, taking your time to think about questions is a critical test taking strategy. In contrast, students tend to rush through tests, possibly to just get them over with. When taking multiple choice tests, they either pick the first answer that sounds good or think of the multiple choice questions as something they either know the answer to or they don't—and they don't take time to stop and think about it.

Advice on taking multiple choice tests:
1) Take your time and THINK.
2) Read each question and each option fully and carefully.
3) BEFORE reading the options, think of a reasonable response on your own.
4) Go through each option as if it were a TRUE/FALSE question.
5) Exclude those that are clearly false.
6) Ask your professor questions, if you find a term ambiguous.
7) Think carefully about your remaining options.

What about essays:
The biggest problem students have with essay tests (and this is true about all students—freshman as well as seniors) is that they don't make their point clearly enough and don't provide clear evidence to support the point. I think students assume professors know the answer so why should you have to explain what you're talking about. Students who do poorly on essay exams either float around describing examples of something without ever clearly stating what point they're trying to make with the examples. OR make some general statement and assume the professor accepts the statement without ever providing examples that demonstrate or clarify the statement. If your answer seems brief, it is probably incomplete!

One method for writing essays is called the X123 method (Kerrigan, 1987). The first thing you write is your X statement: A clear statement of your point. The answer to the essay question. It's what you want to say. The 123 then are each statements that support, demonstrate, and clarify your point. Take this example:

Essay question: What is one major reason students perform less well than they expect on an exam?
X Students are inefficient at studying.
1. Students often wait until right before the exam to do the reading.
2. Students often wait right before the exam to review their notes.
3. Students often try to study what they don't first understand. Then fill out the essay, providing evidence and giving examples to support your 123 statements.

As a final point, the purpose of this Study Guide is to actively engage you in the process of learning about psychology. We hope that as you use this study tool you will develop your ability to think critically, you will become actively engaged in thinking your course material, and you will learn that learning about psychology is both a valuable *and* an enjoyable experience.

References

Dweck, C. S., & Leggett, E. (1988). A social-cognitive approach to motivation and personality, *Psychological Review, 95*, 256–273.

Elliot, A. J., & McGregor, H. A. (1999). Text anxiety and the hierarchical model of approach and avoidance achievement motivation. *Journal of Personality and Social Psychology, 76*, 628–644.

Kerrigan, W. (1987). *Writing to the Point*. New York: Harcourt Brace Jovanovich.

Kuhn, D. (1999). A developmental model of critical thinking. *Educational Researcher, 28*, 16–25, 46.

Nolen, S. B. (1996). Why study? Reasons for learning influence strategy selection *Educational Psychology Review, 8*(4), 335–355.

Schunk, D. H., & Zimmerman, B. J. (2001). *Self-Regulated Learning and Academic Achievement: Theoretical Perspectives*. Mahwah, NJ: Lawrence Erlbaum Associates Publisher.

Cognitive psychology is the scientific study of those behaviors related to thinking. What can cognitive psychology teach you about how to learn? Fortunately, MUCH! A wealth of good evidence shows what works best when it comes to things such as remembering—probably the heart and soul of student life—cramming all that information into your head for longer than just a few days, or even for just a few weeks.

As you will learn in Chapter 7 on Memory, remembering something involves three steps: encoding, storage, and retrieval. First you have to *encode* the information, or you have to get it in. Second, you have to *store* it someplace. Let's not worry about where for now, but how. If you don't store it in such a way that you can find it, well, later, when you need the information, encoding it will have been a wasted effort. Finally, you have to be able to *retrieve* the information, whenever you want to. The information must be available: you got it in and you got it stored somewhere, AND it must be accessible: you can put your (mental) finger right on it.

Because cognitive psychology can teach you so much, picking a starting point could be difficult. Except that it's not: you can begin your studying where cognitive psychologists begin to look at how best to remember, and that is with . . .

ORGANIZATION

LESSON #1: ORGANIZE INFORMATION BEFORE YOU SIT DOWN TO STUDY IT.

How Do We Know?
In a landmark study, Bower, Clark, Lesgold, and Winzenz (1969) gave people four lists of 28 words each, either organized hierarchically or arranged randomly. What did they find? People who studied the organized lists for only 2 minutes per list remembered nearly 100% of the words after only one study session! People who had the randomly organized list remembered less than 80% after four study sessions.

How to Do It:

1. Use the chapter outlines and sections of the textbook to organize material in a hierarchical format.

2. Create concept maps. Concept mapping imposes order on what might seem like TOO MUCH information.

3. Use CHUNKING. To make a "chunk," group together larger units of information into smaller units. For instance, rather than remembering FBICIAKGB as a long string of letters, you could chunk it into FBI, CIA, and KGB.

LESSON #2: CREATE SCHEMAS TO GUIDE YOUR CURRENT LEARNING AND INTEGRATE THE OLD AND THE NEW LEARNING.

How Do We Know?
A "schema" is an organized framework of past experiences. For example, you have a classroom schema. The first time you walked into a college classroom you knew pretty much what to do and what to expect: you dressed a certain way, you came in and took a seat, you might have introduced yourself to people sitting around you, you took out a pen and paper, etc. Schemas provide "cognitive economy," which

means you don't have to relearn everything from scratch each time you need to know about something. Instead, you can call to mind your previous experiences and use them to guide your learning.

How to Do It:

1. Think of similar material you have learned in the past and bring it up from memory. Examine it for relatedness. If you find a match, niche your new information into your existing framework.

2. If you are sure the information is completely new to you, start a new schematic framework, but you will need to access it more often during early learning!

3. Incidentally, the lesson on chunking applies here as well: you can use your schemata (plural of *schema*) to help you integrate new information with old.

LESSON #3: IF YOU CAN'T REMEMBER SOMETHING, SWITCH PERSPECTIVES: CALL UP A DIFFERENT SCHEMA

How Do We Know?
In a clever study, Anderson and Pichert (1978) asked people to remember stories of two boys playing hooky from school. Some people were asked to remember the story from the perspective of a burglar; others were asked to remember the story from the perspective of a potential home buyer. The story involved various details, such as how big the rooms were (homebuyer interest) and different electronic devices (burglar interest) the boys used, such as a television set and small appliances in the kitchen. When Anderson and Pichert asked their participants to recall the stories, they did pretty well, but they performed even better when each group was divided in half. One subgroup recalled the story again, keeping the same perspective. The other subgroup was told to switch perspectives: the potential homebuyers were asked to think of themselves as burglars, and the potential burglars now were asked to think of themselves as homebuyers. What did they find? The people who kept the same perspective recalled just a little less the second time. Those who switched recalled substantially more. Their interpretation: switching perspectives provided a new plan for searching memory.

How to Do It:

If you are stuck in this way, just close your eyes for a minute and deactivate your current path for searching memory; deactivate you schema. Start over again and ask yourself what a related path might be, and go there. For example, maybe you encoded the biological bases of memory with your brain schema, rather than your memory schema. If searching one path doesn't work, try another reasonable path.

IMAGERY

LESSON #1: MAKE PICTORIAL REPRESENTATIONS OF VERBAL KNOWLEDGE WHENEVER POSSIBLE.

How Do We Know?
In another "landmark" study, Shepard (1967) showed subjects hundreds of pictures and 2 hours later gave a recognition task where each "old" picture was paired with a novel picture. Well, here is another no-brainer: Performance was nearly perfect. One week later recognition was still correct at 87%. When the same task was done with words, immediate recognition was only 88%. Yes, we now have evidence we can point to that pictures are better than words for remembering things.

How to Do It:

Create concept maps. It is much easier to bring to mind a picture and remember most of its details, than it is to remember words. Make concept maps for every chapter. This Study Guide will give you some examples, but they are more limited to subsections of chapters, and really, it's best if you make your own.

LESSON #2: TAKE ABSTRACT CONCEPTS AND MAKE THEM AS CONCRETE AND IMAGEABLE AS POSSIBLE.

How Do We Know?
In the 1960s, Alan Paivio conducted a series of studies that showed that memory is stronger for things that are "imageable," such as concrete nouns, than for abstract concepts. In one study Paivio asked people to memorize pairs of words. Among the word pairs were four types: (1) concrete words paired with concrete words, (2) concrete words paired with abstract words, (3) abstract words paired with concrete words, and (4) abstract words paired with abstract words. He found that memory was best, in order, through conditions 1, 2, 3 and 4.

How to Do It:

Remember what we have learned so far: Memory is best if you connect concepts together. It is best to match concrete concepts together. However, much information in psychology is abstract, so you need to go to Paivio's condition 2: match concrete and abstract concepts together. During encoding you need to find related concepts: one concrete and one concrete or abstract. Make a mental image of the first concept: It should be unambiguous. Next, make an image of the abstract concept, even if it is ambiguous. Let's say you want to remember that short-term memory lasts about 30 seconds. "Memory" is a difficult concept for which to form an unambiguous mental image but a stopwatch stopped at 30 seconds can be easy to image. So a stop watch that has a computer memory chip background could work in this case. According to Paivio's dual code theory you will be storing two memories: the verbal one and the visual one. Then, during retrieval, if one path fails, you have a second path to search, and violà—twice the probability of retrieving the information.

MNEMONICS

Mnemonics are well-documented to have positive effects especially at **encoding,** but also at **storage and retrieval.** Many mnemonic devices—techniques to help you remember—are available. Some of these are called technical mnemonics and require you to learn specific techniques and memorize specific information first. Other are called naïve mnemonics because you can make them up as you go along. Whatever works!

LESSON #1: USE INTERACTIVE IMAGERY WHENEVER POSSIBLE.

How Do We Know?
Most of the technical mnemonics make use of imagery, particularly interactive imagery. You've already seen that memory for pictures is superior to that for words, and that dual-coding information for both verbal and imagery cues is superior to a single code. Now you will see evidence that making your images interactive works best. In a creative study examining the use of logos to accompany a company's name, Lutz and Lutz (1977) showed that people better remembered a company when the image of what the company does is integrated with the name of the company.

How to Do It:

Be creative! One common mnemonic is the "peg" system in which first a rhyme is memorized, such as "One is a bun, two is a shoe, three is a tree, four is a door, etc." Then, to-be-remembered ideas are reduced to an image, and these images are "hung" on the "pegs." The simplest example is of a list of errands you need to run. Let's say you needed to go to the grocery store, get gas, pick up the dry cleaning, and stop by the library. You could makes images of a large hamburger bun with groceries sticking out of the middle as the meat, a shoe-shaped car getting gas, with laces going between the gas tank and the pump, a tree with clothes on hangers blowing around in the wind, and a book-shaped door that opens up into shelves of books. This system works very well for memorizing lists or anything in sequence, such as events in history that need to be remembered in the order in which they occurred.

LESSON #2: USE VERBALLY BASED TECHNIQUES WHENEVER POSSIBLE.

How Do We Know?
The research literature is fairly consistent in showing that imagery works best; but some things just cannot be imaged in an unambiguous way. Here is where verbal mnemonics come into play. Reducing the cognitive load makes remembering easier. Psychologists have known this since George Miller first published his classic paper on the capacity of short-term memory in 1956. In addition, a review paper (see Bellezza, 1981; Cook, 1989) on the efficacy of verbally based techniques show that when imagery is not possible, verbal techniques work very well, and certainly MUCH better than just using simple rehearsal. Finally, independent studies of acronym use among introductory psychology students by Stalder (2005) showed that not only were the acronyms effective, but the task of coming up with acronyms, in particular, motivated students to study harder by looking for places where using an acronym would be appropriate, and then implementing their usage.

How to Do It:

Sometimes the material you need to learn is not amenable to images. For these situations, verbally based mnemonics come in handy. They include:
   A. Acrostics – In this type of "first letter mnemonic," you take the first letter of a list of things you need to memorize, such as the musical notes that are written on the "lines." Many a child has learned the sentence—Every Good Boy Does Fine—which stands for the notes E, G, B, D, F written in order from the bottom-most to the top-most line of the music staff.
   B. Acronyms – This "first letter mnemonic" takes the first letter of each word in a list and makes the letters into a word. For instance, "Roy G Biv" stands for the colors in a spectrum: Red, Orange, Yellow, Green, Blue, Indigo, and Violet.
   C. Narrative Methods – In this method you take the terms you need to remember and weave them into a story or a rhyme. For example: to spell correctly most children learn: "I before E, except after C…")
   D. Anything that works for you!

Again, you need some creativity and may need to rearrange concepts, but here is one you can use for the chapter on memory to help you remember the difference between proactive and retroactive interference—most beginning psychology students end up guessing because they just can't remember it: PORN, which is an acronym for Proactive interference Old material dominates Retroactive interference New material dominates. Or you can remember the difference between proactive and retroactive interference this way: _**Pr**_oactive interference occurs because of the _**Pr**_imacy effect and _**Re**_troactive interference occurs because of the _**Re**_cency effect.

DEPTH OF PROCESSING

This approach has its roots in **encoding**, to enhance **retrieval**. Craik and Lockhart (1972) published the seminal paper on depth, or levels of processing. Their basic premise is simple: The type of processing performed on material during encoding predicts later probability of remembering the material. Deep processing—processing for meaning, which focuses on (1) elaboration and (2) making individual bits of material distinct—is far superior to shallow processing, where the material is processed for its physical elements, as occurs during mindless rote repetition.

In describing shallow versus deep processing, Craik and Lockhart suggested two types of rehearsal: In rote rehearsal a person simply repeats to themselves over and over and over again the material, but at the same level of encoding (e.g., just memorizing the sounds of the words, without attaching any real meaning to what is being memorized). In elaborative rehearsal a person works on the material while repeating it, so that meaningfulness is considered—the material is connected to other things that are already known and interpreted in that light; the material is niched into an existing framework, or schema, and takes on a distinctive place in that framework.

LESSON #1: ATTACH MEANING TO NEW INFORMATION BY CONNECTING IT TO WHAT YOU ALREADY KNOW.

How Do We Know?
Here is an example of a study by Hyde and Jenkins (1973). They presented people with lengthy lists of words and asked them to perform one of several tasks. One type of task was a physical task: the person just had to note on paper whether the word was written in uppercase or lowercase letters. Another type of task was a semantic processing task: the person just had to note whether the meaning of the word indicated something pleasant. They were NEVER TOLD TO MEMORIZE the words. Well, in a surprise recall task, those who processed for meaning—that is, they used deep processing during encoding, recalled almost all of the words. Those people who processed only for physical characteristics—that is, they used shallow processing during encoding, recalled almost none of the words. So, without even trying, using deep processing provided strong memory for the material.

How to Do It:

When you study, don't just "memorize" terms. Each time you study a term make sure you are also telling yourself something about the meaning of that term. Later, your chances of remembering that information will be far greater than if you just sat and repeated the terms over and over again to yourself.

LESSON #2: MAKE NEW INFORMATION AS DISTINCT AS POSSIBLE.

How Do We Know?
One of the lessons from studying serial position effects, as well as the reasons for why depth of processing approaches might work other than the focus on meaning has to do with distinctiveness of material. Give a person a list of 20 unrelated words and ask him or her to recall it right away and you will find that they are more likely to remember the first few and the last few words; but are unlikely to remember the words in the middle, UNLESS there is something distinctive about those words in the middle. Then people show a spike in remembering.

How to Do It:

Simply take each concept you need to know and make it unique in some way. For example, you could think about not just the ways that things are alike, but also the ways in which they contrast. In fact, compare and contrast types of essay items are frequently used to assess higher-level thinking. The reasoning is that such items require students both elaborate (compare) the information and make it distinct (contrast).

LESSON #3: RELATE MATERIAL TO YOURSELF WHENEVER POSSIBLE.

How Do We Know?
Rogers, Kuiper, and Kirker (1977) presented a lengthy list of adjectives to people and then asked people to merely decide whether the words described the person. Of course, they had other comparison groups of people who performed other types of encoding tasks. But here is the important thing they found: Those people who performed the self-reference incidental task remember the most words during a surprise recall task.

How to Do It:

Now, you may not always be able to make these self-references, because not all material is going to relate to you. For example, it is hard to learn mathematical formulas in this way (although of course, processing them for meaning is possible, just probably not as a self-reference). However, whenever possible in a class such as psychology, when you learn a principle, think of examples in your own life that relate to the correct principle. THIS IS ESPECIALLY IMPORTANT WHEN YOU MUST OVERCOME INITIALLY INCORRECT PRECONCEPTIONS. Remember what we've told you before: most students come into an introductory psychology class thinking they already know a lot about human behavior—after all they have at least 18 years of human behavior in their own repertoire. But remember this: MUCH of the information reflects naïve science: knowledge based on an extremely limited sample (yourself and the people you know) and tends to be biased. Therefore, whenever you come up to information that seems to go against your existing knowledge, trying to find those examples which in the past you might have thought were exceptions, and dismissed as such, are now really important to focus on.

LESSON #4: IT IS BEST TO COME UP WITH YOUR OWN UNIQUE AND ORIGINAL EXAMPLES.

How Do We Know?
Slamecka and Graf (1978) showed that when people are asked to come up with examples of anything—whether it is generating mental images or schema-based frameworks to find a niche for new information—it always produces MUCH better memory for the information if a person comes up with his or her own image, framework, example, etc. Having the information provided for you is never as good as providing it for yourself.

How to Do It:

When you are studying, it is best to (1) put everything in your own words, (2) come up with your own original examples of the various principles you are reading about. Do not become overly focused on examples provided in your text—they are there as examples to illustrate the principles, but they are not the most important information in your studies. Being able to generate your own examples shows that you understand the principles you are working with—in this class and any other!

ENCODING SPECIFICITY

Tulving and Thomson (1973) stand out in the history of modern cognitive research for providing definitive evidence that **encoding** operations and **retrieval** operations are interwoven, and should not be considered as separate. They called their principles **encoding specificity** because it shows that the conditions and context that are specific to the encoding operations being performed need to be reinstated at retrieval for maximizing the retrieval process.

LESSON #1: MATCHING LEARNING AND RECALL CONTEXTS AND CONDITIONS AS MUCH AS POSSIBLE MAXIMIZES RECALL.

How Do We Know?

Tulving and Thomson asked people to study word pairs. Later, they presented people with two retrieval tasks: one was a recall task in which they presented one of the words originally studied in pairs, and the person had to remember the word that was paired with it. In a second task, recognition, Tulving and Thomson presented all of the to-be-remembered words, but without the paired words to act as cues. Instead, the target words were embedded with other words and only the targets needed to be picked out, i.e., recognized. Now, normally, most people would predict, as many studies do find, that recognition is MUCH easier than recall. However, in the situation that Tulving and Thomson created, of having words studied in pairs, they found that if they reinstated the encoding context by providing one of the words in each pair, people performed MUCH better on the recall task than on the recognition task.

How Do We Know MORE?

Well, in an interesting study Godden and Baddeley (1975) took this hypothesis a step further. They had two groups of participants who were all certified scuba divers. They asked one group of participants to learn a list of words while sitting on land. The other group learned the same list of words while under water. Each group was then split in half again. For the recall phase half of each group recalled the words under the same conditions, and half under the other conditions. So there were four groups: those who learned on land and recalled the words on land, those who learned on land but recalled the words under water, those who learned the words underwater and recalled them on land, and those who learned and recalled the words under water. What did they find? Those whose learning and recall contexts matched, recalled FAR MORE words, than those who changed context between learning and recall.

How to Do It:

Find a place to study that is most like the place in which you will be tested. For many students this might mean studying consistently in a classroom that is much like the classroom they usually have their own class in but that is consistently vacant at a time that the student has free for studying.

LESSON #2: IF YOU MUST CHANGE CONTEXTS BETWEEN LEARNING AND TESTING, IMAGINE YOURSELF IN THE LEARNING CONTEXT.

How Do We Know?

Sometimes, just imaging yourself in a specific location is all it takes. Smith (1979) replicated the classic test of having participants study and learn in the same or different context, but added an extra twist with an extra group of participants. The extra group changed rooms but each individual was asked to imagine him or herself in the learning room—to mentally reinstate the learning context. Smith found that those participants performed just as well as those who did not change rooms at all!

How to Do It:

Now we come to the conventional wisdom often mentioned in study skills Web sites: pick a place to study, study there consistently, and do nothing else in that place. Why? Because you will maximize your ability to remember what you studied if you can recreate your own learning context during a testing situation. Furthermore, if you can pick a seat in class and always sit in that seat, you can also help yourself to retrieve lecture information by literally being in the same context as you were during lecture. Also, don't study with music on, unless you plan to be humming the same music to yourself throughout the test—likely to annoy your classmates should you hum out loud!

LESSON #3: MATCH YOUR INTERNAL STATES AND MOODS AT BOTH LEARNING AND TESTING TIMES.

How Do We Know?

A final tidbit related to all of the cue-dependent learning and forgetting: Ample evidence, as reviewed by Eich (1989), indicates for state-dependent learning is indeed effective. So, what is state-dependent learning? Well, just as context can serve as a retrieval cue, so too can your internal states (and moods for that matter!).

How to Do It:

Are you likely to take your test at about midnight when you are completely mentally drained? Not likely, because classes do not take place at such times. The lesson here is that you should not study in a state of mind that is unlike the state of mind you are likely to be in during the test.

A second lesson can come from this coordination of state and mood as well. Do you suffer from test anxiety? Simulate test anxiety during your study sessions: have a cup of coffee or two to increase arousal levels. But then, during the test, do NOT compound your test anxiety by having coffee on that day! Remember: increasing arousal during study has the purpose of matching encoding and retrieval operations. On the other hand: no test anxiety? Then just be sure to match your internal states as much as possible at encoding and retrieval.

MASSED VERSUS DISTRIBUTED PRACTICE

Studies on the spacing effect go back more than 100 years. The evidence over this time frame has been consistent: for **acquisition** of information, massed practice is good. But for long-term **retention** of material distributed practice is best. This recommendation is partly based on Ebbinghaus's classic forgetting curve, which Ebbinghaus described in the late 1800s, but still holds true today. Ebbinghaus found that most forgetting occurs shortly after initial learning—in fact most new information is rapidly forgotten. What remains tends to be long-lived, but it tends to not be much after a single learning session. Thus, the more learning sessions, the more that is remembered later on. Another reason for the superiority of distributed practice is what is called attenuation of attention. What does this fancy phrase mean? It means that the more you repeatedly study the same exact information, the less you are likely to attend to it—you experience a feeling of already knowing it. Another reason has to do with familiarity. As you repeatedly study the same information it feels familiar; your sense *at that moment* is that you "know" it. But what about the next day or the next week? "LATER" is a better test of what you actually know. Finally, it is difficult to maintain close attention for a long enough study session to master the large amounts of new information you are exposed to in your college classes. You need a break! Take it! Go back LATER.

LESSON #1: DISTRIBUTED PRACTICE IS CONSISTENTLY SUPERIOR TO MASSED PRACTICE (CRAMMING) FOR LONG-TERM RETENTION OF MATERIAL.

How Do We Know?

In one of a series of related studies, Landauer and Bjork (1978) asked students to memorize first and last name pairs. They had different groups of students study the names under different conditions. In one condition they simply used massed practice. In another condition they varied the length of the interval for distributed practice. In a final set of conditions they had what they called expanding and contracting intervals. In the expanding intervals the spacing between learning sessions started out short and was lengthened (expanded) over time. In the contracting interval condition the sequencing was opposite: at first the intervals were long, and then were progressively shortened (contracted). If you had to guess which of these many conditions was best, which would you think? If you thought it was the expanding condition you would be correct: While you are still learning the material, shorter intervals are good.

Remember that massed practice is best for acquisition. But then lengthening the interval progressively is best. It allows the most time for consolidation to take place.

How to Do It:

Don't Cram! PLAN AHEAD and set up times in which you will study; then start out each study session with a review of the previous study session(s). At first you might want to review from the just previous session, but over time, as you accumulate more information you can begin to expand your study sessions. So session 1 you first learn something. Session 2 you go over material from session 1 and then go into new material. Now, at session 3 you might go over session 2 material and learn new material. At session 4 you should probably review material back from study session 1 and then review what you just learned at study session 3 and move on to new material and so on…always review the new material from the previous study session but then go back and review some of the prior material as well before moving on to new material.

METACOGNITION

Metacognition is the big daddy of everything that cognitive psychology can tell us about learning. *Meta* comes from ancient Greek, meaning "behind," "beyond," or "after." Thus, metacognition is knowledge beyond what you know—it is what you know about your own knowledge—and what you don't know! How much control do you believe you exercise over your thinking, and how much of it do you just let "happen"? Remember: Some students who perform poorly study for many more hours than others who perform well. One of the reasons for this appears to be a difference in metacognition—good students spend more time on what they don't yet know well enough, and skimming what they already know. Unfortunately, students who perform poorly tend to not know what they know and don't know and so spend too much time on what they already know, and not enough time on what they don't yet know well.

Most educators discuss metacognition as involving a plan of action, following through with the plan by implementing and maintaining it, and finally, by evaluating the plan—is it producing the desired effect on learning? Good metacognitive awareness requires a LOT of effort, pure and simple, but it is the best guarantee you will ever have of maximizing your learning.

LESSON #1: CONTROLLING YOUR OWN LEARNING IS YOUR BEST CHANCE TO MAXIMIZE YOUR ABILITIES, BUT IT TAKES A LOT OF EFFORT.

How Do We Know?
Dunlosky and Lipko (2007) reviewed studies, as well as carrying out their own research. What they found was that students of all ages need to monitor their progress on an ongoing basis. Time and time again studies show that students overestimate their knowledge and need to remain constantly vigilant to what works and in which situations.

How to Do It:

BEGIN WITH THE PAST: What have you done in the past that has worked for you? Did you read? Memorize? Summarize? Stop and review in your own words? Which study habits have worked best? Worst?

DURING: Throughout the course, ask yourself: How am I doing? Am I on the right track? What information is important to remember? What do I need to do if I do not understand? Does my text have a study guide or a Web site where I can quiz myself?

AFTER: Evaluating your approach to studying answers these questions. How well did you do on assignments/tests? What could you have done differently? Do you need to go back through the task to fill in any "blanks" in your understanding?

BEWARE OF OVERCONFIDENCE: One element resulting in poor metacognition is overconfidence. Dunning, Heath, and Suls (2004) reviewed the literature for the past decades to conclusively show that flawed self-assessment is pervasive. In terms of students: the poorest performing students show the highest confidence in what they think they know.

LESSON #2: DO NOT STOP STUDYING UNTIL YOU HAVE OVERLEARNED THE MATERIAL.

How Do We Know?

In a sense this lesson harkens back to several previous ones, such as distributed practice. Rohrer and Pashler (2007) asked students to memorize word lists until they knew the lists completely. Some of the students continued to memorize them, and others stopped at that point. A week later, those who overlearned the lists remembered them much better. Nine weeks later, it makes no difference. However, in another study they had students either learn the material, and then learn it again after a time lapse. In this case, those students who overlearned by studying again after a time lapse remembered more at both the 1-week and 9-week test dates. Why might overlearning be helpful, especially in the short run? Shiffrin (1988) showed that if you practice a task more, your ability to use the information becomes more automatic, thereby freeing up resources—the task takes less effort. However, for a task to remain automatic it needs continued practice. Thus, distributing the learning sessions is most helpful. Finally, another reason students are often told to overlearn is that for most classroom material there really isn't a "criterion" of understanding that students can study to achieve. The best way to not fall prey to overconfidence that the "criterion" has been reached is to continue to study.

How to Do It:

Probably the easiest way to know what you do and don't know is to quiz yourself—but NOT right after studying. Of course, you know what you just finished studying. Quiz yourself a few days later. THEN go back over what you missed. Briefly gloss over what you think you knew well—you may have heard the saying, "You can never have too much of a good thing." Well, similarly, you can never study your lessons too many times.

References

Anderson, R. C., & Pichert, J. W. (1978). Recall of previously unrecallable information following a shift in perspective. *Journal of Verbal Learning and Verbal Behavior, 17*, 1–12.

Borkowski, J. G., Carr, M., Rellinger, E., & Pressley, M. (1990). Self-regulated cognition: Interdependence of metacognition, attributions, and self-esteem. In B. F. Jones & L. Idol (Eds.), *Dimensions of Thinking and Cognitive Instruction* (pp. 53–92). Mahwah: NJ.

Bower, G. H., Clark, M. C., Lesgold, A. M., & Winzenz, D. (1969). Hierarchical retrieval schemes in recall of categorized word lists. *Journal of Verbal Learning and Verbal Behavior, 8*, 323–343.

Brewer, W. F., & Treyens, J. C. (1981). Role of schemata in memory for places. *Cognitive Psychology, 13*, 207–230.

Craik, F. I. M., & Lockhart, R. S. (1972). Levels of processing: A framework for memory research. *Journal of Verbal Learning and Verbal Behavior, 11*, 671–684.

Dunlosky, J., & Lipko, A. R. (2007). Metacomprehension: A brief history and how to improve its accuracy. *Current Directions in Psychological Science, 16*(4), 228–232.

Dunning, D., Heath, C., & Suls, J. M. (2004). Flawed self-assessment. *Psychological Science in the Public Interest, 5*(3), 69–106.

Eich, E. (1989). Theoretical issues in state dependent memory. In H. L. Roediger & F. I. M. Craik, *Varieties of Memory and Consciousness* (pp. 331–354), Hillsdale, NJ: Lawrence Erlbaum and Associates Publishers.

Godden, D. R., & Baddeley, A. D. (1975). Context-dependent memory in two natural environments: On land and underwater. *British Journal of Psychology, 66*, 325–331.

Hyde, T. S., & Jenkins, J. J. (1973). Recall for words as a function of semantic, graphic, and syntactic orienting tasks. *Journal of Verbal Learning and Verbal Behavior, 12*, 471–480.

Kruger, J., & Dunning, D. (1999). Unskilled and unaware of it: How difficulties in recognizing one's own incompetence lead to inflated self-assessments. *Journal of Personality and Social Psychology, 77*(6), 1121–1134.

Landauer, T. K., & Bjork, R. A. (1978). Optimum rehearsal patterns and name learning. In M. Gruneberg, H. Morris & R. Sykes (Eds.), *Practical Aspects of Memory* (pp. 625–632). London: Academic Press.

Lutz, K. A., & Lutz, R. J. (1977). Effects of interactive imagery on learning: Application to advertising. *Journal of Applied Psychology, 62*(4), 493–498.

Miller, G. A. (1956). The magical number seven, plus or minus two: Some limits on our capacity for processing information. *Psychological Review, 63*(2), 81–97.

Paivio, A., Walsh, M., & Bons, T. (1994). Concreteness effect on memory: When and why? *Journal of Experimental Psychology: Learning, Memory and Cognition, 20* (5), 1196–1204.

Payne, D. G., & Wenger, M. J. (1992). Improving memory through practice. In D. J. Herrmann, H.

Weingartner & A. Searleman, (Eds.), *Memory Improvement* (pp. 187–209). New York: Springer-Verlag.

Rogers, T. B., Kuiper, N. A., & Kirker, W. S. (1977). Self-reference and the encoding of personal information. *Journal of Personality and Social Psychology, 35*(9), 677–688.

Rohrer, D., & Pashler, H. (2007). Increasing retention time without increasing study time. *Current Directions in Psychological Science, 16*, 183–186.

Shepard, R. N. (1967). Recognition memory for words, sentences, and pictures. *Journal of Verbal Learning and Verbal Behavior, 6*, 156–163.

Shiffrin, R. M. (1988). Attention. In R. C. Atkinson, R. J. Herrnstein, G. Lindzey, & R. Dun (Eds.), *Stevens' Handbook of Experimental Psychology* (pp. 739–811). John Wiley & Sons.

Slamecka, N. J., & Graf, P. (1978). The generation effect: Delineation of a phenomenon. *Journal of Experimental Psychology: Human Learning and Memory, 4*(6), 592–604.

Smith, M. S. (1979). Remembering in and out of context. *Journal of Experimental Psychology: Human Learning and Memory, 5*(5), 460–471.

Tulving, E., & Thomson, D. M. (1973). Encoding specificity and retrieval processes in episodic memory. *Psychological Review, 80*, 352–373.

Winn, W., & Snyder, D. (1996). Cognitive perspectives in psychology. In D. H. Jonassen (Ed.), *Handbook of Research for Educational Communications and Technology* (pp. 112–142). New York: Macmillan.

CONCEPT MAPPING

What are all of these "bubble maps"? And why do I need to deal with them?

If you are like my students, you are probably asking yourself these questions. The answer to the first question is that the "bubble" maps are actually concept maps. They represent material in a way that makes learning easier and more efficient, and they make it more likely that the information will stick in your memory. It is a way to organize the material for deeper learning.

The reason you may *want* to deal with the maps (rather than "need" to) is that doing so will maximize the chances that you will actually *learn* the material. That is, if you really want to learn the material (rather than just try to memorize it for a test and forget it) and you want to do so in an efficient way, concept maps can help you achieve your goals.

Why can't I just make an outline?

You could, and some students do, even after being introduced to concepts maps. Remember from the study skills section you just read, that actively engaging in thinking about the information, organizing the information, and relating it to other things you know, results in greater understanding and greater likelihood of retention. Concept mapping does everything outlines do and more. Concept maps organize information, but they also allow you to "visualize" concepts and their relationships in a layout format. This visualization can give you one more cue for retrieval. In addition, unlike an outline, which is organized from top to bottom, concepts maps can be read from top to bottom, but also from bottom to top, left to right and right to left!

How do I know it works? Isn't this just more "busywork?"

In Chapter 7, Memory, you will read about deep and shallow processing and you will see that the research evidence strongly supports deep processing—processing for meaning, based on elaborating the relationships between new and old knowledge. This is how it works—elaborating relationships on many levels. On the other hand, the research evidence is overwhelming that knowledge learned by rote tends to be quickly forgotten because it is not processed deeply. Thinking about how concepts are related to one another helps you encode the information so that it is easier to retrieve the information when you want it.

Another benefit of concept mapping is that a large amount of information can be efficiently summarized so that you can pull together information you already know and understand about a topic, and combine it with new information you are learning. In this way, it is not just more "busywork," which usually does NOT lead to deeper learning. Therefore, summarizing in this way is important because it aids memory, and it encourages high-level, critical thinking, which is so important in university work.

So, tell me again why I want to do these exercises and maybe apply this technique in other classes?

Concept mapping lets you organize information.
Concept mapping lets you see all your basic information on one page.
Concept mapping lets you see the relationships among key ideas more clearly.
Concept mapping lets you add new information as you learn it.
Concept mapping lets you integrate separate maps into larger, more complex structures.
Bottom line: Concept mapping results in better understanding of underlying ideas and, as a result, better retrieval of information.

How do you make a map?

Many concept maps use a hierarchical organization, although that format is not necessary. If hierarchical organization is desired, the most inclusive, most general concepts are placed at the top of the map, with the less general, more specific concepts arranged hierarchically below. Thus, the map will show the relationship of the subordinate (lower) concepts to each superordinate (higher) concept.

Each important term you learn is a node, or concept. A node is usually shown as a circle or bubble, with the term written within it. Lines connect the nodes, to show which concepts are related, and the nature of the relationship. These lines have a one-sided arrow if one concept flows from the other, or a two-sided arrow if there is a back-and-forth relationship between the two concepts, or no arrows at all. Each connecting line is labeled and tells how the concepts relate. A concept might link to another as "a part of," "for example," "located in," or "produces." Map guidelines are flexible—use what helps YOU understand. Here is a simple concept map—as you will see, they can be about any topic, not just psychology.

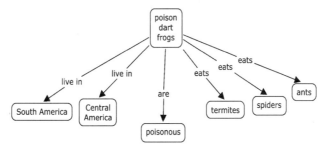

What do I do with the maps in the Study Guide?

In this Study Guide you will sometimes be given a partially completed concept map and your task will be to fill in the remaining circles with concepts, based on the relationships provided to you. Some concept maps will have an answer provided at the end of the chapter's activities. Your maps could differ based on your choice of concepts; it's not a matter of finding the completely "right" or "wrong" answers! Take advantage of the flexibility of concept maps to show multiple relationships.

Sometimes, the answers section will only provide a list of concepts that could be included by you. Other times we will provide you with a set of concepts and ask you to construct the map. The answers section may or may not include a completed map because the final mapping may be related to your prior knowledge, your understanding of the relationships between concepts, and how much information you have gleaned from the text. Most of the time the concept maps are not suggested to you. We encourage you to develop your own maps. You might want to map out entire chapters, linking together the individual maps we are providing you with.

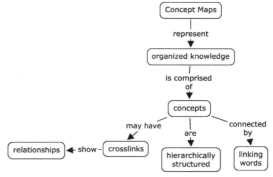

Can you give me an example?

EVALUATING WEB SITES

Throughout this Study Guide, you will be asked to access the Internet—either to find information on your own, or to go to a site that we recommend for a particular activity. The Web is probably among the most wonderful inventions of our time—the information that is now instantly available to you is nothing short of amazing. But it is also the greatest source of misinformation, misconceptions, and just plain old gobbledy-gook imaginable. The following resources provide useful information on evaluating Web sites:

http://lib.nmsu.edu/instruction/evalcrit.html
http://kathyschrock.net/abceval/
http://www.library.cornell.edu/olinuris/ref/research/webeval.html
http://www.lib.msu.edu/link/critical.htm
http://www.lib.berkeley.edu/TeachingLib/Guides/Internet/Evaluate.html

As you read through a few of these recommended Web sites you should keep in mind these basic criteria:

AUTHORITY—Who is the author? What are his or her qualifications or credentials? Who is the publisher? What bias would you expect of this publisher if any? What reputation do these sources have?

VERIFIABILITY—Are the claims made verifiable? Are there accurate, traceable sources?

CURRENCY OR TIMELINESS—Is the information given current? When was the last time the page was updated?

RELEVANCE—Is the material truly related to what you need to know?

BIAS VERSUS OBJECTIVITY—Is the language used loaded? Are points of view given that show a range of opinion? Are you being sold anything?

ORDERLINESS—Is the page arranged in an order that makes sense?

CLARITY—Is the information clearly stated? Does the author use obscure language?

ACCURACY—Is the information given out of context? Are the data used compatible?

NAVIGABILITY—Do all of the links work?

SCHOLASTIC REVIEWS—Has this site received any rewards?

HOUSING—What type of domain houses this Web page?

The bottom line in evaluating Web sites: Use every critical thinking skill you have ever been taught, either in this textbook or in any book you have read or course you have taken. The Web will provide you with quality information, but it will also provide you with the lowest-quality information. It will be up to you to determine the difference.

CHAPTER 1
PSYCHOLOGY AND SCIENTIFIC THINKING

Psychology is the scientific study of the mind, brain, and behavior. It is a field that seems self-evident, but everyday experience doesn't necessarily make us an expert. William James, the founder of American psychology, noted that psychology is difficult to study. Psychology spans multiple **levels of analysis**, from molecules to complex social and cultural influences; from brain to mind.

The challenges in studying psychology reflect the difficulties in studying behaviors that are **multiply determined** and that are interdependent. *Single-variable explanations* are inadequate. **Individual differences** in thinking, emotion, personality, and behavior preclude general rules, and people influence each other, a phenomenon called *reciprocal determinism*. Finally, people's behavior is shaped by culture—often studied from both *emic* (the perspective of a "native" or insider) and *etic* (the perspective of an outsider) approaches.

To understand why others act as they do, most of us trust our common sense. But such understanding of ourselves and the world is often mistaken. We trust our common sense because we're prone to **naive realism**: the belief that we see the world precisely as it is. But appearances can be deceiving, so we need to think scientifically. Most students think that science is just a word for all of the "stuff" they learn in their biology, chemistry, and physics classes. But science is really an *approach* to evidence, a way of thinking, beginning with *empiricism*, the gaining of knowledge through direct observation.

Many people misunderstand what defines a **scientific theory**. A theory is complex and does not explain single events. It is more than an educated guess. A good scientific theory will account for existing data, and for a theory to be scientific, it must generate a testable prediction, called a **hypothesis**, which researchers can test.

Scientists are just as prone to biased thinking as anyone else, so they use safeguards against errors in thinking. One common error in thinking is the **confirmation bias**: the tendency to seek out evidence that supports our beliefs and dismiss evidence that contradicts them. Another common bias is **belief perseverance**, the tendency to stick to our initial beliefs even when evidence contradicts them. It is also important to distinguish scientific claims from **metaphysical claims**: assertions about the world that we can't test, such as assertions about the existence of God, the soul, and the afterlife. It's not that metaphysical claims are wrong or unimportant. They are simply not testable with scientific methods.

The popular psychology industry is growing rapidly. This information explosion has also lead to a *misinformation explosion*. We need to distinguish claims that are genuine from those that are imposters of science, called, **pseudoscience**: a set of claims that seem scientific but aren't. Pseudoscience lacks the safeguards against biased thinking that characterize science. Some of the warning signs of pseudoscience are: (1) overuse of **ad hoc immunizing hypotheses** (loopholes), (2) lack of self-correction, and (3) overreliance on anecdotes.

There are many reasons why people are drawn to pseudoscientific beliefs. Our brains are predisposed to make order out of disorder and find sense in nonsense. This tendency to seek out patterns can lead us to experience **apophenia:** perceiving meaningful connections among unrelated phenomena.

For example, we may attribute paranormal significance (outside the boundaries of traditional science) to coincidences. Another way that we find patterns is the phenomenon of **pareidolia**: seeing meaningful images in meaningless visual stimuli, such as seeing the face of a "man" in the moon. A final reason for the popularity of pseudoscience is motivational: We believe because we want to believe. For example, according to **terror management theory,** many pseudoscientific claims may give us comfort because they seem to offer us a sense of control over an often unpredictable world.

To avoid being seduced by pseudoscience, we must learn to avoid common pitfalls in reasoning—*logical fallacies*. Three important logical fallacies are the **emotional reasoning fallacy**, the **bandwagon fallacy,** and the **not me fallacy**. There are three major reasons why we should be concerned about pseudoscience. These include opportunity cost, direct harm, and an inability to think scientifically as citizens.

One approach to help uncover pseudoscience is to be skeptical—to keep an open mind to all claims, but only accept them after careful scientific testing. One danger is that many of us accept claims simply on the basis of authority. The hallmark of **scientific skepticism** is **critical thinking**. This text emphasizes six scientific thinking principles. These include: (1) ruling out rival hypotheses, (2) correlation isn't causation, (3) falsifiability (a **falsifiable** claim can be disproven), (4) **replicability**, (5) extraordinary claims require extraordinary evidence, and (6) Occam's Razor.

Psychology as a science has existed for only about 130 years. Until the late 1800s the field of psychology was part of the field of philosophy. In 1879, Wilhelm Wundt developed the first psychology laboratory in Germany. Wundt combined experimental methods with **introspection,** a careful reflection of mental experiences. Soon, psychologists around the world opened laboratories in major universities.

Five major theoretical perspectives have shaped contemporary psychological thought. **Structuralists** aimed to identify the basic elements, or "structures," of psychological experience. **Functionalists** wanted to understand the purposes, or functions, of psychological characteristics, such as thoughts, feelings, and behaviors. They were profoundly influenced by Darwin's theory of **natural selection. Behaviorists** focused on uncovering the general principles of learning underlying externally observable behaviors in humans and animals. **Cognitive psychologists** and **cognitive neuroscientists** have argued that thinking is so central to psychology that it merits a separate discipline in its own right. **Psychoanalysis** also focused on internal psychological processes. Today, psychology isn't just one discipline, but rather an assortment of many subdisciplines. These range from biological to cultural. The field of psychology is remarkably diverse, as are the types of careers psychology majors pursue.

Two great debates have shaped the field of psychology since its inception and seem likely to continue to shape it in the future. One, the nature–nurture debate, examines whether our behaviors are attributable mostly to our genes (nature) or to our rearing environments (nurture). *Behavior geneticists* use sophisticated designs such as twin and adoption studies, whereas **evolutionary psychologists** examine the *fitness* of organisms to survive. The second debate concerns free will versus determinism and examines the extent to which our behaviors are freely selected rather than caused by factors outside of our control.

So psychology is all around you, from the changing colors of fire emergency vehicles from red to lime yellow, to the addition of a third, center mounted brake light on cars, to the crafting of commercial messages, to the development of tests, such as the SAT or ACT. **Basic research** examines how the mind works; the goal of **applied research** is to solve real-world problems. To think like a psychologist, you will learn to think scientifically—learning how to collect and interpret evidence.

BEFORE YOU READ … LEARNING OBJECTIVES

After reading Chapter 1 you should be able to:

1.1   Explain why psychology is more than just common sense
1.2   Explain the importance of science as a set of safeguards against biases
1.3   Describe psychological pseudoscience and distinguish it from psychological science
1.4   Identify reasons we are drawn to pseudoscience
1.5   Identify the key features of scientific skepticism
1.6   Identify and explain six key principles of scientific thinking that will be used throughout the text
1.7   Identify the major theoretical frameworks of psychology
1.8   Describe different types of psychologists and identify what each of them does
1.9   Describe the two great debates that have shaped the field of psychology
1.10   Describe how psychological research affects our daily lives

BEFORE YOU READ … TERM IDENTIFICATION

ad hoc immunizing hypothesis (p. 12)
apophenia (p. 14)
applied research (p. 36)
basic research (p. 36)
behaviorism (p. 30)
belief perseverance (p. 9)
cognitive neuroscience (p. 31)
cognitive psychology (p. 31)
confirmation bias (p. 8)
correlation–causation fallacy (p. 23)
critical thinking (p. 21)
evolutionary psychology (p. 34)
falsifiable (p. 23)
functionalism (p. 30)
hypothesis (p. 7)
individual differences (p. 4)

introspection (p. 27)
levels of analysis (p. 2)
metaphysical claims (p. 9)
multiply determined (p. 2)
naïve realism (p. 5)
natural selection (p. 30)
pareidolia (p. 15)
pseudoscience (p. 11)
psychoanalysis (p. 31)
psychology (p. 2)
replicability (p. 24)
scientific skepticism (p. 20)
scientific theory (p. 7)
structuralism (p. 29)
terror management theory (p. 17)
variable (p. 23)

AS YOU READ ... PRACTICE ACTIVITIES

WHAT IS PSYCHOLOGY: SCIENCE VERSUS INTUITION

1. Although coming up with a definition of psychology poses a challenge, coming up with questions that we might expect psychology to answer should be easier. Write down several questions you would like to have answered throughout your journey into psychology. Come back and revisit these questions as the semester goes on. You may find, after reading Chapters 1 and 2, that science cannot answer the questions as asked, and you may need to reframe them; or you may find excellent answers. (LO 1.1)

2. Take the test of popular psychology knowledge in your textbook on page 2. How did you do? If you missed any items, select the one you believed in most strongly or that you have heard the most often. Now look for evidence that supports the right answer. (LO 1.1)

3. Compare "emic" and "etic" approaches to studying the effects of culture on behavior. Note that throughout this Study Guide you will be asked to "compare" two or more concepts rather frequently. When you do so, examine both how the concepts are alike and how they might differ from one another. (LO 1.1)

4. Look at the proverbs and their opposites on p. 5. Pick one pair and research which one of that pair has the better support in terms of both quantity and quality of evidence. Write up your findings here. (LO 1.1)

5. In your own words, describe how a hypothesis is different from a theory. (LO 1.2)

6. Why do scientific psychologists never claim that a theory is proven? Is this need to avoid the use of "proven" only true in psychology, or is it also true in other sciences? (LO 1.2)

PSYCHOLOGICAL PSEUDOSCIENCE: IMPOSTERS OF SCIENCE

1. Draw a relationship between the concepts of falsifiability, metaphysical claims, and pseudoscientific claims. (LO 1.2, 1.3 and 1.6)

2. Read each of the following statements. Which ones ask a legitimate scientific question? Why or why not? (LO 1.2)

   a. People who believe in an afterlife are better adjusted than individuals who do not.

   b. Anxious individuals harbor unconscious sexual urges.

   c. Depressed individuals have sadder memories than do nondepressed individuals.

   d. After death our soul endures and is reborn in a new living being.

3. Self-help books overuse ad hoc immunizing hypotheses, lack self-correction, and over-rely on anecdotes. Check out a "self-help" book from the library. Is the author making a claim that applies to everyone? At all times? Is there any evidence of scientific work supporting the claims? Does it rely on testimonials? Does the author control for or recognize alternative explanations? (LO 1.3)

4. Develop a relationship between illusory correlation (seeing a correlational relationship where none exists—e.g., between gender and how much a person talks) and apophenia. Provide an original example from your own life to support your argument. (LO 1.4)

5. Backward masking is an example of finding patterns in ambiguous auditory information—an auditory analog of pareidolia. Playing words on a recording backward, the sounds have no meaning. Nevertheless, we try to make sense of what we hear. Once we hear a pattern, then confirmation bias takes over. You can listen to many examples at http://www.reversespeech.com/music_reversals.htm. Are you able to hear any of the messages in the backward audio files? (LO 1.2 AND 1.4)

6. Have you ever been thinking of someone and suddenly, they call on the phone?

   How often has this happened in the last month?

   Why do you think this happened?

   Have you ever been thinking of someone and they did not suddenly call you on the phone?

   How often has this happened in the last month?

   Does this observation influence your perception of the first question?

   What phenomenon does this activity demonstrate? (LO 1.4)

7. Draw lines to match the following logical fallacies to their definitions and examples. (LO 1.4)

a. appeal to authority	1. using emotions to guide evaluation of a claim	i) Some people who take Prozac commit suicide, so no one should take it
b. emotional reasoning	2. accepting a claim because many other people do	ii) Everyone I know who drives a Lexus loves it, so it must a good car
c. argument from antiquity	3. seeing an issue as black or white; all-or-nothing	iii) I have a clear head and don't have to worry about being swayed
d. bandwagon	4. accepting a claim because it has been around a long time	iv) Astrology has been around since ancient times, so it must be valid
e. either / or	5. accepting a claim because an authority made it	v) My doctor said so, so it must be true
f. not me	6. believing we are immune from errors in thinking that afflict other people	vi) All cultures believe in an afterlife, so it must exist

SCIENTIFIC THINKING: DISTINGUISHING FACT FROM FICTION

1. Do you believe that critical thinking and scientific thinking are the same or different? Make a case for them being the same and for them being different, both within the context of scientific skepticism. (LO 1.5)

2. Take the case of ESP and apply three of the six critical thinking principles to cast doubt on the reality of ESP. (LO 1.2 and 1.6)

3. Using astrology as an example, briefly discuss one reason why people tend to believe in this pseudoscience, AND at least one reason why psychologists remain skeptical. (LO 1.6)

4. A student receives a bad grade on several tests and subsequently is treated for depression at the campus counseling center. Did the bad grades cause the student's depression? Explain three possible relationships that might actually exist in this situation. (LO 1.6)

PSYCHOLOGY'S PAST AND PRESENT: WHAT A LONG, STRANGE TRIP IT'S BEEN

1. True scientific psychology has always had to coexist with, and differentiate itself from, psychical and spiritualistic studies. Scientific psychologists have been debunking these latter beliefs for well over a century, yet still they persist. What are some modern-day nonscientific disciplines that compete with psychological science? Why do you think that these types of beliefs are so persistent? (LO 1.7)

2. Match these major historical events in the history of psychology to their dates. (LO 1.7 and 1.8)

_____ Neisser launches field of cognitive psychology.

_____ Wilhelm Wundt opens first laboratory devoted to scientific psychology.

_____ Milgram publishes classic studies on obedience.

_____ Ivan Pavlov discovers classical conditioning.

_____ Daniel Kahneman is first psychologist to win a Nobel Prize.

_____ William James writes *Principles of Psychology*.

_____ John Watson starts field of behaviorism

1879; 1890; 1910; 1913; 1963; 1967; 2002

3. Match the following theoretical frameworks to their proponents and to their definitions. (LO 1.7)

Structuralism	Ulric Neisser	focused on understanding that much mental processing goes on outside of conscious awareness
Functionalism	John B. Watson	sought to identify basic purpose of thoughts, feelings, and behaviors
Behaviorism	Sigmund Freud	sought to understand elements of psychology
Cognitivism	Edward Titchener	examined the effects of "thinking" in behavior
Psychoanalysis	William James	uncovered general laws of learning by examining external, objective behavior

4. A public speaking phobia can be interpreted differently by the different types of psychologists. Pick three different types of psychologists and suggest the mechanisms they might use to interpret a public speaking phobia. (LO 1.8)

5. After reading about the "Great Debates of Psychology," skim through the rest of your text and find examples you believe illustrate each of these concepts. The Prologue provides you with many ideas of the chapters that cover the different areas of psychology where good examples can be found. (LO 1.9)

   a. nature

   b. nurture

   c. free will

   d. determinism

AS YOU READ ... CONCEPT MAP ACTIVITIES

ACTIVITY 1: Complete this concept map for the Basic Principles of Critical Thinking

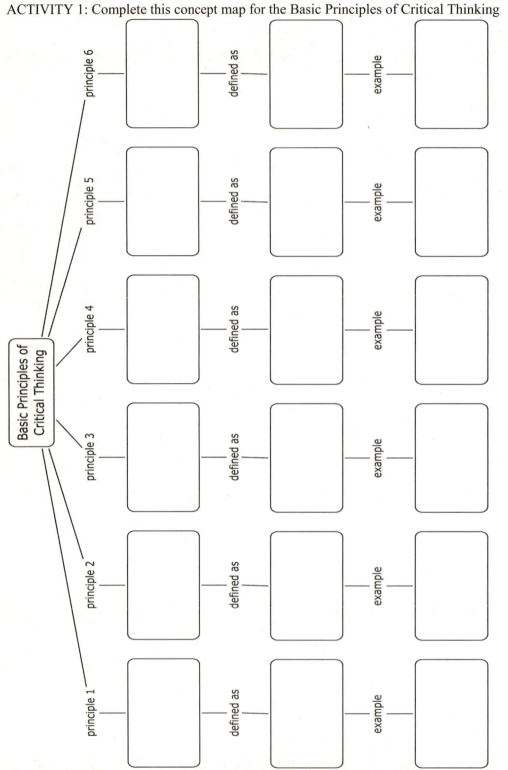

Author activity content supported by *IHMC Cmap Tools* Copyright ©1998-2007 Institute for Human & Machine Cognition

ACTIVITY 2: Provide your own original examples for these 5 things that make psychology challenging.

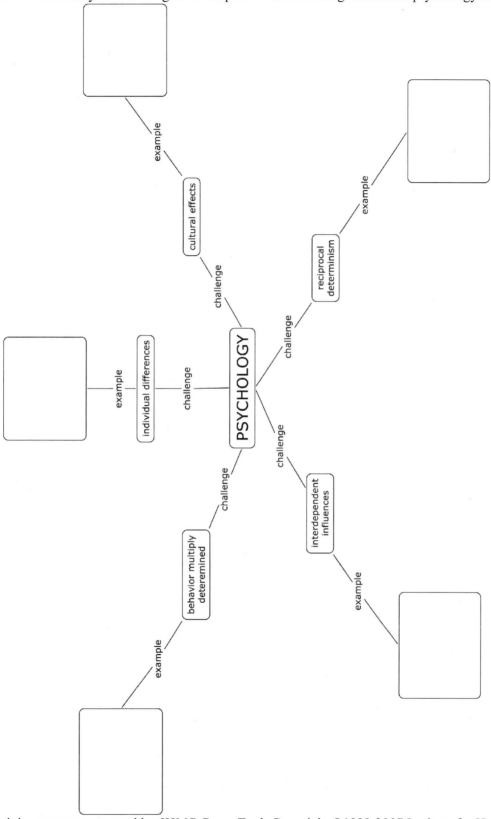

Author activity content supported by *IHMC Cmap Tools* Copyright ©1998-2007 Institute for Human & Machine Cognition

AS YOU READ … MYTH OR REALITY?

Myth: Human behavior is more erratic during a full moon.

Reality: No evidence in terms of crime rates or hospitalizations indicate that human behavior is any more erratic during a full moon than it is during any other phase of the moon.

1. Develop an argument that people's false belief in the negative effects of the full moon can be attributed to confirmation bias.

Myth: People can bend spoons and walk across hot coals just using the power of their minds.

Reality: Of course these feats are not accomplished using the power of mind. People often pay large amounts of money to attend training sessions to help them unleash and connect with the power of their minds to accomplish such activities, but they are just being swindled.

1. Develop several hypotheses, drawing on the combined principles of scientific thinking, the warning signs of pseudoscience, and logical fallacies in scientific thinking, to clearly reason through and provide alternative explanations for what might be happening during these and other sleights-of-mind.

Myth: Parapsychology is the name for a subtype of psychology.
Reality: Parapsychology has little if any true psychological science to back it up.

1. Go to http://www.parapsychology.org and read about parapsychology.
    a. Evaluate the quality of this web site using the guidelines in the Prologue to this Study Guide.
    b. Evaluate parapsychology in terms of psychological science's "Great Theoretical Frameworks" as delineated in your text. Does parapsychology fit in with any of these frameworks? If not, why not? If so, which ones and how?
    c. Which of psychology's subtypes would parapsychology best fit with? Why? Is it easy to "niche" parapsychology into the standard subtypes of psychology? Why or why not?

2. If you accept a definition of psychology as a systematic, scientific consideration of human and animal behavior, then programs in parapsychology may fall short. To get an example of typical programs in parapsychology, see http://www.itp.edu/ and http://www.saybrook.edu/phs/academicprograms/hs/phd and http://www.aiht.edu/catalog/parapsychic_courses.asp At these web sites you will find information about how you can receive a B.S., M.S., or Ph.D. in Parapsychic Science.
    a. How do the descriptions of these programs differ from a standard college program of study? Do they show the same breadth of instruction across disciplines? Compare the requirements to achieve your degree, to the program of study described at the second link. It is a 61-unit program with no general education courses included and culminates in a Bachelor of Science degree.
    b. Why do you think this program might be a detriment to a good education?

As You Read ... Put Your Scientific Thinking Skills to the Test

1. Your text points out in the first fictoid, that physicists and other "hard" scientists are no more skeptical than any other people, and less so than psychologists. Think of the reasons why this might be so. Consider what their education and training might (or might not) entail and how this might affect their degree of scientific skepticism when it comes to human behavior.

2. Psychological scientists always have a null hypothesis (a tacit statement of no differences between examined groups) that underlies each research hypothesis (an explicit statement of expected findings in a research study). How do you think the null hypothesis helps scientists to not fall prey to confirmation bias?

3. Consider each of the six basic scientific thinking principles. For each principle, note one belief that you seriously considered or held in the past, before you rejected it by applying that scientific thinking principle.

4. According to L. Ron Hubbard, author of *Dianetics*, when the body dies, the spirit within will look for a new body. Often it will hang around pregnant women and enter the baby as it takes its first breath. How do you suppose Hubbard knows that events happen this way? What qualifies the claim as pseudoscientific?

5. As the text notes, scientific thinking is not limited to understanding psychology. An understanding of the interrelations among earth's systems as well as the ability to think about scientific data led to an important international agreement to protect the ozone layer, which is critical to protecting life on earth. The agreement resulted in banning substances that would deplete the ozone layer. Today, nations are finding it difficult to agree on the issue of global warming. How can psychological principles discussed in this chapter contribute to understanding the diversity of claims on this subject?

6. Assuming that you know you want to major in psychology, you may not be sure of exactly what you can do with a degree in psychology. After reading in your text about the types of psychologists, you can also go to http://www.apa.org/topics/psychologycareer.html or http://www.uni.edu/walsh/linda1.html to read more about the different careers within psychology. Develop two distinct career paths, one you can pursue with a BA and one for which you'd want to go to graduate school, that you might want to take, and what you will need to do to get from here (where you are now), to there (where you want to be eventually).

AS YOU READ ... MYPSYCHLAB CONNECTION

What Is Psychology? Science versus Intuition
What does a typical student think about psychology? **Watch** the video titled *How much do you know about psychology?* To see how biased we can be in making decisions, complete the **Explore** *Confirmation Bias.*

Psychological Pseudoscience: Imposters of Science
Can people talk to the dead? **Watch** the video titled *Cold reading: Talking to popular heaven medium James Van Pragh.* **Explore** why astrology is considered a pseudoscience and how psychologists study it in *The Pseudoscience of Astrology.* Can you influence the outcome of a coin toss? Participate in the **Explore** *Coin Toss* to learn when events do not predict subsequent outcomes. Want to be a better consumer of information in the media? **Listen** to this podcast and learn how to evaluate reports of psychological findings in the news. *Psychology in the News.*

Scientific Thinking: Distinguishing Fact from Fiction
Can you think yourself wealthy or think yourself to good grades? **Watch** the video titled *The Secret.* Review guidelines for **Explore** *How to Be a Critical Thinker.* Then **Listen** to two psychologists discuss the six critical thinking principles and how they can be applied to scientific and pseudoscientific topics. *Science and Pseudoscience.* To better understand that correlation cannot imply causation **Watch** the videos *Magical Thinking Adults* and *Magical Thinking Children.* Then **Explore** *Accelerated Learning* to help you better understand scientific skepticism.

Psychology's Past and Present: What A Long, Strange Trip It's Been
Why has the percentage of women in the field of psychology increased in recent years? **Watch** the video titled *Women and the Field of Psychology: Florence Denmark.* Take a **Quick Review** quiz on *The Great Theoretical Frameworks of Psychology* to review the various theoretical perspectives. Take a **Quick Review** quiz on *The Great Debates of Psychology* and see if you understand the debates that have helped to shape the field of psychology **Explore** the *Psychology Timeline* to see the timeline of significant events in the field of psychology and biographies of contributors to the field. **Explore** the types of psychologists with *Psychologists at Work* to learn more about the work and various fields of psychologists. Are these exciting times for psychologists and psychology students? **Watch** the video titled *So much to choose from: Phil Zimbardo.* Can psychology change your life? **Watch** the video *The Complexity of Humans: Phil Zimbardo.* **Listen** to learn more about *The Nature-Nurture Debate.*

AFTER YOU READ... PRACTICE TEST #1

Before beginning this practice test, estimate the percent you expect to get correct.
Anticipated percent correct: _____

1. Parents often use different discipline techniques even among their own children, each of whom have a unique personality and temperament. This situation illustrates the principle of
   a. multiple determinism.
   b. introspection.
   c. reciprocal determinism.
   d. reflexivity.

2. Science
   a. is an approach to evaluating evidence.
   b. refers to a body of established knowledge.
   c. is too rigid to help us to overcome preexisting biases in thinking.
   d. refers to what we call the complicated content of fields such as chemistry and biology.

3. Which of the following statements is TRUE regarding "scientific theories"?
   a. A theory is only proven to be a fact when all researchers accept it.
   b. A theory is a general scientific explanation of how the world works.
   c. It is difficult to determine which of several competing scientific theories is better because theories rely largely on personal opinion.
   d. It is difficult to determine which of several competing scientific theories is better because theories rely largely on the degree of authority of the researcher.

4. Jesse believes he sometimes has ESP. For example, just last week he predicted there would be a pop quiz in class, so he studied extra hard, and sure enough, there was a pop quiz. Unfortunately, Jesse forgets about those times when he predicts a pop quiz and there is none. Jesse's behavior illustrates
   a. a metaphysical claim.
   b. confirmation bias.
   c. belief perseverance.
   d. hindsight bias.

5. What percentage of self-help books offer untested advice?
   a. 25%
   b. 50%
   c. 75%
   d. 95%

6. The problem with many pseudosciences is that
   a. just because they can't be falsified doesn't mean they aren't both valid and reliable.
   b. they "sound" scientific, and so fool people into thinking they are truly scientific.
   c. they are often misunderstood by scientists, who demand ridiculously rigorous tests of their scientific value.
   d. if too many people subscribe to them, too many people will develop superior skills and there are not enough jobs "at the top."

7. To support his case for the benefits of Vitamin C, George describes the changes in his health as a result of taking increased doses of Vitamin C. George is using _____ evidence.
   a. unambiguous
   b. correlational
   c. anecdotal
   d. scientific

8. The problem with using anecdotes as evidence is that
   a. they cannot be falsified.
   b. they take into account large amounts of data.
   c. peer-review of anecdotes is a time-consuming process.
   d. they are prone to bias, making them difficult to interpret.

9. When we see the "man in the moon" we exhibit
   a. pareidolia.
   b. apophenia.
   c. the naturalistic fallacy.
   d. terror management.

10. Sometimes people have problems that traditional medicine and psychotherapy don't seem to help. They may then turn to pseudoscience because of its
    a. perceived sense of control in an unpredictable world.
    b. clear and rational explanations.
    c. strong base of empirical research evidence to support it.
    d. independence and lack of connectivity to other sciences.

11. Scientific skepticism means scientists
    a. approach new findings in science with cynicism.
    b. reject ALL claims that fail to match their previous beliefs.
    c. approach ALL claims, even the most outrageous, with an open mind.
    d. reject scientific findings that contradict previously established scientific findings.

12. Phillipe has noticed that every time he dreams about his psychology class, the next day the professor gives a pop quiz in class. Phillipe believes he has a type of ESP in which his dreams are predicting the future. Unfortunately, he has failed to
    a. rule out rival hypotheses.
    b. ask his friends if they would agree.
    c. consider using his ESP to predict other important events in his life.
    d. consult an expert authority on ESP and dreams, to see whether his conclusion could be possible.

13. According to the third variable problem, we often fail to notice
    a. that two variables are truly causally related.
    b. the statistical probability of a relationship between variables.
    c. when a third cause can result from a previous sequencing of cause and effect.
    d. another variable that could be leading two other variables to seem to be causally related.

14. Based on census data, the government finds that people who have more electrical appliances in their homes have fewer children. An "expert" therefore recommends that people who want smaller families should buy more electrical appliances. The expert has failed to consider that
    a. these same people may also believe in pseudoscientific beliefs.
    b. some appliances may be better for birth control than others.

c. the data are probably based on anecdotes.

d. correlation is not causation.

15. Which of these hypotheses can be falsified?
    a. People who believe in a soul live longer.
    b. Babies who die in infancy become angels.
    c. The spirits of our ancestors guide our present lives.
    d. How well we live today determines the life form we will return as in our future lives.

16. The major news media love to report new studies, especially when the findings are dramatic. Newscasters will often joke about not knowing what to believe anymore. In fact, people should know that
    a. even a good skeptic can accept a single, scientifically clean study.
    b. most of these studies need to be replicated before being accepted.
    c. when one study falsifies another study's results, this creates confusion even for scientists.
    d. when a study contradicts a prior study's findings, its results need to be supported by greater authority of the researchers.

17. The year 1879 is often considered the "birth year" of psychology as an independent laboratory science, because in 1879
    a. Ivan Pavlov discovered classical conditioning.
    b. Sigmund Freud wrote, *The Interpretation of Dreams*.
    c. Charles Darwin published, *The Origin of the Species*.
    d. Wilhelm Wundt developed and opened the first psychology laboratory.

18. Carlos is a landscaper who picks plants for outdoor living spaces based on how well the scents and colors of the plants blend together. He tries to understand why some plants are more aesthetically pleasing to his clients. Carlos's approach to landscaping best reflects
    a. functionalism.
    b. structuralism.
    c. behaviorism.
    d. empiricism.

19. Evolutionary psychology
    a. provides readily testable hypotheses.
    b. depends on the overall strength of organisms relative to one another.
    c. applies the theory of natural selection to human and animal behavior.
    d. suggests hypotheses that provide deep explanations of human and animal behavior.

20. Dr. Brown is researching the effects of loud noise on auditory development in monkeys. Dr. Grace is examining how loud noise in the classroom affects test taking. Dr. Brown is doing _____ research, whereas Dr. Grace is doing _____research.
    a. basic; applied
    b. invasive; theoretical
    c. structural; functional
    d. qualitative; quantitative

After completing the test, calculate your percent correct
(/ 20 =) x 100 = _____.

How accurate were your expectations? Does your performance suggest need for additional study? For the items you missed, go back and identify why the "correct" answer is the best answer.

AFTER YOU READ... PRACTICE TEST #2

Before beginning this practice test, estimate the percent you expect to get correct.
Anticipated percent correct: _____

1. According to naïve realism
   a. we think that we perceive the world exactly as it is, although this can be misleading.
   b. reality can never be determined by its physical properties.
   c. our perception of the world comes from its objective properties.
   d. we cannot rely on common sense without risking a distorted view of reality.

2. Common sense
   a. is never accurate.
   b. is not "testable" using scientific methods.
   c. almost always contradicts research evidence.
   d. provides a good starting point for developing scientific hypotheses.

3. A tendency to notice and remember instances in which events match our prior beliefs can strongly contribute to
   a. hindsight bias.
   b. placebo effects.
   c. confirmation bias
   d. illusory correlations.

4. Research shows that many students come into their first introductory psychology class with many misconceptions. Unfortunately, they leave the class with many of these same misconceptions. This illustrates
   a. disinterestedness.
   b. scientific thinking.
   c. scientific skepticism.
   d. belief perseverance.

5. Popular psychology has led to an explosion of
   a. primarily correct information.
   b. primarily misinformation that can be harmful if followed.
   c. some correct information as well as much misinformation.
   d. a small amount of misinformation and, fortunately, much correct information.

6. Ad hoc immunizing hypotheses take advantage of using
   b. facts rather than possibilities.
   b. loopholes that prevent falsification.
   c. testimonial results rather than experimental results.
   d. what is possible rather than what has been demonstrated.

7. People are often drawn to pseudoscience because it
   a. is based on rational thinking, and is more effortful to evaluate.
   b. is based on finding order in an otherwise chaotic world.
   c. follows Hume's dictum by providing extraordinary evidence for its extraordinary claims.
   d. follows Occam's Razor by providing precise explanations for natural and supernatural phenomena.

8. Which of the following statements about pseudoscience is FALSE?
   a. It not only prevents us from seeking proper care but can actually cause direct harm.
   b. It is especially seductive because it uses scientific-sounding language and provides everyday evidence that even laypeople can understand without much effort.
   c. It prevents people from applying a truly scientific approach to both large and small problems that face us as individuals and as a society.
   d. It tends to strengthen the critical thinking skills of those who believe in it.

9. Jeff has been treating his depression with herbal remedies because they are natural and his crystal-healing therapist recommended them. Because his depression is severe, Jeff has not been able to work in more than a year. Jeff's case illustrates
   a. blind spot bias.
   b. opportunity cost.
   c. confirmation bias.
   d. the bandwagon fallacy.

10. Annette has been criticized by her friends as living by the Missouri state motto, "Show me." As a skeptical scientist, Annette most likely
    a. takes this as an insult.
    b. takes this as a compliment.
    c. realizes she might need to change her attitude.
    d. decides to move to Missouri to live among people more like herself.

11. Professor Dakkhi administered a test of learning strategies and a test of motivations for learning. She found a strong positive correlation between the two tests. She can now safely conclude that
    a. the use of learning strategies is directly related to the type of motivation a student has for learning.
    b. no relationship is evident between strategy use and motivations for learning.
    c. the particular motivation a student has for learning causes the student to use a particular strategy.
    d. the particular learning strategies that a student uses cause that student to adopt a certain motivation for learning.

12. Which of the following reflects a true scientific approach, as opposed to being a pseudoscience?
    a. Using lie detector machines to assess a person's honesty.
    b. Using handwriting analysis to assess a person's personality.
    c. Using hypnosis to help a person recover repressed memories of early childhood sexual abuse.
    d. Using replication to show the correlation between watching violent TV programs and playground aggressiveness in elementary school children.

13. If you follow the belief that a simple answer to a problem is usually most accurate, you are using the principle of
    a. Occam's Razor.
    b. falsifiability.
    c. pareidolia.
    d. apophenia.

14. Marilise is convinced that because she sometimes wakes up with bruises on her body, that she has been abducted by aliens who performed tests on her while she is asleep. You tell her that
    a. if she really believes it, and has vivid memories of her abductions, it is probably true.
    b. her extraordinary claim really requires more evidence than waking up with bruises.

    c.   her argument seems sufficiently rational to believe with the evidence of the mysterious bruising.

    d.   she probably needs to be hypnotized to help her remember more details of what was done to her by the aliens.

15. Cyndi and her friends are sitting around a table at the campus coffee shop, systematically comparing their own inner thoughts on how they "know" that they have an ability called "memory." Cyndi and her friends are engaging in
    a.   spiritualism.
    b.   introspection.
    c.   structuralism.
    d.   psychoanalysis.

16. Which approach to psychology was advocated by Edward Titchener in the late 1800s?
    a.   Humanistic psychology
    b.   Psychoanalysis
    c.   Functionalism
    d.   Structuralism

17. The theoretical framework that focused on examining our external, objective responses to environmental stimuli is
    a.   behaviorism.
    b.   structuralism.
    c.   functionalism.
    d.   psychoanalysis.

18. Which of the following is MOST likely to work in a research setting?
    a.   school psychologist
    b.   experimental psychologist
    c.   forensic psychologist
    d.   counseling psychologist

19. These days, the nature–nurture debate is more focused on
    a.   why the debate has been dead since the genome project has now finished mapping out nature's contributions to behavior.
    b.   how nature and nurture work together.
    c.   determining exactly which genes are responsible for which of our behaviors.
    d.   delineating the failures of genetics to predict behaviors, supporting the nurture account.

20. Some scientists argue that free will is an illusion. Support for this notion comes from
    a.   the finding that so many of our behaviors only occur through great effort on our part.
    b.   evidence of our direct access to the cause of our behaviors.
    c.   B. F. Skinner's argument that we are not conscious of all of the stimuli in the environment that elicit a behavioral response from us.
    d.   the effects of mental illness on our ability to act freely.

After completing the test, calculate your percent correct
(/ 20 =   ) x 100 = _____ .

How accurate were your expectations? Does your performance suggest need for additional study? For the items you missed, go back and identify why the "correct" answer is the best answer.

AFTER YOU READ . . . PRACTICE TEST ANSWER KEYS

Practice Test 1.

1. c (p. 4)
2. a (p. 6)
3. b (p. 7)
4. b (p. 8)
5. d (p. 11)
6. b (p. 11)
7. c (p. 13)
8. d (p. 14)
9. a (p. 15)
10. a (p. 16)
11. c (p. 21)
12. a (p. 21-23)
13. d (p. 23)
14. d (p. 23)
15. a (p. 24)
16. b (p. 24)
17. d (p. 27)
18. a (p. 30)
19. c (p. 34)
20. a (p. 36)

Practice Test 2.

1. a (p. 5)
2. d (p. 5)
3. c (p. 8)
4. d (p. 9)
5. c (p. 11)
6. b (p. 12)
7. b (p. 14)
8. d (p. 11-18)
9. b (p. 19)
10. b (p. 21)
11. a (p. 22)
12. d (p. 24)
13. a (p. 25)
14. b (p. 25)
15. b (p. 27)
16. d (p. 29)
17. a (p. 30)
18. b (p. 33)
19. b (p. 34)
20. c (p. 35)

AFTER YOU READ ... CONCEPT MAPPING ACTIVITY ANSWERS

ACTIVITY 1: Complete this concept map for the Basic Principles of Critical Thinking

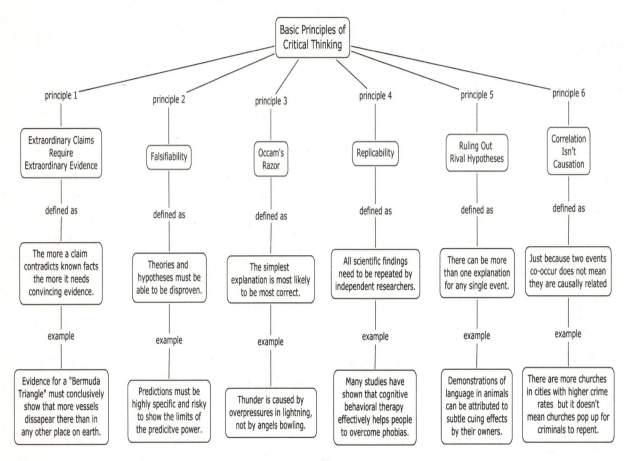

ACTIVITY 2: Provide your own original examples for the 5 things that make psychology challenging.

For this activity there is a wide range of personal examples that you can fill in appropriately.

CHAPTER 2
RESEARCH METHODS
SAFEGUARDS AGAINST ERROR

BEFORE YOU READ ... CHAPTER PREVIEW

Students of psychology often wonder why they are expected to learn research methods when they "just want to learn about people." As you will discover in this text, thinking critically involves understanding that some things that seem to be true may not actually be true. Claims people make about behavior, or observations you may make yourself, may not hold up when looked at objectively. Your task is to learn to tell the difference between the claims that are most likely to be true and the claims that are probably not true. An understanding of research methods can help you with this task.

Because we are *cognitive misers* we tend to *oversimplify* by employing **heuristics**, or mental shortcuts. As a result, we sometimes draw inaccurate and potentially harmful conclusions about human behavior.

Research methods provide tools to help us avoid being tricked by our own **cognitive biases**. For example, we often make decision by using the **representativeness heuristic** (making comparisons to previously developed prototypes) or the **availability heuristic** (what comes to mind easiest). Our observations can also lead us to ignore **base rates,** as in the **hindsight bias** (our tendency to believe we "knew it all along") and by **overconfidence**. **Scientific methods** are designed to counter such tendencies to fool ourselves. Scientific methods permit us to systematically test a *hypothesis* (specific prediction) and to determine whether objective evidence exists to support our hypothesis.

There are several research designs that help us minimize our biases. Each design has advantages and disadvantages. Effective research programs include a variety of designs. **Naturalistic observation** allows us to observe and report on behaviors as they occur naturally in the real world. They are high in **external validity** (the degree to which they can generalize to the real world) but are low in **internal validity** (the degree to which they can make causal claims). **Case studies** allow us to generate hypotheses but not test hypotheses. Case studies provide **existence proofs**—evidence for psychological phenomena. *Self-report measures*, such as *surveys*, allow the collection of large amount of information in a quick time frame. The best surveys use **random selection**, where each person has a known probability of being selected to participate. Self-reports, as is true for all measures in psychology, must have **reliability** (consistency) and **validity** (truly measure what they claim to measure). However, self-reports depend on people truly knowing themselves, and being honest. Some people are prone to **response sets**—answer all the items a particular way—which can result in *positive impression management* (making one's self seem good), or in *malingering* (making one's self seem worse off than is true). Sometimes others are asked to rate us. Here again, problems can arise with *halo effects* (positive responses spill over to other responses).

Correlational studies allow us to determine whether variables are systematically related to one another and allow us to make predictions but do not allow us to make causal claims. We cannot say that one of our variables causes the other because in a correlational study, we have not ruled out alternative explanations. Correlations vary from -1.00 (perfect inverse relationship) through 0.00 (no relationship) through +1.00 (perfect direct relationship). Correlations can be depicted by a **scatterplot,** a graph of all paired outcomes. A bias in thinking to guard against is illusory correlation, the perception of a correlation when in fact there is none. Illusory correlations can lead to superstitious behaviors. Illusory correlations occur because we notice when two things co-occur but forget the less notable failures. The media are notorious for misinterpreting the meaning of correlational studies. Frequently the media will report correlations and suggest the findings imply causation when no such relation is supported by the data.

In order to rule out alternative explanations and be able to make causal statements, a true **experiment** must be conducted. A true experiment assures that the manipulated variable, the **independent variable** (IV), and *only* the IV, caused the variability observed in the **dependent variable** (DV), the measured outcome. Experiments must satisfy certain criteria. They must have a true IV that is manipulated and must **randomly assign** participants to **experimental conditions** and **control conditions.** Each variable must be **operationally defined**—abstract concepts must be made concrete and testable. Experimental control allows the experimenter to make sure everything in the experimental and comparison conditions are exactly the same in every way except in terms of the manipulation and that all **confounding variables** have been controlled.

An experiment is not easy to design and not all questions can be studied with experimental methods. Challenges include avoiding the **placebo effect**, which make it appear that a treatment is effective despite it not having a real effect. Making sure participants are blind—unaware—of the condition they have been randomly assigned to can help. The *nocebo effect* (harm that comes from an expectation of harm) must also be guarded against. Researchers must also be cautious to avoid their own biases. This **experimenter expectancy effect** (called the Rosenthal effect) can be avoided by conducting **double-blind** studies where neither the experimenter nor the participant is aware of which condition individuals are in. Finally, researchers must guard against **demand characteristics.** These are cues that give away the experiment's hypothesis and thereby change the participant's behavior.

Psychologists must attend to the rights of their research participants. Unfortunately, too many examples show how researchers in the past have put their research interest above the interests of the participants. Today, *Institutional Review Boards* review and approve all research with humans and other animals as participants and weigh the benefits of the research against any costs. A key element of ethical treatment is **informed consent**, although sometimes *deception* is used to assure natural behavior. This often involves the use of a *confederate*, and must always be followed by a full *debriefing*.

Much of the misunderstanding of psychology is the result of a failure to understand the role of **statistics** in research claims. Misunderstandings can involve simple **descriptive statistics** as well as **inferential statistics**. For example, although several measures of **central tendency** exist, many people don't realize the degree to which the **mean** is highly misleading when there are **outliers**. In that case, the **median** or the **mode** may better describe central tendency. Similarly, **variability** can be measured in several ways that help avoid confusion, such as the **range** or the **standard deviation**. In terms of **inferential statistics**, the concept of significance is critical in knowing whether an observed difference reflects a real (not chance) difference in the population. At the same time, it is important to know that a difference may be *significant* but may still not have any *practical* value.

Failure to understand such concepts can contribute to the media's ability to lie with statistics. Consumers of information must be critical in evaluating claims. Questions to ask include (1) Who is the source of the information? (2) Are there exaggerations in going from data to claim? (3) Is there balance in the reporting of evidence? The *base rate fallacy* must be avoided.

Better journals have peer review, where other researchers evaluate the studies submitted for publication and focus on avoiding the pitfalls of each research design. Finally, we must consider the source of our information. Some magazines are more scientifically reputable than others. In particular, we need to look out for *sharpening* (exaggeration), *leveling* (minimizing details), and *pseudosymmetry* (balancing science and pseudoscience as if they are equal).

BEFORE YOU READ ... LEARNING OBJECTIVES

After reading Chapter 2 you should be able to:

2.1   Identify heuristics and biases that prevent us from thinking clearly about psychology
2.2   Describe the advantages and disadvantages of using naturalistic observation, case studies, and surveys
2.3   Describe the role of correlational designs and distinguish correlation from causation
2.4   Identify the components of an experiment and the potential pitfalls that can lead to faulty conclusions
2.5   Explain the ethical obligations of researchers toward their research participants
2.6   Describe both sides of the debate on the use of animals as research subjects
2.7   Identify uses of various measures of central tendency and dispersion
2.8   Explain how inferential statistics can help us to determine whether we can generalize from our sample to the full population
2.9   Show how statistics can be misused for purposes of persuasion
2.10   Identify flaws in research design
2.11   Identify skills for evaluating psychological claims in the popular media

BEFORE YOU READ ... TERM IDENTIFICATION

availability heuristic (p. 48)
base rate (p. 47)
blind (p. 63)
case study (p. 51)
central tendency (p. 70)
cognitive biases (p. 48)
control group (p. 61)
correlational design (p. 56)
demand characteristics (p. 65)
dependent variable (p. 61)
descriptive statistics (p. 70)
double-blind (p. 64)
existence proof (p. 51)
experiment (p. 61)
experimental group (p. 61)
experimenter expectancy effect (p. 64)
external validity (p. 51)
heuristics (p. 46)
hindsight bias (p. 48)
illusory correlation (p. 58)
independent variable (p. 61)
inferential statistics (p. 71)

informed consent (p. 67)
internal validity (p. 51)
mean (p. 70)
median (p. 70)
mode (p. 70)
naturalistic observation (p. 50)
operational definition (p. 61)
overconfidence (p. 48)
placebo effect (p. 62)
prefrontal lobotomy (p. 45)
random assignment (p. 61)
random selection (p. 52)
range (p. 71)
reliability (p. 53)
representativeness heuristic (p. 47)
response set (p. 55)
scatterplot (p. 56)
standard deviation (p. 71)
statistics (p. 70)
validity (p. 54)
variability (p. 71)

AS YOU READ ... PRACTICE ACTIVITIES

THE BEAUTY AND NECESSITY OF GOOD RESEARCH DESIGN

1. After reviewing 23 empirical studies on sugar and children, Dr. Mark Wolraich and colleagues concluded that sugar does not affect aggression, mood, motor skills, or cognitive skills (Wolraich, Wilson, & White, 1995). Yet many people claim that despite any research, they know there is a causal relation because they have *seen* it many times. (LO 2.1)

    Why are even multiple observations of children eating sugar and being active not good evidence supporting a causal connection?

    What alternative explanations exist for why one might observe children eating sugar and being active?

2. Maria likes classical music, wears glasses, and dresses plainly. Which is more likely?
    a. She is a librarian.
    b. She plays the piano.
    c. She is a librarian who plays the piano.

    Why did you answer as you did?

    Was your answer influenced by a stereotype you formed of Maria?

    If so, you may have relied on the representativeness heuristic and failed to consider base rates.

    Consider this: is the likelihood of 'a' and 'b' together more or less likely than either 'a' or 'b' alone? (LO 2.1)

3. Our tendency to focus on stereotypes and to ignore base rates contributes to our misuse of the representativeness heuristic. We also ignore base rates when we misinterpret statements like the following: "Most accidents occur around the home." Although the statement is true, does it mean that the home is the most dangerous place to be? Why or why not? (LO 2.1)

4. Which is the more common cause of death in the United States: accidents, asthma, or tornadoes? (LO 2.1)

   On what did you base your answer? If you used the availability heuristic, you likely based your answer on the cause of death for which there was an easily retrieved image from memory. The answer, however, may not have provided such a memory. Asthma causes 16 times more deaths than accidents and 20 times more deaths than tornadoes.

5. Here is an anagram: OSTAT
   On a scale from 1 to 10, how easy do you think it would be for someone to solve this anagram?

   Here is an anagram: AERTW
   On a scale from 1 to 10, how easy do you think it would be for someone to solve this anagram?

   Each of these anagrams is 5 letters, comes from a basic spelling list, and uses the same strategy to mix letters. The first solution is 'toast' and the second solution is 'water.' Why do you think most people rate the first as easier than the second? How does this example demonstrate hindsight bias? (LO 2.1)

THE SCIENTIFIC METHOD: TOOLBOX OF SKILLS

1. Complete this table comparing the types of designs, their advantages, disadvantages, and types of conclusions we can draw from them. (LO 2.2 and 2.3)

	Advantages	Disadvantages	Conclusions
Naturalistic Observation			
Case Study			
Survey			
Correlation			
Experiment			

2. Dr. See teaches statistics and biological psychology. Students see these classes as difficult and Dr. See as a hard teacher. When they finally have an opportunity to interact with Dr. See outside of class, they find that she is really funny and a nice person and they are SHOCKED. What "effect" discussed in the text would explain the students' surprise? (LO 2.2)

3. A bathroom scale that is 5 pounds off can be reliable (consistent), but is it valid? Can a measure be valid but not reliable? Why is reliability so important when we are trying to make predictions? (LO 2.2)

4. Research in Taiwan finds a significant positive correlation between the number of appliances in the home and whether a couple uses birth control (known as the toaster method of birth control). What does this correlation mean? Can you predict whether a couple uses birth control from knowing how many appliances they own? Why or why not? (LO 2.3)

5. Create a scatterplot from the following data set (plot the scores). (LO 2.3)
   What type of correlational relationship do the data suggest?

Cups of Coffee/Day	GPA
1	3.5
2	3.0
3	2.5
4	2.0

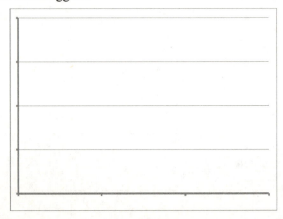

6. As the text indicates, illusory correlations occur because we are poor judges of the degree to which events occur together. We attend to confirming evidence and ignore disconfirming evidence. What are people making the following claims ignoring? (LO 2.3)

    a. Every time I wash my car it rains!

    b. My joints hurt when it rains.

7. Students often confuse random selection with random assignment. To help you keep these concepts distinct in your mind, explain why random selection is important for external validity but not so important for internal validity. Then explain why random assignment is important for internal validity but not so much for external validity. (LO 2.2, 2.3 and 2.4)

8. In the original research on the effect of listening to Mozart's music on abilities, the researcher randomly assigned college students to one of three conditions. Group A listened to 10 minutes of Mozart's piano sonata in G major. Group B listened to a relaxation tape. Group C listened to silence. Group A performed better than group B and C on a task of spatial reasoning when measured immediately after they listened but not when measured 10 minutes after listening. (LO 2.4)

    What is the independent variable?

    What is the dependent variable?

    Based on the sample, the IV, and DV, what could the researchers *appropriately* conclude?

9. Research suggests that 80% of drug effects can be attributed to the placebo effect. Why might the placebo effect be even greater when the placebo produces side effects? (LO 2.4)

ETHICAL ISSUES IN RESEARCH DESIGN

1. What is informed consent? Why is it critical to protecting rights of research participants? (LO 2.5)

2. What is "deception"? When is the use of deception justified in a psychological study? (LO 2.5)

3. What is a "debriefing"? If you have participated in a psychological study as part of your introductory psychology course, were you given such a debriefing? (LO 2.5)

4. Introductory psychology students often participate in research studies. Acacia, an introductory psychology student, shows up for a study and is given a questionnaire about sibling relationships. Her brother was killed in Iraq a year ago and she gets emotional when she thinks about him. She does not want to complete the questionnaire. The researcher tells her she has to complete the form because it is required for her introductory psychology class. Evaluate this scenario in terms of ethical guidelines for research. (LO 2.5)

5. What critical question must a researcher answer if his or her study using animals is to be considered justified? (L.O. 2.6)

6. Research with animals is both critical and controversial. Think about your beliefs about such research. Are there types of research you find acceptable? Are there types of animals you find to be acceptable as subjects? Are there types of regulations that make animal research acceptable? Much of what we know about the function of the neuron has been learned from the study of the squid. Is a squid an acceptable subject of study? Research with invertebrates is not regulated. Should it be? (L.O. 2.6)

STATISTICS: THE LANGUAGE OF PSYCHOLOGICAL RESEARCH

1. Calculate the mean, median, and mode for the following distributions. (LO 2.7)

In a community of 9 households, the annual incomes are as follows:	Women's shoes are sold as follows:
$ 20,000	5
30,000	6
30,000	9
40,000	9
1,000,000	11
_____	_____
mean =	mean =
median =	median =
mode =	mode =

Which measure of central tendency would be most appropriate for someone trying to describe each of the distributions? Why?

2. In comparing distributions, why is it important to know about their central tendency *and* to know about variability? (LO 2.7 and 2.8)

3. Researchers consistently find that men are statistically significantly faster than women in laboratory studies of simple reaction time (signal comes on, push a button—see http://biology.clemson.edu/bpc/bp/Lab/110/reaction.htm#Gender). Generally, across a very wide range of studies men are approximately 40 milliseconds faster than women. Is this a difference that makes a difference? Why or why not? (LO 2.8)

4. For the following claims, identify the information being "left out." (LO 2.9)

   a. No other product is more effective than ours.

   b. Brand X toothpaste users have 27% fewer cavities.

   c. There are more plane accidents today than in 1911.

5. An advertisement claims, "People rate our beer higher than any other beer!" and provides the following graph. Evaluate their claim and the evidence. (LO 2.9)

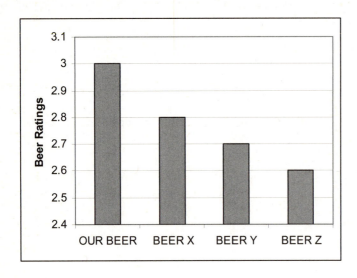

EVALUATING PSYCHOLOGICAL RESEARCH

1. A marriage counselor notices that quite a few of the couples she works with are opposites of one another in a variety of ways. She wonders whether "opposites attract." She gives personality inventories to her clients and finds that in fact, the majority are opposites. She writes a book to show how we are attracted to people who are our opposites. How would you evaluate her study and her claim? (LO 2.10)

2. Dr. Concoctor is interested in the effect of computer games on young boys' aggressive behavior. He randomly assigns a group of young boys to play either a simple ping-pong type computer game or an action-packed combat type computer game for 30 minutes. He then observes the boys' behavior on the playground. (LO 2.10)

   What type of research method did Dr. Concotor use for this study?

   Is there an independent variable? If so, what is it?

   Is there a dependent variable? If so, what is it?

   Do you see any problem(s) with this study? If so, what? Can you think of a way to fix the problem(s)?

3. Evaluate the information on the following web sites:
   http://mozarteffect.com
   http://faculty.washington.edu/chudler/music.html

   How credible are the sites? What are the author's claiming? On what evidence are their claims based? How confident should you be in the Mozart Effect? (LO 2.11)

AS YOU READ ... CONCEPT MAP ACTIVITIES

ACTIVITY 1: Review some of the ways research participants' rights are protected by completing this map.

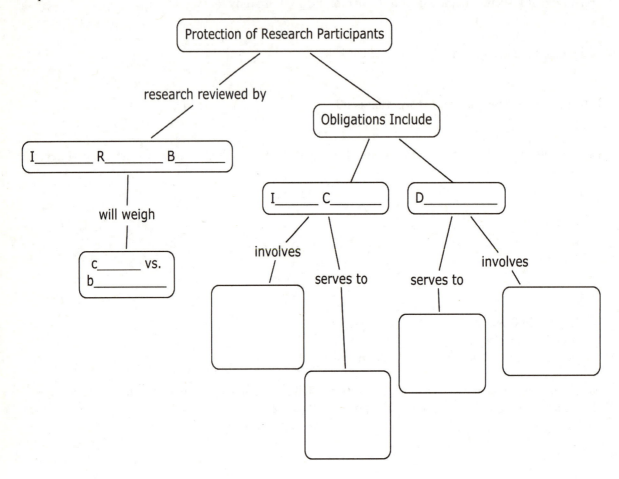

Author activity content supported by *IHMC Cmap Tools* Copyright ©1998-2007 Institute for Human & Machine Cognition

ACTIVITY 2: Try to complete this concept map by referring to the types of research design described in the text and summarized in the table you created for an earlier activity. Compare the ways of summarizing, Table vs. Map. Which do you prefer?

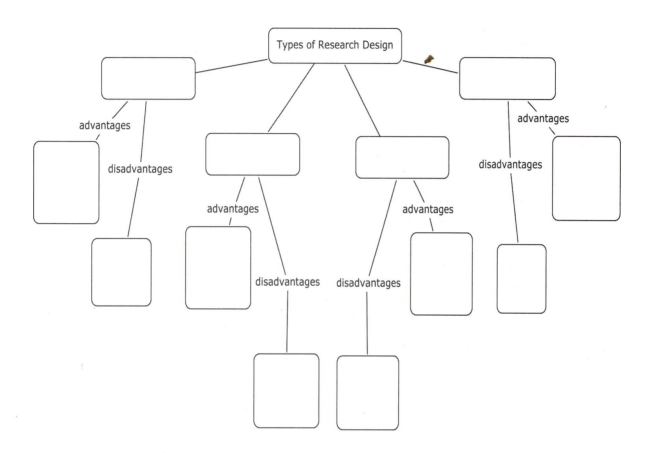

Author activity content supported by *IHMC Cmap Tools* Copyright ©1998-2007 Institute for Human & Machine Cognition

AS YOU READ ... MYTH OR REALITY?

Myth: Sugar causes hyperactivity in children.
Reality: Although many believe they have observed a causal relation between children's consumption of sugary food and high activity level, objective research suggests any carbohydrate would give the same level of energy and "no one has heard of a rice high or potato buzz."

1. What cognitive biases contribute to this misconception?

Myth: 50% of all marriages end in divorce.
Reality: No credible evidence supports the statement that half of all marriages end in divorce. The overall divorce rate is on the decline.

1. Why is this misconception so pervasive?
2. Take a look at this web site for some discussion about how a misreading of statistics is likely to have contributed to the misconception.
   http://www.truthorfiction.com/rumors/d/divorce.htm

Myth: Homework for children boosts academic learning and teaches responsibility.
Reality: Homework in elementary school shows virtually no relation to performance.

Although educators will insist on the benefits of homework for young children, the empirical data do not support the claim. Harris Cooper, the major homework researcher, has shown that limited amounts of homework may contribute to performance in older children, no effect has been shown for young children. In addition, large amounts of homework contribute to negative attitudes toward school. A brief summary of this research can be found at this site: http://www.slate.com/id/2149593/

1. If the evidence fails to support an effect, why do you think educators cling to their beliefs?

As You Read ... Put Your Scientific Thinking Skills to the Test

1. The *Journal of American Pediatrics* reports a link between TV watching and obesity. Does this link imply a causal relation? What alternative explanations can you think of?

2. As your text suggests, statistics describe general tendencies that can be true in most cases even if not true for every case. That is, a claim can be made, based on statistical evidence that is true on average even though exceptions exist. Despite this probabilistic nature of statistics, the exceptional case can sometimes be made to look more persuasive than the typical case. This persuasive technique of misusing "an example" is sometimes called the "person who . . . statistic."
   a. When is the use of examples appropriate and when is it inappropriate? (*Hint*: Think of the difference between reasoning by anecdote and illustrating with anecdote.)
   b. Does your psychology instructor ever use examples? Are they used appropriately?
   c. How do politicians and advertisers use examples? Listen carefully to the next speech or testimonial you hear.

AS YOU READ ... MYPSYCHLAB CONNECTION

The Beauty and Necessity of Good Research Design
Is bias in the mind of the beholder? Learn how to avoid bias in everyday thinking. Participate in the **Simulation** activity titled *Anchoring and Adjustment.*

The Scientific Method: Toolbox of Skills
Challenge your assumptions about explanations of behavior. **Explore** *Correlations Do Not Show Causation.* Be a participant in a psychological experiment and practice your knowledge of research methods. Try the **Simulation** *Distinguishing Independent and Dependent Variables* and **Explore** *Think: Research Methods: Safeguards Against Error.* Test your knowledge of the scientific method. **Review** with *The Scientific Method: A Toolbox of Skills.*

Ethical Issues in Research Design
Can participants die in experiments? **Watch** the video titled *Before Informed Consent: Robert Guthrie.* Research with animals is also governed by ethical principles. **Watch** *Animal Rights Terrorists.*

Statistics: The Language of Psychological Research
How do we know what conclusions we can and cannot draw from data? Practice with this hands-on **Simulation**, *Doing Simple Statistics.* What does it mean to be "normal"? Familiarize yourself with the bell curve and see where you fall under it with the **Simulation** *The Normal Curve.* Is one gender really more intelligent than another? Participate in the **Simulation** titled *Doing Simple Statistics.*

Evaluating Psychological Research
Impress your friends as you apply your skills to critiquing psychological articles in the news by **Listening** to *Reviewing Reports of Psychology in the News.* How ethical would you be as a psychological researcher? Use the **Simulation** *Ethics in Psychological Research* to test your knowledge about research ethics.

AFTER YOU READ ... PRACTICE TEST #1

Before beginning this practice test, estimate the percent you expect to get correct.
Estimated percent correct _____

1. "Why do I need to know statistics and research methods? I just want to help people!" How would you answer this question?
   a. We can only prove our claims by providing statistics.
   b. Statistics are important in conducting research, but clinical observation is important in evaluating the effectiveness of therapies.
   c. Although most psychologists don't use statistics, it is a traditional part of their training.
   d. A failure to objectively evaluate therapies can harm those the therapy is trying to help.

2. The effects of fatigue play a role in an estimated two-thirds of road accidents. Yet we fear drunk drivers and rarely think of sleepy drivers. This example of selective attention reflects
   a. the base rate fallacy.
   b. overconfidence.
   c. the availability heuristic.
   d. hindsight bias.

3. Jane Goodall was the first to observe demonstrations of tool use and homicide among chimpanzees in their natural environment. The observational method she used is generally considered to be
   a. high in external validity.
   b. high in internal validity.
   c. subject to demand characteristics.
   d. difficult to interpret because of observer expectancy.

4. A new book has just come out called *Get Your Brain Fit, Now!* The author, a former Mr. Universe, claims that just as you can get your body in shape, you can get your brain fit through a series of "mental exercises." He describes these exercises and provides evidence for their effectiveness by describing in detail the stories of four people who felt dull before "getting fit" and exciting after "getting fit." The author claims his exercises helped these people and will help you too. Why would you be skeptical of this claim?
   a. We don't know if these four people gave informed consent.
   b. It is clear that these four people did not really improve.
   c. He is making use of the representativeness heuristic.
   d. The author's claim is based on anecdotal evidence.

5. Random selection is most important when
   a. it's easiest to sample the people that we come across naturally.
   b. we want to generalize to a broader population.
   c. we want to control the differences between groups.
   d. the population of interest is small.

6. Anatol is convinced his dreams can tell the future. Just the other night he dreamt of his wife and when he awoke, there she was, sleeping next to him. Anatol's belief is an example of
   a. an illusory correlation.
   b. superstitious behavior.
   c. the halo effect.
   d. hindsight bias.

7. There is a moderately large negative correlation between coffee consumption and grades. Which of the following conclusions is suggested by this finding?
   a. You can predict that if a student is a heavy coffee drinker, it is likely that s/he is getting poor grades.
   b. The correlation coefficient is probably about +.75.
   c. If you observe a good student drinking a lot of coffee, it is evidence that the correlation is wrong.
   d. There is a significant difference between coffee drinking and grades.

8. A study of college students reports finding a strong correlation between coffee consumption and grade point averages, with those drinking more coffee getting lower grades. A possible explanation for this finding is that
   a. high coffee consumption causes students to get lower grades.
   b. getting lower grades causes students to drink more coffee.
   c. a third variable could be causing both high coffee consumption and low grades.
   d. all of the above are possible explanations.

9. Why do researchers randomly assign participants in experiments to experimental and control conditions?
   a. To eliminate negative correlations in the research.
   b. In an attempt to make equivalent groups that differ only in terms of the independent variable.
   c. To avoid doing unethical research in which some participants get preferential treatment.
   d. To keep people from guessing the research question.

10. A researcher wants to see whether caffeine will affect problem solving in rats. One group of rats is fed rat chow containing caffeine. Another group is fed their regular rat chow. In this experiment, the type of rat chow (caffeinated vs. noncaffeinated) fed to the rats is the
    a. control group.   c. independent variable.
    b. dependent variable.   d. confounding variable.

11. In the experiment described above, the rats who ate the regular, noncaffeinated rat chow are the
    a. control group.   c. experimental group.
    b. independent group.   d. the sleepy group.

12. Before participating in a psychological study, Letitia signed an "informed consent," which means
    a. she was told the purposes and hypotheses of the study.
    b. she knew that deception would not be used in the study.
    c. she was given an accurate picture of the risks involved in the research before agreeing to participate.
    d. the study took place before the 1960s.

13. Which of the following statements about ethics in psychological research is TRUE?
    a. In contrast to many other countries, the United States has never conducted studies that violated participants' right to informed consent.
    b. Milgram's study would be approved today because of the knowledge gained.
    c. In the debriefing, participants are informed about the purpose of the study.
    d. Deception is no longer allowed in psychological studies.

14. For which of the following distributions would the MEAN be an appropriate measure of central tendency?
    a. 200, 300, 500, 600   c. 0, 10, 10, 10, 10
    b. 20, 30, 40, 100   d. 2, 8, 9, 10, 11

15. Which of the following statements about animal research in psychology is TRUE?
    a. Ethical issues are of little concern with animals because animals do not have feelings.
    b. Animal researchers must weigh carefully the benefits and costs of such research.
    c. Animals are rarely used in psychological research now that we have computer models.
    d. Recent reports show that the majority of labs using animals in research are violating ethical standards.

16. When psychologists say that their results are statistically significant, they mean that the results
    a. have important practical applications.
    b. have important implications for scientific theory.
    c. are unlikely to be due to the fluctuations of chance.
    d. are positively correlated.

17. A school district superintendent compares an affluent high school that does not have a full health services center with an inner city high school that does. He finds that when compared with the students in the inner city school, students in the affluent school are statistically healthier. He argues that this study provides evidence that school health service centers play no role in student health and that the district does not need to provide such centers. His conclusions are poorly supported because
    a. all campuses deserve equal services depending on the budget.
    b. providing health services serves a basic need regardless of statistical findings.
    c. more money was spent on the full health service center at the inner city high school.
    d. students' family income is likely confounded with school provision of health services.

18. A university administrator wants to demonstrate that the tutoring centers on campus are ineffective. He provides evidence showing that the GPAs of students who receive tutoring are lower than the GPAs of students who do not receive tutoring. Do these data support his claim?
    a. Yes, the averages scores are different.
    b. No, the students are likely to differ in ways other than in their obtaining tutoring.
    c. Yes, because he has a comparison group, he can claim to support his claim.
    d. No, he did not identify the type of tutoring the students received.

19. "Brand X toothpaste users have 27% fewer cavities." The problem with a statement such as this one is that it doesn't give information about
    a. how many cavities an average person has.
    b. who made up the comparison group.
    c. the definition of cavity.
    d. whether there were response sets.

20. A report in a magazine claims "EATING CHOCOLATE CRITICAL FOR GOOD HEALTH." In evaluating this claim, you would
    a. want to know more about the study on which the article is based.
    b. try it out for yourself.
    c. accept the findings as long as the article is not written by a candy company.
    d. accept the article as long as it is balanced by a view of the reasons to avoid chocolate.

After completing the test, calculate your percent correct
(/ 20 =   ) x 100 = _____.

How accurate were your expectations? Does your performance suggest need for additional study? For the items you missed, go back and identify why the "correct" answer is the best answer.

AFTER YOU READ ... PRACTICE TEST #2

Before beginning this practice test estimate the percent you expect to get correct.
Esitmated percent correct: _____

1. Most people believe that when you toss a fair coin HTHHTTHT is a better random sequence than
   HHHHTTTT. As with most heuristics, this use of the representativeness shows that
   a. such short cuts in thinking save cognitive energy for more important thinking.
   b. most people have good intuitive knowledge of probability.
   c. heuristics have survival value.
   d. we tend to oversimplify.

2. Many students who perform poorly on exams might be falling prey to the cognitive bias of
   a. confirmation bias.
   b. hindsight bias.
   c. superstitious behavior.
   d. overconfidence.

3. Alejandro thinks he is quite a good comedian despite most people thinking his jokes are far from
   funny. According to the cognitive biases discussed in the chapter, Alejandro's judgment demonstrates
   a. the Great Fourfold Table of Life.
   b. that people overestimate their level of skill at a task.
   c. that there are individual differences in humor.
   d. the availability heuristic.

4. _____ are useful for providing existence proofs but limited in terms of testing hypotheses.
   a. Experimental studies
   b. Naturalistic observations
   c. Case studies
   d. Correlational studies

5. The College Vegans want to show the administration how concerned the campus is with the
   cafeteria's selling of animal products. They survey their organization and find 100% of the students
   do not want animal products sold on campus. The administration isn't impressed with their findings
   because
   a. no attempt was made to obtain a random selection of students on campus.
   b. the Vegans need to conduct a true experiment to support their point.
   c. their results are correlational.
   d. they did not have random assignment.

6. Joowan just took a personality test in a magazine and found out she was a "Rocker." In reading the
   descriptions of personality types identified by the test, she remembers she took the same test in
   another magazine last week and was identified as a "Slacker." With such diverse results, it is likely
   this test is
   a. high in external validity.
   b. high in demand characteristics.
   c. low in validity and low in reliability.
   d. high in correlation and therefore low in causal attribution.

7. Which of the following is TRUE?
   a. The processes that lead to heuristics are generally maladaptive.
   b. Statistically significant findings are important and large in size.
   c. A correlation of -.80 is just as high as a correlation of +.80.
   d. Mode and standard deviation are both measures of dispersion.

8. Looking over evaluations of communication professors at his college, Ray notices that Dr. Lin has good scores on all measures and is rated HOT! Dr. Smith also has good ratings but is not rated hot. Ray assumes this means Dr. Lin is a better professor than Dr. Smith. One potential influence on Ray's assumption is the
   a. Lake Wobegon effect.
   b. Rosenthal effect.
   c. horns effect.
   d. halo effect.

9. A researcher measured how much time children spent on their homework and their standardized test scores. The researcher found that as the amount of homework increased, the performance on the standardized test increased. The type of relation observed was
   a. a positive linear relation.
   b. a negative relation.
   c. no relation.
   d. impossible to tell from this description.

10. Based on this homework research, which of the following would be an appropriate conclusion?
    a. Increasing homework will increase test scores.
    b. Knowing how much time a student spends on homework allows one to predict test scores.
    c. All children should be given more homework.
    d. The children who don't do their homework will be the ones with low test scores.

11. Mako's parents came to visit him at college and it rained all weekend. Now he is convinced it always rains on weekends so he misses class during the week to entertain visitors. Mako's reasoning reflects
    a. inferring cause from correlation.
    b. hindsight bias.
    c. a belief in an illusory correlation.
    d. the representativeness heuristic.

12. In an experiment, the participants in the control group
    a. don't know whether or not they received the experimental treatment.
    b. differ from the experimental group only in terms of not receiving the experimental treatment.
    c. expect to receive the negative experience.
    d. provide evidence for the existence of some phenomenon.

13. A new medication is given to individuals who experience frequent tension headaches. The researchers in this study should include a placebo group in order to
    a. control for alternative explanations.
    b. save money on medication.
    c. avoid the experimenter expectancy effect.
    d. avoid the nocebo effect.

14. Professor Bryant knows which group of participants in his study received one type of test. Because he really wanted participants in the second group to perform better on their type of test, he was worried and nervous when talking to them. His results failed to support his hypothesis. In fact, the first group scored higher. This outcome is most likely the result of
    a. an experimenter expectancy effect.
    b. the base rate fallacy.
    c. statistical significance.
    d. rigid peer review.

15. During the debriefing period of an experiment, participants
    a. are told about the purpose of the study.
    b. are questioned by the Institutional Review Board about the study.
    c. are paid for their participation.
    d. sign an informed consent.

16. Sample #1: 80, 85, 95, 95, 220
    Sample #2: 95, 95, 98, 99, 100
    Although these two distributions have the same _____, they are likely to have different _____.
    a. means ; modes
    b. modes ; standard deviations
    c. medians; standard deviations
    d. standard deviations; modes

17. Which of the following is an important recommendation made about statistical reasoning?
    a. When looking at statistical graphs, read the scale labels and note scale ranges.
    b. When you have outliers, the mean is the most appropriate measure of central tendency.
    c. Because you can be tricked by statistics, it is important to rely on your own observations.
    d. Either the range or the standard deviation will provide the same important information about variability.

18. Gunter began to feel a stomachache after drinking a beer before dinner and wine with dinner. What factor was responsible for Gunter's stomachache?
    a. Mixing liquors
    b. The cumulative effect of liquors
    c. The food served
    d. You cannot tell the cause of his stomachache from this observation

19. The primary justification for using deception in a study is that
    a. deception never causes psychological stress.
    b. participants who are unaware of the real purpose of the study will act more naturally.
    c. debriefing participants is inefficient.
    d. most studies in psychology use it.

20. Wolfgang is convinced that piano training improves school performance of children. He compares the school performance of his students with the children living in his apartment who do not take piano lessons. He finds his students are getting better grades in school compared with the children in his apartment. He concludes that he is correct in believing the difference is because of the piano training. Is his conclusion warranted?
    a. Yes, he has an independent variable and a control group.
    b. No, the difference demonstrated only applies to his students not to piano training in general.
    c. Yes, musical training teaches discipline.
    d. No, the students were not randomly assigned, so differences other than piano training exist.

After completing the test, calculate your percent correct
(/ 20 =   ) x 100 = _____.

How accurate were your expectations? Does your performance suggest need for additional study? For the items you missed, go back and identify why the "correct" answer is the best answer.

AFTER YOU READ ... PRACTICE TEST ANSWER KEYS

Practice Test 1.

1. d (p. 46)
2. c (p. 48)
3. a (p. 51)
4. d (p. 52)
5. b (p. 52)
6. a (p. 58)
7. a (p. 57)
8. d (p. 59)
9. b (p. 61)
10. c (p. 61)
11. a (p. 61)
12. c (p. 67)
13. c (p. 68)
14. a (p. 70)
15. b (p. 69)
16. c (p. 72)
17. d (p. 73)
18. b (p. 74-75)
19. b (p. 75)
20. a (p. 76)

Practice Test 2.

1. d (p. 46-47)
2. d (p. 48-49)
3. b (p. 48)
4. c (p. 51)
5. a (p. 52)
6. c (p. 53-54)
7. c (p. 56)
8. d (p. 55)
9. a (p. 57)
10. b (p. 57)
11. c (p. 58)
12. b (p. 61)
13. a (p. 63)
14. a (p. 64)
15. a (p. 68)
16. b (p. 70-71)
17. a (p. 73)
18. d (p. 73)
19. b (p. 75)
20. d (p. 75)

AFTER YOU READ ... CONCEPT MAPPING ACTIVITY ANSWERS

ACTIVITY 1

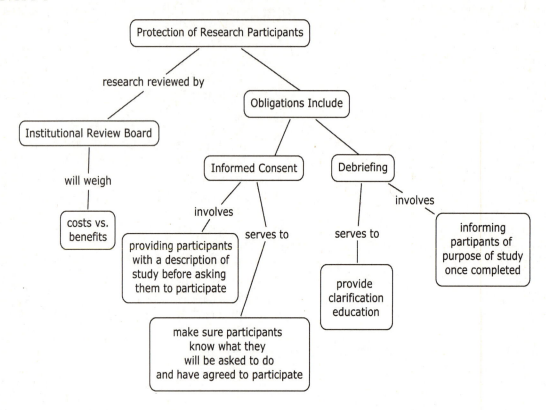

ACTIVITY 2: Here are some of the most important advantages and disadvantages of the various research designs.

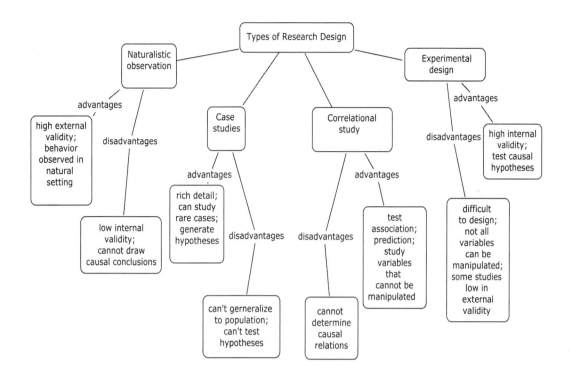

CHAPTER 3
BIOLOGICAL PSYCHOLOGY:
BRIDGING THE LEVELS OF ANALYSIS

BEFORE YOU READ ... CHAPTER PREVIEW

The nervous system is the most complex of human organ systems. It is composed of many parts, any one of which is capable of astonishing feats. Although the information in this chapter may seem daunting, it is included early because of its importance in understanding the mental processes and behavior of human beings.

Activity in the nervous system occurs by the activity of **neurons** and **glial cells**. Neurons are specially designed for communicating with one another, and consist of a cell body, **dendrites** for receiving messages, **axons** for sending messages, and **axon vesicles**, which store **neurotransmitters**. Messages connect between neurons through a microscopic space called a **synapse**. Neurotransmitters are released from the axon terminals into the **synaptic cleft**. Glial cells provide supportive functions for the neurons. Some glia are star-shaped *astrocytes* found in *blood-brain barriers*. Other glia are *oligodendrocytes* which produce the **myelin sheath**; myelin creates *nodes* on the axon which speed up neural transmission.

Neurons communicate in two ways: electrically and chemically. Electrically, all neurons have a **resting potential** that is negatively charged. As messages come into the cell, some of them are excitatory and some are inhibitory, but all are added together. When a **threshold** is reached, an **action potential** occurs, sending a message down the axon to release its neurotransmitter and send a message to subsequent neurons. As neurotransmitters are released into the synapse, the message changes from an electrical message to a chemical message. Neurotransmitters bind to **receptor sites** on the postsynaptic dendrites. Eventually, **reuptake** stops the action of the neurotransmitters. Some neurotransmitters (*glutamate*, acetylcholine, *norepinephrine, dopamine*) primarily **excite** the nervous system. Others **inhibit**, or reduce, activity in the nervous system, i.e., *GABA* and *serotonin*, which also plays a role in mood. **Endorphins** play a role in pain reduction, whereas *anandamine* affects eating, memory, motivation, and sleep. Some drugs, called *psychoactive drugs*, either mimic or enhance a neuron's activity, called *agonists*, and others decrease a neuron's activity, called *antagonists*. Neural **plasticity** refers to how our brains change with experience. During development, this includes *growth* of axons and dendrites, *synaptogenesis, pruning,* and *myelination*. During learning, especially with *long-term potentiation (LTP),* there is much *structural plasticity*. **Stem cells** (undifferentiated neurons) are important in plasticity because they can take on many roles. In addition, we now have evidence for **neurogenesis** well into adulthood.

The major parts of the nervous system include the **central nervous system**, composed of the brain and spinal cord, and the **peripheral nervous system**, composed of the somatic and autonomic nervous systems. The brain is composed of the **forebrain**, or **cerebral cortex**, the midbrain, and hindbrain. The cortex is divided into two **cerebral hemispheres**, covered by thin membranes--the *meninges*--which are connected by the **corpus callosum** and separated by fluid-filled spaces--the **cerebral ventricles**. Each hemisphere is further divided into *lobes*, including the **frontal lobe**, responsible for *executive functions*, with the **motor cortex** at its back margin. The area in front of the motor cortex is the **prefrontal cortex**, which initiates many executive functions, and includes **Broca's area**, a language production area. Behind the motor cortex is a deep groove, the *central sulcus*. The **parietal lobe** is behind the frontal lobe, with a somatosensory area that corresponds to, and is directly behind, the motor cortex. The **parietal lobe** integrates sensory inputs and maintains attention. The **temporal lobe**, located below the parietal and prefrontal areas, is separated by a groove, called the *lateral fissure*. It contains the *auditory cortex*, specialized for sound perception, and **Wernicke's area**, a language area responsible for speech perception. The temporal lobe is also important for memory formation. The **occipital lobe**, at the back of the head, contains the *visual cortex* and is specialized for visual perception. The **association cortex** is spread out and integrates all the messages, especially from the **primary somatosensory cortex**.

Buried beneath the forebrain are the **basal ganglia**, which control movement, as well as **limbic system** structures, the *emotional center*. These structures include (1) the **thalamus**, a set of nuclei through which pass messages into and out of the nervous system; (2) the **hypothalamus**, responsible for homeostasis; (3) **the amygdala**, associated with fear and arousal; and (4) the **hippocampus**, which plays a role in long-term memory consolidation. Connected to the forebrain and going towards the spinal cord is the **brain stem**, which contains the **midbrain** reticular activating system (RAS), which controls arousal. Finally, the **hindbrain**, directly below the midbrain, contains the **cerebellum**, the **pons**, and the **medulla**, which is important for sustaining life functions such as breathing and heartbeat.

The **spinal cord** contains *nerves* that carry messages from the brain to the extremities. *Motor nerves* carry messages from the extremities to the brain and *sensory nerves* carry messages to the extremities. Neurons within the spinal cord called **interneurons**, which allow for a rapid connection of sensory to motor nerves to produce **reflexes**.

The peripheral nervous system has two parts: the **somatic nervous system**, which connects the CNS to muscles throughout the body, and the **autonomic nervous system**, which regulates emotion and internal physical states. The autonomic nervous system is divided into two parts. The **sympathetic nervous system** activates the nervous system for *flight-or-fight* and the **parasympathetic nervous system** restores functions suited to rest and digestion. The **endocrine system** is responsible for controlling **hormones** through a series of glands, including the **pituitary gland**, which controls many of the body's other glands and produces *oxytocin,* and the **adrenal gland**, which produces both *adrenaline* and *cortisol* as well as sex hormones, including *estrogen* and *testosterone*.

Phrenology and lesions studies represent earlier attempts to understand the *localization of function*. Recent technological developments have helped scientists to understand how mind and brain interact. These techniques include the **EEG**, which represents electrical activity in the brain using surface electrodes; various scanning techniques, such as **CT** scans and **MRI** images, which allow clearer pictures of anatomical structures; and functional imaging techniques, such as **PET** scans, **fMRI**, **TMS**, and **MEG**, which allow scientists to see the brain in action. At least one interesting aspect of this work has been to debunk several myths, including the notion that we use only 10% of our brains or are primarily left-brained or right-brained. Neuroimaging techniques have allowed a clearer picture of functions such as language and those that are widely distributed. Furthermore, scientists know that some functions are preferentially performed by one hemisphere or the other, called **lateralization**, but that most human behaviors require the ongoing activity of both hemispheres in concert. Additional insights have come from studies of patients with **split-brain surgery**.

A final consideration regards genetics. **Chromosomes** within the nucleus of every cell contain **genes**, our genetic makeup. With the completion of the *Human Genome Project,* we now know most everything we can about human genetics. One important distinction is made between **genotype**, each person's genetic makeup, and **phenotype**, how that genetic makeup expresses itself in terms of **dominant** and **recessive genes**. Studies of *behavioral genetics* and **heritability**—how much genes contribute to differences *among individuals*, allow scientists to evaluate the effects of environment on genetics. Many organisms make *adaptations* to their environment, a measure of **fitness**. Much new information has come from **family studies**, **twin studies**, and **adoption studies** of twins into different families.

BEFORE YOU READ ... LEARNING OBJECTIVES

After reading Chapter 3 you should be able to:

3.1   Distinguish the parts of neurons and what they do
3.2   Describe electrical responses of neurons and what makes them possible
3.3   Explain how neurons use neurotransmitters to communicate with each other
3.4   Describe how the brain changes as a result of development, learning, and injury
3.5   Identify what roles different parts of the central nervous system play in behavior
3.6   Clarify how the somatic and autonomic nervous systems work in emergency and everyday situations
3.7   Describe what hormones are and how they affect behavior
3.8   Identify different brain-stimulating, -recording, and -imaging techniques
3.9   Evaluate results demonstrating the brain's localization of function
3.10   Describe genes and how they influence psychological traits
3.11   Explain the concept of heritability and the misconceptions surrounding it

---

BEFORE YOU READ ... TERM IDENTIFICATION

---

absolute refractory period (p. 88)
action potential (p. 87)
adoption study (p. 117)
adrenal gland (p. 104)
amygdala (p. 99)
association cortex (p. 98)
autonomic nervous system (p. 102)
axon (p. 86)
basal ganglia (p. 98)
brain stem (p. 100)
Broca's area (p. 96)
central nervous system (CNS) (p. 93)
cerebellum (p. 101)
cerebral cortex (p. 95)
cerebral hemispheres (p. 95)
cerebral ventricles (p. 94)
chromosome (p. 113)
computed tomography (CT) (p. 107)
corpus callosum (p. 95)
dendrite (p. 86)
dominant gene (p.114)
electroencephalography (EEG) (p. 107)
endocrine system (p. 103)
endorphin (p. 90)
family study (p. 116)
fitness (p. 114)
forebrain (p. 95)
frontal lobe (p. 96)
functional MRI (fMRI) (p. 108)
gene (p. 113)
genotype (p. 114)

glial cell (p. 87)
heritability (p. 115)
hindbrain (p. 101)
hippocampus (p. 100)
hormone (p. 103)
hypothalamus (p. 99)
interneuron (p. 101)
lateralization (p. 111)
limbic system (p. 99)
magnetic resonance imaging (MRI) (p. 107)
magnetoencephalography (MEG) (p. 108)
medulla (p. 101)
midbrain (p. 100)
motor cortex (p. 96)
myelin sheath (p. 87)
neurogenesis (p. 93)
neuron (p. 85)
neurotransmitter (p. 86)
occipital lobe (p. 98)
parasympathetic division (p. 103)
parietal lobe (p. 97)
peripheral nervous system (PNS) (p. 93)
phenotype (p. 114)
pituitary gland (p. 103)
plasticity (p. 91)
pons (p. 101)
positron emission tomography (PET) (p. 107)
prefrontal cortex (p. 96)
primary sensory cortex (p. 98)
receptor site (p. 88)
recessive gene (p.114)

reflex (p. 101)
resting potential (p. 87)
reticular activating system (RAS) (p. 100)
reuptake (p. 89)
somatic nervous system (p. 102)
spinal cord (p. 101)
split-brain surgery (p. 111)
stem cell (p. 92)
sympathetic division (p. 102)

synapse (p. 86)
synaptic cleft (p. 86)
synaptic vesicle (p. 86)
temporal lobe (p. 97)
thalamus (p. 99)
threshold (p. 87)
transcranial magnetic stimulation (TMS) (p. 108)
twin study (p. 116)
Wernicke's area (p. 98)

AS YOU READ ... PRACTICE ACTIVITIES

NERVE CELLS: COMMUNICATION PORTALS

1. Draw a neuron and label the major structures within the neuron. Then list the function of each structure. (LO 3.1)

2. You are a glial cell, seldom recognized for all the important work you do. You have an opportunity to be interviewed by a newspaper reporter. Convince him to write up a special report of all the important things that you do. (LO 3.1)

3. Go to http://faculty.washington.edu/chudler/ap.html and watch an action potential. (LO 3.2)
4. Compare (remember that "compare" in this case means you should note how things are similar and also how they are different) the actions of agonists and antagonists and give an example of each. (LO 3.3)

5. Complete the following table of neurotransmitters. Rely on the text, NOT on the table. (LO 3.3)

Neurotransmitter	Selected Roles	Excitatory or Inhibitory
Glutamate		
GABA		
Norepinephrine		
Dopamine		
Serotonin		
Endorphins		
Anandamide		

6. Go to http://stemcells.nih.gov/info/basics/. Note at least three new things you learned about stem cells. Note at least one misconception you might have had for which you now have correct information after reading through this web site. (LO 3.4)

THE BRAIN—BEHAVIOR NETWORK

1. Differentiate between the central nervous system and the peripheral nervous system. (LO 3.5)

2. Which is the primary structure that makes up the forebrain, and what is its function? (LO 3.5)

3. On this silhouette of the brain, indicate each of the four major lobes of each cerebral hemisphere and note the functions associated with each. Then name each of the two major speech centers in the brain and note their locations in the drawing. Finally, add in the locations of motor and somatosensory cortex. (LO 3.5)

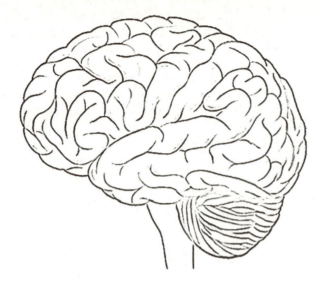

4. An airline "hub" is a transfer point where passengers change planes en route to a distant destination. Develop an analogy between the function of airline hubs and the functions of the thalamus. (LO 3.5)

5. At http://www.med.harvard.edu/AANLIB/home.html you can have some fun navigating around the whole brain atlas and looking at all of the structures you've been reading about! (LO 3.5)

6. At http://thebrain.mcgill.ca/flash/a/a_01/a_01_m/a_01_m_fon/a_01_m_fon.html you can navigate about the web site at several different levels from social to molecular, and from beginner to advanced. (LO 3.5)

7. If you suffer damage to your cerebellum, how might your behavior be affected? (LO 3.5)

8. On this silhouette of the brain, note the location of the corpus callosum (as a reference structure) and then draw and label the four limbic system structures. Note the functions of each. (LO 3.5)

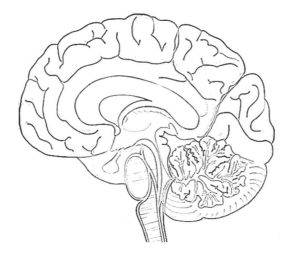

9. Complete this table for the autonomic nervous system's activities. (LO 3.6)

Autonomic Nervous System

Sympathetic Nervous System		Parasympathetic Nervous System	
Organ	**Action**	**Organ**	**Action**
_____	_____	_____	_____
_____	_____	_____	_____
_____	_____	_____	_____
_____	_____	_____	_____
_____	_____	_____	_____

10. Now imagine that you are being chased by a large, angry dog. Go over the various sympathetic nervous system changes that occur and note how these might be quite practical in the need to either flee or stay and fight. (LO 3.6)

THE ENDOCRINE SYSTEM

1. Compare the activities of cortisol to those of adrenaline. (LO 3.7)

MAPPING THE MIND: THE BRAIN IN ACTION

1. Describe the three sources of evidence we use to map brain activity to mind. (LO 3.8)

2. Complete the following table. (LO 3.8)

Technique	Type (Structure or Function)	What It Can Tell Us
Electroencephalograph (EEG)		
Computed tomography (CT scans)		
Magnetic resonance imaging (MR)		
Positron emission tomography (PET)		
Functional MRI (fMRI)		

3. Discuss the problems with using phrenology for assessing localization of function. Also explain phrenology's greatest "virtue." (LO 3.8)

4. Even though this Web site at http://faculty.washington.edu/chudler/image.html is titled, "Neuroscience for Kids," it is definitely appropriate for all age groups. Enjoy surfing around some of the links with more information and more images. (LO 3.8)

5. Before reading your text, how much of your brain did you believe you were using on a regular basis? Describe the evidence that we use more than 10% of our brains. Why do you think that people are willing to believe such misconceptions surrounding limited use of our brain's resources? (LO 3.9)

6. You are having a bite to eat at your favorite diner when the person next to you strikes up a conversation. You mention you are studying psychology, to which this person immediately replies, "I am *so* right-brained!" Although you may want to get up and run away from this half-brained person, describe some of the arguments that favor and counter the belief that we are "right-brained" versus "left-brained." Convince your new friend that we use our whole brain all of the time. (LO 3.9)

7. Complete this table for scientifically verified specializations of the hemispheres. (LO 3.9)

Side of Brain	Specialized Function
Right	
Left	

NATURE AND NURTURE: DID YOUR GENES—OR PARENTS—MAKE YOU DO IT?

1. Compare heredity to heritability. Be sure to consider dominant and recessive genes. (LO 3.10 and 3.11)

2. Describe three major misconceptions about heritability and note the evidence that disconfirms each misconception. (LO 3.11)

3. In terms of behavioral genetics, what can (or cannot) each of the following tell us about the heritability of a trait: (a) family studies; (b) studies of identical (monozygotic) twins; and (c) studies of fraternal (dizygotic) twins? (LO 3.11)

4. Speculate on what we can learn from adoption studies of twins raised together or apart. Then go to http://www.psych.umn.edu/psylabs/mtfs/special.htm. Compare your speculative answers with known findings. (LO 3.11)

AS YOU READ ... CONCEPT MAP ACTIVITIES

ACTIVITY 1: Complete the following concept map of the divisions of the nervous system.

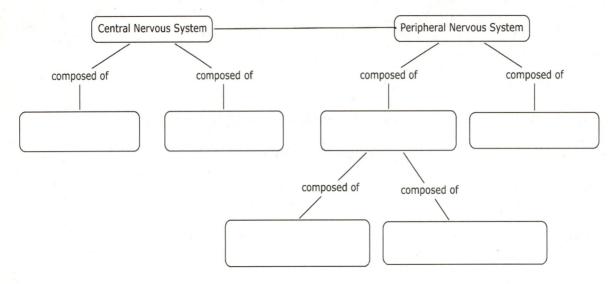

Author activity content supported by *IHMC Cmap Tools* Copyright ©1998-2007 Institute for Human & Machine Cognition

ACTIVITY 2: Complete this concept map for a typical reflex response, such as what happens when you step on a nail.

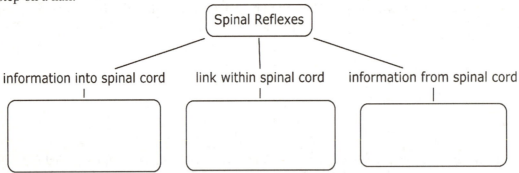

Author activity content supported by *IHMC Cmap Tools* Copyright ©1998-2007 Institute for Human & Machine Cognition

ACTIVITY 3: Complete the following concept map of limbic circuits.

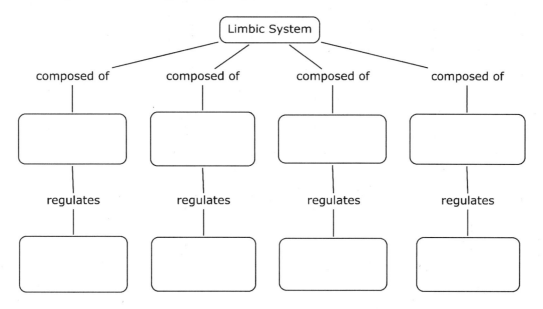

ACTIVITY 4: Complete the following concept map of the endocrine system.

Author activity content supported by *IHMC Cmap Tools* Copyright ©1998-2007 Institute for Human & Machine Cognition

AS YOU READ ... MYTH OR REALITY?

Myth: As adults, we lose about 100,000 neurons each day.
Reality: Although we do lose neurons each day, the actual number is considerably lower, perhaps one tenth of that. (Juan, 2006)

1. At http://www.princeton.edu/pr/news/99/q4/1014-brain.htm and http://www.msnbc.msn.com/id/19096030/ you will find reports of recent studies that suggest that not only may the loss be small, but we do regenerate neurons even into late adulthood. Read this carefully.

2. Discuss how the findings reported at this web site might affect the restoration of function following stroke.

AS YOU READ ... PUT YOUR CRITICAL THINKING SKILLS TO THE TEST

1. In your book you read about Phineas Gage and the effects of frontal lobe damage that he suffered in a work-related accident. What do you think would be the effects of a frontal lobotomy? Frontal lobotomies had a brief popularity in the 1940s and 1950s. Search the Internet for information on the typical effects of frontal lobotomies and compare them to the effects of Phineas Gage's accident and to what you expected to find.
   a.   Were you correct?
   b.   How were your expectations correct, and how were they incorrect?
   c.   How do the descriptions of people who have had a lobotomy compare to the effects of Phineas Gage's accident?
   d.   Can you find more recent examples on the Internet?

2. While you are watching TV, you decide you need a snack, but you want to wait for a commercial to come on before heading out to the kitchen. Describe the activity of your somatic nervous system in helping you to get up and get a snack from the kitchen, and then get back to watching TV. Be sure to consider that you want to inhibit going to the kitchen until the commercial comes on, that you then want to navigate over to the kitchen and remember that you went there to get a snack, that you want to return to the TV room before the commercials are over, and that you finally want to be able to pick up the story on the TV program when you return.

3. An analogy is often made between action potentials and the flushing of a toilet. Develop that analogy here and think of the ways that the two functions have in common. Be sure to consider all aspects of neural transmission of messages.

4. While still an undergraduate student, one of the co-authors of this study guide had the wonderful experience of taking art lessons at California State University, Long Beach, from Betty Edwards (see http://www.drawright.com). She makes a living on promoting her program of "Drawing on the Right Side of the Brain." Knowing what you know about how the hemispheres function together and apart, critique her program.

5. Your text comments on the fact that in the 1800s employers sometimes demanded that potential employees "have their heads examined" by phrenologists before hiring them. This practice relates to modern day use of personality inventories or lie detector tests before hiring potential employees. Go to http://www.skepdic.com and read about lie detectors, as well as personality tests, particularly the Myers-Briggs Temperament Inventory (be sure to click the link to the Forer Effect), which is frequently used by human resources departments. Using the scientific thinking skills you developed in Chapter 1, decide whether we have come very far in this type of pre-employment testing, since the 1800s.

AS YOU READ ... MYPSYCHLAB CONNECTION

Nerve Cells: Communication Portals
For an interactive visual of how neurotransmission and receptor binding works, **Explore** *Structure of a Neuron*, *The Action Potential*, *Neuronal Transmission*, *The Nerve Impulse*, *Afferent and Efferent Neurons*, and *The Synapse* as well as *Brain-Body Communication*. To see the effects of drugs on neurotransmitter binding and the brain, review the **Simulation** *General Model of Drug Addiction*. To learn more about brain communication and neurotransmission by **Watch** the video *Exercise Your Brain*.

The Brain-Behavior Network
For a better understanding of the brain and brain-behavior networks **Watch** *Brain Stem and Limbic System*, participate in the **Simulations** *The Human Cerebrum, Split Brain, Organization of the Nervous System* and *Split Brain*. To test your knowledge of the endocrine and limbic systems, **Explore** the *Autonomic Nervous System, Endocrine System,* and *Limbic System*. To learn more about the structure of the brain, **Explore** *The Visual Cortex*. Apply your knowledge of how the brain affects everyday behaviors with the **Simulation** *Physiological Bases of Behavioral Problems*. To better understand the somatic nervous system, **Watch** *Studying Squid*. For a personal look at neuronal damage and behavioral problems, **Watch** *Connie: Head Injury* and *ALS Lost Nerve Power*. These videos review some behavioral problems associated with neuronal damage resulting from head trauma and degenerative diseases. Can the development of your brain be influenced by exercise? **Watch** the video titled *Brain Building*. You can learn more about the cerebellum's role in balance; **Watch** the video *Balancing*.

Mapping the Mind: The Brain in Action
To see how the brain processes sensory information, such as vision, **Explore** *The Visual Cortex*. To receive a hands-on learning experience of hemispheric functioning and split-brain studies, check out the **Simulations** *Hemispheric Experiments, Physiological Bases of Behavioral Problems* and *Split-Brain Experiments*. How do scientists map the brain? **Watch** the video *MKM and Brain Scans*. **Listen** to *Brain Mapping*.

Nature and Nurture: Did Your Genes—or Parents—Make You Do It?
For an interactive visual on genetics and DNA, utilize and **Explore** *Dominant and Recessive Traits* and *Building Blocks of Genetics* as well as *Healthy versus Unhealthy Behaviors* and *Should You Consult a Genetic Counselor*. For further insight to genetics and DNA, **Watch** the videos *Junk DNA, How the Human Genome Map Affects You,* and *Genetic Time Clock*. Interested in stem cell research and cloning? **Watch** *Cloned Child* and *Human Cloning—The Ethics*.

AFTER YOU READ … PRACTICE TEST #1

Before beginning this practice test, estimate the percent you expect to get correct.
Anticipated percent correct: _____

1. Action potentials send messages from one neuron to another. The progression of an action potential within a single neuron occurs in the following sequence.
   a. Axon, cell body, dendrites, axon terminals
   b. Axon terminals, axon, cell body, dendrites
   c. Dendrites, axon, cell body, axon terminals
   d. Dendrites, cell body, axon, axon terminals

2. Gina suffers from an illness in which the myelin sheath surrounding neurons has deteriorated. She is most likely suffering from
   a. schizophrenia.
   b. multiple sclerosis.
   c. Alzheimer's disease.
   d. Parkinson's disease.

3. Action potentials move more quickly along myelinated fibers because
   a. depolarization can jump the spaces between nodes and does not need to fire the entire length of the axon.
   b. myelin is a fatty substance and the depolarization occurs more quickly in fat than in watery substances.
   c. myelin contains salts that can transmit the message for depolarization more quickly down the axon.
   d. depolarization depends on the presence of glial cells to support the movement of ions within the axon.

4. A frequent analogy used for understanding the transmission of neural signals across a synapse is that of a lock and key mechanism. This analogy arises from the finding that
   a. reuptake is limited to specific neurotransmitters within the synapse.
   b. only specific neurotransmitters can bind to specific postsynaptic membranes.
   c. glial cells can act as a locksmith to prevent confusion in transmitting messages.
   d. the neurotransmitter unlocks the ability of the neuron to generate a new action potential.

5. Agonists work to _____ a neuron's activity, whereas antagonists work to _____ a neuron's activity.
   a. enhance; reduce
   b. reduce; enhance
   c. reduce; increase
   d. decrease; increase

6. When rats are raised in an enriched environment, their brains show
   a. larger neuronal cell bodies.
   b. a reduced need for myelination.
   c. increased size, as determined by weight.
   d. increased branching of neuronal dendrites.

7. The central nervous system is composed of
   a. the autonomic and somatic nervous systems.
   b. the right and left hemispheres of the brain.
   c. the brain and spinal cord.
   d. neurons and glial cells.

8. John suffers from severe epilepsy that did not respond to drug therapy. Doctors have proposed surgery to disconnect the hemispheres of his brain by severing the band of fibers called the _____ that connects the two hemispheres.
   a. corpus callosum
   b. myelin sheath
   c. hippocampus
   d. thalamus

9. Al, who is strongly right-handed, suffered a stroke in Broca's area of his left hemisphere. Al most likely now suffers from
   a. autobiographical amnesia.
   b. personality changes.
   c. language reception.
   d. language production.

10. You are driving along the freeway when another driver suddenly cuts you off, leading you to feel angry and upset with the other driver. This emotional response is mediated by
    a. the thalamus.
    b. the limbic system.
    c. pituitary hormones.
    d. the basal ganglia.

11. The hindbrain is composed of
    a. the pons, cerebellum, and medulla.
    b. the hippocampus, amygdala, an d hypothalamus.
    c. the prefrontal cortex, Broca's area, and motor strip.
    d. the autonomic, sympathetic, and parasympathetic nervous systems.

12. A gazelle is being chased by a hungry lion in the wild. It is quite likely that there is activation of the gazelle's
    a. Broca's area.
    b. endocrine system.
    c. sympathetic nervous system.
    d. parasympathetic nervous system.

13. The _____ is called the "master" gland.
    a. thyroid
    b. adrenal
    c. pituitary
    d. endocrine

14. The EEG has
    a. poor temporal resolution but great spatial resolution.
    b. good temporal resolution but poor spatial resolution.
    c. neither good temporal nor good spatial resolution.
    d. both good temporal and spatial resolution.

15. The PET scan depends on
    a. recording metabolic activity related to oxygen metabolism.
    b. recording metabolic activity related to glucose metabolism.
    c. noninvasive measures of electrical activity on the surface of the scalp.
    d. noninvasive measures of metabolic activity on the surface of the scalp.

16. What is the danger of relying too much on neuroimaging tests?
    a. We will give up using traditional psychological tests for assessing brain functions.
    b. We may focus too much on activity in areas that are not traditionally thought to be specialized for a particular function.
    c. We run the risk of assigning narrowly defined functions to brain regions, rather than remembering that most functions are distributed.
    d. We will pay too much attention to how different parts of the brain work together rather than focusing on individual parts and how they function.

17. Your friend, Kutali, says he is definitely a left-brained person because he excels in his math classes but performs miserably in his art classes. You tell him that
    a. scientific evidence supports some specialization across hemispheres so he must have greater activation of one hemisphere compared to the other if his school grades support his premise.
    b. no scientific evidence supports this type of hemispheric asymmetry for complex tasks, and actually the two hemispheres function together.
    c. he has it backwards: if he likes math but dislikes languages he must be right-brained.
    d. he needs to also assess his handedness before reaching this conclusion.

18. Andrea has brown eyes, but all of her children have blue eyes, which means that
    a. Andrea probably adopted her children, because brown eye color is dominant and her natural children would all have brown eyes.
    b. Andrea's recessive genes combined with her husband's dominant genes to determine eye color in her children.
    c. Andrea's dominant traits are expressed in her children.
    d. Andrea's phenotype does not reflect her genotype.

19. Which of the following is NOT a misconception concerning heritability?
    a. Heritability is a fixed number.
    b. Heritability tells us whether a trait can be changed.
    c. Heritability is a statistic that applies only to groups of individuals.
    d. Heritability applies to a single individual rather than to differences among individuals.

20. The logic underlying twin studies that seek to increase our understanding of the heritability of disorders is that
    a. twins must be separated at birth for the results to be meaningful.
    b. monozygotic are more alike than dizygotic twins because of shared genetics.
    c. dizygotic twins are more genetically alike than any other siblings.
    d. monozygotic twins share the same embryonic sac and, therefore, share more environmental factors than do dizygotic twins.

After completing the test, calculate your percent correct
(_____ / 20 = _____) x 100 = _____ .

How accurate were your expectations? Does your performance suggest the need for additional study? For the items you missed, go back and identify why the "correct" answer is the best answer.

AFTER YOU READ ... PRACTICE TEST #2

Before beginning this practice test, estimate the percent you expect to get correct.
Anticipated percent correct: _____

1. When neurons communicate among themselves,
   a. the absolute refractory period is lengthened.
   b. action potentials are continuously generated.
   c. neurotransmitter is released into the synaptic cleft.
   d. enzymes are required to activate muscle receptors.

2. People with multiple sclerosis often show a slowing of transmission of messages in the nervous system attributed to
   a. a loss of astrocytes in the blood-brain barrier.
   b. degeneration of the myelin sheath, generated by a special type of glial cell
   c. a narrowing of the synaptic cleft.
   d. an overabundance of glial cells, interfering with neural transmission.

3. If glial cells were up for an academy award, one category they could be nominated in would be
   a. best costume.
   b. best musical score.
   c. best visual effects.
   d. best supporting actor.

4. Your friend Joe is a serious runner. He always runs until he feels a good burn in his legs and his chest works hard to provide his body with oxygen. In fact, Joe runs several times a day because he says a good hard run gives him a "runner's high." Which neurotransmitter system is probably responsible for Joe's runner's high?
   a. GABA
   b. Serotonin
   c. Endorphin
   d. Acetylcholine

5. Stem cells carry the potential for replacing damaged cells following spinal cord injury because they
   a. are undifferentiated and can still become any type of cell.
   b. can enhance axon growth.
   c. are primarily found in older adults with Alzheimer's disease.
   d. have more myelin than other neurons.

6. The peripheral nervous system helps us to
   a. think, talk, and reason.
   b. make decisions and use language.
   c. analyze sensory information and think.
   d. control motor behavior and regulate emotion.

7. The frontal lobe of the cortex is responsible for
   a. motor function, executive function, and language.
   b. transferring short-term to long-term memories.
   c. primary processing of auditory inputs.
   d. somatosensory processing.

8. The parietal lobe of the cortex is responsible for
   a. many kinds of perception, including spatial perception.
   b. relaying messages to and from the extremities.
   c. storage of autobiographical memories.
   d. coordination of motor movements.

9. The thalamus can be thought of as
   a. the end of the line of a train station—this is where all trains end up.
   b. an airline hub, with most flights coming and going through the hub.
   c. a map, showing where various nuclei are located relative to one another.
   d. a parking garage, where vehicles are left for a temporary amount of time.

10. In the film *Memento*, the main character, Lenny, compensates for his inability to form new
    memories by taking Polaroid pictures of important people and objects. Lenny clearly has damage to
    his
    a. amygdala.   c. hippocampus.
    b. frontal lobe.   d. cingulated cortex

11. The reason that a blow to the back of the neck can be deadly is that it might result in damage to the
    a. medulla, which controls heartbeat and breathing.
    b. cerebellum, compromising balance.
    c. pons, which connects the cortex and cerebellum.
    d. spinal cord, preventing messages from entering or exiting the spinal cord.

12. _____ are secreted into the blood stream directly, in order to affect behavior.
    a. Neurotransmitters   c. Chromosomes
    b. GABA molecules   d. Hormones

13. You notice smoke coming out of a house and hear a child crying inside. As you run inside to save
    the child your heart muscle contracts, your pupils dilate, and airways open up. All of these effects
    are probably the result of the release of _____ into your bloodstream.
    a. oxytocin
    b. adrenaline
    c. endorphins
    d. testosterone

14. When it comes to testosterone, studies show that
    a. it is not related to a person's sex drive.
    b. one must play, and not just watch sports to show elevated levels.
    c. the ovaries in women produce it.
    d. it is very strongly and reliably related to aggressive behaviors.

15. Your friend Mike wants to go see a phrenologist. You tell him to save his money because
    a. phrenology still needs to be falsified.
    b. your friend could learn much more about himself by visiting an astrologer.
    c. enlarged areas on the outside of the head are only accurate in determining vanity, friendliness,
       and happiness.
    d. bumps on the outside of the head have not been shown to correspond to any known personality
       traits or abilities.

16. The major drawback of CT scans and MRI images is that they both
    a. only provide information about structures, not functions.
    b. carry the risk of overexposure to radioactivity.
    c. do not allow a view of inner brain structures.
    d. are invasive.

17. Evidence against the 10% myth (we only use 10% of our brains) comes from
    a. the general success of courses to improve our brain power.
    b. the effectiveness of self-help books to increase mental capacity.
    c. neuroimaging studies, which fail to find any consistently silent areas.
    d. psychics who are able to perform extraordinary feats of mental powers.

18. Jillian has had her corpus callosum severed. When the written sentence "Stand up" appears in her right visual field-left hemisphere, she will
    a. read the words out loud.
    b. stand up but claim she doesn't know why.
    c. stand up, but not be able to read the words.
    d. be able to read the words but won't understand the words or carry out the command.

19. Genotype refers to _____, whereas phenotype refers to _____.
    a. a person's observable traits; that which is passed on from parents to offspring.
    b. a person's expressed traits; recessive and dominant traits in combination.
    c. a person's actual genetic makeup; a person's observable traits.
    d. recessive traits; dominant traits.

20. Behavioral genetics allows us to study
    a. only the effects of genetics on behavior.
    b. the differences in genetic makeup within a single individual.
    c. the interaction of nature and nurture in the expression of a trait.
    d. behavioral traits, but cannot tell us about the heritability of diseases.

After completing the test, calculate your percent correct
(___ / 20 = ___) x 100 = _____.

How accurate were your expectations? Does your performance suggest the need for additional study?
For the items you missed, go back and identify why the "correct" answer is the best answer.

AFTER YOU READ . . . PRACTICE TEST ANSWER KEYS

Practice Test 1.

1. b (p. 85)
2. b (p. 87)
3. a (p. 87)
4. b (p. 88)
5. a (p. 90-91)
6. d (p. 92)
7. c (p. 93)
8. a (p. 95)
9. d (p. 96)
10. b (p. 99)
11. a (p. 101)
12. c (p. 102)
13. c (p. 103)
14. b (p. 107)
15. b (p. 107-108)
16. c (p. 109)
17. b (p. 112)
18. d (p. 114)
19. c (p. 115-116)
20. b (p. 117)

Practice Test 2.

1. c (p. 86)
2. b (p. 87)
3. d (p. 87)
4. c (p. 90)
5. a (p. 92)
6. d (p. 93)
7. a (p. 96)
8. a (p. 97)
9. b (p. 99)
10. c (p. 100)
11. a (p. 101)
12. d (p. 103)
13. b (p. 104)
14. c (p. 105)
15. d (p. 106)
16. a (p. 107)
17. c (p. 110)
18. a (p. 111)
19. c (p. 114)
20. c (p. 115)

AS YOU READ … CONCEPT MAPPING ACTIVITY ANSWERS

ACTIVITY 1:

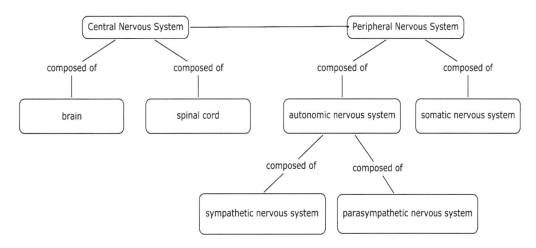

ACTIVITY 2:
You should have entered the terms: *afferent neurons*, *interneurons*, and *efferent neurons* in that order going across the nodes.

ACTIVITY 3:

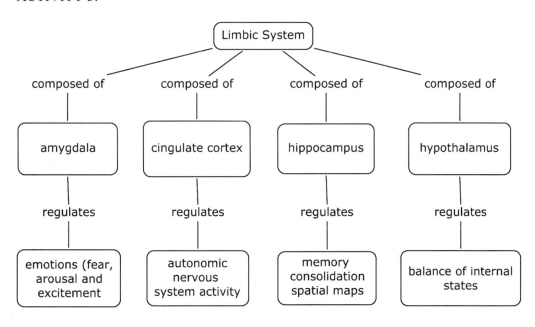

ACTIVITY 4:
Alphabetical list of terms you might have included:

adrenaline	ovaries	vasopressin
boosts energy	oxytocin	
cortisol	regulates cardiac function	
estrogen	testes	
growth	testosterone	

CHAPTER 4
SENSATION AND PERCEPTION:
HOW WE SENSE AND CONCEPTUALIZE THE WORLD

BEFORE YOU READ … CHAPTER PREVIEW

Sensation is the detection of a physical energy by means of specialized **sense receptors**, whereas **perception** is our *interpretation* of these sensory inputs. This process can be complicated when an **illusion** occurs, because our perceptions don't always match the sensations. *Naïve realism* leads us to believe that our perceptions are always correct but our brains will *fill-in* patterns that don't exist. A physical stimulus becomes a psychological reality by the process of **transduction**. Activity is greatest when we first detect a stimulus but declines as **sensory adaptation** starts in. The study of how sensations become perceptions is called **psychophysics**. We now know that sensation requires a minimum amount of intensity of stimulation, called an **absolute threshold**. The smallest difference in intensity that can be detected is called a **just noticeable difference (JND)**, which is governed by **Weber's Law**: the stronger the stimulus, the more change is required to detect it. Sometimes perception occurs in a background of other stimuli, and the signal-to-noise ratio is reduced so that **signal detection** can go wrong. In addition, people have various *responses biases*, so that in the end there can be a *true positive* or a *true negative*, but also a *false positive* (false alarm) or a false *negative* (a miss). In the 1800s people examined *specific nerve energies* related to each sense; in vision, this related to noticing *phosphenes*. Sometimes sensory systems work together, such as for the *McGurk effect* or the *rubber hand illusion*. At other times, rare individuals experiences **synesthesias**—experiencing sensations across modalities, such as *grapheme-color synesthesia* or *lexical-taste synesthesia*. Perception can depend on **bottom-up processing** of sensory information and **top-down processing** to guide perception, as exemplified in **perceptual sets**. Perception can also depend on context, and on **perceptual constancy** of *shape, size,* and *color*. In fact, most things we perceive are composed of many smaller sensations that bind together to form a single perception. For perception to occur, we need **selective attention** to stimuli. The *filter theory of attention* views attention as a bottleneck for further processing and has been demonstrated with *dichotic listening* and *shadowing* tasks. The *cocktail party effect* shows that we can pick out important information when multiple stimuli surround us. When many things are going on around us, it is difficult to focus on only one thing; focusing on more than one thing leads to a quick deterioration of perceptual quality as seen in **inattentional blindness**. How all of incoming messages come together is part of the *binding problem,* for which there are only hypotheses but no explanations. Of course, we cannot consciously perceive a stimulus at all if it is well below threshold, or **subliminal**. Although evidence exists for subliminal perception, the evidence for *subliminal persuasion* is meager at best; no clear evidence indicates that people can be subliminally persuaded to perform certain behaviors. *Parapsychologists* study **extrasensory perception (ESP),** including precognition, telepathy, clairvoyance, and *psychokinesis.* Although belief in ESP is pervasive, scientific evidence for ESP is lacking and it cannot be falsified. People tend to believe in ESP because of *illusory correlation*, confirmation bias, and *missing endpoints*. Most *cold readings* in fact make use of *popular stereotypes*, flattery, and props.

In terms of vision, we respond to a very narrow range of *wavelengths* of light as they reflect off surfaces in the environment. *Brightness* is the intensity of the light that reaches our eyes, and **hue** is the color of light. We're sensitive to three primary colors of light— red, green, and blue. Different parts of the eye have specific functions in transmitting light. The iris, the colored part of the eye, is a set of muscles with *pigments* controlling an opening that modifies the amount of light permitted through the **pupil**, an opening allowing light into the eye. This opening changes size as a result of a *pupillary reflex*. The **cornea** is a curved, transparent layer covering the iris and pupil. **Accommodation** allows the **lens,** which is transparent, to change shape to focus light on the back of the eye. Nearsightedness (*myopia)* and farsightedness *(hyperopia)* result from the curve of the cornea. The **retina** is a thin membrane at the back of the eye that contains receptor cells. The **fovea** is the central part of the retina, responsible for **acuity**. The two types of receptor cells are **rods** and **cones**. Rods are long and narrow and are used in low light; they help us see basic shapes and forms. Cones are used in high light and give us color and detailed vision. **Ganglion cells**, the last cells in the retinal circuit, contain axons that leave the eye as the **optic nerve**, creating a small **blind spot** at their exit point. The optic nerve travels to the brain, half splitting at the *optic chiasm* to travel to the same hemisphere and half crossing to the other side. The optic tracts send most of their axons to the primary visual cortex, V1, but some go to the *superior colliculus* in the midbrain and on to arousal centers.

Perception is more complicated. We have both *simple* and *complex* **feature detector cells** in V1 that respond to external stimuli based on specific orientation or motion, allowing us to see lines, edges, and corners. Several *Gestalt principles*, so named because they were first articulated by the Gestalt psychologists, help us to perceive objects in space, including *subjective contours*, proximity, similarity, good continuation, closure, symmetry, and figure-ground. Face recognition is especially important for humans; cells located in the temporal lobe are specialized for this task. Motion perception is especially complex, involving the *phi phenomenon*, the organization of separate, changing images, into a single, flowing perception. For color perception, the **trichromatic theory** proposes three different types of cones, each of which respond to a different light wavelength. If one of these receptors is faulty, then **color blindness** occurs, either *monochromatic* or *dichromatic*. Another theory of color perception, **opponent process theory**, involves the opposite pairing of colors at the ganglion cell and thalamus levels, and explains why afterimages are of different colors than the actual stimulus. **Depth perception** is complicated because we can perceive depth using either both eyes using **binocular depth cues**, based on the different message that each eye receives (**binocular disparity**), and how the eye muscles move to focus moving images on the retina (**binocular convergence**). **Monocular depth cues** or *pictorial cues* depend on using just one eye and include relative size, texture gradients, interposition, linear perspective, height in plane, and light and shadow. When perception fails to operate as it should, we experience optical illusions, including the *moon illusion*, the *Ames room illusion*, the *Müller-Lyer illusion*, the *Ponzo illusion*, the *horizontal-vertical illusion*, and the *Ebbinghaus-Tichener illusion*. Blindness is the inability to see or perceive either anything at all or very clearly at all. Other types of blindness include motion blindness, *visual agnosia*, and *blindsight*. Evidence as to whether blind individuals' other senses take over to compensate for the loss of vision is inconclusive. Some evidence shows that somatosensory areas, especially for touch, do spread out and take up more space.

Audition results from waves, which have *pitch* and amplitude. Pitch corresponds to the wave frequency with fast waves producing a higher pitch and slow waves producing a lower pitch. The amplitude or height of the sound wave corresponds to *loudness*. **Timbre** refers to the complexity of sound. The *outer ear* has the simplest function for processing sound as it funnels sound waves from the *pinna* onto the *eardrum*. The *middle ear* contains the *ossicles* to amplify the waves. From there, sound is transmitted to the spiral-shaped **cochlea**, in the *inner ear*, where vibration is transduced into neural activity. Waves travel through the cochlea, which is filled with a thick fluid, bending *hair cells* embedded in the **organ of Corti** and a thin **basilar membrane** running down its middle. The hair cells convert acoustic information into action potentials, sending their axons as the **auditory nerve** to auditory cortex in the temporal lobe. According to **place theory,** pitch is perceived because different areas of primary auditory cortex respond selectively to different frequencies of sound waves, which excite hair cells in different areas of the basilar membrane—at least for high-pitched sounds. For very low-pitched sounds, a **frequency theory** suggests that hair cells fire at the speed at which the sound waves arrive. For moderately low pitches, *volley theory* suggests that neurons fire out of sync with one another. Furthermore, we can localize sound because *binaural* information reaches the brain at a slightly offset time frame. There is also a *sound shadow* because the ears are well separated on the head. *Monaural cues* can be used to localize sound based on the clarity and intensity of the sound. Sound illusions can occur, similarly to visual illusions. *Echolocation* helps certain animals that emit a high-pitched sound that then echoes off objects. Deafness can occur for several reasons, most commonly because of damage to the auditory nerve—*nerve deafness*, if the ossicles malfunction—*conduction deafness*, or if there is a prolonged exposure to loud noise—*noise-induced hearing loss*.

Smell, called **olfaction**, results when odors (airborne chemicals) interact with receptors in the lining of our nasal passages. Odors have a lock-and-key mechanism for smell perception and humans can detect possibly thousands of specific odors. Once the receptors are activated, then the information goes to the olfactory cortex and on to the limbic system. Smell is especially important for sexual behavior in many species. **Pheromones** are odorless chemicals that serve as social signals and are processed by the olfactory system. Taste is also called **gustation.** We detect taste with taste buds, which are found in *papillae* on the tongue. We're sensitive to five basic tastes— sweet, salty, sour, bitter, and umami. Fat is being investigated as a sixth basic taste. The "taste map," which many students learn about in school, is a myth—all tastes are spread out throughout the taste buds on our tongue. From the taste buds, messages are sent to the gustatory and somatosensory cortex, and also on to the limbic system. To a great extent, taste is strongly influenced by odors. Smell and taste are very important to add an essential "zest" to life.

We have three body senses. The **somatosensory system** responds to stimuli applied to the skin, such as touch (from *mechanoreceptors*), pain (primarily via *free nerve endings*), or temperature. Free nerve endings send their messages to the spinal cord, to the brain, and to the somatosensory cortex. Sometimes pain results in a *withdrawal reflex*, a spinal reflex that results in a rapid response to a painful stimulus. Each pain-producing stimulus has its own *threshold*. The **gate control model** of pain proposes a gating mechanism wherein touch sensations can precede pain sensations to the brain, reducing the perception of pain. Researchers have documented cultural differences in pain perception. Finally, amputees often experience **phantom pain.** *Proprioception* keeps track of body position via two types of receptors: stretch detectors in muscles and force detectors in tendons. This information also eventually goes to the somatosensory cortex and even to the motor cortex if quick movement is necessary. Finally, the **vestibular sense** is our sense of balance. The **semicircular canals**, attached to the cochlea, send information on motion and orientation. The sense receptors are similar to those for hearing but their message is sent via the brainstem to the cerebellum, as well as the somatosensory cortex. How our bodies interact with the external world is the purview of *human factors*, also called *ergonomics*.

BEFORE YOU READ ... LEARNING OBJECTIVES

After reading Chapter 4 you should be able to:

4.1   Identify the basic principles that apply to all senses
4.2   Track how our minds build up perceptions
4.3   Analyze the scientific support for and against ESP
4.4   Explain how the eye starts the visual process
4.5   Identify the different kinds of visual perception
4.6   Describe different visual problems
4.7   Explain how the ear starts the auditory process
4.8   Identify the different kinds of auditory perception
4.9   Identify how we sense and perceive tastes and odors
4.10   Describe the three different body senses
4.11   Explain how pain perception differs from touch perception
4.12   Describe the field of psychology called human factors

BEFORE YOU READ ... TERM IDENTIFICATION

absolute threshold (p. 125)
accommodation (p. 138)
acuity (p. 138)
audition (p. 148)
basilar membrane (p. 149)
binocular depth cues (p. 144)
blind spot (p. 138)
bottom-up processing (p. 127)
cochlea (p. 149)
cornea (p. 136)
color blindness (p. 142)
cones (p. 138)
dark adaptation (p. 138)
depth perception (p. 144)
extrasensory perception (ESP) (p. 132)
feature detector cells (p. 140)
fovea (p. 138)
frequency theory (p. 150)
gate control model (p. 156)
gustation (p. 152)
hue (p. 136)
illusion (p. 124)
inattentional blindness (p. 129)
just noticeable difference (JND) (p. 125)
lens (p. 136)
monocular depth cues (p. 144)
olfaction (p. 152)
opponent process theory (p. 143)
optic nerve (p. 138)

organ of Corti (p. 149)
parallel processing (p. 127)
perception (p. 124)
perceptual constancy (p. 128)
perceptual set (p. 128)
phantom pain (p. 157)
pheromone (p. 154)
place theory (p. 150)
proprioception (p. 158)
psychophysics (p. 125)
pupil (136)
retina (p. 138)
rods (p. 138)
selective attention (p. 129)
semicircular canals (p. 158)
sensation (p. 124)
sense receptor (p. 125)
sensory adaptation (p. 125)
signal detection theory (p. 126)
somatosensory (p. 154)
subliminal perception (p. 130)
synesthesia (p. 127)
taste bud (p. 152)
timbre (p. 149)
top-down processing (p. 127)
transduction (p. 125)
trichromatic theory (p. 142)
vestibular sense (p. 158)
Weber's Law (p. 125)

AS YOU READ … PRACTICE ACTIVITIES

<u>TWO SIDES OF THE COIN: SENSATION AND PERCEPTION</u>

1. Differentiate between sensation and perception. Use an original example to illustrate the difference. (LO 4.1)

2. Differentiate between subliminal perception and subliminal persuasion. Based on your reading of the text, do you believe that you could be subliminally persuaded by an advertiser to purchase a product? Why or why not? (LO 4.2)

3. Provide an original example from your everyday life of size constancy, color constancy, and shape constancy. (LO 4.2)

4. Do you believe that some people at some times have ESP? Have you ever thought you had an instance of ESP? Explain how an instance of precognition could be alternatively explained as an instance of illusory correlation. (LO 4.3)

SEEING: THE VISUAL SYSTEM

1. Using the following silhouette of the eyeball, label the cornea, pupil, iris, lens, retina, fovea, and blind spot. (LO 4.4)

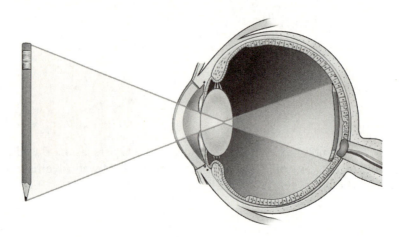

2. Briefly note the function of each of the structures you have labeled in the above drawing. (LO 4.4)

3. Compare the functions of rods and cones. Remember to discuss both the similarities and differences between them. Does the concentration of cones near the fovea make sense to you? Why or why not? (LO 4.4)

4. Go to http://desktoppub.about.com/od/gestalt/Gestalt.htm and explore different ways that Gestalt principles are used in everyday life in various public media, such as advertising and developing company logos. (LO 4.5)

5. Draw a simple, but original picture or line drawing to illustrate the following Gestalt principles: (LO 4.5)

    a. proximity

    b. similarity

    c. closure

6. Go to http://www.michaelbach.de/ot/col_lilacChaser/index.html to experience a great example of opponent process theory. (LO 4.5)

7. Make a line drawing of a landscape, even if you can only make stick figures and geometrical shapes. Incorporate the following aspects of depth perception into your drawing: relative size, texture gradient, interposition, linear perspective, light and shadow, and height in plane. Draw a line to, and label, each of these elements in your drawing. (LO 4.5)

8. Go to http://www.exploratorium.edu/exhibits/depth_spinner/index.html and enjoy the motion-related visual illusions. (LO 4.6)

HEARING: THE AUDITORY SYSTEM

1. Label the parts of the ear designated by the letters A, B, C, D, and E. Note a function of each part. (LO 4.7)

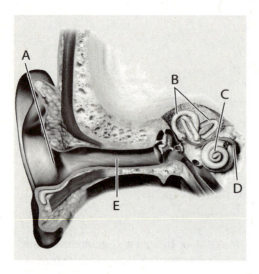

A _____

B _____

C _____

D _____

E _____

2. Compare place theory of pitch perception with frequency theory of pitch perception. When would one be more likely to dominate perception over the other? (LO 4.8)

3. Your text discusses both blindsight and echolocation as separate explanations for why some blind people don't bump into objects more often than they do. How do you believe the input from different sensory systems might interact to help the blind? (LO 4.8)

SMELL AND TASTE: THE SENSUAL SENSES

1. You may have noticed that when you have a cold and a sore throat you can taste sweet or salty tastes but not much else. For example, if you have some popsicles to soothe your sore throat they probably all taste the same. Why do you think this happens? (LO 4.9)

2. Buy a small box of flavorful jelly beans (Jelly Bellies work well). Now, shut your eyes and reach into the package. With your eyes shut, hold your nose tightly shut and with the other hand put the jelly bean into your mouth. Try not to breathe so that air is not pushed up the backside of your nasal passages. Chew up the jelly bean. What flavor was it? How sure are you? Was it easy to tell what the flavor was? Why or why not? (LO 4.9)

3. What do you think about including "fat" as a basic taste? Do you believe it is a taste that is affected by smell? Do you believe that you can taste "fat"? If not, then how would you describe what you experience when you taste something that has fat in it, versus something that does not, such as fat-free yogurt compared to a creamy yogurt? (LO 4.9)

OUR BODY SENSES: TOUCH, BODY POSITION, AND BALANCE

1. What are the three different body senses? Describe each one briefly. (LO 4.10)

2. Go back to Chapter 3 and review what happens during a spinal reflex (withdrawal reflex). Why is a faster turnaround time for the motor response more important than the psychological realization of what is happening? Think of the last time you did something like step on a tack. Have you ever been consciously aware of this time difference? If so, explain what happened. (LO 4.10)

3. Describe the ways proprioception and the vestibular system work together to help you maintain balance. (LO 4.11)

4. Motion sickness results from a mismatch between the messages sent by two sensory systems. Surf the web on your own and find information on which two sensory systems are most likely to be implicated, and explain in your own words what causes motion sickness. If you ever go on a cruise, what could you do to minimize this effect? (LO 4.11)

5. Go to http://faculty.washington.edu/chudler/pain.html and read about the gate-control theory of pain. Based on the information at this web site, what could you do to at least minimize pain perception when you know in advance that something painful will happen to you? (LO 4.11)

6. Ergonomics, or human factors, are important in almost everything we do in our mechanized society. Think about the standard QWERTY keyboard. Do you think an ABCDEF keyboard makes more sense? Why or why not? (LO 4.12)

AS YOU READ ... CONCEPT MAP ACTIVITIES

ACTIVITY 1: See how well you can fill in this fairly complicated map of the sensory systems.

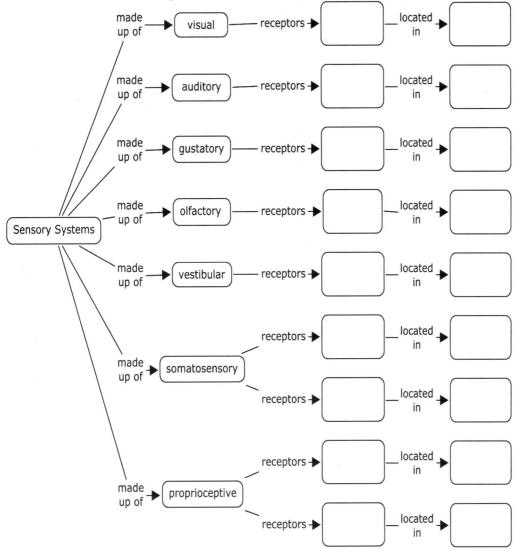

Author activity content supported by *IHMC Cmap Tools* Copyright ©1998-2007 Institute for Human & Machine Cognition

ACTIVITY 2: This map shows the visual system and should simplify your understanding of the complexities of both sensation and perception in vision.

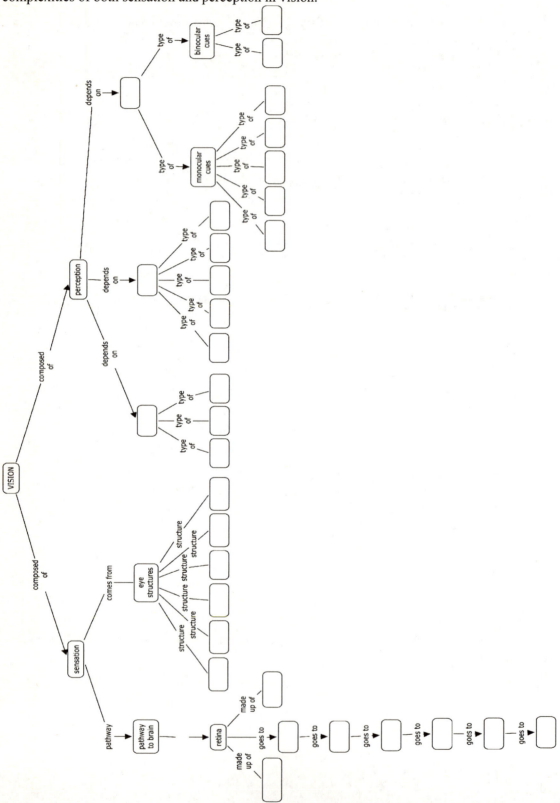

Author activity content supported by *IHMC Cmap Tools* Copyright ©1998-2007 Institute for Human & Machine Cognition

AS YOU READ ... MYTH OR REALITY?

Myth: People can be persuaded to buy certain products by subliminally hiding sexual messages in the product's labeling or advertising.

Reality: Being frequently exposed to the labeling or advertising might make a person feel more comfortable with the product and that could lead to increased purchasing (the mere exposure effect). However, by definition, if something is *sub*liminal, people will not be consciously aware of the presence and meaning of the sexual symbols and thus will not be persuaded to buy the products.

1. Explore the following four sites:
   http://www.planetperplex.com/en/img.php?id=308
   http://www.snopes.com/disney/films/lionking.htm
   http://www.planetperplex.com/en/item277
   http://www.planetperplex.com/en/item265
   How convinced are you that people can really "see" sexual innuendos in any of these ads on a normal day-to-day basis?

2. In some of them, such as the Pepsi ad, the image is more blatant if the cans are positioned just right. Do you believe it is still, then, "subliminal"?

Myth: Vision occurs because our eyes emit a light that interacts with objects outside of ourselves.
Reality: No evidence supports this belief.

1. Read a summary of early beliefs about vision.
   http://findarticles.com/p/articles/mi_m0PAL/is_509_159/ai_n6153266/
   Early master painters, such as Leonardo da Vinci, believed that vision occurs because of a ray emitted by the eyes. It was not until Helmholtz (who developed the trichromatic theory of color vision you have read about) that scientists understood how vision works.

2. In addition, http://en.wikipedia.org/wiki/History_of_scientific_method provides a discussion of the scientific method. Read one of the nice examples of how the scientific method was able to lead scientists to the correct conception of vision: that objects reflect light, not that the eyes emit light.

3. Finally, if you go to
   http://www.cartage.org.lb/en/themes/sciences/Physics/Optics/briefhistory/briefhistory.htm you will notice that even early Greek philosophers argued back and forth about how vision works: light waves into the eyes or light waves out of the eyes. However, by the early 1800s scientific doubt had been eliminated.

4. So, if science has conclusively shown since the 1800s that vision occurs because of light waves reflected INTO the eye, why do you think some people still persist in believing that vision occurs because of light rays emitted from the eyes?

AS YOU READ ... PUT YOUR SCIENTIFIC THINKING SKILLS TO THE TEST

1. Signal detection theory is applied to a variety of psychological phenomena, including recognition memory, and diagnosis of psychopathology.
    a. Go to http://epsych.msstate.edu/deliberate/sig_det/index.html. Read the explanatory text and do the exercise. How did you do relative to what the theory would predict? If your results are not as predicted, where did they differ? Why do you think this happened—be honest!
    b. Now provide a hypothesis based on signal detection theory of what should happen with the diagnosis of psychopathology. For which disorders would you shift the criterion more so than for other disorders?

2. Psychic readings are sleight of mind (much like we talk about "magic" tricks as "sleight-of-hand") using a technique called "cold reading." Your text describes several cold reading techniques.
    a. Go to http://www.youtube.com/watch?v=saTR3r297ys
        Watch a few minutes' worth of the video—no need to watch all 10 minutes. Were you convinced by the reading? Why or why not?
    b. Go back over the list of cold reading techniques in your text and find a few of the techniques that you saw used in this video.

3. Go to http://www.youtube.com/watch?v=voAntzB7EwE and watch the video. Do not look ahead at the questions.
    a. What did you notice the first time?
    b. Watch the video again. What did you fail to notice the first time?
    c. Based on this exercise, what can you conclude about eyewitness accuracy? Remember that in addition to any normal viewing conditions, eyewitness events are witnessed in a context of emotional upset, occur very quickly, and our attention is often diverted by other important events, such as the presence of a weapon.

AS YOU READ ... MYPSYCHLAB CONNECTION

Two Sides of the Coin: Sensation and Perception

To better understand top-down processing, **Explore** *Top-Down Processing* and *Perceptual Sets*. In the **Simulation** *Ambiguous Figures*, you can see how visual perception and sensation work together and sometimes how one overrides the other. **Listen** to the podcast *Sensation and Perception,* which contains a lively conversation between two psychologists to help you better understand how these processes work together to help you see, hear, smell, and taste.

Seeing: The Visual System

Explore your knowledge of different types of visual illusions with *Five Well-Known Illusions*. Review how the optical system processes light waves; **Explore** on *Light and the Optic Nerve*, which presents a visual simulation of how light is processed through the eye. Also **Watch** the video *Blindspot*. For more on how light is processed through the retina, **Explore** *Receptive Fields*. To learn more about opponent processes in action, **Watch** the video *After Image*. **Explore** *Normal Vision, Nearsightedness*, to see what causes the need for corrective lenses. Your stereotypes about the way the world works or even expectancies that you have can influence what you see. Participate in a visual **Simulation** on *Perceptual Sets* that demonstrates how what we see can be influenced by what other people say or do with perceptual sets. *Gestalt Laws of Perception* is another **Simulation** that will help you review the Gestalt principles. *Distinguishing Figure-Ground Relationships* **Simulation** provides you with an opportunity to test your ability to not succumb to visual illusions. To learn more about depth perception, participate in the **Simulation** *The Visual Cliff*. Can you tell the difference between two images? If you think you can, try the **Simulation** *Methods of Constant Stimuli*. Do you believe that subliminal messages influence your behavior? **Listen** to *Subliminal Messages*.

Hearing: The Auditory System

Explore different sound waves with *Frequency and Amplitude of Sound Waves*. Test yourself on all the structures of the ear with the interactive **Explore** *Major Structures of the Ear*. **Watch** the following five video clips on how the brain processes auditory information: *Cochlear Implants, Ear Ringing, Listening to Blues Test, Mosquito*, and *Noise and the Brain*. To learn more about cochlear implants, **Listen** to the podcast *Cochlear Implants*.

Our Body Senses: Touch, Body Position, and Balance

Watch the video *Brain Pain* to see how distraction in virtual reality games can decrease how much pain patients report and result in fewer pain signals in the brain.

Smell and Taste: The Sensual Senses

Watch *Alzheimer's Smell Test* to see how a decline in sensitivity to smell may signal onset of Alzheimer's disease. **Watch** *Aromatherapy* to see how odors, such as vanilla, modify your emotions.

AFTER YOU READ ... PRACTICE TEST #1

Before beginning this practice test, estimate the percent you expect to get correct.
Anticipated percent correct: _____

1. Sensation is to perception as
   a. global is to specific.
   b. complex is to simple.
   c. normal is to abnormal.
   d. physical is to psychological.

2. Sense receptors are
   a. more numerous in people with extrasensory perception.
   b. specialized cells that transduce physical inputs into neural activity.
   c. hairs in your ears and nose that improve hearing and smell, respectively.
   d. undifferentiated across sensory modalities; visual receptors look just like auditory ones.

3. According to signal detection theory, if you are an air traffic controller
   a. a "miss" is preferred to a "hit."
   b. a "false alarm" is preferred to a "hit."
   c. a "false alarm" is preferred to a "miss."
   d. a "miss" is preferred to a "false alarm."

4. Caroline is sitting in a lab with stereo headphones on, and hears two different stories playing simultaneously in the right and left channels. Caroline is probably a participant in a study of
   a. dichotic listening.
   b. sensory adaptation.
   c. perceptual constancy.
   d. subliminal persuasion.

5. Anika has blue eyes; Jose has brown eyes. The difference in eye color is the result of different pigments in the
   a. cornea.
   b. pupil.
   c. lens.
   d. iris.

6. The process by which the shape of the lens changes to focus on things that are either close by or far away is called
   a. laxity.
   b. constriction.
   c. assimilation.
   d. accommodation.

7. Rods are specialized for _____, whereas cones are specialized for _____.
   a. low light; color vision
   b. color vision; negative afterimages
   c. bright light conditions; dark adaptation
   d. detecting details; detecting overall shapes

8. Hubel and Weisel earned a Nobel Prize for their lifetime work on defining feature detector cells in cats, which
   a. are cells in the retina that fire in response to specific features in the environment.
   b. correspond to human ganglion cells, showing early perceptual decoding in the eye.
   c. detect specific lines and edges, responding to specific length, orientation, and motion.
   d. are clusters of cells distributed in somatosensory cortex that only respond to specific stimuli.

9. The Gestalt principles of organization
    a. are rules that help us to organize elements into something that is complete.
    b. are binocular cues for perceiving three-dimensional objects.
    c. help us to understand the perception of different colors.
    d. illustrate how illusions lead to inaccurate perceptions.

10. If you stand at the edge of a cornfield, the stalks will look coarse close to you and finer if you look into the distance. This phenomenon is called
    a. relative size.
    b. relative motion.
    c. texture gradient.
    d. linear perspective.

11. A person who is blind in one eye uses more _____ cues than _____ cues.
    a. disparity; size
    b. monocular; binocular
    c. convergence; texture
    d. memory; perceptual

12. Depth perception develops
    a. at birth.
    b. as soon as children start to walk.
    c. about the age children start kindergarten.
    d. about the same age as toddlers begin to crawl.

13. In regards to pitch, fast waves produce a _____-pitched sound, and slow waves produce a _____-pitched sound.
    a. high; low
    b. loud; soft
    c. true; fuzzy
    d. deep; shallow

14. The auditory sensory receptor cells are located in the
    a. cochlea.
    b. ossicles.
    c. oval window.
    d. tympanic membrane.

15. As the decibels of a sound increase, the
    a. amplitude increases.
    b. frequency increases.
    c. amplitude decreases.
    d. frequency decreases.

16. A chemical released by one animal that changes the social behavior or another animal is called a
    a. steroid.
    b. pheromone.
    c. testosterone.
    d. photopigment.

17. Katie is going out tonight with a guy she just met and is interested in romantically. To assure herself that he will also be attracted to her, Katie bought a bottle of a new perfume, "FER-O-MOAN," advertised to excite a man's sexual instincts.
    a. Smart Katie. This is a sure way to make this new guy at least show a sexual interest in her.
    b. Silly Katie. Just because she uses the perfume doesn't mean his sexual excitation will be toward her.
    c. Silly Katie. No scientific evidence indicates that pheromone molecules actually "work" with humans.
    d. Smart Katie. Good evidence shows that all mammals, including humans, respond to pheromones.

18. Dennis is sitting in the dentist's chair. As he receives an injection of lidocaine, the dentist jiggles and pulls his cheek near the gum area. The dentist probably does this because
    a. touch messages, sent faster than pain messages, reach the brain first, and reduce the pain messages from the injection.
    b. the anesthetic will spread out more evenly to numb the desired area more quickly.
    c. the anesthetic will spread out and cover a larger area so that less is needed overall.
    d. he wants to distract Dennis from what he is doing, so he will not clench his jaws.

19. Which of the following structures is related to our sense of balance?
    a. Ossicles
    b. Otoliths
    c. Semicircular canals
    d. Basilar membrane

20. Wanda recently had a spell during which she could not keep her balance and kept throwing up. She thought she had food poisoning and went to the Emergency Room. The doctor told her that she had
    a. a middle ear infection—the ossicles could not move freely to transmit messages within the ear.
    b. an outer ear infection and that her ear canal had filled with fluid, putting pressure on the tympanic membrane.
    c. an inner ear infection—her semicircular canals were filled with excess fluid and the vestibular system could not respond.
    d. an inner ear infection, causing the fluid in her semicircular canals to be spinning wildly out of control.

After completing the test, calculate your percent correct
(/ 20 =   ) x 100 = _____ .

How accurate were your expectations? Does your performance suggest the need for additional study?
For the items you missed, go back and identify why the "correct" answer is the best answer.

AFTER YOU READ ... PRACTICE TEST #2

Before beginning this practice test, estimate the percent you expect to get correct.
Anticipated percent correct: _____

1. Amelia is watching TV. When listening to the show, hearing the various sounds of the actors' words would be _____. Interpreting the meaning of these words is an example of _____.
   a. sensation; perception
   b. perception; sensation
   c. assimilation; accommodation
   d. accommodation; assimilation

2. The absolute threshold is
   a. the highest level of perception that can be tolerated.
   b. the highest level of perception that can be responded to.
   c. the lowest level of stimulation that is detected only 50% of the time.
   d. the lowest level of stimulation that can be detected nearly 100% of the time.

3. You are watching an old movie when the sound track offsets from the visual track. The lip movements of the speakers lag behind the words you hear. This is bothersome for you because of
   a. the rubber hand illusion.   c. the octave illusion.
   b. the tritone illusion.   d. the McGurk Effect.

4. Because we organize information into perceptual sets,
   a. we see something like A13C as A-B-C, and not as A-13-C.
   b. we see things as constantly changing in size and color, until it stops moving.
   c. we primarily use incoming sensory information to interpret the world around us.
   d. we can separate our biases and expectations from the processing of a physical stimulus.

5. Antwon is at a family picnic at the beach talking to his cousins near the water's edge. He hears his mother say his name in conversation with her sisters, although she is up by the picnic tables cooking hamburgers. This ability to pick up unattended but personally important information exemplifies the
   a. Ganzfield effect.   c. von Restorff effect.
   b. cocktail party effect.   d. illusory placebo effect.

6. The problem with ESP studies is that
   a. people with pure ESP are seldom aware of their ability, and so we miss testing the right people.
   b. under strict testing conditions the evidence for ESP is extremely weak.
   c. laboratory conditions disrupt the flow of psychic energies.
   d. scientists are so skeptical, that they miss the signs of ESP.

7. Hue is simply a more technical name for
   a. color.   c. reflection.
   b. intensity.   d. brightness.

8. When images are focused on the fovea
   a. we see nothing ; it's the blind spot.
   b. acuity is greatest.
   c. they have no color.
   d. they can best be seen in low light.

9. Light waves are entering your eye. As they do so, they proclaim, "Here we come,
    a. through the pupil, past the lens, through the vitreous, and on to the retina!"
    b. past the lens and through the pupil, through the vitreous and on to the sclera!"
    c. from the retina, through the vitreous, out the lens and the cornea, to freedom, back outside!"
    d. from the ganglion cells, out the vitreous, escaping through the lens, look out world, here we come!"

10. Although the visual sensory receptors are _____, the optic nerve is made up of the axons of the _____.
    a. ganglion cells; fovea
    b. in the lens ; the retina
    c. rods and cones ; ganglion cells
    d. at the blindspot ; rods and cones

11. The point at which the optic nerve exits the eye is the _____ of the eye.
    a. fovea
    b. cornea
    c. blind spot
    d. basilar membrane

12. Kim just put up her Christmas tree and meticulously arranged the lights to form star shapes when they flash sequentially. She steps back in delight to watch the individual lights flash on and off to make the patterns of stars. This kind of motion reflects
    a. motion parallax.
    b. subjective contours.
    c. the psi phenomenon.
    d. the phi phenomenon.

13. The idea that we have three different types of cone cells, each responding to a different wavelength of light, is called
    a. trichromatic theory.
    b. opponent-process theory.
    c. feature detection theory.
    d. RYB (red/yellow/blue) theory.

14. Because of the difference in the images that reach each eye, we receive two slightly different views of the world. This phenomenon is known as
    a. accommodation.
    b. binocular disparity.
    c. interposition.
    d. convergence.

15. _____ is to the frequency of sound waves, as _____ is to the frequency of visually perceived waves.
    a. Pitch; hue
    b. Pitch; timber
    c. Timbre; intensity
    d. Loudness; saturation

16. The primary function of the ossicles is to
    a. assemble sensations into perceptions.
    b. transform sound waves into impulses.
    c. gather sound waves and send them into the middle ear.
    d. pass sound waves from the ear drum to the inner ear.

17. Jimmi is walking down the street when she hears someone behind and slightly to her right call her name. She turns and sees her friend waving at her. How did Jimmi know where to look?
    a. Jimmi's past experiences (top-down processing) told her where to look.
    b. Jimmi first saw the waving out of the corner of her eye and then associated the sound with it.
    c. The sound of her name arrived at each ear at slightly different times because of how they are separated on her head.
    d. As sound waves bounce off objects in the environment, they created echoes that Jimmi used to help her locate the sound.

18. Humans can detect
    a. slightly more smells than tastes.
    b. many more tastes than smells.
    c. many more smells than tastes.
    d. about the same amount of smells and tastes.

19. Smell and taste perception come together when messages from both the olfactory receptors and the gustatory receptors are sent on and reach
    a. the frontal lobes.
    b. the limbic system.
    c. association cortex.
    d. somatosensory cortex.

20. Fixing the problem of Florida's famous "hanging chads" in the 2000 presidential election—where the punched out cardboard squares didn't always fall out completely from the voting cards—has fallen to _____ psychologists.
    a. organizational
    b. political
    c. Gestalt
    d. human factors

After completing the test, calculate your percent correct
(/ 20 =   ) x 100 = _____.

How accurate were your expectations? Does your performance suggest the need for additional study?
For the items you missed, go back and identify why the "correct" answer is the best answer.

AFTER YOU READ . . . PRACTICE TEST ANSWER KEYS

Practice Test 1.

1. d (p. 124)
2. b (p. 125)
3. c (p. 126)
4. a (p. 129)
5. d (p. 136)
6. d (p. 138)
7. a (p. 138)
8. c (p. 139-140)
9. a (p. 140)
10. c (p. 144)
11. b (p. 144)
12. d (p. 145)
13. a (p. 148)
14. a (p. 149)
15. a (p. 149)
16. b (p. 154)
17. c (p. 154)
18. a (p. 156-157)
19. c (p. 159)
20. c (p. 159)

Practice Test 2.

1. a (p. 124)
2. c (p. 125)
3. d (p. 126)
4. a (p. 128)
5. b (p. 129)
6. b (p. 133)
7. a (p. 136)
8. b (p. 138)
9. a (p. 137)
10. c (p. 138)
11. c (p. 139)
12. d (p. 142)
13. a (p. 142)
14. b (p. 144)
15. a (p. 136, 148)
16. d (p. 149)
17. c (p. 150-151)
18. c (p. 152)
19. a (p. 153-154)
20. d (p. 159)

AFTER YOU READ ... CONCEPT MAPPING ACTIVITY ANSWERS

ACTIVITY 1: Here is a list of terms in alphabetical order that you might have included in this concept map.

basilar membrane	muscles	skin
eye	nasal receptors	stretch receptors
free nerve endings	nose	tendons
force detectors	papillae	tongue
inner ear	retina	
mechanoreceptors	semicircular canals	

ACTIVITY 2: Here is a possible completed concept map. This complicated map for vision certainly could have had more links and you should feel free to add some!

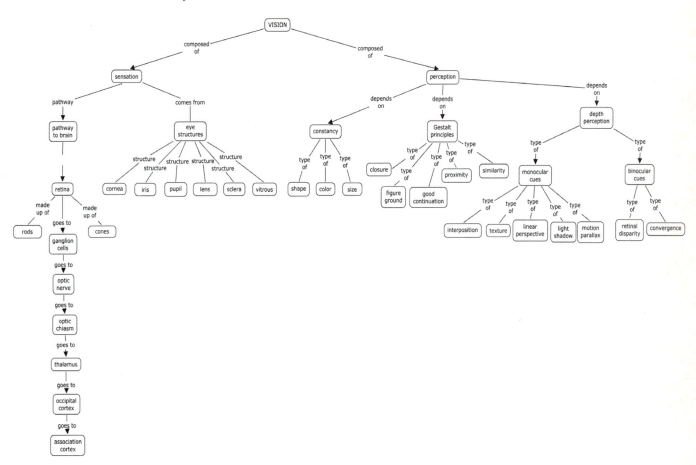

CHAPTER 5
CONSCIOUSNESS
EXPANDING THE BOUNDARIES OF
PSYCHOLOGICAL INQUIRY

BEFORE YOU READ ... CHAPTER PREVIEW

This chapter will introduce you to many different states of **consciousness**. About a third of our lives is spent asleep, so it's important to understand sleep problems such as **sleep paralysis**. We have an internal **biological clock** that operates on a **circadian rhythm**. The biological clock is located in the *suprachiasmatic nucleus* and is related to levels of the hormone *melatonin*. Most young adults, up through about age 25, need an average of 9 hours of sleep per night. After that, adults still need about 7 hours of sleep per night. Many adults don't get the required amount of sleep, including from events such as *jet lag,* and suffer from sleep deprivation and sleep debt, which has many serious mental and physical health risks. Research using electrical recording devices, such as EEG, shows that sleep progresses through a series of five stages with changes related to **rapid eye movements (REM)**. During REM sleep, people more often report vivid dreams than they do during **non-REM (NREM) sleep**. Stage 1 occurs when you first fall asleep, and is often accompanied by *hypnagogic imagery*, followed by Stage 2, which is a light sleep state in which we spend most of our time asleep and which is characterized by *sleep spindles* and *K-complexes*. Stages 3 and 4 represent increasingly deep sleep stages that are necessary to feel rested the next day. Stage 5 represents *paradoxical* or **REM sleep**. When deprived of REM sleep, most people experience a *REM rebound*. EEG sleep waves include *delta waves* (1-2 cycles per second), *theta waves* (4-7 per second), *alpha waves* (8-12 per second), and *beta waves* (13+ times per second). When deprived of sleep, we get to REM sleep the fastest and spend the most time in it. REM sleep is a time of elevated brain activity (the brain does *not* rest during sleep); however, muscles may become paralyzed. Sleep and waking are not completely separate. In lucid dreaming, a person becomes aware of the dream and can take control of its outcome. Sleep can be disrupted by various disorders. Insomnia, the most common sleep disorder, is characterized by an overall lack of sleep. Short-term psychotherapy offers the best treatment; sleeping pills do not, often producing *rebound insomnia*. Other sleep disorders include **narcolepsy** and *cataplexy*, both of which might be affected by the hormone *orexin*, **sleep apnea, night terrors**, and **sleepwalking.**

Dreaming is universal and evidence indicates that even blind people dream. Several theories and hypotheses try to account for why we dream. The oldest is Freud's theory of dream protection and *wish fulfillment*. Freud suggested that dreams have an obvious, *manifest content* and a hidden, *latent content.* Research evidence has failed to support Freud's theory. Another theory, **activation-synthesis theory,** suggests that dreams start out as random brain activation that we weave into a meaningful interpretation. Evidence supports the forebrain as being an important area for initiating dreams. The **neurocognitive theory** suggests that our cognitive capacities shape what we dream about. In terms of content, many dreams are associated with emotional concerns and everyday preoccupations. About 50–80% of people report recurrent dreams. Despite some disagreements, scientists generally concur that an intimate connection occurs between brain activity and dreaming, that acetylcholine turns on REM sleep, and that the forebrain plays an important role in dreams.

Consciousness is complicated by other phenomena, such as *hallucinations*, which are perceptual experiences in the absence of physical sensation. In addition, about 25% of college students report **out-of-body experiences (OBEs)** in which they have the sensation of seeing their bodies from outside of themselves. Similarly, **near-death experiences (NDEs)** occur in about one-fourth of people who were near death. The reports are often similar, consisting of the sense of a bright light, floating upward, and a *life review.* People often think it is a mystical experience, but scientists are now able to replicate it in the lab. The bright light and sense of floating may result from a release of endorphins when some brain areas become oxygen starved. Another insight into consciousness comes from **déjà vu**, the sense of reliving an experience. More than 66% of all people claim to have had this experience. Many people also have had a **mystical experience**, a sense of oneness with the world. **Hypnosis** is a confusing state of conscious, filled with many misconceptions. It is a technique to increase suggestibility across a variety of feelings, beliefs, and behaviors. It is not a "trance state" in which "amazing" behaviors can be performed, nor is it unique. It is not a sleeplike state in which people are unaware of their surroundings and forget what happened; and most importantly, it does NOT improve memory—in fact, evidence suggests it may actually lead to false memories. According to the **sociocultural theory** of hypnosis, people's expectations and level of suggestibility affect the individual response to hypnotic induction. However, **dissociation theory** focuses on a *dissociation* between personality functions that are otherwise integrated, reflecting either a *hidden observer* or a *flexible observer.* The best use of hypnosis has been in clinical practice, where it has been shown to help with pain control, but other legitimate uses are questionable.

  Psychoactive drugs alter consciousness by changing chemical processes in neurons. A person's mental set (expectation) can either magnify or reduce the effects of these drugs. Whereas *substance abuse* results in problems with family, friends, and at work, *substance dependence* is characterized by **tolerance** (a need for more and more to reach the same level of intoxication) and **withdrawal symptoms** (uncomfortable symptoms when the drug is stopped) as well as **physical dependence** and **psychological dependence**. Explanations for drug use and abuse include sociocultural influences, learning and expectations (the *tension reduction hypothesis*), and genetic influences. Evidence fails to support the idea of an addictive personality. Depressant drugs, categorized as either **sedative** or **hypnotic**, depress the nervous system. Alcohol is probably the psychoactive drug that has been used by mankind for the longest time and is a depressant, but can be a stimulant at low doses. Other sedative-hypnotic drugs include the *barbiturates, nonbarbiturates,* and *benzodiazepines.* Stimulant drugs such as nicotine, cocaine, and amphetamines (the most abused of all drugs), including *methamphetamine*, excite the nervous system. Another category of psychoactive drugs include the opiate **narcotics**: **heroin** and **morphine**. These drugs are very effective for controlling pain, but are highly addictive. A final category of drugs includes the *psychedelic drugs*—primarily *hallucinogenic* drugs that alter perception, mood, and thought. These drugs include marijuana, the illegal drug most people have used, which has sedative and hypnotic qualities, and is a mild hallucinogen. A more potent hallucinogen is LSD. Even tiny amounts alter our perceptions and consciousness. Although the effects may be simply curious or unusual, they can also be extremely unpleasant, producing psychosis-like symptoms.

BEFORE YOU READ ... LEARNING OBJECTIVES

After reading Chapter 5 you should be able to:

5.1   Explain the role of the circadian rhythm and how our bodies react to a disruption in our biological clocks

5.2   Identify the different stages of sleep and the neural activity and dreaming behaviors that occur in each

5.3   Identify the features and causes of sleep disorders

5.4   Describe the research on dream content

5.5   Explain three major theories of dreaming

5.6   Determine how scientists explain seemingly "mystical" alterations in consciousness

5.7   Distinguish myths from realities concerning hypnosis

5.8   Identify possible influences on alcohol abuse and dependence

5.9   Distinguish different types of drugs and their effects on consciousness

BEFORE YOU READ ... TERM IDENTIFICATION

activation–synthesis theory (p.175)
biological clock (p. 167)
circadian rhythm (p. 167)
consciousness (p. 166)
déjà vu (p. 180)
dissociation theory (p. 185)
hallucinogenic (p. 193)
insomnia (p. 171)
hypnosis (p. 181)
hypnotic (p. 189)
lucid dreaming (p. 171)
mystical experience (p. 180)
narcolepsy (p. 172)
narcotic (p. 193)
near-death experiences (NDE) (p. 179)
neurocognitive theory (p. 176)
night terrors (p. 173)

non-REM (NREM) sleep (p. 169)
out-of-body experience (OBE) (p. 178)
past life regression therapy (p. 184)
physical dependence (p. 187)
psychoactive drug (p. 186)
psychological dependence (p. 187)
rapid eye movement (REM) (p. 169)
REM sleep (p. 169)
sedative (p. 189)
sleep apnea (p. 172)
sleep paralysis (p. 166)
sleepwalking (p. 173)
sociocognitive theory (p. 184)
stimulant (p. 191)
tolerance (p. 187)
withdrawal (p. 187)

AS YOU READ ... PRACTICE ACTIVITIES

THE BIOLOGY OF SLEEP

1. What is commonly called the "biological clock" is really a nucleus of neurons. (LO 5.1)

    a. Where is it located?

    b. How many neurons typically make up this nucleus?

    c. Go back to Chapter 3 and remind yourself how many neurons are typically present in the human brain. Calculate the percentage of neurons that are dedicated to maintaining consciousness.

    d. What is the importance of your biological clock relative to the action of melatonin—and what IS melatonin?

2. Keep a sleep log for the next week, then come back to this item. Answer each question fully, not with a simple "yes" or "no." (LO 5.1)

    a. How many hours per night did you sleep?

    b. Did you sleep through the night, or wake up and go back to sleep again?

    c. Was this a typical week for you?

    d. Are you in sleep deprivation?

    e. Are you in sleep debt? (Make sure you know the difference.)

    f. How might this affect your day-to-day life?

    g. Develop a plan of what you will do the next time you find yourself unable to sleep, giving yourself several options. Write out this plan on an index card and place it by your bed.

3. REM sleep is interesting because of the paradoxical activities that occur. Describe several here and note the reasons why scientists believe these events occur. Were you familiar with some of them before reading your text? Which ones? Were some of the paradoxical events new to you? Which ones? (LO 5.2)

4. Complete this table for the sleep stages. (LO 5.2)

	Lasts	Characterized by
Stage 1		
Stage 2		
Stages 3, 4		
Stage 5		

5. Go to http://www.sleepnet.com/sleeptest.html where you can take a sleep disorders test. Go ahead and take it! Then you can also play around with different symptoms and see what the test results show. You will see that most sleep disorders do follow closely along the lines described in your text. (LO 5.3)

6. Complete this table for the disorders of sleep. Describe each disorder in the space provided. (LO 5.3)

Insomnia	
Narcolepsy	
Sleep Apnea	
Night Terrors	
Sleepwalking	

DREAMS

1. Table 5.1 lists the most common dream themes that scientists have compiled based on extensive survey data. Have you experience any of these dreams? Are there other themes that you commonly experience? (LO 5.4)

2. In Chapters 1 and 4 you read about how people have an innate tendency to create order from chaos, for example, seeing images of faces in random patterns, such as the "man in the moon." Which theory of dreaming picks up this theme? Note specific aspects that lead you to this conclusion. (LO 5.5)

3. Map out the pathway of neurotransmitter activity during REM sleep. Note the various brain structures that are involved and how all of this might lead to the experience of a "dream." (LO 5.5)

4. Your text lists several functions of dreams. Summarize them and provide an example of your own dreams that exemplify that function. (LO 5.5)

OTHER ALTERATIONS OF CONSCIOUSNESS AND UNUSUAL EXPERIENCES

1. Evaluate the quality of the evidence that out-of-body experiences (OBEs) are a "real" experience. (LO 5.6)

2. True or False? All near-death experiences (NDEs) are described as spiritual and pleasant. What is the evidence for your answer? Explain some of the brain's biochemical events that could explain several typical NDE elements, following severe trauma. (LO 5.6)

3. Your text discusses three testable explanations for the déjà vu experience. Summarize them here in your own words. Which one do you favor? Why? (LO 5.6)

4. In your own words, list the six commonly held misconceptions about hypnosis. Then briefly suggest evidence that contradicts each misconception. In addition, some known benefits to hypnosis are legitimate. List a few of them here. Do you think you would be a good candidate for hypnosis? Why or why not? (LO 5.7)

5. Compare the two most accepted models of hypnosis: the sociocognitive and the dissociative. Which model do you favor? Why? (LO 5.7)

DRUGS AND CONSCIOUSNESS

1. Complete this table with the four drug types. For the "Effects," include more details than are included in the table in your text—note specific effects. (LO 5.8)

Drug Type	Effect	Examples

2. Using alcohol as a model, describe the signs and symptoms of substance dependence. (LO 5.8)

3. Table 5.5 lists a number of alcohol-related misconceptions. Which of these have you heard of? Which of these did you believe in? Pick the one you most believed in, then surf the Internet for evidence to disconfirm your belief. Summarize the information from the web site in your own words. Be sure to include the URL here, as well as a brief review of the quality of the web site. (LO 5.9)

AS YOU READ ... CONCEPT MAP ACTIVITIES

ACTIVITY 1: This concept map covers many of the ideas within this chapter. It could include many more links, and you can draw in more nodes and label the links.

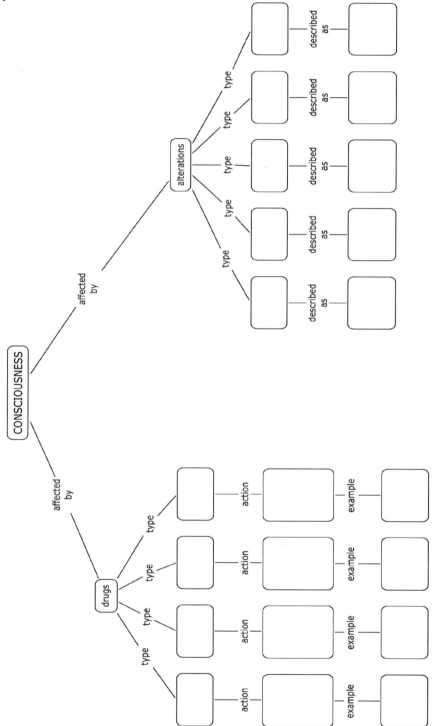

ACTIVITY 2: This concept map limits itself to sleep because there are so many interrelated concepts.

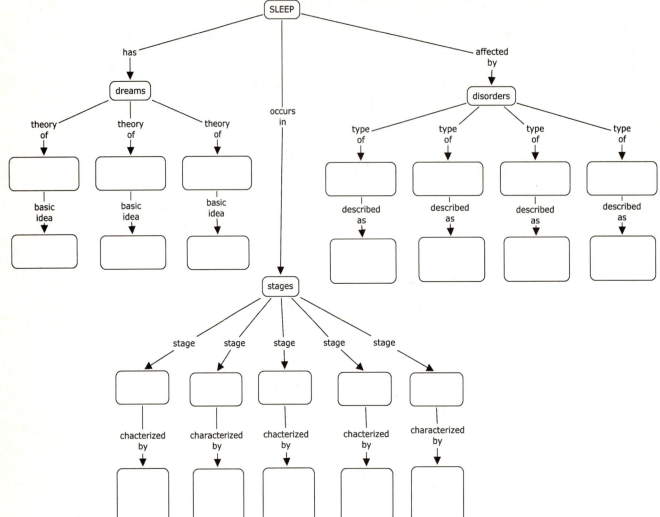

Author activity content supported by *IHMC Cmap Tools* Copyright ©1998-2007 Institute for Human & Machine Cognition

AS YOU READ … MYTH OR REALITY?

Myth: Some people don't dream.
Reality: All people dream, probably every night, they just don't remember their dreams.

1. We have all met people who tell us they don't dream. Do you know anyone who makes this claim? This statement contradicts the research evidence, starting with an important study by Dement (1978). He noted that all people show REM sleep at various times during the night. Indeed, when he woke people up during REM sleep they consistently reported that they were dreaming.

   a. Surf the Internet on your own. You will find a wealth of web sites devoted to discussions of dreaming. Be sure you review your scientific thinking principles and web-evaluation criteria!

   b. Make an argument for why people might not remember their dreams. Although this issue probably has no completely "correct" answer, many hypotheses are certainly available—some better than others.

Myth: Mixing different types of alcoholic beverages, for example, drinking beer and then switching to whiskey, will give you a greater hangover than if you just stick with one type of alcoholic beverage.
Reality: It makes no difference what you are drinking or how you mix your alcohols together. What matters is the overall alcohol content—the more you drink the greater the hangover.

   1. Go to http://health.ninemsn.com.au/article.aspx?id=113108 and http://www.madsci.org/posts/archives/1998-05/896646552.Me.r.html but see http://www.realbeer.com/edu/health/hangovers.php (funded by beer producers) and read about it.

   2. Develop an argument you could use to convince your friends, the next time they tell you that mixing different alcoholic beverages, or drinking them in a particular sequence will give you a worse hangover.

AS YOU READ ... PUT YOUR SCIENTIFIC THINKING SKILLS TO THE TEST

1. Many people believe in biorhythms—the cycling of your physical, emotional, and intellectual well-being. Biorhythm charts can illustrate this concept. Some people monitor the highs and lows of these cycles and plan their lives around them.
   a. Find a web site where you can calculate your biorhythm chart. Go ahead and calculate it! What did you find out about yourself?
   b. Now evaluate the web site using the criteria in the start of this Study Guide. What can you conclude about the overall quality of the web site?
   c. Go to http://skepdic.com/biorhyth.html and read this critique of biorhythms. Does your assessment of the web site quality, taken together with the skepdic.com entry influence your belief in the accuracy of your "biorhythms"?

2. Young adults, generally between the ages of 15 and 23, undergo a phase shift in their circadian cycle, called the "Circadian Shift." During this time, young adults are at their peak performance from later in the morning until later at night, compared to other age groups. However, the need for total sleep hours is increased, averaging about 9.2 hours per night.
   a. You can read more about circadian phase shifts and their effects on behavior:
   http://www.apa.org/monitor/oct01/sleepteen.html and
   http://www.sleepfoundation.org/article/sleep-topics/sleep-drive-and-your-body-clock

   b. Keep track of the times of day when you feel you are at your best, and the times of day when you feel you are slowing down. Does your behavior reflect a circadian shift? However, how does your life schedule affect your overall sleep deficit? Do you have early morning classes? Are you able to fall asleep early enough to get your 9 hours of sleep before you get up for school, ON A REGULAR BASIS? If not, what could you do to rearrange your schedule?

3. In Chapter 1 you read about six principles of scientific thinking. Put these skills to the test. Here are three different web sites with three slightly different, albeit somewhat overlapping, interpretations of what it means to dream about guns. How can you reconcile the differences? Consider the different theories of dreaming presented in your text.
   http://www.dreamloverinc.com/g.htm#Guns
   http://www.experienceproject.com/dream-dictionary/Guns-dreams
   http://www.dreamhawk.com/dyd-g2.htm#gun

As You Read ... MyPsychLab Connection

The Biology of Sleep

To learn more about circadian rhythms, **Listen** to *Brain Time*. **Watch** the video *Lucid Dreaming*, which covers the physiology of lucid dreaming and how scientists have learned to induce lucid dreaming in a laboratory setting. You can also **Listen** to the podcast *Lucid Dreaming*. To review topics such as sleep disorders, **watch** *Robert: Insomnia*, the real case of a man suffering from a sleep disorder.

Dreams

Gain a better understanding of the various theories of dreams by utilizing the **Explore** *Theories of Dreaming*. Through this explore, you can learn more about the psychodynamic, cognitive, and physiological theories of dreams.

Other Alterations of Consciousness and Unusual Experiences

Learning about hypnosis? Check out the **Simulation** *Hypnosis*, where you can experience an induction method used in hypnosis. Not only will you receive hands-on experience on how one is inducted into the hypnotic state, but this activity will also help dispel the myths of hypnosis by allowing you to think critically about what actually constitutes the hypnotic state. So why do people become hypnotized? In trying to understand hypnosis, you may also wish to **Watch** the video *Hypnosis*.

Drugs and Consciousness

When reviewing how drugs and alcohol affect consciousness and behavior, **Explore** *Behavioral Effects Associated with Various Blood Alcohol Levels*. What to know more about the effects of smoking and nicotine on your behavior? **Watch** the video *Smoking Damage* and **Listen** to the podcast *Smoking*. When learning about drugs and consciousness, **Watch** the video *Kathy: Substance Abuse*. This video features a real case study of a woman who has a history of abusing substances and who talks about the deleterious effects that the substances have had on her everyday life.

AFTER YOU READ ... PRACTICE TEST #1

Before beginning this practice test, estimate the percent you expect to get correct.
Anticipated percent correct: _____

1. On average, about _____ of college students report they have experienced sleep paralysis, accompanied by feelings of anxiety or terror, feeling vibrations, or hearing humming noises.
   a. 10% to 25%
   b. 33% to 50%
   c. 60% to 75%
   d. 75% to 90%

2. Most animals have a biological clock that regulates sleep/wakefulness cycles. In humans we refer to this as the _____ rhythm.
   a. circadian.
   b. diurnal.
   c. melatonin.
   d. sleep/wake.

3. Although research suggests that college students need about _____ hours of sleep per night, surveys show that on average they only sleep about _____ hours per night, accumulating a sleep deficit.
   a. 9 / 6
   b. 10 / 7
   c. 9 / 5
   d. 10 / 5

4. Sleep deprivation can lead to
   a. weight loss.
   b. excess non-REM sleep.
   c. difficulties with attention and learning.
   d. increased risk of low blood pressure.

5. Hypnagogic imagery refers to
   a. bizarre dream-like images in stage 1 sleep.
   b. the vivid images of stage 5 (REM) sleep.
   c. images induced during hypnosis.
   d. the images present in lucid dreaming.

6. Research suggests that an important sleep stage for humans is
   a. stage 1 sleep because deprivation makes it difficult to fall asleep, so less time is spent in any of the other sleep stages.
   b. stage 5 (REM)—when animals or people are sleep-deprived they get into REM sleep more quickly and spend more time in REM sleep than they would otherwise.
   c. stage 2 (light sleep)—when sleep-deprived, humans and animals spend almost all of their time in Stage 2 sleep, maybe only going through the full cycle once, after several hours.
   d. stage 3 or 4 deep sleep—when animals or people are sleep-deprived they get into Stages 3 and 4 sleep more quickly and spend more time in deep sleep than they would otherwise.

7. Many dreams have disturbing themes, so some therapists train people to control dream content during times that they are aware of dreaming. This awareness of dreaming is called
   a. light dreaming.
   b. lucid dreaming.
   c. aware dreaming.
   d. awake dreaming.

8. Milana recently traveled from her home in California to a wedding in Europe. When she got back her boyfriend broke up with her. She is now having trouble sleeping. Because you are her good friend you advise her to
   a. take a pill like *Lunesta* or *Ambien*.
   b. turn up the thermostat so the room is nice and warm, or even hot.
   c. put away the clocks in her house so she isn't preoccupied with the time.
   d. have a cup of hot coffee or tea because the warm liquid in her stomach will help her fall asleep.

9. Jose's wife complains that his snoring and frequent turning over in his sleep are keeping her awake at night. Yet Jose insists that he sleeps well, despite often feeling tired in the morning. Jose probably suffers from
   a. insomnia.
   b. narcolepsy.
   c. night terrors.
   d. sleep apnea.

10. According to Freud, dreams have two aspects. The actual content of the dream is called _____ content, and the hidden, underlying meaning is called the _____ content.
    a. outer; inner
    b. overt; covert
    c. manifest; latent
    d. external; internal

11. While asleep, Kendra's brain is busy. As acetylcholine surges and activates the pons random messages travel to the thalamus and throughout the cortex. As she enters Stage 5 sleep, Kendra has a dream of talking to friends in class. This process reflects the _____ theory of dreaming.
    a. neurocognitive
    b. wish fulfillment
    c. dream protection
    d. activation-synthesis

12. Near-death experiences (NDEs) are not a purely biological phenomenon because evidence shows that
    a. they are spiritually bound.
    b. they are influenced by culture.
    c. they have never been reported by neither agnostics nor atheists.
    d. they provide a glimpse into the afterlife, suggesting a religious component.

13. John was in an accident and was seriously injured. He tells his friends that he felt his consciousness leave his body, and he watched from above as the doctors worked on him. He saw his deceased grandparents were there, smiling at him and the pain went away. Then, as the doctors finished working on him his consciousness returned to his body. John experienced a(n)
    a. mystical experience.
    b. déjà vu experience.
    c. hypnotic regression.
    d. near-death experience.

14. Déjà vu experiences might be attributed to
    a. memories of a past life.
    b. an excess of serotonin in the visual cortex.
    c. a coping mechanism when feeling anxious in a new situation.
    d. small seizures in the right temporal lobe.

15. You are a movie reviewer and just saw a film in which stage show volunteers received posthypnotic suggestions to rob jewelry stores and mail the jewels to the hypnotist. You title your review,
    a. "Entertaining, and Realistic!"
    b. "Plot Follows Known Research Evidence."
    c. "Entertaining, But Goes Against the Known Facts."
    d. "A 'How-To' for Getting Rich Quickly and Safely."

16. A criticism of past life regression is that people's memories from their past lives reflect
    a. the role of the "hidden observer."
    b. frequent inaccuracies of historical details.
    c. child-like EEGs in their adult brains, making it impossible to interpret.
    d. a belief in reincarnation that provides an alternative explanation for the success of the regression.

17. Support for the sociocognitive theory of hypnosis comes from the finding that
    a. a "hidden observer" within the hypnotized individual retains full awareness.
    b. psychoactive drugs can enhance a person's hypnotic suggestibility.
    c. hypnotic suggestibility is a stable trait.
    d. there is an inhibition of activity in the frontal lobes during hypnosis.

18. Alcohol is primarily a
    a. psychedelic.
    b. stimulant.
    c. anesthetic.
    d. depressant.

19. The most powerful natural stimulant is
    a. cocaine.
    b. alcohol.
    c. amphetamine.
    d. methamphetamine.

20. Jasmine says she will never smoke marijuana because it leads to the use of other stronger and more addictive drugs. You tell Jasmine that
    a. she is right. Good research evidence suggests that marijuana is a gateway drug.
    b. she might be right, but the direction of cause and effect has not been established; and other reasons perhaps explain why some people start out with marijuana and move on to more potent drugs.
    c. she is wrong. The research evidence clearly contradicts Jasmine's beliefs; in fact, in studies of addicts, the direction of progression was TO marijuana, not FROM it.
    d. she is right. Even though you know that no research evidence supports Jasmine's belief, you figure it's best if Jasmine doesn't take any chances that way.

After completing the test, calculate your percent correct
(/ 20 =   ) x 100 = _____.

How accurate were your expectations? Does your performance suggest the need for additional study?
For the items you missed, go back and identify why the "correct" answer is the best answer.

AFTER YOU READ ... PRACTICE TEST #2

Before beginning this practice test, estimate the percent you expect to get correct:

Anticipated percent correct: _____

1. Janelle has recently started therapy because she believes that she has been visited by aliens who held her down and examined her, usually right after she fell asleep, or just before she woke up. Her therapist, who is a scientific psychologist, explains that
   a. she probably suffers from night terrors.
   b. she probably suffers from sleep paralysis.
   c. she was in a state of paradoxical sleep and dreamed it.
   d. she was probably sexually abused by a family member.

2. We normally cycle through _____ stages of sleep each night, with each cycle lasting approximately _____ minutes.
   a. 5 / 15   c. 5 / 90
   b. 4 / 120   d. 4 / 60

3. Children spend most of their time asleep, about 40% in
   a. stage 5, REM sleep.
   b. stages 3 & 4, deep sleep.
   c. stage 2 sleep.
   d. stage 5, NREM sleep.

4. As adults we spend most of our time asleep, about 65%, in
   a. stage 5, REM sleep.
   b. stages 3 & 4, deep sleep.
   c. stage 2 sleep.
   d. stage 5, NREM sleep.

5. We spend the least time in REM sleep _____ in an entire night's sleep cycle, and more _____ in the sleep cycle.
   a. early and late; midway
   b. midway; early and late
   c. late; early
   d. early; late

6. Which of the following is TRUE?
   a. Dolphins sleep with one of their hemispheres awake and the other asleep.
   b. Dreams only last for a few seconds even if they seem to last longer.
   c. When humans are asleep, their brain rests.
   d. Many people never dream.

7. People with narcolepsy
   a. usually fall asleep if they remain calm for too long.
   b. go directly into REM sleep, suggesting their sleep-wake cycle is disordered.
   c. will fall asleep for about an hour at a time but then wake up feeling refreshed.
   d. have a good response to caffeine, and can stave off attacks during working hours by taking caffeine pills.

119

8. Whether someone is dreaming in New York or Beijing or anywhere else, that person is likely to have
   a. dreams that have more friendliness than aggressiveness.
   b. dreams that have more good fortune than misfortune.
   c. more aggressive dreams if it is a man, but more positive dreams if it is a woman.
   d. more emotional dreams if it is a woman, but more dreams about men if it is a man.

9. Which of the following is FALSE? The best evidence suggests several reasons for why we dream, including
   a. expressing built up anger (catharsis).
   b. consolidating memories.
   c. processing our emotions.
   d. learning new ways of doing things.

10. Research tests of Freud's wish fulfillment and dream protection explanations of dreams failed to find
    a. negative content; most people's dreams are primarily positive.
    b. much sexual content—only 10% of dreams are sexual in nature.
    c. frequent nightmares, which Freud predicted should occur regularly.
    d. common events; about 90% of dreams reflect bizarre themes in disguise.

11. Hallucinations
    a. are the experience of a sensation without perception.
    b. are limited to visual and auditory modalities.
    c. occur in as many as 39% of normal, sober college students.
    d. occur only in individuals who are mentally ill or taking psychoactive drugs.

12. As finals approach, Kareem has been studying day and night. He is under intense pressure to raise his grades to keep his scholarship. He tells you that earlier in the library he felt himself "float" over himself and "saw" himself studying. This experience frightened him, but you tell him not to worry
    a. at least 90% of all people report experiencing at least one OBE in their lifetime.
    b. he can now develop this ability and will be able to have frequent mystical experiences.
    c. as long as he doesn't "fall" while feeling that he is floating, he will not be in danger during such experiences.
    d. high stress, such as he is under right now, is related to increased reports of OBEs.

13. Near-death experiences (NDEs) are really misnamed because they can also occur with
    a. alcohol intoxication.
    b. NREM state dreams.
    c. electrical stimulation of the temporal lobes.
    d. rapidly rising to the surface from a deep underwater dive.

14. Most of the misconceptions about hypnosis seem to originate from
    a. police interrogations under hypnosis.
    b. media reports of recovered memories under hypnosis.
    c. movies and stage shows that misrepresent true hypnotic states.
    d. scientific studies which replicate hypnotic states in fully aware and awake subjects.

15. Hypnosis can be accurately portrayed as
    a. a sleep-like state.
    b. an altered state during which amazing feats are possible.
    c. increasing people's confidence for memories recalled under hypnosis.
    d. an aid to increasing memory accuracy for repressed traumatic events in the past.

16. Substance abuse is characterized by
    a. tolerance requiring increasingly higher doses of the drug.
    b. a pattern of problems with family, friends and work, associated with the drug.
    c. having withdrawal symptoms when the drug is taken away.
    d. committing crimes in order to support one's 'habit.'

17. In trying to explain drug use, researchers have found that
    a. there is an addictive personality type that predisposes people to use drugs.
    b. no genetic factors can be identified for the development of most addictions or alcoholism.
    c. many commonly used drugs help people to self-treat problems with tension and anxiety.
    d. sociocultural influences actually reflect an underlying biological effect and have been discounted.

18. The psychoactive drug that has probably been used for the longest time by humans is
    a. alcohol.
    b. cocaine.
    c. marijuana.
    d. mescaline.

19. Omar, who is 6' tall and weighs 200 pounds, and Deolinda, who is 5'2" and weighs 110, are at a bar. They each drink 3 beers in an hour. Who is drunker?
    a. Deolinda; because BAC is affected by body mass, and Deolinda simply has less of it.
    b. Omar; because he has more lean body mass, and will not metabolize the alcohol as well.
    c. Omar; because beer has less effect on women, who are more sensitive to hard liquor.
    d. Deolinda; because women's expectations result in their becoming drunk on smaller amounts of alcohol.

20. Although the most commonly used illegal drug is _____, the most commonly abused drug is _____.
    a. cocaine / heroin
    b. alcohol / benzodiazepine
    c. methamphetamine / marijuana
    d. marijuana / amphetamine

After completing the test, calculate your percent correct

(____ / 20 = ____) x 100 = _____.

How accurate were your expectations? Does your performance suggest the need for additional study?
For the items you missed, go back and identify why the "correct" answer is the best answer.

AFTER YOU READ . . . PRACTICE TEST ANSWER KEYS

Practice Test 1.

1. b (p. 166)
2. a (p. 167)
3. a (p. 168)
4. c (p. 168)
5. a (p. 169)
6. b (p. 170)
7. b (p. 171)
8. c (p. 172)
9. d (p. 172-173)
10. c (p. 175)
11. d (p. 175-176)
12. b (p. 179)
13. d (p. 179)
14. d (p. 180)
15. c (p. 182)
16. b (p. 184)
17. c (p. 185)
18. d (p. 189)
19. a (p. 191)
20. b (p. 194-195)

Practice Test 2.

1. b (p. 166)
2. c (p. 169)
3. b (p. 169)
4. c (p. 169)
5. d (p. 170)
6. a (p. 171)
7. b (p. 172)
8. d (p. 174)
9. a (p. 174)
10. b (p. 175)
11. c (p. 178)
12. d (p. 178)
13. c (p. 180)
14. c (p. 181)
15. c (p. 183)
16. b (p. 187)
17. c (p. 188)
18. a (p. 189)
19. a (p. 189-190)
20. d (p. 192-193)

AFTER YOU READ ... CONCEPT MAPPING ACTIVITY ANSWERS

ACTIVITY 1:

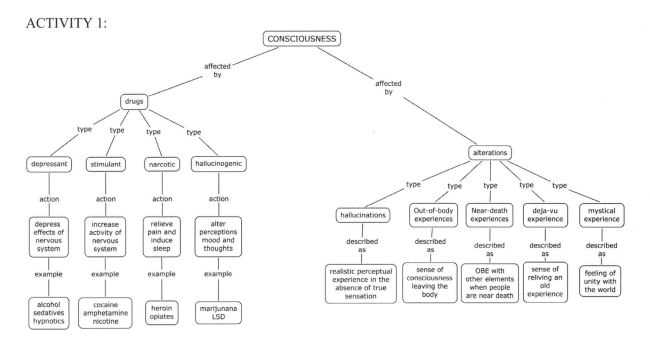

ACTIVITY 2: For this map you should have included the following terms, listed here in alphabetical order, as well as descriptions:

activation-synthesis
dream protection
insomnia
narcolepsy
neurocognitive
night terrors
REM
sleep apnea
sleep walking
stage1
stage 2
stages 3 & 4
wish fulfillment

CHAPTER 6
LEARNING
HOW NURTURE CHANGES US

BEFORE YOU READ ... CHAPTER PREVIEW

Learning is defined as a change in an organism's behavior or thoughts as a result of experience. It is fundamental to everything else we do. **Habituation** is the simplest form of learning. It allows us to keep from becoming overloaded with stimulation from the environment and is seen in the most basic life forms. Eric Kandel, who won a Nobel Prize for his work with a very simple organism, the sea slug *Aplysia,* discovered much of what we know about learning, including habituation, and its opposite, *sensitization.*

The *British Associationists* were the first to systematically study learning. They noted that stimuli come to be connected together. In modern times, this association is best seen in the work of the Russian physiologist, Ivan Pavlov, who studied digestion in dogs. He noticed that the dogs often salivated before being fed. The process by which the dogs learned to anticipate food is now called **classical conditioning.** During **acquisition** a neutral stimulus comes to elicit a **conditioned response (CR)**—a response that is similar to a naturally occurring, **unconditioned response (UCR)**. Thus, the neutral stimulus becomes a **conditioned stimulus (CS)** when it is paired with an **unconditioned stimulus (UCS)** that naturally elicits a UCR. **Extinction** of a CR occurs when we stop pairing the CS with the UCS, so that the connection between the two is lost. **Spontaneous recovery** of the CR can occur, however, when we are again put in the situation in which the original conditioning occurred. However, without continued pairing of the CS and UCS, it will quickly extinguish. In the **renewal** effect, extinction occurs in a novel context, which may help us to understand and explain *phobias*. When a CR occurs to a stimulus that is very similar to the original CS, this is called **stimulus generalization**. At other times, the CS is seen as clearly distinct from other stimuli and the CR occurs only to that precise CS, a process called **stimulus discrimination**. In **higher-order conditioning,** a new CS can be created by pairing an old CS with a new CS. For example, with *occasion setters* for addictive behaviors, just being in a situation in which the behavior was frequently engaged in will elicit the craving for the addictive substance, although it in other situations will not do so. Many additional applications of classical conditioning to everyday life include the acquisition of fears, **fetishism** and phobias (as seen in the case of "Little Albert"), in disgust reactions, and in advertising where **latent inhibition** prevents the acquisition of a new response to an old product. Finally, we need to watch out for *pseudoconditioning* where the CS also triggers the UCR.

Another type of conditioning is called **operant conditioning** (*instrumental conditioning)*. Operant conditioning depends on the consequences of behaviors and is based on the **Law of Effect**: positive consequences strengthen behavior, negative consequences weaken it. This is unlike insight, which results in a sudden shift in behavior. Although classical conditioning depends on natural responses of the nervous system, with operant conditioning, almost any behavior can be learned and maintained. A prominent psychologist, important to the history of operant conditioning, was B. F. Skinner. Using a **Skinner Box**, he recorded the behaviors of animals following different consequences. **Reinforcement** always increases behavior, and can be a reward (**positive reinforcement**) or removal of something unpleasant (**negative reinforcement**). Punishment, however, involves either giving an unpleasant stimulus (**positive punishment**) or removing something pleasant (**negative punishment**). Any external stimulus that signals the presence of reinforcers is called a **discriminative stimulus**. Reinforcement is more effective than punishment for changing behavior. *Acquisition, extinction, spontaneous recovery*, and *stimulus generalization* and *discrimination* are all found in operant conditioning. Reinforcement can be either **continuous** or **partial**, and can be given consistently based either on time (**fixed interval, FI**) or on the number of times a behavior is performed (**fixed ratio, FR**), or it can be given inconsistently, on average over a set amount of time (**variable interval, VI**) or the average of a number of times a behavior is performed (**variable ratio, VR**). These different **schedules of reinforcement** result in different patterns of responding. One last aspect of acquisition is that behaviors need to be **shaped by successive approximations** (*shaped*), and do not occur spontaneously, as with classical conditioning. An everyday example is that operant conditioning can explain *superstitious behaviors*: you did something that was followed by a positive outcome, and now you repeat the initial behavior, anticipating again the positive outcome. In addition, so-called *token economies* take advantage of using secondary reinforcers, such as tokens, or stars, which a person can accumulate to earn desired rewards. The tokens are **secondary reinforcers** that can be associated with **primary reinforcers.** In considering how operant and classical conditioning differ, one interesting new finding is that they are each mediated by different brain areas. Finally, *two-process theory* shows how both classical conditioning and operant conditioning work together to explain behaviors such as phobias.

Cognitive models of learning take into account *thinking*. Whereas strict models of conditioning, *radical behaviorism,* are called stimulus-response (S-R) models, cognitive models are often called S-O-R models because they take into account the organism's assessment of a stimulus. An early challenge to S-R models came from Edward Tolman, who demonstrated **latent learning**, learning that can't result from a specific stimulus. A second type of cognitive learning is called **observational learning** because it occurs from simply watching others do a task, or from watching the consequences others receive for a particular behavior. An early researcher in this area was Albert Bandura, who showed that children can learn to act aggressively by watching others act aggressively. In more recent years, similar studies have examined the effects of media violence on real-world aggression with similar conclusions. Recent research has identified **mirror neurons** that are active during observational learning. A final type of cognitive learning, documented by Wolfgang Kohler, a Gestalt psychologist, involves **insight**—the *aha reaction* when a solution to a problem suddenly comes to us after other strategies have failed.

In recent years, the focus has been on the biological influences on learning. For example, in *conditioned taste aversion* we learn to strongly dislike foods whose eating is followed by illness—even if the food itself was safe and clean. Such a strong form of learning often occurs after just one instance of illness and remains for a long time and contradicts assumptions of *equipotentiality* in classical conditioning. Taste aversion has been a problem for patients undergoing chemotherapy. Another important biological aspect of conditioning concerned **preparedness**—a predisposition to respond a certain way to some stimuli. Preparedness is also related to the concept of **instinctive drift**, which is characterized by great difficulty in trying to operationally condition some behaviors based on an organism's predisposition to respond in certain ways to environmental stimuli.

Finally, it is important to consider learning fads. One such fad is *sleep-assisted learning,* in which learning supposedly occurs during sleep. Scientific studies show that this kind of learning is not possible. Another fad concerns *accelerated learning,* in which varied techniques supposedly help people learn more quickly. Again, scientific studies have not supported these methods. In educational circles, *discovery learning* has been promoted. It requires students to teach themselves deep scientific principles based on their own inquiries. An assessment of discovery learning shows that the solutions to problems that students generate in this way are more often incorrect than correct, and are never corrected by the teacher, leading to life-long misconceptions. A final area to consider is that of "**learning styles**." Here again, the research evidence is clear: no scientific evidence supports the notion that students learn better when provided with one type of material versus another and furthermore, this might delay students' effective learning in a different mode.

BEFORE YOU READ ... LEARNING OBJECTIVES

After reading Chapter 6 you should be able to:

6.1   Describe Pavlov's model of classical conditioning and discriminate conditioned stimuli and responses from unconditioned stimuli and responses

6.2   Explain the major principles and terminology associated with classical conditioning

6.3   Explain how complex behaviors can result from classical conditioning and how they emerge in our daily lives

6.4   Distinguish operant conditioning from classical conditioning

6.5   Describe Thorndike's law of effect

6.6   Describe reinforcement and its effects on behavior and distinguish negative reinforcement from punishment

6.7   Identify the four schedules of reinforcement and the response pattern associated with each

6.8   Describe some applications of operant conditioning

6.9   Outline the evidence that supports latent learning and observational learning

6.10   Identify evidence of insight learning

6.11   Explain how biological predispositions can facilitate learning of some associations

6.12   Evaluate popular techniques marketed to enhance learning

BEFORE YOU READ ... TERM IDENTIFICATION

acquisition (p. 206)
classical (Pavlovian) conditioning (p. 204)
cognitive map (p. 225)
conditioned response (CR) (p. 204)
conditioned stimulus (CS) (p. 204)
continuous reinforcement (p. 217)
discriminative stimulus (p. 216)
extinction (p. 206)
fetishism (p. 209)
fixed interval (FI) schedule (p. 218)
fixed ratio (FR) schedule (p. 218)
habituation (p. 202)
higher-order conditioning (p. 207)
insight (p. 213)
instinctive drift (p. 232)
latent inhibition (p. 208)
latent learning (p. 224)
law of effect (p. 212)
learning (p. 202)
learning style (p. 235)
mirror neuron (p. 227)

negative reinforcement (p. 213)
observational learning (p. 225)
operant conditioning (p. 211)
partial reinforcement (p. 217)
positive reinforcement (p. 213)
preparedness (p. 231)
primary reinforcer (p. 221)
punishment (p. 214)
reinforcement (p. 213)
renewal effect (p. 206)
schedule of reinforcement (p. 217)
secondary reinforcer (p. 221)
shaping by successive approximations (p. 219)
Skinner box (p. 213)
spontaneous recovery (p. 206)
stimulus discrimination (p. 207)
stimulus generalization (p. 207)
unconditioned response (UCR) (p. 204)
unconditioned stimulus (UCS) (p. 204)
variable interval (VI) schedule (p. 219)
variable ratio (VR) schedule (p. 218)

As You Read ... Practice Activities

CLASSICAL CONDITIONING

1. Compare habituation and sensitization. What do these processes suggest about learning? (LO 6.1)

2. Go to http://nobelprize.org/educational_games/medicine/pavlov/ and condition a dog to salivate. Did you earn your certificate? (LO 6.1)

3. Provide an original example of how a behavior could be classically conditioned—do not use one from your text or lecture. Show all the steps of how the conditioning occurs and identify the unconditioned stimulus, conditioned stimulus, unconditioned response, and conditioned response. (LO 6.2)

4. Compare acquisition, spontaneous recovery, and the renewal effect. Provide an original example of how each might occur in simple terms. (LO 6.2)

5. Beer commercials often show people having a good time.
    a. Discuss how the marketing companies are taking advantage of higher-order conditioning. (LO 6.2)

    b. Discuss how their plan could fail on account of latent inhibition. (LO 6.3)

6. In the famous case of Little Albert, Watson and Reyner (1920) showed how phobias can be classically conditioning. Describe this study in terms of the following criteria. (LO 6.3)

Design:

Findings:

Lesson learned:

OPERANT CONDITIONING

1. Go to https://pantherfile.uwm.edu/johnchay/PL06/OC/OC.html and have some fun conditioning a pigeon. Examine the effects of different schedules of reinforcement and be sure to extinguish your pigeon's pecking behavior before you leave! (LO 6.4)

2. Complete this table to help distinguish between classical and operant conditioning. (LO 6.4)

	Classical Conditioning	Operant Conditioning
Target behavior is		
Reward is		
Behavior is produced because		

3. Describe the critical aspect of operant conditioning, and provide an original example that highlights that aspect of the conditioning process. (LO 6.5)

4. Complete the following table. Be sure to use your own, ORIGINAL example from your everyday life. (LO 6.6)

	Definition	Effect on Behavior	Original Example
Positive Reinforcement			
Negative Reinforcement			

5. Match each scenario to the type of consequence. (LO 6.6)

Students come to class unprepared to discuss assigned readings. The professor cancels class and sends them to the library to read. The rest of the semester they show up prepared for discussions.

a. negative reinforcement

You forget to replace the batteries in your smoke alarm. As the batteries start to drain, the smoke alarm goes off with an ear-splitting buzzer. You subsequently replace the batteries every time you change your clocks for daylight savings time.

b. positive reinforcement

You spend hours in the library researching original sources for your term paper, rather than limiting yourself to the ones you can easily access online. Your teacher is impressed with the depth of your review and assigns you an A on the paper. You now do in-library research for all your papers.

c. negative punishment

d. positive punishment

Your roommate leaves his/her dirty underwear lying around in the common bathroom in your dorm suite. You throw it away in disgust. Your roommate now takes the dirty underwear back to his/her room.

6. Complete this table with important concepts in both classical and operant conditioning. Make sure your definitions can fit either classical or operant conditioning and that your examples are original and indicate whether it is drawn from classical or operant principles of conditioning. (LO 6.2 and 6.6)

Term	Definition		Example	
	Classical	Operant	Classical	Operant
Acquisition				
Extinction				
Spontaneous Recovery				
Stimulus Generalization				
Stimulus Discrimination				

7. Complete this table indicating the effect on behavior of each partial reinforcement schedule. (LO 6.7)

	RATIO	**INTERVAL**
FIXED		
VARIABLE		

8. The first year after negotiating a high salary contract, many athletes have an "off year" in their sport, leaving many fans criticizing the high salary. Explain the athlete's behavior in terms of the effects of a fixed interval reinforcement schedule on behavior. (LO 6.7)

9. Describe one of your own superstitious behaviors you have now, or have engaged in, in the past. Discuss how that behavior might have been reinforced. (LO 6.8)

10. Differentiate between primary and secondary reinforcers. Which do you think will maintain a behavior for a longer time, and why? (LO 6.8)

COGNITIVE MODELS OF LEARNING

1. Discuss how Tolman's (1932) studies on latent learning opened the door for "thinking" to be considered essential to learning by addressing the following aspects of his study. (LO 6.9)

   Design:

   Findings:

   Lesson learned:

2. Discuss these important aspects of Albert Bandura's studies of observational learning of aggression. (LO 6.9)

   Design:

   Findings:

   Lesson learned:

3. Insight learning is often accompanied by the "aha" feeling when the solution to a problem you have been unable to solve for a while finally comes to you. Describe such an occurrence in your own life. (LO 6.10)

BIOLOGICAL INFLUENCES ON LEARNING

1. What are the three ways in which conditioned taste aversion differs from other types of classical conditioning? (LO 6.11)

2. Connect the concepts of "equipotentiality" and "preparedness." (LO 6.11)

LEARNING FADS: DO THEY WORK?

1. In considering sleep-assisted learning, accelerated, and discovery learning, why do you believe people are willing to spend their time and money on trying such programs? Consider several biases in thinking that you learned about in Chapters 1 and 2 when answering this question. (LO 6.12)

2. What is a major confound that has not been considered in studies of sleep-assisted learning? How could you control for this confound? (LO 6.12)

3. Most students have experienced some form of "discovery learning" in their classes. Think of an example from your own education in which a teacher allowed you to come up with your own conclusions. Did the teacher also provide direct instruction along with the discovery learning to help you reach a correct solution? (LO 6.12)

As You Read ... Concept Map Activities

ACTIVITY 1: Complete this concept map as an overview of different learning and conditioning models.

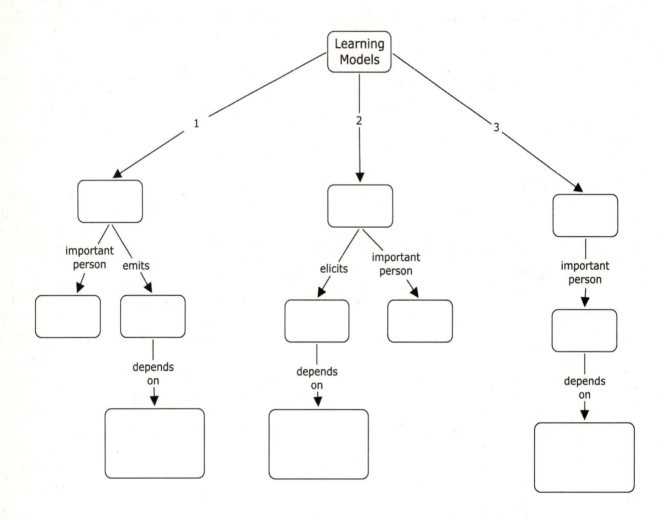

Author activity content supported by *IHMC Cmap Tools* Copyright ©1998-2007 Institute for Human & Machine Cognition

ACTIVITY 2: Complete this concept map for classical conditioning with an example from your own life.

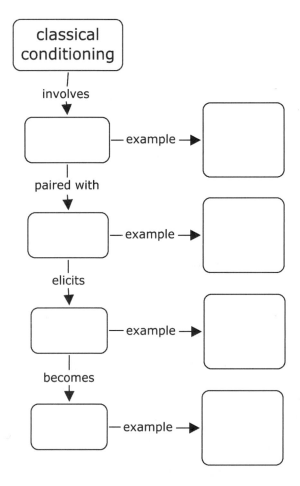

ACTIVITY 3: Complete this concept map for operant conditioning reinforcement schedules.

```
                        ┌─────────────────────────┐
                        │ reinforcement schedules │
                        └─────────────────────────┘
                   can be          can be
              ┌──────────┐              ┌──────────────┐
              │          │              │              │
              └──────────┘              └──────────────┘
                              can be              can be
                         ┌──────────┐          ┌──────────────┐
                         │          │          │              │
                         └──────────┘          └──────────────┘
                    based        based on      based        based on
                    on time      trials        on time      trials
                  ┌───────┐    ┌───────┐     ┌───────┐    ┌───────┐
                  │       │    │       │     │       │    │       │
                  └───────┘    └───────┘     └───────┘    └───────┘
                    for          for           for          for
                    example      example       example      example
                ┌─────────┐  ┌─────────┐   ┌─────────┐  ┌─────────┐
                │         │  │         │   │         │  │         │
                │         │  │         │   │         │  │         │
                └─────────┘  └─────────┘   └─────────┘  └─────────┘
```

Author activity content supported by *IHMC Cmap Tools* Copyright ©1998-2007 Institute for Human & Machine Cognition

AS YOU READ … MYTH OR REALITY?

Myth: Spare the rod and spoil the child.
Reality: Punishment is not as effective at long-range behavior change, as is reinforcement.

Many people believe that punishment is almost necessary for raising children properly. Others believe that any form of physical punishment, no matter how mild, constitutes abuse and creates a potential for future aggression in the child.

1. Reread page 215 in your text and synthesize the arguments both in favor of and against physical punishment.
2. Which side are you more inclined to side with? Why?

Myth: People have distinct learning styles, such as auditory, visual, or kinesthetic, and it is best if they tailor their learning environments to match their style.
Reality: No scientific evidence supports this hypothesis, and, in fact, because students have to interact in a world that is multifaceted, it is to their advantage to learn by all the different possible styles. In addition, some tasks are intrinsically of one "type" more than another.

1. First write down what you honestly believe to be your primary learning style: Auditory learners prefer to learn through hearing the spoken word. Kinesthetic learners prefer to learn through doing, touching, and interacting. Visual learners prefer to learn by examining images, demonstrations, and body language.
2. Go to the following three web sites and complete each learning style inventory and note your style in terms of verbal, auditory, or kinesthetic—you may need to surf around the web site for some of them to find how to "translate" your scores into these criteria:

   http://www.usd.edu/trio/tut/ts/style.html
   Resulted in learning style _____
   http://www.calstatela.edu/faculty/jshindl/plsi/taketest.htm
   Resulted in learning style _____
   http://www.vark-learn.com/english/page.asp?p=questionnaire
   Resulted in learning style _____

3. How did you do? Did you get the same analysis from each web site? If not, why do you think that might be so? Did your answer to question 1 match the analysis in question 2? If not, why do you suppose that what you intuitively thought about yourself did not match what the questionnaires suggested?

4. If you still need convincing, go to http://www.youtube.com/watch?v=sIv9rz2NTUk. Are you now convinced?

AS YOU READ ... PUT YOUR SCIENTIFIC THINKING SKILLS TO THE TEST

1. You have a close friend who is having trouble with test anxiety. Although she studies hard and knows the material, she often performs poorly on exams. How can you help your friend overcome her test anxiety and really perform to the best of her ability?

a. By examining the classically conditioned responses that maintain her test anxiety

b. By examining the law of effect and the principles of operant conditioning that maintain her test anxiety in terms of schedules of reinforcement and both primary and secondary reinforcers

c. By examining cognitive models of learning

2. Drugs such as Antabuse are often used to help people with a substance abuse disorder--in this case, alcohol abuse--stop the negative behavior. Antabuse acts by inducing severe vomiting whenever alcohol is consumed. Consider how the effects of such drugs might continue long after the drugs have been stopped, in helping people to avoid drinking alcohol.

AS YOU READ ... MYPSYCHLAB CONNECTION

Classical Conditioning

Watch *Classic Footage of Pavlov* to learn more about the discoverer of classical conditioning. **Explore** *Classical Conditioning of Little Albert* to see how this classic study used the principles of conditioning to learn a phobia. Review the process of classical conditioning as you **Explore** *Three Stages of Classical Conditioning*. Once an organism learns to have a response to one stimulus, will they respond that way to similar stimuli? To find out, **Explore** *Process of Stimulus Generalization and Stimulus Discrimination in Classical Conditioning*. To see how classical conditioning can lead to the same conditioned response to new stimuli, **Explore** *Higher-Order Conditioning*. Can you unlearn a response? You can **Explore** *Process of Extinction and Spontaneous Recovery* to find out.

Operant Conditioning

Watch the video *B. F. Skinner Biography* to learn more about B. F. Skinner, what led up to his research on operant conditioning, and to see a Skinner Box in action. **Explore** *Stimulus Generalization and Stimulus Discrimination in Operant Conditioning* to see how pigeons in a Skinner Box can learn to respond to red lights but not to green lights. To learn more about whether punishment is effective in producing change in behavior, **Listen** to the podcast *Punishment and Reinforcement*. If you have ever wondered how animal trainers condition the animals to perform, **Explore** *Dolphins at Sea World* to see how the technique of shaping is used with dolphins. Then try the **Simulation** on *Shaping*. Try your hand at gambling and see how different schedules of reinforcement affect your response with a **Simulation** titled *Schedules of Reinforcement*.

Cognitive Models of Learning

Explore, *Banduras Study on Observational Learning*, provides visual animations to describe a classic study on modeling and its implications. Complete the **Simulation** *Latent Learning* to experience learning that occurs but is not observable until some incentive or reinforcer is present. How would you define media violence? Test your critical thinking skills by completing the **Simulation** *Media Violence*, which allows you to provide your interpretation of different studies on aggression. **Watch** *Banduras Bobo Doll Experiment*, a re-creation of the widely known experiment, in which you can see the actual stimulus, the Bobo Doll, in action and witness how children model an adult's violent behavior. **Listen** to the podcast *Mirror Neurons*, which was first introduced in Chapter 3, "Biological Psychology," and think about how these cells may affect learning.

Biological Influences on Learning

Explore *Taste Aversions* to examine how conditioned taste aversions affect cancer patients undergoing chemotherapy.

Learning Fads: Do They Work?

Can you really speed up the process of learning that some products claim? Evaluate these claims in the **Explore** *Accelerated Learning*.

AFTER YOU READ ... PRACTICE TEST #1

Before beginning this practice test, estimate the % you expect to get correct.
Anticipated % correct: _____

1. Learning results from
   a. nature.
   b. spontaneous recovery.
   c. preparedness.
   d. experience.

2. Habituation occurs to
   a. stimuli we conclude are safe to ignore.
   b. any stimulus with equal likelihood.
   c. stimuli that are dangerous and irritating.
   d. loud and painful stimuli, as a protective mechanism.

3. Learning, as the association of one stimulus with another, was first systematically studied by
   a. Gestalt psychologists.
   b. the British Associationists.
   c. William James, the "father of American psychology."
   d. structuralists, such as Wilhelm Wundt, the "father of psychology."

4. Jane wants to use classical conditioning to teach her dog to wag his tail whenever he hears the house phone ring. She plans to pet her dog, which always makes his tail wag, and then immediately call the house phone with her cell phone. How successful will she be?
   a. Very successful; this is a correct pairing of events.
   b. Very successful, as long as she varies the interval between petting the dog and ringing the house phone.
   c. Not very successful at all; tail wagging to a sound cannot be conditioned.
   d. Not very successful at all; this describes backwards conditioning.

5. Carina has a great fear of tarantulas. However, yesterday Carina saw a scorpion and also became very fearful. This is probably due to
   a. stimulus renewal.
   b. spontaneous recovery.
   c. stimulus generalization.
   d. stimulus discrimination.

6. Sometimes classical conditioning fails when a CS has been strongly extinguished—presented without the UCS for a prolonged time—a phenomenon called
   a. latent inhibition.
   b. advertiser's block.
   c. occasion setting.
   d. backwards conditioning.

7. Operant conditioning is also called
   a. classical conditioning.
   b. cognitive conditioning.
   c. two-process conditioning.
   d. instrumental conditioning.

8. When a behavior occurs as an automatic reflex, it is called _____ but when it occurs as a voluntary behavior it is called _____.
    a. illicit; emetic
    b. elicited; emitted
    c. intentional; automatic
    d. generalized; discriminant

9. Every time you eat chocolate you enjoy the taste and feel great afterwards—your mood improves and you have more energy. You often eat chocolate in the afternoon. This situation best illustrates
    a. latent inhibition.
    b. a conditioned response.
    c. the law of effect.
    d. an occasion setter.

10. In theory, negative reinforcement ALWAYS _____ a target behavior; whereas punishment ALWAYS _____ a target behavior.
    a. inhibits; enhances
    b. increases; decreases
    c. removes; establishes
    d. helps acquisition of; helps extinction of

11. Once a behavior is established, the best way to maintain it for the long run is to reinforce it
    a. often.
    b. never.
    c. always.
    d. occasionally.

12. You are a sportscaster announcing a race between people reinforced on different schedules. You announce, "With a rapid rate of response, difficult to extinguish, the person with the highest rate of response is going to be
    a. Granny, playing slot machines."
    b. Hildegard, going to church every Sunday."
    c. Samantha, going to the movies a couple of times each month."
    d. Jones, accumulating frequent flyer miles for a free airfare ticket."

13. Joachim's mother is potty training him. At first she praises him when he approaches his potty chair, and then only when he sits on it. Next she praises him if he "goes" in the potty chair, even if he sometimes has a wet diaper. Finally, she praises him only if he goes in the potty chair *and* keeps his diaper dry. Joachim's mother is using
    a. shaping.
    b. habituation.
    c. preparedness.
    d. the Premack Principle.

14. Brana always wears a religious medal around her neck on exam days because she believes the saints help her to perform well. You think to yourself,
    a. "Good for her, she is sure to do better!"
    b. "Geez, Brana will never be a well-educated person with this type of belief."
    c. "Well, on some past exam Brana must have performed well while wearing that medal."
    d. "Brana must also be an athlete, because athletes are known for such superstitious behaviors."

15. Two-process theory explains the persistence of some phobias as a combination of operant and classical conditioning in which the feared stimulus
    a. causes a person to emit a classically conditioned response, whereas avoidance becomes an operantly conditioned response.
    b. elicits positive reinforcement for the feared item, followed by a return to homeostasis of the autonomic nervous system.
    c. elicits a classically conditioned autonomic response, and an operantly conditioned negative reinforcement to removing one's self from the target stimulus.
    d. is feared less in the long run (classical conditioning effect), but more in the short term (operant conditioning effect).

16. Early behaviorists, who developed the models of conditioning,
    a. did not believe that thinking played a causal role in learning.
    b. considered thinking to be a special class of behaviors, unrelated to learning.
    c. denied "thinking," but accepted "emotion" as an important contributor to learning.
    d. believed that "thinking" only applied to human learning, and so they only studied animals.

17. A critical component of observational learning is that it occurs
    a. in just a single trial.
    b. without reinforcement.
    c. only with partial reinforcement.
    d. only with continuous reinforcement.

18. Modern neuroimaging studies of _____ show brain activity in the same areas when we watch activities as when we participate in them.
    a. mirror neurons
    b. instinctive drift
    c. primary reinforcers
    d. pseudoconditioning

19. Sometimes a solution to a problem suddenly comes to us. This event is called
    a. trial-and-error.
    b. latent learning.
    c. insight learning.
    d. instinctive learning.

20. We are evolutionarily predisposed to fear some things more than others, a phenomenon called
    a. instinctive drift.
    b. preparedness.
    c. natural selection.
    d. béarnaise syndrome.

After completing the test, calculate your percent correct
(/ 20 =   ) x 100 = _____.

How accurate were your expectations? Does your performance suggest the need for additional study? For the items you missed, go back and identify why the "correct" answer is the best answer.

Before beginning this practice test, estimate the % you expect to get correct.
Anticipated % correct: _____

1. When Jill first got glasses they felt uncomfortable around her nose and behind her ears, and she was constantly aware of having them on. Now, weeks later, she doesn't even know she has them on. Jill has _____ to wearing her glasses.
   a. habituated
   b. generalized
   c. become sensitized
   d. become conditioned

2. Pavlov's primary research interest was in
   a. digestive processes in dogs.
   b. pecking behavior in pigeons.
   c. bar-pressing behavior in rats.
   d. taste aversion training in dogs.

3. For something to become a CS, it be must be
   a. directly meaningful in its context.
   b. preferably at a subliminal level of stimulation.
   c. easily perceived but neutral in its original context.
   d. very specific and distinct (i.e., louder or brighter than other things in its context).

4. Every time Annette drops her son, Jay, at school, he says "Good-bye!" and then slams the car door. Now whenever Jay says, "Good-bye!" Annette winces. How can you explain this?
   a. Jay has a loud booming voice that hurts Annette's ears.
   b. Annette knows that she is going to miss her son all day.
   c. Because the original CS-UCS pairing was constant, it resulted in a higher-order conditioning.
   d. Wincing has become a conditioned response to the prior pairings of hearing Jay say "Good-bye!" and then slamming the car door.

5. Dasan has trained his dog, Speck, to drool to the sound of the cell phone ring tone. However, Dasan has noticed that Speck also drools whenever the house phone rings, probably because of
   a. the renewal effect.
   b. spontaneous recovery.
   c. stimulus generalization.
   d. stimulus discrimination.

6. Shanaya has successfully quit smoking. However, whenever she goes to a nightclub, her cigarette cravings return because the nightclub comes to act as a(n)
   a. renewal stimulus.
   b. discriminative stimulus.
   c. addiction trigger.
   d. occasion setter.

7. In pseudoconditioning
   a. the CR actually triggers the CS.
   b. the CS directly triggers a UCR.
   c. the UCS fails to trigger the UCR.
   d. the backwards pairing of UCS-CS elicits the CR.

8. Every time Chris went ice-skating he fell hard on his backside, sometimes even hitting the back of his head on the ice. Because of this experience, Chris no longer goes ice-skating. This situation is an example of
   a. latent inhibition.
   b. an occasion setter.
   c. the law of effect.
   d. a conditioned response.

9. The advantage of using a Skinner Box when studying operant conditioning in rats is that
   a. the studied animals cannot escape, as they could in Thorndike's puzzle box.
   b. it accurately records all behaviors on its own, so you can do other things at the same time.
   c. the floor can be electrocuted so you can readily punish undesired behaviors during training.
   d. it provides constant food and water so you don't have to attend to the animals over the weekend.

10. By definition, negative reinforcement ALWAYS acts to
    a. provide rewards.
    b. provide punishment.
    c. increase target behavior.
    d. decrease target behavior.

11. Cha believes that if you spare the rod, you spoil the child. So she spanks her children when they misbehave. You convince her to stop this because
    a. punishment has been shown to actually increase unwanted behaviors.
    b. this type of punishment lets them know that the behavior is wrong, but doesn't show them what they should be doing instead.
    c. her children will stop the behavior in the long run, but in the short run behavior will be worse.
    d. she is classically conditioning her children to elicit the unwanted behavior when she isn't looking.

12. When Shane's dog was a puppy he always gave him a treat if he used a specific part of the backyard for his bathroom. Shane eventually ran out of treats and the puppy started using the entire backyard as his bathroom. This change in behavior can be attributed to
    a. stimulus generalization.
    b. stimulus discrimination.
    c. acquisition of the new behavior.
    d. extinction of the original behavior.

13. If your professor gives you 5 quizzes over the course of a 15-week semester, your diligent studying is best reinforced if the professor uses a _____ schedule of reinforcement.
    a. fixed ratio
    b. variable interval
    c. fixed interval
    d. variable ratio

14. An important thing to understand about operating conditioning is that
    a. shaping is rapid and can lead to unintended behaviors.
    b. shaping is best applied to applications of animal training.
    c. shaping can result in superstitious behaviors if the trainer is not careful.
    d. shaping can take a long time and requires great patience on the part of the trainer.

15. Chuck's teacher gives him a gold star every time he reads a book and turns in a book report. The top three readers in the class will earn a gift certificate to a toy store. Chuck's teacher is using
    a. a token economy.
    b. pseudoconditioning.
    c. classical conditioning.
    d. applied behavior analysis.

16. The best current evidence, that classical and operant conditioning are distinct processes, comes from
    a. brain imaging studies that show different areas of activation for each type of conditioning.
    b. the qualitative differences between elicited versus emitted responses.
    c. the quantitative differences between elicited versus emitted responses.
    d. some phobias can only be explained by classical conditioning, and others can only be explained by operant conditioning.

17. The "O" in S-O-R psychology stands for
    a. original.
    b. orienting.
    c. organism.
    d. organized.

18. A husband who observes his wife in pain during labor might very well exhibit some of the same brain activity his wife. This best illustrates the functioning of
    a. preparedness.
    b. mirror neurons.
    c. instinctive drift.
    d. insight learning.

19. A close friend is about to undergo chemotherapy. She is worried about the side effects, including the nausea and vomiting that will surely occur. You advise her to
    a. avoid eating anything at all.
    b. eat only the foods she likes the best.
    c. eat foods she doesn't like, just as she starts the chemo.
    d. eat foods she doesn't like, after she starts to feel nauseous.

20. Your cousin, Jamala, is struggling in school so your aunt wants to invest in several learning aids, including some tapes your cousin can listen to while asleep, and a SuperLearning course. You tell her,
    a. Great idea! Anything you can buy will certainly help.
    b. Great idea! Even if the research evidence isn't very strong, at least it's all positive.
    c. Save your money! Just go online and have Jamala complete a learning styles inventory and study to that style.
    d. Save your money! The research evidence fails to support any of these methods.

After completing the test, calculate your percent correct
(/ 20 =   ) x 100 = _____ .

How accurate were your expectations? Does your performance suggest the need for additional study?
For the items you missed, go back and identify why the "correct" answer is the best answer.

AFTER YOU READ . . . PRACTICE TEST ANSWER KEYS

Practice Test 1.

1. d (p. 202)
2. a (p. 203)
3. b (p. 204)
4. d (p. 206)
5. c (p. 206)
6. a (p. 208)
7. d (p. 211)
8. b (p. 212)
9. c (p. 212)
10. b (p. 213-214)
11. d (p. 217)
12. a (p. 218)
13. a (p. 219)
14. c (p. 220)
15. c (p. 222)
16. a (p. 223)
17. b (p. 225)
18. a (p. 227)
19. c (p. 228)
20. b (p. 230)

Practice Test 2.

1. a (p. 202-203)
2. a (p. 204)
3. c (p. 205)
4. d (p. 204-205)
5. c (p. 207)
6. d (p. 207)
7. b (p. 210)
8. c (p. 212)
9. b (p. 213)
10. c (p. 214)
11. b (p. 215)
12. d (p. 216)
13. b (p. 218)
14. d (p. 219)
15. a (p. 221)
16. a (p. 222)
17. c (p. 224)
18. b (p. 227–228)
19. c (p. 229)
20. d (p. 233-235)

AFTER YOU READ … CONCEPT MAPPING ACTIVITY ANSWERS

ACTIVITY 1:

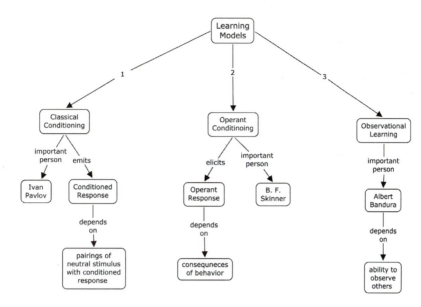

ACTIVITY 2:
conditioned stimulus (ex: metronome sound)
unconditioned stimulus (ex: gun shot)
unconditioned response (ex: eye blink)
conditioned response (ex: gun shot)

ACTIVITY 3:

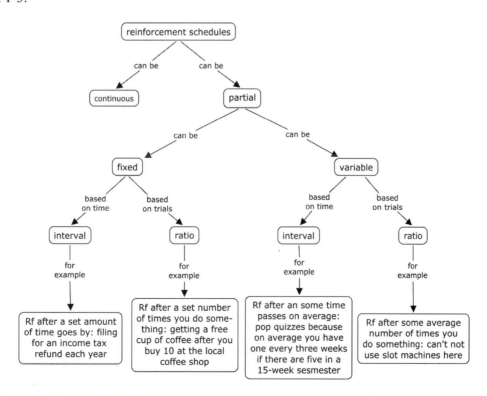

CHAPTER 7
MEMORY
CONSTRUCTING AND RECONSTRUCTING OUR PASTS

BEFORE YOU READ ... CHAPTER PREVIEW

Memory is defined as the retention of information over time. The *paradox of memory* is that it can be excellent sometimes, with individuals showing remarkable feats of memory; and it can be extremely poor at other times, even resulting in **memory illusions**—false but forceful memories. The evidence strongly supports the *reconstructive* nature of memory. It is not *reproductive* like a tape or video recording. Our memories of ourselves can reflect *observer memory* or *field memory*. Memory has three *systems* defined by differences in *span* and *duration*. **Sensory memory** holds incoming information for less than half a second. **Iconic memory** is the name for visual sensory memory, which was defined using the *method of partial report* and holds about 12 items, except in rare cases of *eidetic imagery* (photographic memory). Auditory sensory memory is called **echoic memory.** If the information is attended to, it passes to **short-term memory** (*working memory*), which holds 7 ± 2 **chunks** of information for less than half a minute. Forgetting in STM is either by **decay** or by **interference**—**retroactive** (forgetting old information) or **proactive** (forgetting new information). The duration of STM can be extended with **rehearsal—maintenance rehearsal** (rote repetition) or **elaborative rehearsal** (adding meaning). The **levels-of-processing** model posits that rehearsal can reflect *phonological* processing or *semantic* processing, and this level affects memory strength. If the information is further encoded, it passes to **long-term memory,** where it tends to be coded for its *semantic* properties, as opposed to *acoustic* properties, typical of STM. Memory that is permanent and very long-term is called **permastore**. The **serial position curve**—the increased likelihood of remembering items at the beginning (**primacy effect**) and the end (**recency effect**) of a list of items—provides insight into differences in short-term and long-term memory. Types of LTM include **semantic memory** (for general facts) and **episodic memory** (for personal facts). LTM can also be partitioned into **explicit memory** (including *declarative memory*) and **implicit memory** (including **procedural memory**) and **priming**.

For information to be remembered, it passes through a series of *processes* that include *encoding, storage,* and *retrieval*. **Encoding** is the process of getting information into memory, which requires us to pay attention. Attention is necessary for information to become encoded. When we pay less attention to someone whose turn comes before us, we may forget what they said because of the *next-in-line effect*. **Mnemonic** techniques such as the *pegword method, method of loci,* and *keyword method* are associated with encoding. **Schemas** are frameworks based on past experiences to help us interpret and store new information with similar, old information, so that later we can access it more readily. They are helpful with **storage**, the process of holding information in memory. Schemas can contribute to memory errors because they can lead us to *oversimplify*. **Retrieval** gets at the heart of memory: determining whether information made it through the encoding and storage processes and, if so, whether it can be accessed as needed. Sometimes we need a **retrieval cue** to help us locate a memory.

Memory retrieval is difficult to study because it's nearly impossible to determine whether the memory is there but inaccessible, or whether the information is simply not there. **Recall**—generating previously stored information—is usually harder than **recognition**—a conscious recognition of the information as being "correct." Another way of testing memory, called **relearning**, was first developed by Hermann Ebbinghaus in the 1880s. In this testing, you learn some information, time passes until you have "forgotten" the information, and then you are asked to relearn it. The speed with which you can relearn is thought to be a measure of *savings* from the first learning episode. Relearning may be a more sensitive measure of memory, but the way we test it may be confounded with the use of **distributed practice**—learning spread out over several sessions. This approach is in contrast to **massed practice**, where information is learned in one sitting—cramming! Research consistently shows that distributed practice is better for long-term retention, and massed practice for short-term retention. The **tip-of-the-tongue (TOT) phenomenon** occurs when we know that we know some information, but cannot remember it; it provides useful insights into memory. Usually a hint will immediately elicit the correct information, indicating that the information was available but not accessible. Another factor that affects retrieval is **encoding specificity**: the match between learning and retrieval conditions and operations. **Context-dependent learning** is a type of encoding specificity in which memory is maximized when the external context of learning and testing are similar. In **state-dependent learning,** a person's internal states match at learning and testing; states can even extend to moods in what is called *mood-dependent learning.*

Biology plays a major role in memory. In the 1920s, Karl Lashley looked for the *engram*, a physical trace of memory. He was unable to find specific areas devoted to memory and concluded that memory was distributed throughout the brain. Over 60 years ago, Hebb suggested that memory is located in *assemblies*, organized groups of neurons. More recently, researchers have focused on **long-term potentiation (LTP)**, a phenomenon in which the repeated stimulation of single cells results in a gradual strengthening of connections. Studies of LTP suggest the hippocampus is an important brain structure for the formation of memory. The amygdala and parts of association cortex are also implicated. Glutamate is an important neurotransmitter for memory, as is adrenaline, which appears important for consolidation of emotional memories. We've learned much about memory by studying people whose memory is severely lacking, a condition called **amnesia**, of which there are two types, **retrograde amnesia** (loss of memory for the past) and **anterograde amnesia** (inability to form new memories). Many amnesia myths are perpetuated by movie-makers. For example, *generalized amnesia* is very rare. Case studies of amnesiacs support the importance of the hippocampus in memory consolidation and point to an important role of the amygdala. Finally, serious memory loss, as seen in Alzheimer's-type *dementia,* provides insights into normal memory functioning.

So how does memory develop? Research evidence shows that even fetuses show *habituation.* Children's memories develop increasing sophistication from about 3 years old through 12 years old, especially in **meta-memory skills**—what children know about their own memories. But we know that even 2-month-old infants have memory, as found from their responses to items in their environment, such as a mobile. We remember little from our early lives because of **infantile amnesia**, which is attributed to several causes. First, the hippocampus is not fully developed before age 2 or 3. Second, we don't develop a sense of self until after the age of 18 months. A final problem involves increased suggestibility. Children's schemas are more malleable and it is easier to misguide their memory.

So how do researchers examine memory accuracy? One line of evidence comes from the study of **flashbulb memories**, which are vivid memories of how we learned of emotional events, such as 9/11. These memories were once thought to be quite accurate, but we have learned that these vivid memories, in which people have high confidence, are just as distorted as any other memories. We also tend to forget where a memory came from, called **source monitoring confusion**. A good example of a source memory error is **cryptomnesia**, where a person unwittingly plagiarizes another's work. Another finding concerning memory accuracy is that it is relatively easy to distort memory, or to implant a completely false memory intentionally, using **suggestive memory techniques**. Studies of eyewitness testimony have provided a wonderful source of information on false memories because they tend to be for events that are brief, emotionally charged, and often filled with threatening stimuli, which may distract attention from more relevant information. The **misinformation effect** refers to the distortion of memory with post-event information. It is quite easy to instill elaborate false memories. Finally, we all make some common memory errors, including absentmindedness, suggestibility, bias, blocking, transience, persistence, and misattribution.

BEFORE YOU READ ... LEARNING OBJECTIVES

After reading Chapter 7 you should be able to:

7.1   Identify the ways that memories do and do not accurately reflect experiences
7.2   Explain the function, span, and duration of each of the three memory systems
7.3   Differentiate the subtypes of long-term memory
7.4   Identify methods for connecting new information to existing knowledge
7.5   Identify the role that schemas play in the storage of memories.
7.6   Distinguish ways of measuring memory.
7.7   Describe how the relation between encoding and retrieval conditions influences remembering
7.8   Describe the role of long-term potentiation in memory
7.9   Distinguish different types of amnesia and the relevance of amnesia to the brain's organization of memory
7.10   Identify the key impairments of Alzheimer's disease
7.11   Identify how children's memory abilities change with age
7.12   Identify factors that influence people's susceptibility to false memories and memory errors
7.13   Describe some of the real-world implications of false memories and memory errors

---

BEFORE YOU READ ... TERM IDENTIFICATION

---

anterograde amnesia (p. 265)
chunking (p. 249)
context-dependent learning (p. 262)
cryptomnesia (p. 273)
decay (p. 247)
distributed versus massed practice (p. 261)
echoic memory (p. 247)
elaborative rehearsal (p. 250)
encoding (p. 255)
encoding specificity (p. 262)
episodic memory (p. 252)
explicit memory (p. 252)
flashbulb memory (p. 272)
iconic memory (p. 246)
implicit memory (p. 252)
infantile amnesia (p. 270)
interference (p. 248)
levels of processing (p. 250)
long-term memory (p. 251)
long-term potentiation (LTP) (p. 264)
Magic Number (p. 249)
maintenance rehearsal (p. 249)
memory (p. 242)
memory illusion (p. 244)
meta-memory (p. 270)
mnemonic (p. 255)

misinformation effect (p. 274)
permastore (p. 251)
primacy effect (p. 251)
priming (p. 253)
proactive interference (p. 248)
procedural memory (p. 253)
recall (p. 260)
recency effect (p. 251)
recognition (p. 260)
rehearsal (p. 249)
relearning (p. 260)
retrieval (p. 259)
retrieval cue (p. 260)
retroactive interference (p. 248)
retrograde amnesia (p. 265)
schema (p. 258)
semantic memory (p. 252)
sensory memory (p. 246)
serial position curve (p. 252)
short-term memory (p. 247)
source monitoring (p. 272)
state-dependent learning (p. 262)
storage (p. 258)
suggestive memory technique (p. 273)
tip-of-the-tongue (TOT) phenomenon (p. 262)

AS YOU READ ... PRACTICE ACTIVITIES

HOW MEMORY OPERATES: THE MEMORY ASSEMBLY LINE

1. Look up the words *fallible* and *malleable* in a dictionary. How do their definitions fit with the notion of memory being prone to error? (LO 7.1)

2. Compare iconic and echoic memory. Think of an original everyday example for how each of these facilitate STM or LTM. (LO 7.2)

3. Describe Sperling's study of sensory memory. (LO 7.2)

    Design:

    Findings:

    Lesson learned:

4. *Short-term memory* and *working memory* are two names for essentially the same memory store. Each of these ways of naming this memory process suggests something unique about the process. Discuss what each of the names suggests about the function of this memory store. (LO 7.2)

5. Why do you think Peterson and Peterson (1959) asked their participants to count backwards by threes during the interval between hearing three letters and recalling them? (LO 7.2)

6. Compare proactive interference effects and retroactive interference effects. Provide an original example of each from your own life. (LO 7.2)

7. Compare maintenance and elaborative rehearsal. Provide original examples of how each of these types of rehearsal might be the best technique to use in a specific situation. (LO 7.2)

8. Complete this table for the three memory systems. (LO 7.2)

	Sensory Memory	Short-Term Memory	Long-Term Memory
Purpose			
Duration			
Capacity			
Forgetting Mechanism			

9. What are serial position effects? Describe the different component effects. What does each effect tell us about memory? (LO 7.2)

10. Compare explicit and implicit memory. To which subtypes of long-term memory are they related? (LO 7.3)

THE THREE PROCESSES OF MEMORY

1. How do "systems" of memory differ from "processes" of memory? (LO 7.4)

2. Go to http://www.exploratorium.edu/memory/dont_forget/playing_games_3.html. After completing the exercise, use the method of loci to create a path to help you remember these terms: proactive interference, retroactive interference, episodic memory, semantic memory, procedural memory. Why is this task for 5 concepts so much more difficult than the task for 20 terms on the web site? (LO 7.4)

3. What is your classroom schema? Write it out and compare notes with several of your classmates. Which elements were most often shared? How do you think having a classroom schema affected your classroom behavior on your first day of college? (LO 7.5)

4. Relearning is seldom used these days to test memory. Think of some reasons why recall and recognition are favored as measures of memory. (LO 7.6)

5. Complete the following table by providing an example of how you could apply each of these memory concepts to your own study needs. (LO 7.2 – 7.6)

Memory Concept	Application
Distributed vs. Massed Practice	
Elaborative Retrieval	
Levels of Processing	
Mnemonic Devices	
Encoding Specificity	
Context-Dependent Learning	
State-Dependent Learning	

THE BIOLOGY OF MEMORY

1. It has been difficult to localize memory in any specific brain area. Instead, various aspects of memory seem to be widely distributed throughout our brains. What do you think might be the advantages and disadvantages of such a distribution of function? (LO 7.8)

2. Compare anterograde and retrograde amnesia. (LO 7.9)

3. Go to http://www.youtube.com/watch?v=coZK-t7lbp8 and think about the kind of life that Clive Wearing lived. Compare what you learn about Clive to what you can learn about another patient with similar brain damage at http://ahsmail.uwaterloo.ca/kin356/episodic/LifewithoutEP.htm What can you conclude about memory systems from these case studies? (LO 7.9)

4. Older adults can develop dementia or dementia-like symptoms for a variety of reasons. For example, depression can affect mental abilities as can medication to control high blood pressure, which has a side effect of the loss of sodium and potassium. As you should remember from Chapter 3, these minerals are important for neural transmission. Why is it important to reject other diagnostic possibilities in older adults who seem to be less mentally sharp? (LO 7.10)

THE DEVELOPMENT OF MEMORY: ACQUIRING A PERSONAL HISTORY

1. Memory abilities change with development from childhood through adulthood. Discuss three reasons for this change. (LO 7.11)

2. Describe research evidence that infants have implicit memory. (LO 7.11)

3. Discuss some of the evidence that speaks in favor of infantile amnesia and against the notion of good memory back to early infancy. (LO 7.11)

FALSE MEMORIES: WHEN GOOD MEMORY GOES BAD

1. Write down your flashbulb memory for 9/11. Check with the people you believe can verify the accuracy of your memory. Remember, the "flashbulb" is an episodic memory for all of the circumstances under which you heard the news. This is distinct from your semantic memory of the actual events of 9/11. (LO 7.12)

2. List three conditions under which eyewitness testimony is likely to be faulty, and provide an original example of each to illustrate the effect of these on memory. (LO 7.13)

3. Go to http://www.exploratorium.edu/exhibits/wig/index.html and have fun playing around and learning more about eyewitness memory. (LO 7.13)

4. List Schacter's (2001) "Seven Sins of Memory" and provide an original example from your own life to illustrate each one. (LO 7.13)

AS YOU READ ... CONCEPT MAP ACTIVITIES

ACTIVITY 1:   Complete the following concept map for the stages of memory:

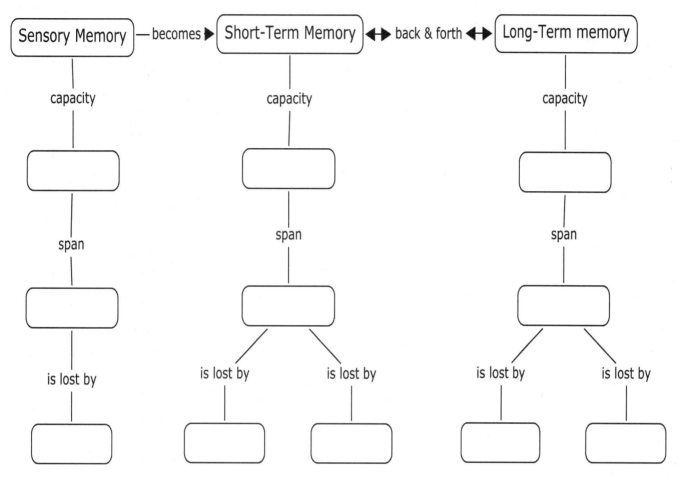

Author activity content supported by *IHMC Cmap Tools* Copyright ©1998-2007 Institute for Human & Machine Cognition

ACTIVITY 2:   Complete this concept map for the organization of long-term memory.

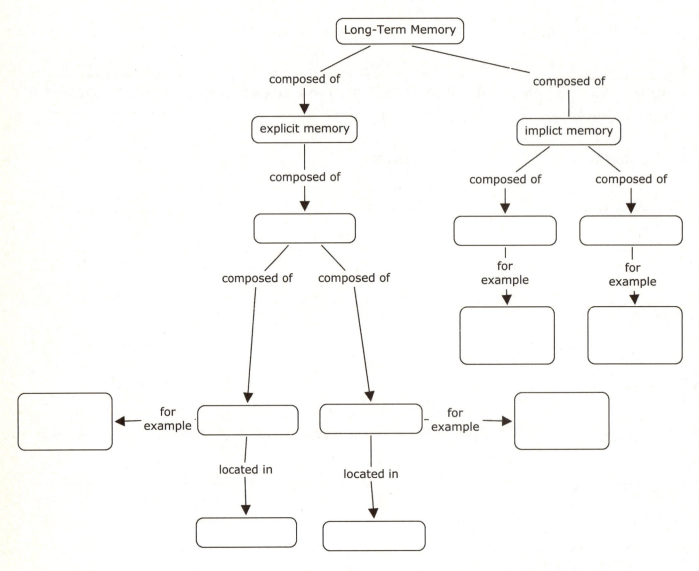

Author activity content supported by *IHMC Cmap Tools* Copyright ©1998-2007 Institute for Human & Machine Cognition

AS YOU READ ... MYTH OR REALITY?

Myth: In criminal eyewitnesses, confidence is closely related to accuracy.
Reality: There is very little relationship between accuracy and confidence among criminal eyewitnesses.

1. If you go to the Internet you can find dozens of articles that explain situations in which this is particularly true. Imagine that you are an expert witness testifying in court for the benefit of a jury regarding the relationship between confidence and accuracy of eyewitnesses. Present a case for why line-ups, in particular, are particularly prone to errors of identification and why confidence should *not* be taken into account.

Myth: If you live long enough, you will develop Alzheimer's disease (AD).
Reality: Many centenarians are as sharp mentally as they were throughout their lives, yet some people in their fifties develop Alzheimer's disease. Age is not so much directly related, as indirectly related to AD: the longer you live, the more opportunity you have for an environmental event to trigger a genetic predisposition to AD.

A great explanation of AD can be found at http://www.alz.org/brain/01.asp As you go through the slide show, you should be aware of the constant comparisons that are made between the brain of a person with AD and the brain of a healthy, normal older adult. What are some of the changes that occur with AD? Make sure to also read through the myths about AD at http://www.alz.org/alzheimers_disease_myths_about_alzheimers.asp.

Not only is it NOT the case that AD is inevitable if you live long enough, but this site can dispel many other myths.

1. Do you know any older adults? How would you describe this person's mental status?

2. Do you know anyone with dementia? In what ways are you better able to understand their condition now?

As You Read ... Put Your Scientific Thinking Skills to the Test

1. At some fundamental level, both the levels of processing framework and the encoding specificity effect are conceptually similar. Consider the elements of processing that connect these two processing effects.

2. The text presents a wealth of evidence that memory is reconstructive.
    a. How then might you explain the extraordinary accuracy with which actors learn long parts, especially in stage plays?
    b. Think of another example where memory is primarily reproductive rather than reconstructive.

3. At http://www.cbsnews.com/stories/2006/11/02/national/main2143883.shtml you will find the story of a man who was identified as an amnesia victim, found wandering in Denver. The man was actually missing from western Canada, near the U.S. border. In the end, the man most probably was not an amnesia victim, but suffered from a dissociative amnesia.
    a. Find information on dissociative amnesia and differentiate between dissociative amnesia and the type of amnesia suffered by people such as Clive Wearing and H. M.

How Memory Operates: The Memory Assembly Line

To learn more about memory systems, **Explore** the *Key Processes in Stages of Memory*. When reviewing the capacity of short-term memory, participate in the **Simulations** *Digit Span, How Good Is Your Memory for Stories?* and *Delay and Interference on Short-Term Memory*. To learn more about the levels-of-processing approach, complete the **Simulation** *Depth of Processing*. Learn more about the serial position effect by completing the **Simulations** *Serial Position Effect* and *The Serial Position Curve*.

The Three Processes of Memory

Explore *Key Processes in Stages of Memory* and *Encoding, Storage and Retrieval in Memory* to learn more about the key processes of memory. What is the best way to study for exams? **Watch** the video entitled *Cramming*. Learn more about imagery and mnemonics. **Watch** the videos *Penny* and *Mnemonics*.

The Biology of Memory

To learn about an experiment conducted on the biology of Alzheimers, **Watch** *What Happens with Alzheimers?* Other videos on memory deterioration that you can **Watch** include *Memory Hazards* and *Dementia: Judy*. To learn more about the effects of stress on memory, **Watch** *The Effects of Sleep and Stress on Memory: Jessica Payne*.

The Development of Memory: Acquiring a Personal History

It is often difficult to believe in the suggestible nature of memory. In order to learn about this phenomenon, **Watch** *Memory: Elizabeth Loftus* and see several of these experiments conducted. The results may surprise you!

False Memories: When Good Memory Goes Bad

When reviewing how false memories are created, review the **Simulation** *Creating False Memories* and see if you are tricked!

AFTER YOU READ … PRACTICE TEST #1

Before beginning this practice test, estimate the percent you expect to get correct.
Anticipated percent correct: _____

1. Salvador Dali created a classic painting of memory titled, "The Persistence of Memory" in which images of time-pieces are stretched and distorted. This image of memory is correct in as much as
   a. all memories are time-locked to their acquisition.
   b. memories become somewhat distorted over time.
   c. memory accurately represents events at the time of their formation.
   d. memories are often so distorted and stretched as to be "unreadable," as are the clocks in this painting.

2. Katy is studying for a history exam. As Katy reads her textbook and tries to memorize important dates, visual information she picks up from her textbook flows from her
   a. iconic memory to short-term memory to long-term memory.
   b. iconic memory to long-term memory to short-term memory.
   c. short-term memory to long-term memory to iconic memory.
   d. short-term memory to iconic memory to long-term memory.

3. Information loss in short-term memory is attributed to
   a. primarily decay.
   b. exclusively decay.
   c. primarily interference.
   d. exclusively interference.

4. Many ice hockey players play roller hockey in the summer. Although the basic game skills are similar, stopping on ice versus stopping on wheels requires a different technique. When making the transition from ice to wheels, some players end up spinning in circles on wheels. This is probably a result of
   a. poor procedural memory.
   b. proactive interference.
   c. retroactive interference.
   d. anterograde inhibition.

5. John just met a girl whom he finds attractive. Unfortunately he doesn't have a pen handy and will have to remember her phone number. Which method would be most effective?
   a. Rote rehearsal
   b. Repetitive rehearsal
   c. Elaborative rehearsal
   d. Maintenance rehearsal

6. The serial position curve reflects the operation of
   a. phonological processing and semantic processing.
   b. sensory, short-term, and long-term memory systems.
   c. long-term memory, seen in the recency effect; and short-term memory, seen in the primacy effect.
   d. long-term memory, seen in the primacy effect; and short-term memory, seen in the recency effect.

7. While you are at home, sick, you call your best friend to bring you a few things from the store. Your friend is driving and cannot write down your items that you read from a list, "tissues, a newspaper, gelatin, cough syrup, chicken soup, apple juice, aspirin, ginger ale, ice pops, Sudafed, menthol rub, and the TV Guide." Which items is your friend most likely to forget?
   a. Menthol rub and the TV Guide
   b. Tissues, a newspaper, gelatin, cough syrup
   c. Chicken soup, apple juice, aspirin, ginger ale
   d. Ice pops, Sudafed, menthol rub, and the TV Guide

8. Mnemonics help primarily to aid in
   a. transfer.
   b. storage.
   c. retrieval.
   d. encoding.

9. If Jessie remembers the errands she needs to run today by imagining a grocery store in the shape of a large bun, a gas pump shaped like a tennis shoe, with the laces acting as a hose, and clothes hanging from a tree in dry-cleaner plastic bags, she is using
   a. the method of loci.
   b. a pegword method.
   c. the keyword method.
   d. an "external" memory aid.

10. Linda believes that all cheerleaders are thin, pretty, energetic, and promiscuous. When she notices from a distance that her boyfriend is talking to a cheerleader, she later remembers that the distance between him and the cheerleader was
   a. closer than it really was because encoding was biased by her schema.
   b. closer than it really was because her encoding was disrupted once her emotions kicked in.
   c. greater than it really was because she stored the memory based on a distorted visual perception.
   d. greater than it really was because her cheerleader schema stored the memory along with her baseball schema, where individuals are usually located far apart.

11. Marcus is studying for his history final by using a mnemonic of connecting the actual contours of the numbers to a pictorial representation of the event that occurred on that date. Later, during the test, when he needs to remember the events, the dates can act as
   a. states.
   b. TOTs.
   c. engrams.
   d. retrieval cues.

12. According to the classic Ebbinghaus forgetting curve
   a. how much we remember is strongly based on wide individual differences.
   b. much of what we learn is forgotten very shortly after learning it for the first time.
   c. how quickly we forget depends on how long we know we will need to remember it.
   d. much of what we learn we remember for a relatively long time, and then we forget it.

13. Elaborative rehearsal is often recommended as a good study habit because it
   a. reduces source confusion for new information.
   b. makes rote memorization of facts much easier.
   c. creates connections between new and old knowledge.
   d. keeps information active in short-term memory for a longer time.

14. Encoding specificity is the basis for the study habit advice that you
   a. relax yourself before you study, so you can improve encoding.
   b. study in as many different places as possible for each class.
   c. study only in the classroom in which your class is held, at times when it is not in use.
   d. process information as deeply as possible, using in your own words.

15. Generalized amnesia
   a. is extremely rare.
   b. usually shows rapid recovery.
   c. includes a loss of memory about one's self.
   d. is limited to procedure knowledge but spares episodic memory.

16. Children's memory improves with age, probably due to
    a. better meta-memory—knowledge of their own memory ability.
    b. increasing use of rote repetition.
    d. the increasing development of their sense of self.
    c. an increasing ability to remember events from early infancy.

17. Infantile amnesia
    a. is greatest in children who fail to recognize themselves in a mirror at a younger age.
    b. shows some individuals can remember events as early as birth.
    c. is rare, and often due to psychological repression of traumatic events early in life.
    d. probably occurs because brain structures such as the hippocampus are not yet sufficiently developed.

18. In source monitoring confusion,
    a. we might confuse our dreams with our actual experiences.
    b. our memory for earlier learned information dominates our memory for later learned information.
    c. our memory for later learned information dominates our memory for earlier learned information.
    d. we discriminate whether information was obtained from an electronic medium, such as a computer, or from a print medium, such as a book.

19. According to the misinformation effect,
    a. we remember false information more readily than true information.
    b. people readily confuse the source of information, even mistaking dreams as factual events.
    c. we sometimes truly fail to recognize someone else's ideas, and confuse them as being our own.
    d. inaccurate information received after an event can become incorporated into the original memory.

20. According to Schacter's (2001) "seven sins of memory," even memory errors have a practical side. For example,
    a. suggestibility allows us to remember our inferences about events.
    b. blocking might prevent us from saying something embarrassing.
    c. absentmindedness prevents our prejudices from coloring our memories.
    d. transience is practical because remembering everything we've ever experienced would be burdensome.

After completing the test, calculate your percent correct
(/ 20 =   ) x 100 = _____.

How accurate were your expectations? Does your performance suggest the need for additional study? For the items you missed, go back and identify why the "correct" answer is the best answer.

Before beginning this practice test, estimate the percent you expect to get correct.
Anticipated percent correct: _____

1. As Janice helps her daughter prepare for her senior prom, she describes the events of her own senior prom. Her memory is likely to reflect
   a. reproduction: Janice's memory is much like a photocopy or snapshot of what occurred, and once activated, Janice can "read it out."
   b. reproduction: Janice can retrieve her memory of her own senior prom much like one downloads and opens a stored document on a computer.
   c. reconstruction: Janice uses the experiences of helping her daughter to prepare for senior prom to create a memory for Janice's own senior prom.
   d. reconstruction: Janice can retrieve some information and then fills in the missing information with probable details, so as to provide a coherent story.

2. The different systems of memory differ in terms of two dimensions. These dimensions are
   a. span and scan.
   b. span and duration.
   c. scan and forgetting mechanisms.
   d. duration and forgetting mechanisms.

3. You are a participant in a memory study in which you hear three letters, followed by a 3-digit number, and must immediately start counting backwards by threes from this number. After counting backwards for 3 seconds, you are likely to remember _____ of the numbers, and after 30 seconds you are likely to remember _____ of the numbers.
   a. most; none
   b. most; most
   c. none; most
   d. none; none

4. Joe Montana, a member of the football Hall of Fame, would probably recall each player's position after a briefly presented video image of football game, better than would Tony Gwynn, a member of the baseball Hall of Fame. This difference is probably accounted for by differences in
   a. chunking.
   b. athleticism.
   c. interference.
   d. visual memory.

5. You have an important test tomorrow. As you review your notes, you find you don't remember a few of the concepts. Your best strategy to memorize this information is to
   a. try to keep the information "alive" as long as possible.
   b. extend the duration of short-term memory until test time.
   c. repeat the information over and over and over to yourself.
   d. connect these new concepts to other ones already firmly in your memory.

6. You are exposed to a word list and are asked to determine whether each word, individually, evokes an emotional reaction. Your friend is exposed to the same words and is asked to note whether each word appeared in black or blue ink. Later, when asked to recall the words
   a. you recall more words than your friend because you processed them more deeply to begin with.
   b. you recall more words than your friend because the encoding and recall conditions are more alike.
   c. your friend recalls more words than you do, because your friend processed them more deeply to begin with.
   d. your friend recalls more words because the emotional overtones inhibit your ability to encode the words very well.

7. You jump into a car with a stick shift for the first time. You remember your dad telling you to gently let up on the clutch while depressing the gas pedal. You follow his directions exactly but stall the engine several times before getting going. The problem is that driving a stick shift requires you to develop a(n) _____ memory, so the verbal instructions are not very helpful.
   a. explicit
   b. episodic
   c. semantic
   d. procedural

8. The three important processes of memory are
   a. encoding, storage, and retrieval.
   b. priming, encoding, and retrieval.
   c. attention, elaboration, and storage.
   d. perception, attention, and elaboration.

9. As everyone goes around the room giving their names on the first day of class, you are LEAST likely to remember the name of
   a. the first person, because of the primacy effect.
   b. the person just before you, because of the next-in-line effect.
   c. the last person, because of the method of loci effect.
   d. the person just after you, because of priming.

10. Storage is enhanced by our schemas because
    a. nature has given us natural ways of storing information most economically.
    b. we can toss our new memories in quickly, and sort them out later, when we need them.
    c. they help us encode new information so it becomes associated with related, old information.
    d. they are like a filing cabinet, with no ambiguity about which "drawer" to use for filing new information.

11. During recognition, a person only needs to confirm that the presented information is "correct," but with recall a person
    a. also needs to decide if it is "incorrect."
    b. needs a cue to trigger memory for the information.
    c. needs to see how long it takes to relearn the material.
    d. must first generate previously stored information, and can then confirm that the generated information is "correct."

12. "Sensitivity" of memory measures from most sensitive (most likely to truly accurately detect a memory), to least sensitive (most likely to miss accurately detecting a memory) goes from
    a. recall, to recognition, to relearning.
    b. relearning, to recognition, to recall.
    c. recognition, to recall, to relearning.
    d. recognition, to relearning, to recall.

13. You and your roommate are both taking intro psych and have an exam next week. This course has a cumulative final. You distribute your practice sessions over several days, but your roommate crams the night before the exam. How will this affect each of your learning the course material?
    a. You should perform better on both the next exam and on the final.
    b. Your roommate should perform better on both the next exam and on the final.
    c. Your roommate should perform just slightly better on the next exam but you should perform much better on the final.
    d. You should both perform equally well on the final, but you roommate should perform much better on the next exam.

14. According to encoding specificity
    a. recognition is always easier than recall.
    b. encoding and retrieval processes are clearly distinctive and independent.
    c. learning is an activity independent of the conditions under which it occurs.
    d. we are more likely to remember information, if cues present at learning are also present at recall.

15. Loss of memory for past events is called _____; whereas the inability to form new memories is called _____.
    a. proactive amnesia; retroactive amnesia
    b. retroactive amnesia; proactive amnesia
    c. retrograde amnesia; anterograde amnesia
    d. anterograde amnesia; retrograde amnesia

16. Dementia is the progressive decline of cognitive/mental functions and
    a. is especially prevalent among aging Catholic nuns.
    b. can occur for many reasons, only one of which is Alzheimer's disease.
    c. typically begins in most people around an average age of 65.
    d. begins with distant memories and then progresses to affecting more recent memories.

17. Infants' memory is often tested by examining how much they kick in response to a familiar versus a new toy, such as a mobile. This behavior is governed by principles of
    a. operant conditioning.
    b. social learning theory.
    c. classical conditioning.
    d. hippocampal development.

18. Flashbulb memory—memory for the events surrounding our reception of important, surprising information—is
    a. vivid, and usually stable and accurate.
    b. vivid, but no more accurate that standard memory.
    c. like a permanent snapshot of the event, captured by a flash on a camera.
    d. so strongly tied to the facts of the event, that we remember both very well.

19. Sometimes even famous people like George Harrison of the Beatles plagiarize another persons' works, having a completely honest source monitoring confusion. This is called
    a. a mnemonics effect.
    b. hypermnesia.
    c. cryptomnesia.
    d. the misinformation effect.

20. When it comes to criminal identification, studies of eyewitnesses lead to the conclusion that
    a. false memories are so prevalent that accurate identification simply isn't possible.
    b. children should never be asked to identify criminals because of their greater suggestibility.
    c. because most crimes are very traumatic events, most people repress many elements of the crime.
    d. sequential line-ups lead to more accurate identification than do simultaneous line-ups.

After completing the test, calculate your percent correct
(/ 20 =   ) x 100 = _____ .

How accurate were your expectations? Does your performance suggest the need for additional study?

For the items you missed, go back and identify why the "correct" answer is the best answer.

AFTER YOU READ . . . PRACTICE TEST ANSWER KEYS

Practice Test 1.

1.   b (p. 243)
2.   a (p. 245)
3.   c (p. 248)
4.   b (p. 248)
5.   c (p. 250)
6.   d (p. 251-252)
7.   c (p. 251-252)
8.   d (p. 255)
9.   b (p. 256)
10. a (p. 258-259)
11. d (p. 260)
12. b (p. 260-261)
13. c (p. 250, 261)
14. c (p. 261)
15. a (p. 265)
16. a (p. 270)
17. d (p. 270)
18. a (p. 273)
19. d (p. 274)
20. d (p. 279)

Practice Test 2.

1.   d (p. 244)
2.   b (p. 245)
3.   a (p. 247)
4.   a (p. 249)
5.   d (p. 250)
6.   a (p. 250)
7.   d (p. 253)
8.   a (p. 254)
9.   b (p. 255)
10. c (p. 258-259)
11. d (p. 260)
12. b (p. 261)
13. c (p. 261)
14. d (p. 262)
15. c (p. 265)
16. b (p. 268)
17. a (p. 270)
18. b (p. 272)
19. c (p. 273)
20. d (p. 276)

AFTER YOU READ ... CONCEPT MAPPING ACTIVITY ANSWERS

ACTIVITY 1: Complete the following concept map for the stages of memory.

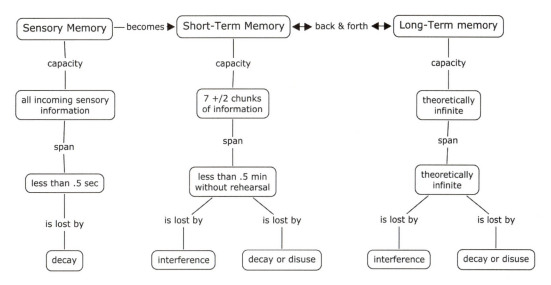

ACTIVITY 2: Complete this concept map for the organization of long-term memory.

The following terms, listed in alphabetic order, should appear in your concept map along with your own original examples for episodic, semantic, and procedural memories and priming.
cerebellum
cerebrum
episodic memory
priming
procedural memory
semantic memory

CHAPTER 8
LANGUAGE, THINKING, AND REASONING
GETTING INSIDE OUR TALKING HEADS

BEFORE YOU READ ... CHAPTER PREVIEW

Language plays a critical role in much of what makes us human. Language is involved in the maintenance of social relationships as well as in the organization of experience. We can think about language at four levels. At the simplest level are **phonemes** (sounds), followed by **morphemes** (smallest meaningful units), **syntax** (word order, sentence structure, *morphological markers*), and **extralinguistic information** (facial expression, posture, gestures, tone of voice). Research on language acquisition suggests that language development begins early and follows a regular sequence. Humans tune into the melody and rhythm of their native language before birth. Although first sounds reflect unintentional vocalizations, increased control of the vocal tract leads to intentional vocalizations such as **babbling**, which still lacks specific meaning. *Comprehension precedes production*: Children don't produce their first words until around their first birthday and begin to combine words by their second birthday.

Misconceptions regarding **sign language** are numerous. It is a linguistic system, not "just gestures." In acquiring sign language, children follow the same developmental path as do *monolingual* children. **Bilingual** children may experience some delays in syntactical development, but delays are offset by **metalinguistic** insight and proficiency. Children appear to be more proficient in second language use when they are exposed to the language earlier in life. Some children deprived of language develop their own **homesign**. Researchers investigated such children to help them determine whether there are *critical periods* for language development and have concluded that these are not rigidly defined and seem to more correctly reflect a *sensitive period*.

Theories of language acquisition all tend to differ in their emphasis on nature versus nurture. The imitation account fails to take account of *generativity*: we can make infinite combinations of communications; this **generative** nature of language could not be explained by imitation. **Nativist** accounts suggest there is a **language acquisition device** that accounts for *overregularization*. **Social pragmatics** accounts point to the importance of social interactions in language development. The *general cognitive processing* accounts link general cognitive abilities with language development. Each reflects only part of the picture. Although nonhuman animal species use communication systems primarily in the contexts of mating and aggression, some exchange other types of information. Efforts to teach language to nonhumans suggest that the basics of language can be taught, but the language never reaches the syntactic complexity of a three-year-old human.

Linguistic determinism is the view that no thought is possible without language. Evidence against this view includes findings that children can perform complex tasks before language. The more moderate view of **linguistic relativity** suggests that language shapes rather than determines thought. Linguistic relativity may be true for some but not all aspects of cognition.

Learning to read requires mastery of both **whole word recognition** and **phonetic decomposition.** Before children can learn to read, they must master prereading skills. For example, they must learn that printed words have meaning, that it moves in a set direction, and that printed letters correspond to particular sounds. Proficient readers tend to be both faster at reading and better at comprehending than poorer readers but "speed reading" has been demonstrated to result in a speed/comprehension trade-off.

Thinking can be defined as any mental activity or processing of information. Although the mind has been compared with a computer, human information processing is more flexible and creative than computer processing. Because as humans we tend to be cognitive misers, we also tend to use thinking shortcuts, or *heuristics*, to increase efficiency. Techniques to streamline processing include *top-down processing* and the use of chunking, schemata, and **concepts** (objects and actions that share core properties). These techniques impose order on information by relying on previous experience.

Two examples of how we use thinking are decision making and problem solving. In **decision making,** we select one or more options from several possible options. Many decisions we make are based on a "gut" feeling about it. **Framing** is also important. In **problem solving,** we have to generate a plan to reach a goal. In contrast to using heuristics, many problems can be solved with **algorithms**, which guarantee a correct solution. But many times there is no algorithm and there are obstacles to problem solving that can lead to faulty solutions, including a tendency to focus on surface properties rather than underlying properties of problems and the use of **mental sets,** in which **functional fixedness** leads us to only see objects for their most common uses. Thus, although many people use a computer analogy for human thinking, and it can be useful, such an analogy is highly limited as a model of the mind. Recent models focus more on *embodied* accounts of thinking, which rely more on individual experiences.

BEFORE YOU READ ... LEARNING OBJECTIVES

After reading Chapter 8 you should be able to:

8.1   Describe the four levels of analysis that make up language
8.2   Trace the development of language acquisition in children
8.3   Determine how sign language in deaf individuals relates to spoken language acquisition in hearing individuals
8.4   Identify the pros and cons of bilingualism
8.5   Compare and contrast theories of language acquisition
8.6   Distinguish human language from nonhuman animal communication.
8.7   Identify how our language may influence our thinking
8.8   Identify the skills required to learn to read, and understand the debate concerning reading strategies
8.9   Analyze the relationship between reading speed and reading comprehension
8.10   Identify methods for achieving cognitive economy
8.11   Describe what factors affects how we make decisions
8.12   Describe some of the common problem-solving strategies and challenges
8.13   Describe various models of the human mind

BEFORE YOU READ ... TERM IDENTIFICATION

algorithm (p. 308)
babbling (p. 290)
bilingual (p. 293)
concept (p. 307)
decision making (p. 307)
dialect (p. 288)
extralinguistic information (p. 287)
framing (p. 307)
functional fixedness (p. 311)
generative (p. 296)
homesign (p. 294)
language (p. 287)
language acquisition device (p. 296)
linguistic determinism (p. 300)
linguistic relativity (p. 301)

mental set (p. 311)
metalinguistic (p. 293)
morpheme (p. 287)
nativist (p. 296)
one-word stage (p. 290)
phoneme (p. 287)
phonetic decomposition (p. 302)
problem solving (p. 308)
semantics (p. 288)
sign language (p. 292)
social pragmatics (p. 296)
syntax (p. 287)
thinking (p. 305)
whole word recognition (p. 302)

AS YOU READ ... PRACTICE ACTIVITIES

HOW DOES LANGUAGE WORK?

1. List the levels of speech analysis from the smallest to the largest unit, then match the level of speech analysis with its description. (LO 8.1)

Levels of Speech   Description

Smallest   1._____   _____

            2._____   _____

            3._____   _____

Largest   4._____   _____

Phoneme   elements of communication context
Extralinguistic information   grammatical rules of language
Syntax   smallest unit of meaningful speech
Morpheme   sounds of language

2. Look at the examples of ambiguous headlines and sentences with multiple meanings in Table 8.1 of the text. Can you find additional examples in a local newspaper? Can you make up some others? How do these examples illustrate the complexity of our linguistic system? What are the pros and cons of such a complex linguistic system? (LO 8.1)

3. Language development is a process—it doesn't happen all at once. Look at the language development of the children described here. Would any of these observations concern you? Why or why not? (LO 8.2)

Yara is a 13-month-old who does not yet comprehend any spoken words, including her name.

Alicia is a 2-year-old who uses the word *duck* to refer to all birds.

Mako is almost 3 and still says "poon" for *spoon*.

4. How is the learning of sign language for a deaf child similar to language learning by a hearing child? (LO 8.3)

5. Although some evidence indicates that bilingual children experience some delay in each of their languages relative to their monolingual counterparts, bilingualism offers some advantages. List at least two advantages. (LO 8.4)

6. What is the evidence both for and against the existence of a "critical period" for language acquisition? (LO 8.5)

7. For each of these theories of language development, identify the main idea, whether the theory emphasizes the source of language as nature or nurture, and the major criticism of the theory. (LO 8.5)

	Main Idea	Source	Criticism
Imitation			
Nativist			
Social Pragmatics			
General Cognitive Processing			

8. What are the similarities and differences in human and nonhuman animal communication? (LO 8.6)

DO WE THINK IN WORDS? THE RELATION BETWEEN LANGUAGE AND THOUGHT

1. Using your own words, briefly describe the idea of "linguistic determinism." (LO 8.7)

2. Had you heard the claim that Eskimos (Inuits) have 1,000 different words for snow? Give at least two reasons to doubt this view. (LO 8.7)

3. How does the idea of linguistic relativity differ from linguistic determinism? (LO 8.7)

4. What makes cross-cultural research on language and thinking challenging? (*Hint*: Remember confounds?) (LO 8.7)

READING: RECOGNIZING THE WRITTEN WORD

1. Try out the Stroop effect at http://faculty.washington.edu/chudler/words.html
   Why is it difficult? (LO 8.8)

   Why is the Stroop effect greater for adults than for children?

   Would the Stroop effect hold for a bilingual adult? Would it be greater for one language than another?

2. What are the prereading skills a child needs to master before learning to read? Why do you think these skills are important? (LO 8.8)

3. Phonological awareness is important in the development of reading as well as in the development of spelling. As young children learn to spell, they will often represent all of a word's phonemes in the spelling. For example, what might this child be trying to say about "ways to travel"? (LO 8.8)

    "u kan tak a kar or chran or chip."

4. Proficient readers tend to be both faster at reading and better at comprehending than poorer readers. Does this finding imply that faster reading speed causes better comprehension? Explain your answer. (LO 8.9)

THINKING AND REASONING

1. Without looking back at the book, how would you define thinking? (LO 8.10)

    Now check the text's definition.
    Did your definition capture the essence of *thinking* as defined by the text?

2. What are the benefits of cognitive economy? (LO 8.10-8.12)

3. We encounter framing everyday in our lives. Give a real-world example of framing that you have noticed. (*Hint:* If you are stuck coming up with an answer, go grocery shopping.) (LO 8.11)

4. Functional fixedness involves seeing objects in their usual way and not being able to see alternative functions, even when the alternatives would be practical and useful. Can you think of a time when you "suffered from" or "overcame" functional fixedness? If not, try to create an example. (LO 8.12)

5. College students often claim that they used memorization successfully in high school and are reluctant to give up this low-level strategy despite finding it to be an ineffective way of studying in college. Why might students have difficulty giving up an ineffective strategy? (LO 8.12)

6. OK … you probably heard this one as a kid: Ask someone to spell the word *joke*. Then ask him to spell *folk*. Next ask him to spell *poke*. Finally ask him to spell the white of an egg. He will probably spell "y-o-l-k." But the yolk is the yellow part of an egg. The white part is called albumin. What problem-solving hurdles discussed in your text make this question tricky? (LO 8.12)

7. Many people have compared the human brain with a computer. But despite their similarities, they also have differences. Discuss two ways human brains differ from computers. (LO 8.13)

AS YOU READ ... CONCEPT MAP ACTIVITIES

ACTIVITY 1: Complete the following concept map for reading.

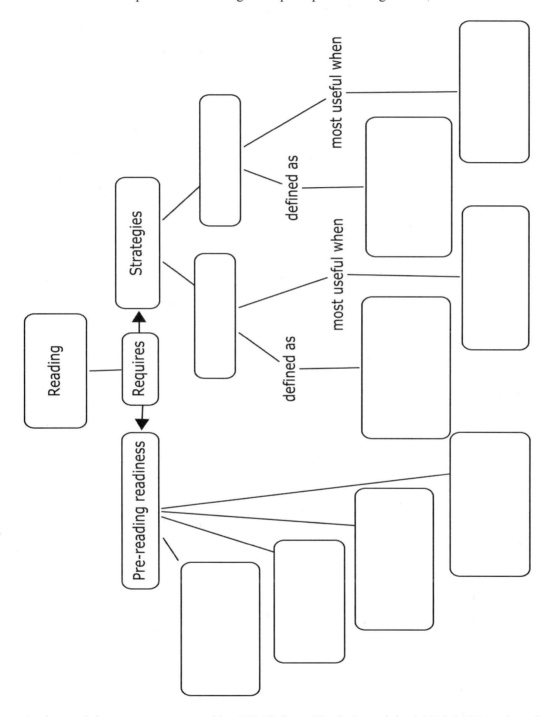

Author activity content supported by *IHMC Cmap Tools* Copyright ©1998-2007 Institute for Human & Machine Cognition

ACTIVITY 2: In this concept map, consider the different explanation that different theories provide for language development.

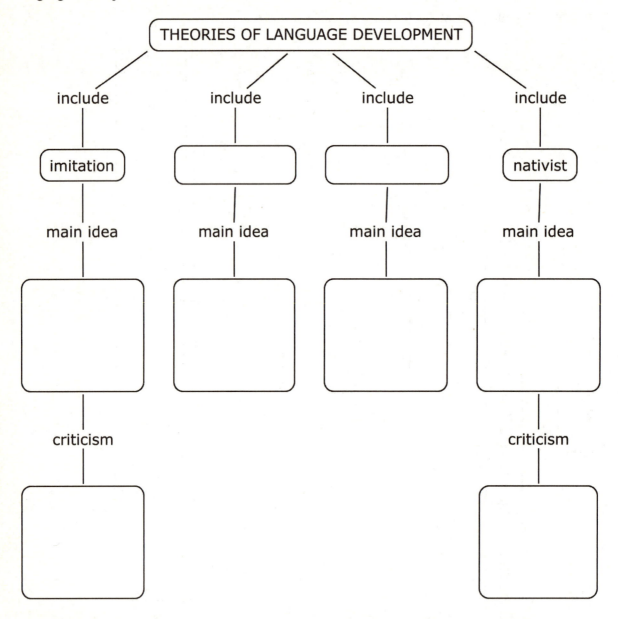

ACTIVITY 3: Create your own concept map in the space provided below by organizing the following concepts from the chapter. Be sure to include superordinate terms, links, and examples that may not be included in the list but are necessary to make the map meaningful.

Theories of Language Development: Imitation, Nativist, Social Pragmatic, General Cognitive Processing

Language Development: Course, Prelinguistic abilities, Babbling, One-Word Stage, Two-word combinations

Features of Language: Four Levels of Analysis, Phonemes, Morphemes, Syntax, Extralinguistic information

AS YOU READ ... MYTH OR REALITY?

Myth: Dyslexia is a perceptual problem caused by children making reversal errors when they read (e.g., reading *was* for *saw*).

Reality: All children reverse letters when learning to read. Dyslexic children make more reversal errors than other children because they make more overall reading errors.

1. In drawing the conclusion that reversal errors cause the dyslexia, what errors in thinking are occurring? (*Hint*: The observation that dyslexic children make reversal errors is missing what important element of the scientific method?)

Myth: Learning difficult subjects such as Latin has broad effects on thinking.

Reality: Little evidence shows that we can develop "mental muscle" by learning difficult subjects.

1. Rather than developing general skills, people seem to learn things that are more specific. What concepts discussed in this chapter support the claim that transfer of learning across context is difficult? (Hint: Transfer between initial and later learning depends not only on the similarity of elements across the two experiences but on the individual noticing the similarity.)

AS YOU READ … PUT YOUR SCIENTIFIC THINKING SKILLS TO THE TEST

1. Teaching hearing infants to use sign language has become popular recently. Try using Google to search for Internet sites on "Baby Sign Language." Review a few of these sites.
   a. What are the claims they are making?
   b. What is their support?
   c. Now look at one of the articles below by Johnston, Durieux-Smith, and Bloom. How are the conclusions these authors draw different from the Internet sites? Why?
      http://fla.sagepub.com/cgi/content/abstract/25/2/235
      http://www.cllrnet.ca/Docs/Programs/GraduateStudentResearchReviews/2003/CRR.pdf

2. If some is good, is *more* necessarily better? Based on the text's description of factors contributing to reading development, which of the following do you think would be a better choice for a preschool-aged child and why?

   A copy of the book, *Read Aloud Rhymes for the Very Young* (Prelutsky & Brown, 1986) for $13.57.
      Or *The Hooked on Phonics Pre-K Kit* with 3 CD ROMS, Audio CD, 6 workbooks, Bingo Cards, 5 sets of Flashcards, and Progress Poster for $99.95.

AS YOU READ ... MYPSYCHLAB CONNECTION

How Does Language Work?
To know more about how language works, **Explore** *Getting Inside Our Talking Heads*. Have you ever wondered how slips of the tongue occur? Participate in the brief **Simulation** on *Lexical Bias in Slips of the Tongue* to show how slips of the tongue can be artificially created. If you would like to see how we learn language, **Watch** *Stimulating Language Development, Literacy,* and *Language Learning*. Have you ever wondered what it might be like to learn in a bilingual environment? **Watch** *Teaching in a Bilingual Classroom, Bilingual Families,* and *Bilingual Education* to find out. To learn more about how other animals communicate, **Watch** *Birds and Language* and *Sign Language*. Are gestures intentional? What is the purpose of gestures? **Watch** *Hand Gesturing Study* and *Susan Goldwin-Meadow: The Role of Gesture in Thinking* to learn about research on gesturing.

Do We Think in Words? The Relation between Language and Thought
How does advertising really work? To understand the theory of linguistic relativity and see how words influence the impressions you form of products, news, other students, and so on, engage in the **Simulation** *Power of Words*.

Reading: Recognizing the Written Word
Want to incorporate a fun activity into your learning? Check out the **Simulation** *Experiencing the Stroop Effect*. This activity will demonstrate how interference affects your speed of processing information.

Thinking and Reasoning
Are you creative enough to solve a problem that seems as if it has no solution? Try the **Explore** *The Two-String Problem*, to find out. Schemas help us organize knowledge on many levels, as you can experience in the **Simulation**, *Schemas*. **Watch** the video, *Water Lily*, to learn more about problem-solving; and participate in the **Simulation** *Intuition and Discovery in Problem Solving*. Psychologists tap into how your mind organizes information in this classic reaction-timed **Simulation** called *The Mind's Organization of Conceptual Knowledge*.

AFTER YOU READ … PRACTICE TEST #1

Before beginning this practice test, estimate the percent you expect to get correct.
Anticipated percent correct: _____

1. The levels of speech analysis from smallest to largest unit are
    a. morpheme, phoneme, extralinguistic information, syntax.
    b. phoneme, morpheme, syntax, extralinguistic information.
    c. morpheme, syntax, extralinguistic information, phoneme.
    d. phoneme, morpheme, extralinguistic information, syntax.

2. Misunderstandings can occur in phone conversations and e-mails because _____ information is missing from the communication.
    a. extralinguistic
    b. syntax
    c. morphemes
    d. phonemes

3. _____ are variations within a language used by a group of people who share geographic proximity or ethnic background.
    a. Babbles
    b. Morphemes
    c. Phonetic decompositions
    d. Dialects

4. Which of the following children would be of greatest concern to you?
    a. Nico at 12 months can comprehend several words, but does not yet speak.
    b. Rubin at 18 months calls all gray-haired men "grandpa."
    c. Mato at 13 months does not recognize his name.
    d. All of these children are experiencing significant delays.

5. One-year-old Lenita says "cookie" while pointing to a cookie just out of reach. She is demonstrating
    a. overgeneralization.
    b. syntax.
    c. the one-word stage.
    d. babbling.

6. When children reach the "two-word" stage of language development,
    a. they are usually a year old.
    b. they rarely combine words in the correct order.
    c. they understand more about syntax than they can produce.
    d. they rely on babbling to communicate.

7. The learning of sign language for a deaf child is similar to the learning of spoken language by a hearing child. Which of the following is NOT one of the ways these processes are similar?
    a. Both language systems have the same linguistic features and complexity.
    b. Acquisition follows a similar developmental sequence beginning with babbling.
    c. Sign language use activates the same brain areas as those involved in spoken language.
    d. Both hearing and deaf children learn language from native speakers.

8. Two-year-old Pippa is growing up in a bilingual family—her parents speak both English and Spanish with her. Some evidence indicates that, as a bilingual child, Pippa will
   a. experience serious delays in vocabulary acquisition.
   b. have the advantage of greater metalinguistic awareness.
   c. will only develop proficiency in one language.
   d. will only be able to learn both languages because she is under the age of seven.

9. Evidence AGAINST a strict critical period for language development includes:
   a. second language acquisition drops off rapidly after age 7.
   b. cochlear implants in deaf children are most effective when implanted at a very young age.
   c. children deprived of all exposure to language early in life never develop full language skills.
   d. even older adults can learn a new language, it's just more effortful and less syntactically fluent.

10. The theory of language that puts the greatest emphasis on innate sources focuses on
    a. imitation.
    b. social pragmatics.
    c. the language acquisition device.
    d. cognitive processing.

11. The theory of language development that would be the most difficult to falsify is the
    a. nativist theory.
    b. general cognitive processing theory.
    c. social pragmatics theory.
    d. imitation.

12. Although chimpanzees can learn to communicate with sign language, they never really master
    a. syntax.
    b. vocabulary.
    c. the use of signs to make requests.
    d. responding to rewards.

13. _____ is the view that all thought is represented verbally and thinking is limited by language.
    a. Linguistic relativism
    b. Covert speech
    c. Linguistic determinism
    d. The verbal-thought theory

14. A major reason it is difficult to draw conclusions from research on cross-cultural differences in language and thought is because
    a. cross-linguistic comparisons are correlational rather than experimental.
    b. language and culture are seldom confounded.
    c. there is no thought without language.
    d. language shapes nearly all aspects of perception and memory.

15. Of the two major reading strategies, _____ is more efficient when reading familiar words, and_____ is critical for less-familiar words.
    a. linguistic relativity; linguistic determinism
    b. whole word recognition; phonetic decomposition
    c. linguistic determinism; linguistic relativity
    d. phonetic decomposition; whole word recognition

16. You are an avid reader and want your child to develop her reading skills. Which of the following would best prepare a child for reading?
    a. Use flashcards displaying whole words.
    b. Have the child sit on your lap while you read nursery rhymes.
    c. Show the child lots of children's videos.
    d. Have the child hear lots of different people speaking.

17. Several students from your Introductory Psychology class are looking at an ad for a speed reading course and debating its claims. Which of the following statements about reading speed is actually TRUE?
    a. Learning to speed read will improve your comprehension.
    b. Proficient readers tend to be both faster at reading and better at comprehending than poorer readers.
    c. Subvocalizing is critical to comprehension.
    d. Reading speed cannot be increased.

18. Top-down processing and heuristics
    a. free us to engage in tasks of greater complexity.
    b. have not been studied empirically.
    c. are usually more accurate than careful analysis.
    d. are accurate only in rare situations.

19. Students' failure to realize that memorization techniques that worked in high school may not help them understand material at the college level may be thought of as an example of the problem-solving hurdle known as
    a. salience of surface similarities.   c. mental set.
    b. correlation is causation.   d. the consequence effect.

20. Bianca could not find a vase for the rose Mic brought her. Her failure to realize that her water bottle would have served the purpose is an example of
    a. salience of surface similarities.
    b. functional fixedness.
    c. availability heuristic.
    d. the consequence effect.

After completing the test, calculate your percent correct
(/ 20 =   ) x 100 = _____.

How accurate were your expectations? Does your performance suggest the need for additional study?
For the items you missed, go back and identify why the "correct" answer is the best answer.

AFTER YOU READ ... PRACTICE TEST #2

Before beginning this practice test, estimate the percent you expect to get correct.
Anticipated percent correct: _____

1. Which of the following statements about phonemes is TRUE?
   a. Phonemes are categories of sounds that our vocal apparatus produces.
   b. A one-to-one correspondence occurs between individual letters of the alphabet and the phonemes in the language.
   c. All languages use the same phoneme categories.
   d. Phonemes include the smallest units of meaning in a language.

2. Syntax
   a. is a set of rules that is rarely violated in spoken language.
   b. is universal across languages.
   c. includes morphological markers that change the meaning of existing words.
   d. reflects the speaker's nonverbal cues.

3. People have begun to use signs such as ☺ and ;-) in their e-mails as partial compensation for
   a. a lack of syntactical information.
   b. a lack of extralinguistic information.
   c. confirmation biases.
   d. availability heuristics.

4. The complexity of human language
   a. contributes to its flexibility.
   b. facilitates a brief learning period.
   c. holds true only for certain languages.
   d. supports sound symbolism.

5. Research suggests that, before birth, infants
   a. cannot hear inside the womb.
   b. can learn to read if read to regularly.
   c. can learn about the melody and rhythm of their native language.
   d. can hear but cannot make out characteristics of language.

6. Babbling
   a. refers to unintentional vocalization.
   b. evolves over the first year of life.
   c. initially includes only sounds of an infant's native language.
   d. is not dependent on control of the vocal tract.

7. Which of the following statements about sign language is TRUE?
   a. Deaf people don't need sign language because they can lip-read.
   b. Learning to sign impedes a deaf child's ability to learn to speak.
   c. American Sign Language is English translated word-for-word into signs.
   d. Deaf babies pass through the same stages in language acquisition as do hearing babies.

8. A child who is learning a second language
   a. will develop greater proficiency if exposed to the second language early in life.
   b. will experience delays in learning the vocabulary of each of his/her languages.
   c. will never learn the syntax of the second language if first exposed later in life.
   d. will perform more poorly on language tasks compared with monolingual children.

9. Which of the following statements regarding children's errors in language use is TRUE?
   a. Children rarely make errors they do not hear.
   b. Children's errors are not part of normal development and require speech therapy.
   c. Using the word *grandpa* for any gray-haired man is an example of an undergeneralization.
   d. Errors tell us children are generating language from their understanding of its rules.

10. The nativist account of language acquisition
    a. claims that children come into the world knowing how to speak.
    b. proposes a specific human organ for language acquisition.
    c. makes claims that are largely unfalsifiable.
    d. cannot explain overregularization.

11. The social pragmatics account of language acquisition
    a. holds that children learn language by being directly reinforced by their parents.
    b. holds that children infer word meanings from the context of social interaction.
    c. is a nativist account of language development.
    d. is unfalsifiable.

12. Nonhuman primate and human infant language learning are both similar and different. Which of the following statements is FALSE?
    a. Human babies get better and faster at word learning; chimpanzees do not.
    b. Chimpanzees require thousands of trials of paired associations with rewards; human children do not.
    c. Human children use words to request food and other pleasurable activities; chimpanzees do not.
    d. Chimpanzees never fully master syntax; human children combine words to form complex sentences.

13. Research on the relation between language and cognition
    a. suggests that language shapes all aspects of perception, thought, and memory.
    b. shows that some aspects of thinking are more vulnerable to language influence than others.
    c. finds that cultures that have only two "color" words, dark and bright, cannot distinguish other colors.
    d. demonstrates that language cannot affect thinking.

14. The reading strategy that involves sounding out words by drawing correspondences between printed letters and sounds is known as
    a. phoneme identification.   c. phonetic decomposition.
    b. word decomposition.   d. whole word recognition.

15. The Stroop effect naming task
    a. requires attending to both printed words and their printed color.
    b. demonstrates that reading is automatic.
    c. is more difficult for young children who are just learning to read.
    d. is a task in which it is easier to read words than to name the color in which the word is written.

16. Many factors are critical in children developing the ability to read. Which of the following statements about reading is FALSE?
    a. In learning to read, children must learn to recognize whole words.
    b. In learning to read, children must learn to recognize how printed letters correspond to sounds.
    c. In learning to read, children must learn that written words are meaningful.
    d. In learning to read, children must listen to books read in utero.

17. Sarah believes that sugar causes hyperactivity. She has frequently noticed that her daughter gets excited when eating ice cream at Ben & Jerry's. Sarah has failed to notice, however, that her daughter also gets excited when eating French fries at McDonald's. Sarah's differential attention best illustrates
    a. functional fixedness.
    b. the availability heuristic.
    c. confirmation bias.
    d. hindsight bias.

18. Once a child is labeled dyslexic, teachers and parents notice the reversal errors the child makes in his/her reading (e.g., reading *was* for *saw*), but fail to notice that all children make reversal errors when learning to read. This tendency to see the dyslexic child's errors is an example of
    a. mental set.
    b. confirmation bias.
    c. functional fixedness.
    d. salience of surface similarity.

19. Top-down processing
    a. begins with the analysis of sensory data.
    b. fails to explain the mechanism underlying chunking.
    c. is an example of a cognitive error in information processing.
    d. uses preexisting knowledge to help streamline information processing.

20. Searching for a hammer and not thinking of using your shoe is an example of
    a. functional fixedness.
    b. availability heuristic.
    c. consequence effect.
    d. confirmation bias.

After completing the test, calculate your percent correct
(/ 20 =   ) x 100 = _____.

How accurate were your expectations? Does your performance suggest the need for additional study?
For the items you missed, go back and identify why the "correct" answer is the best answer.

AFTER YOU READ . . . PRACTICE TEST ANSWER KEYS

Practice Test 1.

1. b (p. 287)
2. a (p. 288)
3. d (p. 288)
4. c (p. 291)
5. c (p. 291)
6. c (p. 291-292)
7. d (p. 292-293)
8. b (p. 293)
9. d (p. 294-295)
10. c (p. 296)
11. a (p. 296)
12. a (p. 298)
13. c (p. 300)
14. a (p. 301)
15. b (p. 302)
16. b (p. 303)
17. b (p. 303-304)
18. a (p. 305-306)
19. c (p. 310)
20. b (p. 310)

Practice Test 2.

1. a (p. 287)
2. c (p. 288)
3. b (p. 288)
4. a (p. 289)
5. c (p. 290)
6. b (p. 290)
7. d (p. 292-293)
8. a (p. 293)
9. d (p. 295)
10. b (p. 296)
11. b (p. 296)
12. a (p. 298)
13. b (p. 301)
14. c (p. 303)
15. b (p. 302)
16. d (p. 302–303)
17. c (p. 305)
18. b (p. 305)
19. d (p. 306)
20. a (p. 310)

AFTER YOU READ ... CONCEPT MAPPING ACTIVITY ANSWERS

ACTIVITY 1: Complete the following concept map for reading.

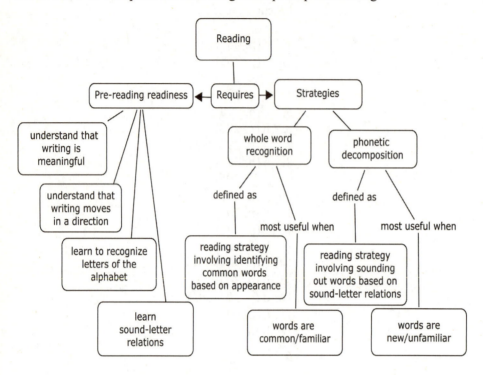

ACTIVITY 2: In this concept map, consider the different explanation that different theories provide for language development.

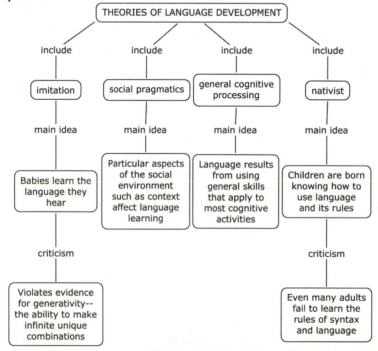

CHAPTER 9
INTELLIGENCE AND IQ TESTING
CONTROVERSY AND CONSENSUS

BEFORE YOU READ ...CHAPTER PREVIEW

The most difficult concept for psychologists to define is intelligence. The first **intelligence tests** sought to measure overall thinking ability. In 1905, Binet and Simon had a practical problem: to identify school children who needed educational assistance. They developed a battery of tests that would predict school success. One element that still defines intelligence since those earlier times is a focus on **abstract thinking**. In addition, most psychologists include the ability to adapt to new environments, to acquire knowledge, and to benefit from experience. Spearman was interested in what is common among intellectual abilities and proposed a single capacity underlying intelligence he called *g* **(general intelligence)**, in addition to *s* **(specific abilities).** Other theorists emphasize how the correlations among the abilities form clusters. Cattell and Horn, for example, proposed a distinction between **fluid intelligence** (the mechanics of solving novel problems) and **crystallized intelligence** (the accumulation of knowledge). Validity for this distinction comes from evidence that fluid intelligence tends to decline with age while crystallized intelligence can continue to increase in healthy adults and is associated with the personality trait of *openness to new experiences*. Some theorists, including Gardner, have proposed **multiple intelligences** that are distinct from one another. Finally, Sternberg proposed a **triarchic model** composed of analytical intelligence (the ability to reason logically), practical intelligence (the ability to solve real world problems), and creative intelligence (the ability to find novel answers to questions). Criticism of these theories include observations that many of these so-called separate intelligences are in fact positively correlated and some of these intelligences are more appropriately seen as talents. Search for neural correlates of intelligence suggests that "brainy" people tend to have somewhat larger brains, although the cause and effect are unclear. Imaging studies show that intelligent people do have more efficient brains. Brain activity related to intelligence seems to be within the prefrontal cortex, an area involved in planning. More intelligent people also have somewhat faster *reaction times* (.3 to .4 correlation), as well as somewhat more efficient working memory.

Measuring a concept that is poorly defined is extremely challenging. Just asking people how smart they think they are doesn't work well because research evidence shows that most people have poor *metacognitive skills*—people consistently over-estimate what they think they know. In addition, there is *the double curse of incompetence*: if you are wrong but unaware of it, you can't correct your knowledge. The early form of the **intelligence quotient** in the **Stanford-Binet IQ test** was calculated as *mental age / chronological age* x 100. **Mental age** depended on one's score on the IQ test. Because of problems with this index, today IQ reflects a person's **deviation IQ,** for which each person's score is calculated relative to norms for that person's age group. IQ testing has a history of abuse. Tests were given to populations for which they were not designed and were used to label and sort people. The **eugenics** movement took sorting to extremes, encouraging people with high IQs to reproduce and those with low IQs to be sterilized. Today the most popular test is the Wechsler Adult Intelligence Scale (WAIS), which is composed of six verbal and five performance subscales. There are also several **culture-fair IQ tests** used to help prevent abuses in testing. College admissions tests (SATs) also correlate highly (between .7 and .8) with IQ tests. Some students take prep classes that slightly improve SAT scores, mostly attributed to *practice effects*. In terms of *validity,* IQ tests predict performance on other IQ tests as well as many real-world behaviors in the classroom and the workplace. However, IQ is tempered by motivation, intellectual curiosity, effort, and *mental energy*. There is a *threshold effect* for IQ: above a certain level, it stops predicting real-world performance.

Scores on IQ tests are distributed normally in the population. A score of 100 reflects the average for people at that age. Ninety-five percent of people score between 70 and 130 and this remains stable because of *assortative mating*: people tend to have children with others who are similar to them genetically. Scores below 70 reflect **mental retardation**; scores above 130 reflect giftedness. Mental retardation may result from a variety of influences including genetic errors (e.g., Down syndrome or Fragile X syndrome) and environmental teratogens (e.g., FAS). One clear finding is that the more serious the retardation, the less likely it is to run in families. The environment after birth also plays a role, particularly in influencing the mild forms of retardation. Among the classification of mental retardation, 85% fall within the mild category and can be *mainstreamed* into typical classrooms. Terman's study of gifted children dispelled several myths, including the idea that gifted individuals are physically fragile, "burn out" at an early age, and are predisposed to mental disorders.

Effects on IQ include both genetics and environment. From *family studies,* researchers have concluded that studies of intact families don't allow them to distinguish between the effects of environment and the effects of genetics. From *twin studies,* researchers have observed that IQs of identical twins correlated between .7 and .8 whereas the IQs of fraternal twins correlate between .3 and .4. This observation suggests that genetics influence IQ because identical twins are more alike than fraternal twins; but also suggests that the environment also influences IQ because the correlation for identical twins is less than 1.00. *Adoption studies* also suggest the influence of genetics on intelligence because adopted children's IQs are more similar to their birth mothers compared with their adopted mothers; such studies also suggest the influence of environment because children adopted from deprived environments into enriched environments show higher IQs. A caveat here regards *selective placement,* in which children tend to be placed into families most like their biological families. Research has shown that birth order effects are very small and primarily show up in large families. There is a modest correlation between amount of education and IQ, but the direction of relationship is not clear. Other environmental effects include early intervention, expectancy effects, nutrition, and poverty. The **Flynn effect** reflects a steady rise in average IQ. Most psychologists believe the effect can be partly explained by various environmental factors.

Individual differences need to considered in light of *group differences*. Group differences focus on differences between genders and across races. More variability can be found in IQ scores among members of the same sex than between members of opposite sexes, especially for men. The few sex differences in IQ scores that do exist include higher performance on some verbal measures for women and higher performance on some spatial measures for men. Although group differences do appear between races, there is substantial overlap in the distributions. When considering racial differences in IQ, both **within-group heritability** and **between-group heritability** must be considered. *Within-group heritability does not predict between-group heritability.* There is strong evidence that environmental factors—such as poverty, social discrimination, and characteristics of the testing situation–rather than genetic differences underlie racial differences in IQ. In addition, **test bias** is an important factor to consider. Finally, individuals of minority groups may simply not test well because of **stereotype threat**.

Psychologists generally require creative accomplishments to be both *novel* and *successful*. Creativity has been measured by tests of **divergent thinking** (e.g., the capacity to generate many solutions to a problem), but creativity also involves **convergent thinking** (e.g. finding the best answer to a problem). Creative people do tend to have higher rates of some mental illnesses, such as bipolar disorder. **Emotional intelligence** refers to the ability to understand one's own and others' emotions. Despite its popularity, the concept does not predict variability between individuals beyond general intelligence and basic personality measures. The **ideological immune system**—the tendency to defend against views that contradict one's own—provides one explanation of why "smart" people may come to believe strange things. **Wisdom** has been defined as an application of one's intelligence for the common good. Wise people balance their own and others' interests. Wisdom does not necessarily come with age.

BEFORE YOU READ ... LEARNING OBJECTIVES

After reading Chapter 9 you should be able to:

9.1   Identify different models and types of intelligence
9.2   Describe the connection between intelligence and brain size and efficiency
9.3   Determine how psychologists calculate IQ
9.4   Explain the history of misuse of intelligence tests in the United States
9.5   Describe tests of intelligence used today and evaluate the reliability and validity of IQ scores.
9.6   Distinguish the unique characteristics of mental retardation and genius
9.7   Explain how genetic influences can be determined from family, twin, and adoption studies
9.8   Identify potential environment influences on IQ
9.9   Identify similarities and differences in mental ability between men and women
9.10   Evaluate the evidence concerning racial differences in IQ
9.11   Describe how creativity and emotional intelligence relate to intelligence
9.12   Identify reasons why intelligence doesn't protect us from errors in thinking

BEFORE YOU READ ... TERM IDENTIFICATION

abstract thinking (p. 319)
bell curve (p. 345)
between-group heritability (p. 347)
convergent thinking (p. 350)
crystallized intelligence (p. 320)
culture-fair IQ tests (p. 330)
deviation IQ (p. 327)
divergent thinking (p. 350)
emotional intelligence (p. 351)
eugenics (p. 329)
fluid intelligence (p. 320)
Flynn effect (p. 341)
g (general intelligence) (p. 320)
ideological immune system (p. 353)

intelligence quotient (p. 327)
intelligence test (p. 319)
mental age (p. 327)
mental retardation (p. 334)
multiple intelligences (p. 322)
s (specific abilities) (p. 320)
Stanford-Binet IQ Test (p. 327)
stereotype threat (p. 348)
test bias (p. 347)
triarchic model (p. 322)
Wechsler Adult Intelligence Scale (WAIS) (p. 329)
wisdom (p. 352)
within-group heritability (p. 347)

AS YOU READ ... PRACTICE ACTIVITIES

WHAT IS INTELLIGENCE? DEFINITIONAL CONFUSION

1. Most psychologists would agree that intelligence has something to do with higher mental processes. What are the four abilities generally believed to demonstrate intelligence behavior? (LO 9.1)

2. The first intelligence test developed in 1905 by Binet and Simon was designed to solve what practical problem? Are they still primarily used for this purpose? (LO 9.1)

3. Intelligence tests include a variety of items tapping mathematical and verbal ability and spatial and verbal reasoning. Despite this variety, items tend to correlate positively with one another. Does this finding suggest that intelligence is one thing or many? Could it be both? Explain your answer. (LO 9.1)

4. Gardner proposes that multiple intelligences are different from and independent from one another. (LO 9.1)
    Gardner's claims are based on evidence from…

    Despite popular appeal, researchers remain critical of Gardner's claims because…

5. Sternberg proposes three domains of intelligence in his triarchic model. List and give an example of these domains. (LO 9.1)
    1. _____

    Example_____

    2. _____

    Example_____

    3. _____

    Example_____

    Criticism of his claims include:

6. Research on the biological basis of intelligence and information processing suggests at least some validity to the idea that people who are intelligent are "quick minded." What sort of evidence supports this view? (LO 9.2)

7. A moderate correlation can be demonstrated between brain size and IQ. What does this correlation mean? (LO 9.2)

INTELLIGENCE TESTING: THE GOOD, THE BAD, AND THE UGLY

1. What is the main lesson of Kruger and Dunning's work on how well we know whether we know? (LO 9.3)

   What implications does this work have for studying in college? (Hint: What do we ask you before and after each quiz?)

2. What was Wilhelm Stern's original formula for calculating IQ? (LO 9.3)

3. What were two problems with the eugenics movement relative to IQ? Can you think of similar types of abuses that are on-going? (LO 9.4)

4. Fill in this outline describing the most commonly used IQ test today. (LO 9.5)

   The _____ _____ _____ (or WAIS)

   Yields three scores
   Verbal Scale consisting of

   Performance Scale consisting of

   Full Scale combining

5. The Raven's Progressive Matrices is a "culturally fair test." What does this mean? (LO 9.5)

6. The chapter brings up the standardized test, the SAT, at several points. Summarize these findings by answering the following questions: (LO 9.5)
   How are SAT scores affected by training courses?

   Are SAT scores correlated with college grades?

   What factors might explain these observed relations?

7. "IQ-type" assessments taken in the first few years of life do not correlate with later IQ, yet measures of speed of habituation do show moderate correlations with later IQ. Why do you think early IQ measures do not predict later IQ measures but a measure of information processing does predict later IQ? (LO 9.5)

8. Terman's study of exceptional individuals with IQs above 135 dispelled several myths about individuals with high IQs. List the myths and the realities. (LO 9.6)

Myths:

Realities:

Research on genius also provided evidence that becoming a genius in one's chosen field takes ….

GENETIC AND ENVIRONMENTAL INFLUENCES ON IQ

1. Complete this sentence: Studies of the correlations between IQs of twins show that identical twins' IQs are generally [higher/lower] compared with correlations between IQs of fraternal twins. (LO 9.7)

These observations suggest that IQ is genetically influenced because…

These observations also suggest that IQ is environmentally influenced because…

2. Findings from adoption studies include the following: (LO 9.7)
   a. Adopted children tend to be more similar to their _____ parents.

   b. Resemblance to adoptive parents _____ with age.

   c. Contributions of the environment are suggested by the observation that adoptive children from deprived environments show _____ IQ when adopted into enriched environments.

   What conclusions can be drawn from these studies?

3. How do adoption studies allow us to separate genetic from environmental influences? (LO 9.7)

4. **T or F**: Later-born children tend to have slightly lower IQs than earlier-born children. Explain. (LO 9.8)

5. Carol Dweck and others study people's beliefs about the nature of intelligence and how these beliefs relate to behavior. According to this research, how does the behavior of people who believe in a fixed (unchanging) intelligence tend to differ from the behavior of people who believe intelligence is flexible? (LO 9.8)

Do you tend to see intelligence as fixed or flexible? Do you see the same relation between your belief and your behavior as the relations observed by Dweck?

6. What evidence supports the claim that schooling influences intelligence? (LO 9.8)

7. Discuss the ways that poverty might influence children's IQ scores. (LO 9.8)

8. What is the Flynn effect? (LO 9.8)

What possible explanations for the effect have been proposed?

Can you think of others?

GROUP DIFFERENCES IN IQ: THE SCIENCE AND THE POLITICS

1. Complete this sentence, and then draw and label overlapping bell curves (i.e., men, women) to reflect your answer. Finally, check your answer and drawing with Figure 9.15.

Although gender differences [do/do not] appear in average IQ scores, more [men/women] are at both the low and the high ends of the IQ bell curve. (LO 9.9)

2. Men and women tend to score at the same level on most intellectual tasks. However, women tend to score higher on tasks involving _____, and men tend to score higher on tasks involving _____. (LO 9.9)

3. Complete this sentence, then *explain* your answer.
   The variability [within/between] races tends to be greater than the variability [within/between] races. (LO 9.10)

4. Herrnstein and Murray's book, *The Bell Curve*, contributed to a controversy because it claimed … (LO 9.10)

   Evaluate the evidence that contradicts the book's claim.

   a. Test bias

   b. Misinterpretation of heritability

   c. Stereotype threat

5. T or F: Heredity may contribute to individual differences in intelligence but not necessarily to group differences. Explain your answer. (LO 9.10)

THE REST OF THE STORY: OTHER DIMENSIONS OF INTELLECT

1. Differentiate divergent and convergent thinking and link each with its example. (LO 9.11)

   _____ thinking is . . .

   An example question would be "How many ways could you use a paper cup?"

   _____ thinking is . . .

   An example question would be "What is the area of a 3 x 5 rectangle?"

2. Evaluate the following statement: "The best predictor of the quality of a person's creative accomplishment is the quality of that person's output." (LO 9.11)

3. The personality trait, "openness to experience," is moderately positively correlated with crystallized intelligence. The observation is correlational, which means that several explanations are possible for the relation. Describe at least two possible explanations. (LO 9.12)

4. Emotional intelligence refers to … (LO 9.12)

    Despite its popularity, the concept does not predict variability between individuals beyond …

5. Why might "smart" people nevertheless believe strange things? How is the ideological immune system involved? (LO 9.12)

6. What are the three characteristics of wisdom? Do you know someone you would consider wise? What is it about this person that reflects the characteristic of wisdom? (LO 9.12)

AS YOU READ ... CONCEPT MAP ACTIVITIES

ACTIVITY 1: The various components of intelligence can be summarized by what is called the "hierarchy of mental abilities." Try to describe such a hierarchy. Start with *g* at the top, include the "clusters" or "facets," and then give an example of "specific abilities."

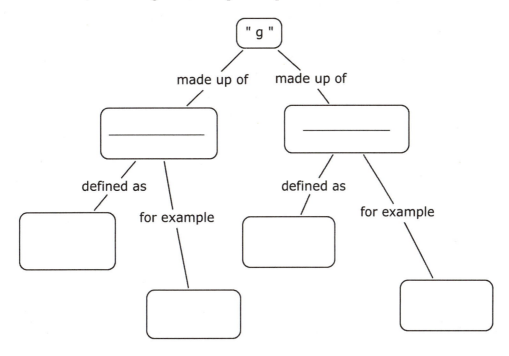

ACTIVITY 2: Summarize the criteria and categories for classifying the degrees of mental retardation.

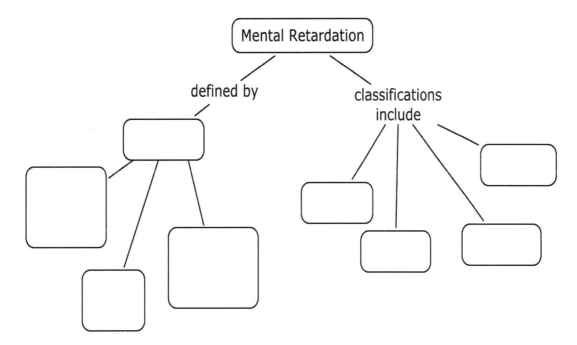

ACTIVITY 3: There are several models of multiple intelligences. Consider how they fit into this concept map but also DRAW LINES CONNECTING the different types across the different models. Clearly, whatever "intelligence" is, it is the same thing that each model is trying to clarify, and there should be connections between them.

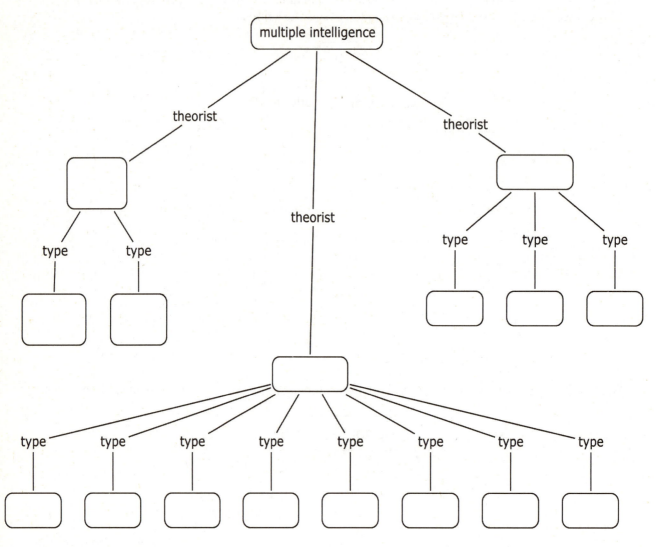

Author activity content supported by *IHMC Cmap Tools* Copyright ©1998-2007 Institute for Human & Machine Cognition

---

AS YOU READ … MYTH OR REALITY?

Myth: Fifty percent of a child's intelligence is acquired by age 4.
Have you heard this claim?
Have you ever thought about what it "means"?
When you do think about it, do you still think it makes sense?

Reality: Not only does the brain remain malleable throughout life, some abilities continue to develop well into late adulthood.

1. The 50% claim is partly based on a misinterpretation of "mental test data." As the text notes, developmental tests before the age of 4 tend to have low reliability and to be unrelated to (poor predictors of) later IQ scores. By age 4, however, you can predict with about 50% accuracy what a child's IQ test score will be at age 17. Why does this statistical finding not translate to the claim as stated?

Myth: Highly stimulating early environments are critical for infant intellectual development.
Reality: Most normal environments provide adequate stimulation for infant development.

1. Like the 50% misconception, infant stimulation claims are partly based on a misinterpretation of research. Research does show a negative effect of deprived environments on intelligence. However, adding more stimulation to already normal environments is an overextrapolation of the findings. It is the overextrapolation that seems to dominate the market for infant products. Look for websites marketing "infant stimulation" products. How have these marketers misinterpreted the scientific research?

AS YOU READ ... PUT YOUR SCIENTIFIC THINKING SKILLS TO THE TEST

1. The Flynn effect reflects the observation that average IQ scores have been rising. Based on your understanding of the factors influencing IQ, is it possible "We are getting less dumb" rather than "We are getting smarter"? What evidence would support such an interpretation?

2. If Dweck's work on the relations between perceptions of ability and effort are correct, why might the current obsession with performance and testing students be undermining their learning?

3. As the text notes, early intervention programs result in positive effects such as lower high school dropout rates but do not produce lasting increases in IQ. Reflecting on these findings, Brooks-Gunn stated, "It is unrealistic, given our knowledge of development, to expect short-term early interventions to last indefinitely, especially if children end up attending poor quality schools. It is magical thinking to expect that if we intervene in the early years, no further help will be needed by children in the elementary school years and beyond."
    http://www.srcd.org/Documents/Publications/SPR/spr17-1.pdf
    How do concepts presented in this chapter support this statement?

As You Read … MyPsychLab Connection

What Is Intelligence? Definitional Confusion

To become familiar with and to compare non-traditional methods of intelligence, **Explore** *Gardner's multiple intelligences* and *Sternberg's triarchic model of intelligence*.

Intelligence Testing: The Good, the Bad, and the Ugly

Watch the classic video *Assessment of Memory with the Stanford-Binet Intelligence Scale*. The SAT is used for college admissions decisions, but **Watch** *SAT Alternatives: Robert Sternberg* to learn more about academic achievement tests. **Watch** Robert Guthrie, author of <u>Even the Rat Was White,</u> discuss the validity of intelligence tests and what they measure in *Are Intelligence Tests Valid?: Robert Guthrie*.

Genetic and Environmental Influences on IQ

How well do you understand the influences on IQ? Test yourself by **Exploring** *Factors Affecting Intelligence*. What's more important when it comes to intelligence – nature or nurture? To find some clues, **Explore** *Correlations between IQ Scores of Persons of Varying Relationships*.

Group Differences in IQ: The Science and the Politics

Try the **Simulation** *Mental Rotation*, which explains how spatial abilities are tested and allows you to participate. Are there gender differences in IQ? **Watch** *Gender/Spatial Ability: Nora Newcombe* and *Gender Differences: Robert Sternberg*. Did you know that knowledge of a stereotype has been shown to impact scores on tests? **Listen** to the podcast *Stereotype Threat* to find out how. Learn more about spatial abilities with the **Simulation** on *Mental Rotation*.

The Rest of the Story: Other Dimensions of Intellect

Do you think "out of the box?" Test yourself with the **Simulation** *Creativity*.

AFTER YOU READ … PRACTICE TEST #1

Before beginning this practice test, estimate the percent you expect to get correct.
Anticipated percent correct: _____

1. The first intelligence test developed in 1905 by Binet and Simon was designed to solve what practical problem?
   a. To determine which military recruits would serve as officers and which would serve on the front lines.
   b. To identify those who were from "good stock."
   c. To identify school children in need of educational assistance.
   d. To predict career success.

2. In general, experts agree intelligence is demonstrated by
   a. social, emotional, verbal, and artistic ability.
   b. abstract reasoning, adaptive learning, knowledge acquisition, and the ability to learn from experience.
   c. the sensory capacities: visual, auditory, gustatory, and olfactory.
   d. practical, analytical, emotional, and creative ability.

3. Which of the following reflects crystallized intelligence?
   a. Your ability to solve a puzzle you've never seen
   b. Your ability to answer the question "What's the population of the United States?"
   c. Your ability to "size up" people you've just met
   d. Your reaction time

4. Which of the following statements about Gardner's theory of multiple intelligences is NOT true?
   a. He has demonstrated that the eight forms of intelligence are independent from one another.
   b. His claims are partly based on evidence from people with brain damage.
   c. Critics claim that several of his intelligences reflect nonmental talents.
   d. He believes the ability to recognize, identify, and understand animals is an intelligence.

5. Brain volume correlates positively (between .3 and .4) with measured intelligence. What can you say based on this finding?
   a. It's likely that brain size has nothing to do with thinking.
   b. Large brain volume is necessary for high intelligence.
   c. A third variable underlies the observed relation.
   d. We don't know whether these findings reflect a direct causal relation.

6. Modern IQ scores
   a. are calculated as MA/CA x 100.
   b. rely on a statistic called deviation IQ.
   c. reflect simple mental age.
   d. = CA/MA.

7. Although "IQ-type" measures from the first few years of life do not correlate with later IQ, _____ shows moderate correlations with later IQ.
   a. age at which the infant reaches motor-milestones
   b. age at which the child speaks his/her first words
   c. speed of habituation
   d. visual acuity

8. Of those classified as having mental retardation, 85% fall into the _____ category.
    a. mildly retarded
    b. moderately retarded
    c. severely retarded
    d. profoundly retarded

9. Abdul is considered a child genius with an IQ of 145. Based on the research with people with exceptional abilities, which of the following is likely to be TRUE?
    a. He probably spends much time practicing and working on his interests.
    b. He is likely to develop severe psychopathology in adulthood.
    c. He will achieve brilliance with little effort.
    d. He will burn out and become "average" by age 25.

10. IQ studies of adopted children find
    a. adopted children tend to be more similar to their adoptive parents compared with their biological parents.
    b. adopted children's resemblance to their adoptive parents decreases with age.
    c. children adopted from deprived environments are unaffected by their enriched adoptive environments.
    d. IQs of unrelated adopted children, raised in the same family, are highly correlated

11. According to Dweck and others who have studied people's beliefs about intelligence, people who believe that intelligence is a fixed entity tend to
    a. become energized after failure.
    b. believe that effort contributes to the development of knowledge.
    c. persist on difficult tasks.
    d. avoid challenging tasks.

12. Although _____ gender differences are found in average IQ scores, more _____ are at both the low and the high ends of the IQ bell curve.
    a. few; men.
    b. few; women.
    c. some; men.
    d. some; women.

13. Herrnstein and Murray's book, *The Bell Curve*, contributed to a controversy because it claimed that
    a. the dominant culture had created tests that were biased against subcultures.
    b. the media had a tendency to misinterpret the concept of heritability racial differences.
    c. intelligence was the result of genetic differences between races.
    d. observed racial differences in IQ were really the result of stereotype threat.

14. Which of the following statement about heritability is TRUE?
    a. The variability between races tends to be greater than the variability within races.
    b. Because IQ is heritable, differences between groups are the result of genetic differences.
    c. Because IQ is heritable, racial difference in IQ are heritable.
    d. Within-group heritability doesn't necessarily imply between-group heritability.

15. Stereotype threat can become a self-fulfilling prophecy when
    a. people perform on IQ tests to match racial stereotypes.
    b. one considers race independent of gender.
    c. people intentionally perform in a way to match a stereotype for the ethnic group.
    d. teachers teach differently to children of different races.

16. Which of the following ideas do you think psychologists would consider creative?
    a. Washing your car by driving it into a lake
    b. Developing a liquid paper to cover mistakes in typing
    c. Killing flies with darts
    d. Correctly identifying all 50 U.S. state capitals

17. Proponents of emotional intelligence point to the fact that
    a. people high in emotional intelligence effectively use their understanding of others' emotions in their everyday lives.
    b. this concept measures a general personality trait.
    c. measures of EQ are better than tests of general intelligence to predict job performance.
    d. different measures of EQ each provide a unique assessment.

18. Which of the following individuals demonstrates LOW levels of emotional intelligence?
    a. Lupe can tell from a distance when her husband is angry.
    b. Alicia goes for a walk when stressed by work.
    c. Mikhail ignores his mother when she is angry because he feels she gets angry for no reason.
    d. Anna knows her father will be mad if she leaves a mess in the kitchen.

19. What are the three characteristics of wisdom?
    a. Concern for self, concern for others, and concern for society
    b. Practical intelligence, analytic intelligence, and creative intelligence
    c. Age, IQ, and creativity
    d. Verbal ability, social concern, and emotional intelligence

20. Which of the following reflects the text's discussion of "smart" people?
    a. Smart people are immune to the belief in strange things.
    b. The strength of the ideological immune system is negatively related to IQ.
    c. People with high IQs are vulnerable to the sense of knowing everything.
    d. The higher the IQ, the more likely one is to consider alternative explanations.

After completing the test, calculate your percent correct
(/ 20 =   ) x 100 = _____ .

How accurate were your expectations? Does your performance suggest the need for additional study?
For the items you missed, go back and identify why the "correct" answer is the best answer.

AFTER YOU READ ... PRACTICE TEST #2

Before beginning this practice test, estimate the percent you expect to get correct.
Anticipated percent correct: _____

1. The personality trait, "openness to experience," is moderately positively correlated with crystallized intelligence, which indicates that
    a. intellectually curious people expose themselves to more knowledge and learn more.
    b. people who know more find learning difficult as their knowledge increases.
    c. with only a moderate correlation, no real link is likely between the trait and intelligence.
    d. people who are "open to experience" lack "street smarts."

2. Which of the following is TRUE?
    a. Although some abilities cluster together, little evidence indicates a "general intelligence."
    b. Correlations among the variety of items assessing intelligence prove that a single common factor underlies individual differences in IQ.
    c. Our ability to solve spatial problems is due to our general problem-solving ability and also to our specific spatial ability.
    d. The finding that items on intelligence tests do not correlate supports the notion of multiple intelligences.

3. Fluid intelligence
    a. increases steadily through adulthood.
    b. reflects the accumulation of information.
    c. is uncorrelated with crystallized intelligence.
    d. is measured by items such as the ability to solve novel puzzles.

4. Which of the following is one of Sternberg's proposed three domains of intelligence?
    a. practical intelligence, or "street smarts."
    b. *g,* or global intelligence.
    c. spatial intelligence, or the ability to think about objects in three dimensions.
    d. emotional intelligence, or the ability to understand and control emotion.

5. Research on the biological basis of intelligence and information processing suggests at least some validity to the idea that people who are intelligent are "quick minded." What sort of evidence supports this view?
    a. Measured intelligence correlates negatively with reaction time.
    b. A moderate correlation is evident between brain volume and measure of intelligence.
    c. Most items on intelligence tests tend to be intercorrelated.
    d. Psychologists refer to thinking as information processing.

6. What is the main lesson of Kruger and Dunning's work on how well we know whether we know?
    a. Most people are able to accurately estimate their own level of intelligence (IQ).
    b. People with low levels of skill in a given domain may overestimate their performance because they don't know that they don't know.
    c. People who perform poorly on a job are clearly aware of their poor level of performance.
    d. Self-reports can be used to estimate IQ

7. The eugenics movement
   a. was based on careful redesign of childhood IQ tests to make them appropriate for use with adults.
   b. recommended but never required the sterilization of low IQ individuals.
   c. was an effort to improve a population's "genetic stock."
   d. highly implicated in the Flynn effect.

8. The Raven's Progressive Matrices test
   a. is considered a "culturally fair test."
   b. provides both verbal and performance scores.
   c. includes questions such as "How is a dog and a rose alike?"
   d. assesses memory for lists of digits.

9. According to the text's discussion of the standardized test,
   a. SAT scores are uncorrelated with IQ scores.
   b. SAT scores are uncorrelated with first-year college grades.
   c. SAT scores are strongly correlated with later college grades.
   d. SAT scores' modest improvement with prep courses is likely due to practice effects.

10. The reason that many studies fail to show a predictive relationship between standardized admissions test scores and school grade point average (GPA) may be that
    a. there truly is no predictive relationship to be demonstrated.
    b. all too often only a restricted range of test scores is examined.
    c. the type of material on admissions tests does not represent real school work.
    d. they are frequently examined with scatterplots rather than true statistical tests.

11. The threshold effect refers to the finding that
    a. above a certain level of intelligence, IQ stops being differentially predictive of real-world behavior.
    b. one must have a certain minimal amount of intelligence for IQ tests to accurately determine one's IQ.
    c. the mean is set at 100 because those who score above 100 are more likely to be successful in life than are those who score below 100.
    d. people tend to have children with other people who are of similar IQ to their own.

12. Terman and others who study exceptional individuals have found that children with high IQs
    a. demonstrate exceptional abilities with little effort.
    b. burn out at an early age.
    c. suffer from poor physical health.
    d. demonstrate normal mental health.

13. Which of the following findings provides evidence that the family environment influences the development of intelligent behavior?
    a. Identical twins are more similar in IQ than fraternal twins.
    b. Siblings reared together are more similar in IQ than are siblings reared apart.
    c. Identical twins reared apart are more similar in IQ than are siblings reared together.
    d. Adopted children are more similar in IQ to their biological mother than to their adopted mother.

14. Which of the following family members would likely be the MOST similar in IQ?
    a. Mother and father
    b. Mother and biological child
    c. Identical twins
    d. Fraternal twins

15. Which piece of research provides the strongest evidence that schooling exerts an influence on IQ?
    a. Number of years in school correlates .60 with IQ.
    b. Individuals with high IQ scores enjoy taking classes more than individual with low IQ scores.
    c. When comparing children of the same age who differ in years in school, children who've attended an extra year of school tend to have higher IQs.
    d. Children's IQs increase significantly during the summer months.

16. Poverty can influence children's IQ scores
    a. by influencing quality of nutrition.
    b. by providing special services, such as Head Start.
    c. because poverty is influenced by genetic factors.
    d. because they are more often breast-fed as infants.

17. What is the Flynn effect?
    a. The finding that earlier-borns score higher on tests of intelligence compared with later-borns.
    b. The finding that the least competent are likely to have the most confidence in their competence.
    c. The finding that average intelligence scores have been rising over time.
    d. The finding that crystallized intelligence can increase throughout adulthood.

18. Which of the following statements about gender differences in IQ is TRUE?
    a. Men and women tend to score at the same level on most intellectual tasks.
    b. Women tend to score higher on tasks requiring spatial abilities.
    c. Men tend to score higher on tasks requiring verbal abilities.
    d. More women fall at the lower end and more men fall at the higher end of the IQ distribution.

19. IQ tests have been shown to be good predictors of _____, but NOT good predictors of _____.
    a. school performance; crime-proneness
    b. health literacy; health-related outcomes
    c. job performance; school performance
    d. school performance; creativity

20. Avery is developing a measure of creativity. Which of the following questions would she be likely to include in her assessment?
    a. You have 2 pair of black and 2 pair of brown socks in a drawer. The room is pitch black. How many socks to you need to pull out to be sure you have at least one pair?
    b. 7,695 x 15,480 = ?
    c. How many uses can you think of for a shoe?
    d. In order to duplicate this pattern *#^#*#^#*____ , what shape would come next?

After completing the test, calculate your percent correct
(/20 =   ) x 100 = _____.

How accurate were your expectations? Does your performance suggest need for additional study? For the items you missed, go back and identify why the "correct" answer is the best answer.

AFTER YOU READ ... PRACTICE TEST ANSWER KEYS

Practice Test 1.

1. c (p. 319)
2. b (p. 320)
3. b (p. 321)
4. a (p. 322-323)
5. d (p. 324)
6. b (p. 327)
7. c (p. 333)
8. a (p. 335)
9. a (p. 336)
10. b (p. 338)
11. d (p. 339)
12. a (p. 343)
13. c (p. 345-346)
14. d (p. 347)
15. a (p. 349)
16. b (p. 350)
17. a (p. 351)
18. c (p. 351)
19. a (p. 352)
20. c (p. 353)

Practice Test 2.

1. a (p. 321)
2. c (p. 322)
3. d (p. 321)
4. a (p. 323)
5. a (p. 325)
6. b (p. 326)
7. c (p. 327-328)
8. a (p. 330)
9. d (p. 330-331)
10. c (p. 332)
11. a (p. 334)
12. d (p. 336)
13. b (p. 337)
14. c (p. 337-338)
15. c (p. 339)
16. a (p. 340-341)
17. c (p. 341)
18. a (p. 344)
19. d (p. 334, 350)
20. c (p. 350)

AFTER YOU READ ... CONCEPT MAPPING ACTIVITY ANSWERS

ACTIVITY 1: In this hierarchy of mental abilities, several "examples" of abilities are possible.

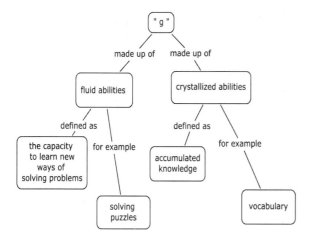

ACTIVITY 2: Summarize the criteria and categories for classifying the degrees of mental retardation.

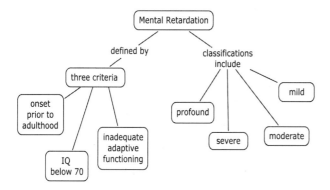

ACTIVITY 3: There are several models of multiple intelligences. Consider how they fit into this concept map.

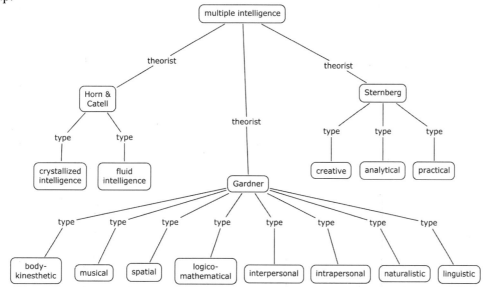

CHAPTER 10
HUMAN DEVELOPMENT
HOW AND WHY WE CHANGE

BEFORE YOU READ ... CHAPTER PREVIEW

Developmental psychology is the study of how behavior changes over the lifespan. It is a particularly complex division of psychology. One of the challenges is avoiding the **post hoc fallacy**—the belief that because one event preceded another the two are causally related. In fact, human development is *bidirectional*. Parents may influence their children's behavior, but children also influence parents' behavior. Two important misconceptions regarding child development are the ideas of *infant determinism* and *childhood fragility*.

Recognizing the difficulties in studying development, researchers draw conclusions cautiously. **Cross-sectional methods** compare individuals of different ages measured at the same point in time so they can tell us about age differences but not age-related changes, and might be susceptible to **cohort effects** because the comparisons are between different people (different *cohorts*) who may differ in ways other than age. **Longitudinal designs** examine the same people over time and can tell us that the people we observed changed over time. The *nature* or *nurture* question generally asks how these two combine to influence development. It is likely that the two *interact*. The **gene-environment interaction** is complex. In **nature via nurture,** a genetic predisposition may lead a person to create a favorable environment. In **gene expression,** the environment may influence the expression of genes.

Understanding child development begins with an understanding of **prenatal** development. During the *germinal stage,* the fertilized egg, or zygote, forms a **blastocyst.** In the *embryonic stage,* the **embryo** takes on human shape. In the *fetal stage,* the **fetus** continues physical maturation. There is tremendous *proliferation* of neurons. Development can be derailed by genetic errors, by environmental influences (**teratogens**—for example, **fetal alcohol syndrome**), and by premature birth. A full-term pregnancy is 40 weeks and a full-term baby weighs 7.5 pounds. Before 36 weeks, babies are considered premature. *Viability* occurs around 22-25 weeks. Babies are born with *reflexes*, including the *sucking* and *rooting reflex* that play survival roles. Self-initiated **motor behaviors** develop over time; motor milestones vary but have a generally uniform sequence. The head-to-body ratio decreases until **adolescence** in a relatively continuous fashion, with a few spurts, when bodies reach full physical maturity. At this time, individuals go through **puberty**, or *sexual maturation*. Both **primary** and **secondary sex characteristics** develop, with **menarche** in girls and **spermarche** in boys. After a physical peak in the twenties, there is a slow but steady decrease in muscle tone and increase in body fat. Fertility in women declines until **menopause**.

Cognitive development refers to the study of how we develop the ability to think, reason, and remember. In Piaget's *stage theory,* children are active participants in their acquisition of knowledge about their world, with cognitive change marked by *equilibration* and *schema* development. **Assimilation** (using an existing schema to interpret new information) and **accommodation** (changing one's schema based on new information) are the cornerstones of this framework. Piaget believed that individuals progress through qualitatively different cognitive stages: a **sensorimotor stage** when children develop *mental representations*, **object permanence,** and *deferred imitation*; a **preoperational stage** where **egocentrism** dominates and **conservation** develops; a **concrete operational stage** where mental operations develop; and a **formal operations stage,** which involves the ability to reason logically about abstract problems. Although Piaget made an enormous contribution to the study of cognitive development, his model cannot be falsified because of *horizontal decalage* and culturally biased methods.

Vygotsky saw children as active participants in the acquisition of knowledge, but emphasized the role of the social environment in cognitive development, especially in developing **scaffolding**. He identified the **zone of proximal development** as a level of performance the individual is capable of achieving with assistance. Children develop many incorrect conceptions of how the world operates, especially obvious with *naïve physics*, and many of which persist into adulthood. By age one, children show a sense of self. By age four, children begin to develop a **theory of mind**—the understanding that one person can know something another does not—often tested with the *false-belief task*. By adolescence, the frontal lobes fully develop so well-reasoned decisions can be made. However, many adolescents still fall prey to the *personal fable*. College-aged individuals can realize that truth and reality "depend" on different perspectives. With advancing age, cognitive functions decline somewhat. Free recall and crystallized intelligence decline with age, but cued recall and recognition do not.

Infants are predisposed to develop social relationships. Around eight months of age, they develop **stranger anxiety**. **Temperament** is *early appearing* and *largely genetic* in origin and reflects an infant's basic emotional style (*easy, difficult, slow-to-warm-up, behaviorally inhibited*). Infants' temperament can be bidirectional to influence **attachment**. Although many animals show *imprinting* that occurs during a *critical period*, this is not true for humans. The attachment bond in many mammals is based on **contact comfort**. Using various techniques, such as the *Strange Situation*, researchers have identified several patterns of attachment styles: secure (infant freely explores from a *secure base*), insecure-avoidant, insecure-anxious, and disorganized. These patterns depend on caregiver responsiveness and infant temperament. The Strange Situation is prone to a **mono-operation bias** and isn't especially *reliable*.

In assuming child behavior is monodirectional, much parenting advice is at odds with research evidence. Some recommendations are *child-centered*, and others are *parent-centered*. Optimal development appears in children whose parents are *authoritative* rather than permissive, uninvolved, or authoritarian. Children growing up in *individualistic cultures* respond differently to parenting styles than children growing up in *collectivist cultures*, with most parents providing an **average expectable environment.** According to **group socialization theory**, peers can be more important than parents.

Researchers have examined **self-control**. The ability to delay gratification in childhood predicts coping in adolescence. Gender concepts affect children's understanding of themselves as social beings. The term "sex" refers to individuals' biological status; the term "gender" refers to psychological characteristics. **Gender identity** refers to people's sense of being male or female. Some people have a *gender identity disorder*, sometimes called *transsexualism*. **Gender role** refers to the behaviors that accompany being male or female. Some gender differences are seen in early infancy and toy preferences may reflect differences in biological predispositions. *Sex segregation* suggests that children understand differences between genders very early. Research supports the effects of nurture: parents often encourage children to engage in gender-stereotyped behaviors. The teenage years are a time of dramatic changes in body, brain, and social activities as well as a time of discovery, participation in adult-like activities, and deep friendships. The idea of adolescence as turbulent is a myth. Erik Erikson developed a comprehensive theory of how identity develops and coined the term *identity crisis*. Erikson believed we confront different **psychosocial crises.** Researchers now define the period of life between 18 and 25 as **emerging adulthood**, during which there is much *role experimentation*.

Young children develop ideas of right and wrong but *moral dilemmas* arise more often later in life. Moral understanding appears rooted in fear. Piaget believed moral development depends on cognitive development, comparing *objective responsibility* with *subjective responsibility*. Kohlberg identified how morality unfolds across the life span, suggesting three stages: *preconventional morality (*focused on punishment and reward), *conventional morality* (focused on societal values), and *postconventional morality (*focused on internal moral principles). Kohlberg's work has been widely criticized.

There is no single trajectory in adulthood. Fewer than 25% of adults live in conventional nuclear families. American workers change jobs frequently. People in serious long-term relationships are generally happier. Parenthood is the biggest transition for adults. Middle age presents new challenges; however, a **midlife crisis**, including the **empty nest syndrome,** is a myth. Life expectancy of the average American man is 75.3; for the American woman, it's 80.4. Contrary to popular belief, depression is less common among the elderly than it is among younger people. Some indices other than chronological age include biological age, psychological age, functional age, and social age. Remaining physically and mentally active can promote a younger body and mind.

BEFORE YOU READ ... LEARNING OBJECTIVES

After reading Chapter 10 you should be able to:

10.1   Identify ways to think scientifically about developmental findings
10.2   Clarify how nature and nurture can contribute to development
10.3   Track the trajectory of prenatal development and identify barriers to normal development
10.4   Describe how infants learn to coordinate motion and achieve major motor milestones
10.5   Describe physical maturation during childhood and adolescence
10.6   Explain which aspects of physical ability decline during aging
10.7   Understand major theories of how children's thinking develops
10.8   Explain how children acquire knowledge in important cognitive domains
10.9   Describe how attitudes toward knowledge change during adolescence
10.10   Describe how and when children establish emotional bonds with their caregivers
10.11   Explain the environmental and genetic influences on social behavior and social style in children
10.12   Determine how morality and identity develop during adolescence and emerging adulthood
10.13   Identify developmental changes during major life transitions in adults
10.14   Summarize different ways of conceptualizing old age

BEFORE YOU READ ... TERM IDENTIFICATION

accommodation (p. 372)
adolescence (p. 368)
assimilation (p. 372)
attachment (p. 384)
average expectable environment (p. 389)
blastocyst (p. 364)
cognitive development (p. 371)
cohort effect (p. 362)
concrete operations stage (p. 374)
conservation (p. 374)
contact comfort (p. 386)
cross-sectional design (p. 362)
developmental psychology (p. 361)
egocentrism (p. 374)
embryo (p. 364)
emerging adulthood (p. 394)
empty-nest syndrome (p. 398)
fetal alcohol syndrome (p. 366)
fetus (p. 364)
formal operations stage (p. 375)
gender identity (p. 392)
gender role (p. 392)
gene expression (p. 364)
gene-environment interaction (p. 364)
identity (p. 392)

longitudinal design (p. 362)
menarche (p. 369)
menopause (p. 371)
midlife crisis (p. 398)
mono-operation bias (p. 387)
motor behavior (p. 367)
nature via nurture (p. 364)
object permanence (p. 372)
post hoc fallacy (p. 361)
prenatal (p. 364)
preoperational stage (p. 372)
primary sex characteristic (p. 369)
psychosocial crisis (p. 392)
puberty (p. 368)
scaffolding (p. 376)
secondary sex characteristic (p. 369)
self-control (p. 391)
sensorimotor stage (p. 372)
spermarche (p. 369)
stranger anxiety (p. 383)
temperament (p. 383)
teratogen (p. 366)
theory of mind (p. 379)
zone of proximal development (p. 376)
zygote (p. 364)

As You Read ... Practice Activities

SPECIAL CONSIDERATIONS IN HUMAN DEVELOPMENT

1. What is the post hoc fallacy? Why do we need to be particularly attentive to this fallacy when studying development? (LO 10.1)

2. Describe the following myths and realities: (LO 10.1)

   Myth: Infant determinism

   Reality:

   Myth: Childhood fragility

   Reality:

3. Why should we be particularly cautious in drawing conclusions from developmental designs? (Hint: Is either the longitudinal or cross-sectional design a "true experiment"?) (LO 10.1)

4. List three ways nature and nurture can interact. Give an example of how nature and nurture can have reciprocal (bidirectional) effects. (LO 10.2)

THE DEVELOPING BODY: PHYSICAL AND MOTOR DEVELOPMENT

1. Match the stage of prenatal development with its description. (LO 10.3)

   a. blastocyst _____ period during which limbs, features, and organs take form

   b. embryo _____ ball of identical cells that have not yet begun to take on specific functions

   c. fetus _____ period of physical maturation of organs

2. Why might teratogens have their greatest effect on the development of major structures if exposure occurs during the embryonic period? (LO 10.3)

3. Motor movements at birth include several reflexes. Describe the adaptive value of the two discussed in your text. (LO 10.4)

   a.

   b.

4. T or F: Children tend to achieve motor milestones in the same order even though the age of acquisition may vary. Explain your answer (i.e., the factors that might contribute to this statement being true or false). (LO 10.4)

5. Think about both the advantages and disadvantages of early maturation and complete this grid. How would these differ for boys and girls? (LO10.5)

Advantages		Disadvantages		
Boys	**Girls**	**Boys**	**Girls**	
				Early Puberty
				Late Puberty

6. Describe the normally experienced changes that are associated with old age. (LO 10.6)

THE DEVELOPING MIND: COGNITIVE DEVELOPMENT

1. Complete this chart of the Piagetian Stages of Cognitive Development with their primary achievement. (LO 10.7)

Stage	Age	Primary Way of Thinking
		Thinks in terms of physical interactions with objects
		Thinks in terms of representations Does not understand that objects retain identity despite transformation
		Operates on physical representations Cannot operate on the abstractions
		Can reason in terms of the hypothetical and abstract; thinks systematically

2. Use the following terms to complete this chart comparing the similarities and differences between Piaget's and Vygotsky's theories of cognitive development. (LO 10.7)

Claims: active learner; social environment key; physical environment key; ZPD; domain-general development; domain-specific development; stages of cognitive development

Piaget claims	Both claim	Vygotsky claims

3. Why would Vygotsky suggest that playing with a child would do more to foster cognitive development than would playing Mozart music or showing a *Baby Einstein* video? (LO 10.7 & 10.8)

4. Discuss the concept of "theory of mind." What is it? How is it assessed? Why do you think the structure of the assessment affects the child's performance? (LO 10.8)

5. What is the evidence that calls into question the concept of a "personal fable"? (LO 10.9)

6. About the time that young adults begin college, most begin to realize that some answers are more "right" than others, even if something being "right" often "depends on" other things. How might this impact learning across the college years? (*Hint:* Read about Perry's research in your text.) (LO 10.9)

THE DEVELOPING PERSONALITY: SOCIAL AND MORAL DEVELOPMENT

1. T or F: Infants differ from one another in terms of personality, at birth. Explain your answer. (LO 10.10)

2. What are the patterns of attachment? How is the attachment relationship generally studied? Why is it important to understand the method by which attachment is studied in order to understand the limitations of the claims made from these studies? (LO 10.10)

3. Contact comfort rather than nourishment appears to underlie the attachment relationship. What implication does this finding hold for fathers? (LO 10.10)

4. T or F: Stranger anxiety demonstrates a problem in the attachment relationship. Explain your answer. (LO 10.10)

5. Match the parenting "style" with its example. (LO 10.10)

    a. Authoritative   _____ "You will do it because I told you to!"

    b. Authoritarian   _____ "Sure honey, you can stay up as long as you want."

    c. Permissive   _____ "We want you to call if you will be late because we worry about the irresponsible drivers out there."

    d. Uninvolved   _____ "I don't care what you do. Just leave me alone!"

6. Authoritative parents tend to have competent children. Because this finding is correlational, the parents may not be the cause or the only cause of child behavior. What other factors are likely to account for the observed relation? (Don't forget bidirectional influences.) (LO 10.10)

7. Discuss how gender roles might have a "nurture" effect on gender identity. (LO10.11)

8. Summarize the five major criticisms of Kohlberg's model of moral development. (LO 10.12)

    a.

    b.

    c.

    d.

    e.

9. Briefly summarize these three major life transitions in adulthood: (LO10.13)

    a. Careers:

    b. Love & Commitment:

    c. Parenthood:

10. Discuss each of these myths of adult development and their reality. (LO 10.13)

Myth: Most men experience a midlife crisis in which they try to regain their youth.
Reality:

Myth: Menopause is a period of increased depression for women.
Reality:

Myth: Depression in mothers follows "flight of their children" and their empty nest.
Reality:

Myth: Mental decline in all cognitive domains is inevitable with old age.
Reality:

11. Describe the four ways we can measure "age" as we get older. (LO 10.14)

AS YOU READ ... CONCEPT MAP ACTIVITIES

ACTIVITY 1: Please complete this concept map which allows you to compare developmental research designs.

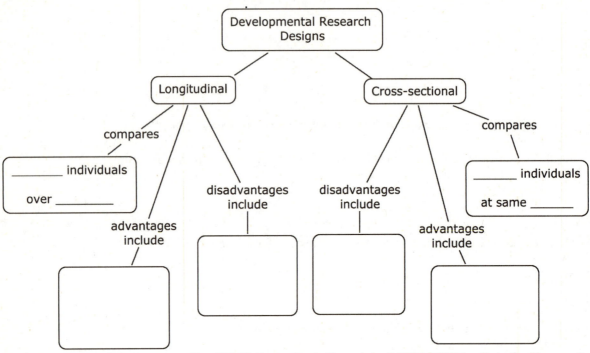

Author content activity supported by *IHMC Cmap Tools* Copyright ©1998-2007 Institute for Human & Machine Cognition

ACTIVITY 2: Complete this concept map with important details of both prenatal and perinatal development.

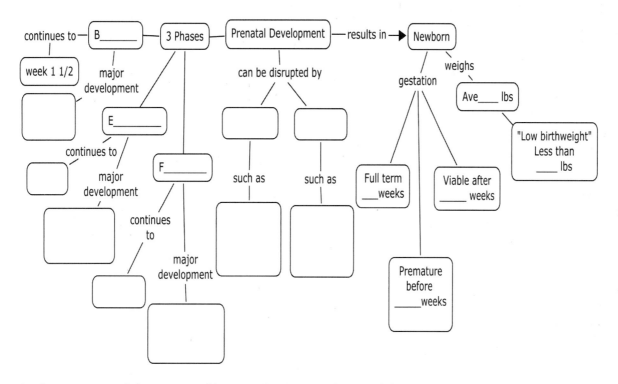

Author content activity supported by *IHMC Cmap Tools* Copyright ©1998-2007 Institute for Human & Machine Cognition

AS YOU READ… MYTH OR REALITY?

Myth: Mozart music increases the intelligence of infants.
Reality: Music may influence performance by influencing arousal but has no demonstrated, lasting effect on intelligence.

A good brief description of the original research may be found at http://faculty.washinton.edu/chudler/. Look at the researchers' operational definition of variables, the research design, and the sample studied. How do the claims go way beyond the data?

Myth: Many children have been killed by poisons or dangerous objects put into their Halloween candy.
Reality: Few documented injuries have been caused by Halloween candy.

As the discussion of the availability heuristic in Chapter 2 suggested, we tend to worry about the wrong things because our attention is grabbed by the dramatic or the memorable. For example, compare the number of deaths per year from Halloween candy with the number of deaths due to diarrhea. Why do you think we pay more attention to Halloween candy?

http://www.livescience.com/strangenews/051025_halloween_candy.html
http://www.time.com/time/magazine/article/0,9171,901061016-1543876,00.html
http://rehydrate.org/

AS YOU READ … PUT YOUR SCIENTIFIC THINKING SKILLS TO THE TEST

---

1. Extraordinary claims require extraordinary evidence. The following claims are made in *Child Genius Magazine*. Check out the website and evaluate whether the claims have empirical support. http://www.internationalparentingassociation.org/BrainDevelopment/mobility1.html

How would the average reader know whether these claims are actually supported? For example, this passage comes from the website:

> The moment a child is conceived is not too early to start focusing on the child's vast learning potential. In the fetus, the brain is developing rapidly. The right hemisphere is highly active while the left hemisphere is relatively dormant. In this manner, the soul of the child is endowed with extrasensory perception, which is carried out through the phenomenal fetal right brain in connection with every single cell of the fetal body—the cells themselves being ESP receptors.

2. The site also claims that crawling is not only essential for brain development but that promoting early crawling can promote intellectual development, or super babies. How do the following claims reflect a misunderstanding and an overgeneralization from correlational data?

> It is important to understand that these … areas of child development are related … if a child improves in one area, such as hearing, [one] would find some improvement in all the other areas as well. This demonstrates how physical achievement is associated with mental achievement. The amount of crawling and creeping a baby does will have an effect on how well that child can see and hear and how well he will be able to speak and read.

AS YOU READ ... MYPSYCHLAB CONNECTION

Special Consideration in Human Development

To become a better consumer of developmental research, **Explore** *Cross-Sectional and Longitudinal Research Designs*, which explains the advantages and disadvantage of each design. **Listen** to the podcast *Research Designs*, an interactive conversation about the conclusions we can draw from cross-sectional and longitudinal designs.

The Developing Body: Physical and Motor Development

Many videos illustrate key concepts in fetal development. **Watch** *Fetal Development* for an overview. **Watch** *Period of the Zygote* to see the cells after fertilization and *Brain Development and Nutrition* to see how brain growth is affected by diet. Learn how brain development occurs, **Explore** *Dendritic Spreading: Forming Interconnections in the Brain*. After learning about embryonic development, **Explore** *The Embryonic Period: a Critical Period of Human Development* to see what changes occur during this stage. To examine what an infant should be doing developmentally, **Explore** *Infants Perceptual & Cognitive Milestones*. What reflexes do newborns have? **Watch** *Reflexes: Babinski, Reflexes: Moro, Reflexes: Palmar Grasp, Reflexes: Sucking,* and *The Newborns Reflexes* to learn about and see the reflexes in action. Is motor development a progressive series of stages? **Watch** *Motor Development in Infants and Toddlers: Karen Adolph* to find out. The **Simulation** *Teratogens and Their Effects* allows you to role-play a physician in diagnosing what medication, chemical, or environmental agent has interfered with normal development. **Explore** Erikson's theory with *Erikson's First Four Stages of Psychosocial Development.* For a summary of physical and cognitive changes, **Explore** the interactive table in *Major Changes in Important Domains of Adult Functioning* and **Watch** *Aging and Changes in Physical Appearance.* For a direct perspective on aging, **Watch** an interview with a *Centenarian.*

The Developing Mind: Cognitive Development

To grasp Piagetian concepts, **Explore** *Piaget's Stages of Cognitive Development* then **Watch** *The Sensorimotor Stage, Conservation of Liquids,* and *The Preoperational & Concrete Operational Stage.* To understand Vygotsky's model, **Watch** *Zone of Proximal Development.*

The Developing Personality: Social and Moral Development

Test your knowledge of attachment styles with the **Simulation** *Attachment Classifications in the Strange Situation.* A set of videos demonstrates different temperaments of infants: **Watch** *Temperament: Difficult* and *Temperament: Easy.* There are also two videos that illustrate attachment and separation issues of infants: **Watch** *Attachment in Infants, Stranger Anxiety* and *Separation Anxiety.* Then participate in the **Simulation** of *Attachment Classifications in the Strange Situation.* To examine the effects of divorce on children, **Watch** *Pam: A Divorced Mother of a Nine-Year Old. Early Gender Typing* recreates research by Patricia Bauer, showing that children as young as two prefer gender type toys. Next, **Watch** *Erikson's Last Four Stages of Psychosocial Development.* The **Simulation** *Kohlberg's Stages of Moral Reasoning* provides another interactive test of children's responses on the Heinz moral dilemma task. Then, **Watch** *Moral Development: Postconventional.* To learn more about parenthood, **Watch** *Jess: Expecting First Child.* See the different ways aging can be defined. **Watch** *A 92-Year Old Volunteer.*

Before beginning this practice test, estimate the percent you expect to get correct.
Anticipated percent correct: _____

1. Children often change their environment by acting in ways that influence their parents to respond differently from how they might have otherwise. This is an example of
   a. unidirectional effects.
   b. infant determinism.
   c. bidirectional effects.
   d. group socialization effects.

2. If we wanted to know whether aggressive 10-year-old boys will grow up to be aggressive 15-year-old teenagers, we would most likely conduct
   a. a clinical study.
   b. a true experiment.
   c. a cross-sectional study.
   d. a longitudinal study.

3. One advantage of the cross-sectional design over the longitudinal design is
   a. one doesn't have to worry about the cohort effect confound.
   b. it is simpler to conduct than the longitudinal design.
   c. it allows the researcher to observe individuals change over time.
   d. the need to track the same people over a lengthy period of time.

4. An ad for an infant computer program claims it provides important early stimulation for your infant because "The first three years of life are the most critical for brain development." This ad reflects
   a. the belief in childhood resilience.
   b. the empirical research on infant brain development.
   c. the myth of infant determinism.
   d. the average expectable environment claim.

5. Which of the following occurs during the embryonic period?
   a. Fertilization of the ovum
   b. Development of the heart and lungs
   c. Cell division
   d. Final maturation of the organs

6. Children acquire motor developmental milestones
   a. pretty much in the same order for all normal infants.
   b. pretty much at the same rate for all normal infants.
   c. at a faster rate if they are heavier.
   d. faster if they are swaddled throughout the first year of life.

7. According to Piaget's theory, cognitive development
   a. proceeds through a series of qualitatively different stages.
   b. is dependent on the sociocultural context in which the child is embedded.
   c. is characterized as a passive process of behavior acquisition.
   d. moves through the zone of proximal development.

8. The preoperational stage of cognitive development is an advance over the sensorimotor stage because now the preschool-aged child can think in terms of
   a. representations.
   b. operations.
   c. the hypothetical.
   d. only the here-and-now.

9. One of the criticisms made of Piaget's claims is that
   a. his observations of children's performance seems to be influenced by task demands.
   b. his theory reflects a passive child.
   c. development seems to be more stage-like than he proposed.
   d. development seems to be more general across domains than he proposed.

10. Which of the following would be an example of a scaffold?
    a. Allowing a child to explore a set of graduated size blocks on his/her own
    b. Helping a child solve a puzzle by suggesting he first find all the edge pieces
    c. Reinforcing a child with praise when she brushes her teeth
    d. Using flashcards to teach a child math facts

11. Research indicates that one way the average 17-year-old teenager differs from the average adult is
    a. the teen is in a stage of role confusion while the adult is in a stage of integrity.
    b. the teen is experiencing the most stressful period of the lifespan.
    c. areas of the teen's brain involved in inhibitory control are not fully mature.
    d. the teen has not yet reached sexual maturity.

12. Which of the following students is at the highest level of understanding according to Perry?
    a. "I appreciate professors who help me see the right answers."
    b. "Everyone has a right to his or her own opinion."
    c. "Some opinions are supported by better arguments and evidence."
    d. "If I say the right things, then I'll get a good grade."

13. Which of the following accurately reflects cognitive changes with age?
    a. Compared with younger adults, older adults perform worse on tests of analogies and vocabulary but perform better on tests that require memory for a random list of words.
    b. Elderly people's hearing, sight, and other senses decline but their reaction times are the same as those of younger adults.
    c. Older adults show significant declines in both free recall and cued recall.
    d. Many of the changes associated with aging are more apparent in fluid than crystallized intelligence.

14. Temperament
    a. seems to have genetic and early origins.
    b. is the result of parental responsiveness.
    c. refers to the observation that most babies are temperamentally challenging.
    d. is unrelated to later personality.

15. Research on attachment suggests that
    a. securely attached children are most likely to remain in close proximity to their parents or caregivers.
    b. parents or caregivers who provide nourishment for the infant become primary attachment figures.
    c. early imprinting is important for secure attachment.
    d. temperament can influence the attachment relationship.

16. "We want you to be in by midnight or call and tell us you will be late. We worry about you because we know that there can be many irresponsible drivers on the roads at night." This statement demonstrates what Baumrind characterized as _____ parenting.
    a. permissive
    b. authoritative
    c. authoritarian
    d. restrictive

17. Arnold expects obedience from his children. He often says, "You will do it because I told you to!" According to Baumrind, Arnold's parenting style is
    a. authoritative.
    b. permissive.
    c. authoritarian.
    d. neglectful.

18. Which of the following reflects research based on Kohlberg's theory of moral development?
    a. Moral level seems to have a low correlation with moral behavior.
    b. The assessment of moral reasoning is uncorrelated with verbal intelligence.
    c. People pass through Kohlberg's stages in different orders in different cultures.
    d. Studies clearly show that men perform at higher moral levels compared with women.

19. Adult development differs from child development in that
    a. physical maturation plays a greater role in adulthood compared with childhood.
    b. the course of development in adulthood reflects greater variety in trajectories and in the timing of transitions.
    c. adulthood involves stability while childhood involves change.
    d. adult development is characterized by decline while childhood is characterized by progression.

20. If you wanted to assess the readiness of older adults to retire, it would be appropriate to use
    a. biological age.
    b. social age.
    c. chronological age.
    d. functional age.

After completing the test, calculate your percent correct
(/ 20 =   ) x 100 = _____.

How accurate were your expectations? Does your performance suggest the need for additional study? For the items you missed, go back and identify why the "correct" answer is the best answer.

AFTER YOU READ... PRACTICE TEST #2

Before beginning this practice test, estimate the percent you expect to get correct.

Anticipated percent correct: _____

1. You conduct a study comparing the computer game–playing skill of 10-year-old, 30-year-old, and 50-year-old participants. You find the 10-year-olds outperform the 30-year-olds who outperform the 50-year-olds. Although skill could decline with age, an alternative explanation for your finding is
   a. the post hoc fallacy.
   b. conservation.
   c. the cohort effect.
   d. the habituation effect.

2. Which of the following statements is a valid example of the nature via nurture concept?
   a. Most children exposed to severe stress grow up with severe psychological problems.
   b. Research suggests that highly fearful children tend to seek out environments that protect them from their anxieties.
   c. Children raised in almost total isolation during the first year of life will suffer significant delays through adulthood.
   d. Children with both the low MAO gene and a history of maltreatment are at heightened risk for antisocial behaviors.

3. Which of the following statements regarding early brain development is TRUE?
   a. The fetus ends up manufacturing many more neurons than it will need as an infant.
   b. Neurons do not sort themselves out and move into their final position until well after birth.
   c. Mylenization, pruning, and synaptogenesis are completed by the 36th week of gestation.
   d. Because the brain has a long period of maturation, it is the organ least vulnerable to teratogens.

4. Why might teratogens have their greatest effect on the development of major structures if exposure occurs during the embryonic period?
   a. Major organs are developing during this period.
   b. Fertilization occurs during this period.
   c. Cell division and differentiation occur during period.
   d. Neurons are sorting and organizing themselves during this period.

5. Studies of the effects of teratogens on prenatal development
   a. are cross-sectional studies.
   b. are true experiments.
   c. show there are environmental effect on neural development.
   d. involve exposing pregnant women to various substances.

6. Children tend to achieve motor milestones in the same order even though the age of acquisition may vary. Which of the following statement is the *best* description of what underlies motor development?
   a. Motor development is the result of an innate and inflexible motor program.
   b. Motor development is the result of physical maturation of body.
   c. Motor development is the result of physical maturation and environmental factors.
   d. Motor development is the result of parental practices that encourage or discourage exploration.

234

7. Compared with sensorimotor infants, the preoperational child can
   a. understand the permanence of objects.
   b. perform conservation tasks.
   c. think in terms of representations.
   d. can see the world from outside herself.

8. Based on problems with physical science, such as the pendulum problem, Piaget concluded that adolescents can
   a. problem solve, but only with trial and error.
   b. manipulate abstract ideas and think systematically.
   c. understand that despite the relativity of much knowledge, it is possible to commit to an answer.
   d. solve problems, but with lower levels of formal reasoning compared with adults.

9. Vygotsky would likely recommend
   a. providing lots of toys for your child because the physical environment promotes cognitive development.
   b. playing with your child because social interaction promotes cognitive development.
   c. buying stimulating toys for your infant because early brain stimulation is critical for later brain development.
   d. playing Mozart music for your infant because music promotes intellectual development in infants.

10. Vygotsky and Piaget agreed that
    a. learning mostly occurs because of physical interactions with the environment.
    b. individuals are active in the construction of knowledge.
    c. social interactions are a primary source of learning.
    d. development occurs in four qualitatively different stages.

11. The ability called "theory of mind"
    a. is key in perspective-taking.
    b. does not seem to develop until age 7 or 8.
    c. appears to be innate.
    d. depends on the child's cognitive level and not how researchers structure the task.

12. The development of counting _____ across cultures, whereas stranger anxiety _____ across cultures.
    a. varies greatly; appears identically
    b. appear identically; varies greatly
    c. appears in stages; appears gradually
    d. appears gradually; appears in stages

13. According to Perry's studies of how people understand the concept of "knowledge," college freshmen
    a. enter college with a realistic understanding of knowledge.
    b. see knowledge as relative—there are no right or wrong answers.
    c. develop their views of knowledge over the course of their college years.
    d. find it easy to accept that answers will often depend on the situation.

14. Kagan's studies of temperament found that infants categorized as behaviorally inhibited
    a. were at a heightened risk for shyness and anxiety disorders in childhood.
    b. were at increased risk for impulsive behaviors in later childhood.
    c. are mostly found in collectivist cultures.
    d. account for about 40% of infants.

15. _____ appears to underlie the attachment relationship.
    a. Nourishment
    b. Imprinting
    c. Contact comfort
    d. Reinforcement

16. The attachment relationship is influenced by
    a. infant temperament.
    b. relationships with peers.
    c. parental responsiveness.
    d. the interaction of infant temperament and parental responsiveness.

17. When it comes to non-traditional families,
    a. divorce has long-term negative emotional after-effects.
    b. children raised with two same-sex parents have more problems in school.
    c. children raised by a single-father have the highest rates of criminal behaviors.
    d. most of the children fare quite well when poverty and life-stress are accounted for.

18. Gender identity and gender roles
    a. always strongly covary.
    b. are both primarily socially determined.
    c. are both primarily biologically determined.
    d. affect how others in a society interpret and respond to children's behaviors.

19. Which of the following statements about the study of moral development is TRUE?
    a. When evaluating moral dilemmas, the answers the person gives are less important than the reasoning.
    b. Compared with individualist cultures, cultures that favor collectivism are more likely to demonstrate postconventional morality.
    c. An individual who believes that speeding is only bad when cops are around is at the conventional stage of moral development.
    d. A strong positive correlation is evident between moral level and moral behavior.

20. Which of the following is supported by evidence?
    a. Most men experience a midlife crisis in which they try to regain their youth.
    b. Menopause is a period of increased depression for women.
    c. Depression in mothers follows "flight of their children" and their resulting "empty nest."
    d. Older adults experience less depression when compared to younger adults.

After completing the test, calculate your percent correct
(/ 20 =   ) x 100 = _____.

How accurate were your expectations? Does your performance suggest the need for additional study? For the items you missed, go back and identify why the "correct" answer is the best answer.

AFTER YOU READ ... PRACTICE TEST ANSWER KEYS

Practice Test 1.

1. c (p. 361)
2. d (p. 362)
3. b (p. 362)
4. c (p. 362)
5. b (p. 365)
6. a (p. 367)
7. a (p. 372)
8. a (p. 373)
9. a (p. 375)
10. b (p. 376)
11. c (p. 381)
12. c (p. 382)
13. d (p. 382)
14. a (p. 383)
15. d (p. 383-384)
16. b (p. 388)
17. c (p. 388)
18. a (p. 396)
19. b (p. 396-397)
20. d (p. 399)

Practice Test 2.

1. c (p. 362)
2. b (p. 364)
3. a (p. 365)
4. a (p. 365)
5. c (p. 366)
6. c (p. 367)
7. c (p. 373)
8. b (p. 374)
9. b (p. 376)
10. b (p. 376)
11. a (p. 379)
12. a (p. 381, 383)
13. c (p. 382)
14. a (p. 384)
15. c (p. 386)
16. d (p. 387-388)
17. d (p. 390-391)
18. d (p. 392)
19. a (p. 394)
20. d (p. 399)

AFTER YOU READ ... CONCEPT MAPPING ACTIVITY ANSWERS

ACTIVITY 1: Please complete this concept map which allows you to compare developmental research designs.

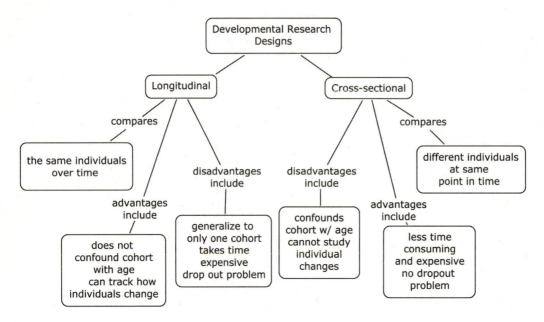

ACTIVITY 2:
The Prenatal/Perinatal Map should include the following terms and concepts:

Blastocyst: cell differentiation, implantation
Embryo: eight week; organ development
Fetus: physical maturation
Teratogens: alcohol
Genetic disruptions: Down syndrome or Fragile X Syndrome
Gestation: full-term at 40 weeks; viable at 25 weeks; premature before 36 weeks
Weighs: average 7.5 lbs; low birth weight less than 5.5 lbs

CHAPTER 11
EMOTION AND MOTIVATION
WHAT MOVES US

Emotions (feelings associated with experiences) and reason are often portrayed as opposites, but theories of emotion each describe the interactive relation between emotion and thinking. **Discrete emotions theory**, with an evolutionary emphasis, proposes that humans are biologically programmed to experience a set of emotion-behavior links. For example, disgust motivates us to avoid substances perceived as harmful; fear motivates us to be vigilant. Many emotions show cross-cultural *universality*. Ekman believes a set of **primary emotions** are universal and can be recognized through facial expressions. This universality as well as brain imaging studies and physiological measures show some support for the theory. Cultures, however, do differ in **display rules**—that is, they differ in how and when emotions are expressed. In fact, emotion theorists can distinguish genuine happiness, expressed in the so-called *Duchenne smile,* from the fake, or *Pan Am smile.* Other explanations for emotion are **cognitive theories of emotion.** In the **James-Lange theory**, emotions result from our bodily reactions to stimuli—we are afraid because we are running away. **Somatic marker theory** proposes that we use our physical responses to know what we are feeling. **Cannon-Bard theory** proposes that the emotion-provoking event triggers a bodily reaction and emotional reaction simultaneously—we are afraid and we are running at the same time. **Two-factor theory** suggests that events trigger arousal but we look to the situation to label the arousal with the appropriate emotion. Evidence also suggests that *unconscious influences* act on emotion. For example, the **mere exposure effect** reflects the finding that we *like* stimuli we are exposed to repeatedly. The **facial feedback hypothesis** suggests we are more likely to feel emotions corresponding to facial features—smile and you'll feel happier.

Nonverbal expressions of emotion, as in gestures and posture, can be more valid indicators of emotion than words because of **nonverbal leakage**. Gestures can be *illustrators, manipulators,* or *emblems.* Because we are less aware of these nonverbal cues to our emotions, they are more difficult for us to conceal. Written communication often suffers from *the curse of knowledge*—we assume that others know what we know. **Proxemics**, personal space, are also important components of emotional expression. Distance can be public, social, personal, or intimate. Some people are able to use nonverbal cues to tell whether a person is lying. Most of us, however, are not very good at detecting lies. The polygraph is also not as good at detecting lies as its proponents believe. It assumes a **Pinocchio response**—that there can be a perfect physical indicator of lying. The polygraph is better at detecting arousal, which can result from reasons other than lying. The polygraph, therefore, yields many *false positives* and is *biased against the innocent.* But there are also many *false negatives*, despite *countermeasures*, by people trained to beat the polygraph. An alternative, the **guilty knowledge test** seems more promising. More recently, brain scan technology has been used for lie detection using *brain fingerprinting*. Support for this technique is still preliminary. Finally, many employers use **integrity tests**, self-report pencil-and-paper questionnaires.

Positive psychology emphasizes human strengths, including resilience, coping, and happiness. Like the emphasis on wellness in general, these strengths can help people avoid distress. Happiness predicts longevity and broadens thinking and problem solving. Popular theories of happiness reflect many misconceptions. Some people use **defensive pessimism** to prepare mentally for negative events. **Broaden and build theory** suggests happiness predisposes us to see a "bigger" picture. There are many myths about happiness, and many realities: How we react to life events is a better indicator of our happiness than the actual events we experience. Money does not make us happy. Even the old are happy. In fact, according to the **positivity effect** we have more positive than negative memories with age. Happy people do tend to be married, have friends, are religious, giving, grateful, exercise, and experience *flow;* however, these relations are correlational and not causal. People are poor at **affective forecasting**, *over-estimating the impact of events on mood*, which creates a **durability bias**. In reality, we adjust our happiness to external circumstances, a process called the **hedonic treadmill**. **Self-esteem** does not predict happiness, achievement, social skills, or drug use, but is related to **positive illusions** such as the belief that one is more likeable than one really is.

Motivation refers to drives that propel us in specific directions. According to **drive reduction theory**, *drives* such as hunger and thirst motivate us to minimize aversive states. Motivation is to obtain *homeostasis* or equilibrium. One factor that affects the strength of our drives is arousal. The **Yerkes-Dodson law** proposes that optimal arousal is at moderate levels—neither too high nor too low. Drives can conflict when the desire to *approach* and to *avoid* situations occur simultaneously. Some behaviors are not easily explained in terms of drives. **Incentive theories** propose how we are motivated by goals. These goals can reflect incentives that come from within us—*intrinsic motivation* (e.g., interests)—or incentives from outside of us—*extrinsic motivation* (e.g., money). Sometimes too much extrinsic motivation can diminish intrinsic motivation. Needs can be categorized as *primary needs* (e.g,, biological necessities) and *secondary needs* (e.g., psychological desires, such as the *need for achievement*). Maslow developed a model of a **hierarchy of needs**. Unfortunately, support for his model is poor.

Although we believe we feel hunger in our stomachs, hunger is actually quite complicated and involves a variety of additional factors including the brain, blood, glucose levels, and hormones. The ventromedial hypothalamus appears to be a "satiety" center, whereas the lateral hypothalamus appears to be a "feeding" center, with *gherlin*, a hormone, mediating this relationship. According to **glucostatic theory**, blood sugar levels also affect hunger. Obesity involves biological predispositions such as differences in sensitivity to the hormone **leptin** that sends signals to reduce appetite. **Set point** theory suggests that people differ by their number of fat cells and metabolic rate. According to **internal-external theory,** overweight people are more sensitive to environmental cues to eat and are affected by *portion distortion*. **Bulimia nervosa** is an eating disorder that involves periods of *binge eating* followed by efforts to minimize weight gain (including *purging* by vomiting or abusing laxatives). The disorder affects 1–3% of all people, with higher percentages among college-aged women. **Anorexia nervosa**, involving a refusal to maintain normal weight, is less common. The disorder is affected by both biology and culture. With a 5–10% mortality rate, it is the most life threatening of the psychological conditions.

The hormone testosterone can enhance sexual interest, but neurotransmitters also play a role in sexual desire, called *libido*. Masters and Johnson's pioneering work on human **sexual response cycle** reported that basic sexual arousal was the same for men and women and involved four phases: (1) **excitement**, (2) **plateau**, (3) **orgasm (climax)**, and (4) *resolution*. Many married men and women continue to be sexually active over age 60. Cultures differ in their approval of premarital sex. Same-sex romantic relations develop in all cultures. About 2.8% of males and 1.4% of females identify themselves as gay or lesbian. Psychologists don't fully understand the biological-environment interactions influencing sexual orientation, but it is clear that sexual orientation cannot be changed. Twin studies show a fairly high *concordance* rate in identical twins, when compared to fraternal twins. As with most psychological processes, biology, cultural, and social factors all play a complex, interactive role. Three principles guide attraction and relationships: **proximity**, **similarity**, and **reciprocity**. Physical attractiveness also plays a role, especially for men. Women tend to be attracted to those with financial resources. Some psychologists suggest that these preferences have adaptive, evolutionary bases. According to *social role theory*, physical attractiveness may predict fertility; resources enhance offspring survival. Average faces tend to be seen as most attractive. Sternberg has proposed three dimensions of love—passion, intimacy, and commitment—which combine so that **passionate love** is distinct from **companionate love**. The opposite of love, hate, can be seen as the opposite of these three dimensions.

BEFORE YOU READ ... LEARNING OBJECTIVES

After reading Chapter 11 you should be able to:

11.1   Describe the major theories of emotion
11.2   Identify unconscious influences on emotion
11.3   Explain the importance of nonverbal expression of emotion
11.4   Identify major lie detection methods and their pitfalls
11.5   Describe the emerging discipline of popular psychology
11.6   Identify common myths and realities about happiness and self-esteem
11.7   Explain basic principles and theories of motivation
11.8   Describe the determinants of hunger, weight gain, and obesity
11.9   Identify the symptoms of bulimia and anorexia
11.10   Describe the human sexual response cycle and factors that influence sexual activity
11.11   Identify common misconceptions and potential influences on sexual orientation
11.12   Identify principles and factors that guide attraction and relationship formation
11.13   Describe the major types of love and the elements of love and hate

---

BEFORE YOU READ ... TERM IDENTIFICATION

---

affective forecasting (p. 426)
anorexia nervosa (p. 436)
broaden and build theory (p. 423)
bulimia nervosa (p. 436)
Cannon-Bard theory (p. 412)
cognitive theories of emotion (p. 410)
companionate love (p. 448)
defensive pessimism (p. 423)
desire phase (p.439)
discrete emotions theory (p. 407)
display rules (p. 408)
drive reduction theory (p. 429)
durability bias (p. 426)
excitement phase (p. 438)
facial feedback hypothesis (p. 415)
glucostatic theory (p. 433)
guilty knowledge test (p. 420)
hedonic treadmill (p. 427)
hierarchy of needs (p. 431)
homeostasis (p. 429)
incentive theories (p. 431)
integrity tests (p. 421)
internal-external theory (p. 435)
James-Lange theory of emotion (p. 410)

leptin (p. 433)
mere exposure effect (p. 414)
motivation (p. 429)
nonverbal leakage (p. 416)
orgasm (climax) phase (p. 438)
passionate love (p. 447)
Pinocchio response (p. 419)
plateau phase (p. 438)
positive illusions (p. 428)
positive psychology (p. 422)
positivity effect (p. 425)
primary emotions (p. 408)
proxemics (p. 417)
proximity (p.445)
reciprocity (p. 445)
resolution phase (p. 439)
self-esteem (p. 427)
set point (p. 434)
sexual response cycle (p. 438)
similarity (p.445)
social identity support (p. 445)
somatic marker theory (p. 411)
two-factor theory (p. 412)
Yerkes-Dodson law (p. 429)

AS YOU READ ... PRACTICE ACTIVITIES

THEORIES OF EMOTION: WHAT CAUSES OUR FEELINGS?

1. According to discrete emotions theory, our feelings are linked to physical responses. Your text gives the example of disgust. Similarly, apply this example to what you think might go on physically when you experience surprise. (LO 11.1)

2. Compare primary and secondary emotions. List some additional examples of secondary emotions that are not listed in your text. (LO 11.1)

3. Paul Ekman, whose work is discussed in several sections of this chapter, has partnered with Disney's Pixar animation studios to help them with facial expressions for such animated feature films as *Toy Story, Cars,* and *Monsters, Inc.* You can read about some of his work at http://www.sfgate.com/cgi-bin/article.cgi?f=/c/a/2002/09/16/MN241376.DTL&type=science. (LO 11.1)

Discuss how you would draw a new character's facial expressions so that he or she could convey the following—and then draw it!

(a) Happiness

(b) Sadness

(c) Surprise

(d) Anger

(e) Fear

4. You have probably had some experiences in your life where you've observed different cultural display rules. Describe such an experience and the situation surrounding it. (LO 11.1)

5. Compare the James-Lange, somatic marker, facial feedback, Cannon-Bard, and Schachter-Singer two-factor theories of emotion. You should make a table to help you organize your comparisons. Which of these do you personally favor? Why? (LO 11.1)

6. Oftentimes people follow the wisdom of everyday proverbs. What is the research evidence regarding the proverb, "Familiarity breeds contempt"? (LO11.2)

NONVERBAL EXPRESSION OF EMOTION: THE EYES, BODIES, AND CULTURES HAVE IT

1. Recall from Chapter 3 that for most right-handers the right hemisphere is important for processing extralinguistic aspects of language. If you are having a conversation with someone who has right hemisphere damage near the areas that normally correspond to speech areas in the left hemisphere, how do you think the conversation might be affected? (LO 11.3)

2. Think of a time when you had to stand in line. You have probably experienced the feeling that the person in front of you was not "moving along"; or you may have felt that the person behind you was "crowding." Relate a personal experience for each of these situations. Estimate the distance that you found annoying and what you think would have been a more appropriate distance. How do these distances match up with the guidelines on p. 417 of your text? (LO 11.3)

3. Explain why a polygraph is not truly a "lie detector" test. Include in your explanation how the polygraph is supposed to detect lies, the procedure and types of questions asked by the polygraph examiner, and the limitations and accuracy of these devices. (LO 11.4)

4. Your professor comes to class the day after an exam and announces that several students cheated on the exam and that he is going to give a lie-detector test to find out who the main culprit was. Would you take the test? Why or why not? (LO 11.4)

5. How does "truth serum" work to get people to tell the truth, and what are the potential problems with using this method of getting at the truth? (LO 11.4)

HAPPINESS AND SELF-ESTEEM: SCIENCE CONFRONTS POP PSYCHOLOGY

1. One could make the argument that happiness is really a pathological state—a psychological disorder. Look ahead to Chapter 15, where you will find several approaches that psychologists use to determine whether a particular behavior is "normal" or "abnormal." Then, make the case that happiness is really an abnormal state. (LO 11.5)

2. Bozena is really excited; she just won the lottery! How long do you think her happiness will last, and why? (LO 11.5)

3. Examine the four misconceptions that people have about happiness. Which of these did you know was a misconception? Why? Which of these did you most believe in? Are you now convinced that it is, in fact, a misconception? Why or why not? (LO 11.5)

4. Relate the concept of "hedonic treadmill" to the concept of "durability bias." How might the former predict the latter? (LO 11.5)

5. Happiness can predict many positive lifetime outcomes. Consider each of the variables discussed in the chapter that correlate with happiness and note how you can implement each one to enhance the quality of your life. Some of them may go against your basic values, on the surface, so think about how each can fit your life (e.g., "religion" can be defined in different ways). (LO 11.5)

6. Which myth about self-esteem did you find most surprising? Does the research evidence the authors of your text provide convince you of the correct conception? If not, what else would you need to know to change your belief? (LO 11.6)

MOTIVATION: OUR WANTS AND NEEDS

1. Apply the Yerkes-Dodson law to test anxiety. What would you tell a person with low test anxiety about drinking coffee just before an exam? What about a person with high test anxiety? Why? (LO 11.7)

2. Describe a situation in your life when you experienced an approach-avoidance conflict. How did you resolve the conflict? Did you have to completely give up on one option? (LO 11.7)

3. Compare intrinsic and extrinsic motivation. Suggest some ways that we can increase children's internal motivation to read. (LO 11.7)

4. Discuss the evidence for each of the following theories of hunger. (LO 11.8)

    (a) Stomach contraction hypothesis

    (b) Separate "satiety" and "feeding" centers in the brain (including their locations)

    (c) Glucostatic theory

5. Discuss the role of each of the following factors in affecting eating behaviors. (LO 11.8)

    (a) Leptin

    (b) Set point

    (c) Genes

    (d) Internal-external theory

6. Compare anorexia and bulimia in terms of symptoms, frequency rates, underlying causes, gender differences, and effects on overall health. Making a table should help you to organize your comparison. (LO 11.9)

7. T or F: Men have a stronger sex drive than women. Explain your answer. (LO 11.10)

8. As with many human characteristics, sexual orientation appears to be part nature and part nurture. Discuss the evidence for each contribution. In the end, do you believe the evidence is stronger for nature or for nurture? (LO 11.11)

ATTRACTION, LOVE, AND HATE: THE GREATEST MYSTERIES OF THEM ALL

1. Summarize the effects of proximity, similarity, and reciprocity in intimate relationships. (LO 11.12)

2. At http://www.soc.ucsb.edu/sexinfo/article/attraction-theories you can read about romantic love and some of the factors that influence relationships (in contrast to popular belief, opposites do NOT attract and, in fact, birds of a feather DO flock together). Given this information, how might the mere exposure effect influence the relationships between similarity, proximity, familiarity, and love? (LO 11.2, LO 11.12)

3. Compare social role theory to evolutionary models of attraction. (LO 11.12)

4. What is the evidence that an average face is actually most often labeled as "attractive"? (LO 11.12)

5. Summarize Sternberg's six varieties of love, and relate them to other types of love, such as "Hollywood" love or friendship. (LO 11.13)

As You Read ... Concept Map Activities

ACTIVITY 1: Complete this concept map for the theories of emotion.

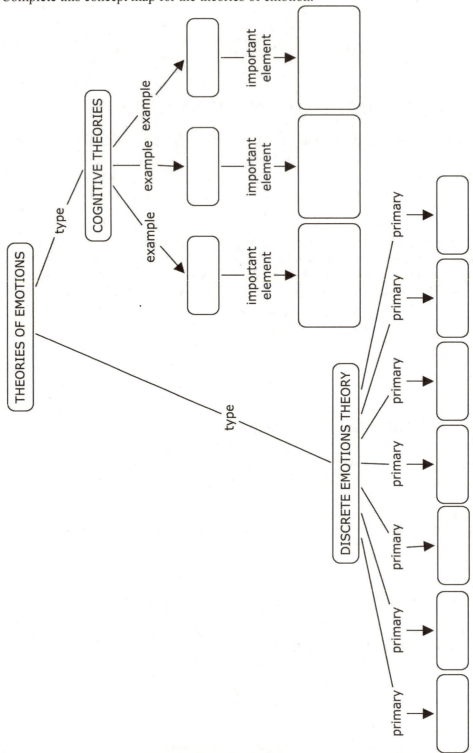

ACTIVITY 2: Complete this concept map for the variables associated with hunger.

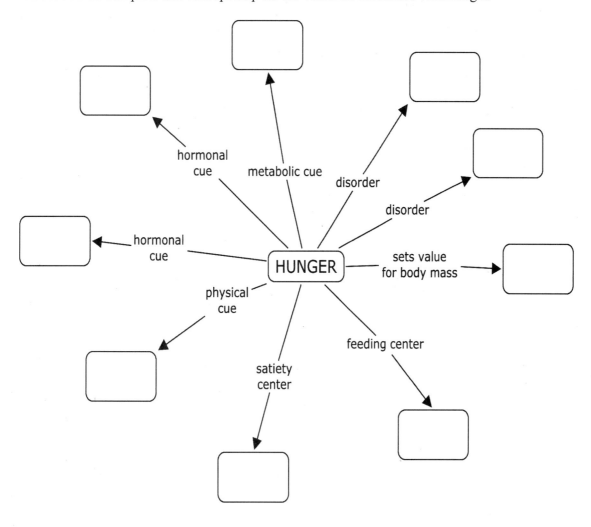

ACTIVITY 3: For this concept map, make your own, using the following terms:

ATTRACTION, social influences, proximity, similarity, reciprocity, models, evolutionary, social roles; LOVE, Hollywood love, passionate love, companionate love, friendship, intimacy, passion, consummate love, romantic love, liking, intimacy, commitment, empty love, fatuous love

---

AS YOU READ ... MYTH OR REALITY?

Myth: Women talk more than men.
Reality: Men and women use the same amount of words in a fixed time frame.

1. Have you heard any everyday wisdom about differences in men's and women's communication styles? In what aspects of language have you heard that men and women differ? Do you believe that the similarity of language usage is a good measure of whether men and women experience emotions similarly? Why or why not?

2. Your text notes in a "Fictoid" box the myth that men and women have distinctly different styles of emotional communication. In reality, research studies fail to find any such differences. Indeed, as your text notes, there is great similarity in the communication styles of men and women.

   To bolster this finding, recent independent studies have provided clear evidence that men and women also talk about the same amount. You can find the results of two studies, each conducted independently of the other and using a different methodology, at:
   http://www.sciencedaily.com/releases/2007/11/071108171518.htm
   http://www.npr.org/templates/story/story.php?storyId=11762186

Myth: Fat people are fat because they are lazy and lack willpower.
Reality: Obesity is a complicated disorder that is an aggregate of many variables.

1. Your text notes many of the factors that contribute to obesity. You can also read much more about obesity at:
   http://www.obesityinamerica.org/understandingObesity/index.cfm
   http://www.weight.com/causes.asp

   Synthesize all your readings into an argument that would speak against fat people being lazy or lacking willpower, and instead make an argument for other factors that contribute to obesity.

AS YOU READ ... PUT YOUR SCIENTIFIC THINKING SKILLS TO THE TEST

1. Because current lie detection technology is flawed, a new technology is now being developed for lie detection: the use of functional MRIs.
    a. Read about this new technology at these websites:
        http://www.usatoday.com/tech/science/2006-06-26-mri-lie_x.htm
        http://www.sciam.com/article.cfm?id=lie-brain-fmri-polygraph&page=1
    b. Read about the potential ethical problems with this type of technology at
        http://ethicsinthenews.typepad.com/practicalethics/2007/11/lie-detection-u.html
    c. After reading the information at these websites, what do you think about the usage of functional MRIs versus current technology? Would you want to rely on either one if a critical life decision depended on it? If you had to pick one technique and were given a choice, which one would you pick? Why?

2. Maslow's hierarchy of needs has often been criticized.
    a. Read about some of these criticisms by scrolling through these two websites:
        http://www.abraham-maslow.com/m_motivation/Hierarchy_of_Needs.asp
        http://webspace.ship.edu/cgboer/maslow.html.
    b. Maslow based his model on cases of individuals he considered to have achieved self-actualization; can you think of cases that contradict this model?
    c. How could you reformulate the model to better explain a wider range of human achievements?

As You Read... MyPsychLab Connection

Theories of Emotion: What Causes Our Feelings?

When reviewing different theories of emotions, **Explore** *Physiological, Evolutionary, and Cognitive Theories of Emotion* and learn about the universality of emotions and how cognitive appraisal influences emotional states. Why does familiarity breed liking? Complete the *Mere Exposure* **Simulation** to find out. To further illustrate the universal nature of emotional expression, complete the **Simulation** *Recognizing Facial Expressions of Emotions*. In this simulation, you will have a chance to identify the emotion being expressed.

Nonverbal Expressions of Emotion: The Eyes, Bodies, and Cultures Have It

Watch *Lie Spy* to see new techniques in lie detection—a heat-sensitive camera.

Happiness and Self-Esteem: Science Confronts Pop Psychology

Complete the **Simulation** *Survey on Happiness*. By taking this survey, you may learn what factors truly make you happy.

Motivation: Our Wants and Needs

To master the theories of motivation, **Explore** *Maslow's Hierarchy of Needs* and *Theories of Motivation and Job Performance*. To learn about how the brain plays a role in eating, **Watch** *The Effects of the Hypothalamus on Eating Behavior* and *Your Brain on Food*. Learn about various eating disorders by **Watching** *Eating Disorders* and *Anorexia Nervosa: Kim*. To learn more about the physiology of the sexual response, **Explore** *The Sexual Response Cycle*.

Attraction, Love, and Hate: The Greatest Mysteries of All?

To learn more about social influences on interpersonal attraction, **Watch** the video *Interpersonal Attraction*. **Watch** *Dating and Finding a Mate: Ralf, 33*, to learn more about factors that affect attraction. Complete the **Simulation** *Perceptions of Attractiveness*. **Explore** *Passionate Love Scale* when reviewing different types of love. **Watch** *Triangular Theory of Love: Robert Sternberg*.

After You Read ... Practice Test #1

Before beginning this practice test, estimate the percent you expect to get correct.
Anticipated percent correct: _____

1. Science fiction characters are sometimes portrayed as being emotionless and rational, with expert decision-making skills. This depiction
   a. underscores how emotions are opposite of clear, rational thinking.
   b. is consistent with scientific evidence from brain-damaged individuals.
   c. is in contrast to real case studies where brain damage leaves people emotionless but also less rational.
   d. fails to show that despite the rational thinking of brain-damaged individuals, their relationships with others are often unsuccessful.

2. Worldwide, the easiest emotion to recognize is
   a. anger.
   b. surprise.
   c. contempt.
   d. happiness.

3. Ekman conducted many studies of facial expressions associated with emotions and concluded that
   a. across cultures people disagree on how to name the different emotions.
   b. almost everyone agrees on seven fundamental emotions.
   c. only happiness and sadness have common expressions across cultures.
   d. expression of the same emotion varies from culture to culture.

4. Fear has been shown to be associated with several physical markers, including
   a. digestive system activation.
   b. slowing of heart rate.
   c. brain activation of the amygdala.
   d. a curling up of both corners of the mouth.

5. Markeesah reads an article that informs her that "if you see a bear, you are frightened because your heart is pounding." She immediately recognizes this statement as describing the
   a. James-Lange theory.
   b. somatic marker theory.
   c. Schachter-Singer theory.
   d. facial-feedback theory.

6. According to the Cannon-Bard theory of emotion,
   a. different types of arousal exist, and they are each named to correspond to an emotion.
   b. the amygdala is most important in experiencing the correct emotion, given a particular situation.
   c. the thalamus simultaneously triggers both an emotion and bodily reactions.
   d. the experience of emotion depends on cognitive interpretation of arousal.

7. Crystal's mother buys store-brand sodas that come in red cans. When offered Coke (which comes in a red can) or Pepsi (which comes in a blue can), Crystal always picks Coke. Crystal's behavior might best be explained as the result of
   a. somatic markers.
   b. autonomic arousal.
   c. affective forecasting.
   d. the mere exposure effect.

8. Which of the following statements regarding lie detectors is TRUE?
   a. Polygraph examiners make correct decisions 99% of the time.
   b. Evidence from lie detectors is admissible in most courts of law.
   c. Lie detectors assume a Pinocchio response: a perfect physiological indication of lying.
   d. Examiners are more likely to produce false negatives (i.e., to identify liars as truthful people).

9. It is most accurate to describe a polygraph as
   a. a confidence detector.   c. a truth detector.
   b. an arousal detector.   d. a lie detector.

10. Unlike a polygraph test, the integrity test
    a. is a pencil and paper test.
    b. yields few false positives.
    c. is a valid "honesty" detector.
    d. corrects for the shortcomings of the polygraph test.

11. Hector just won the Pennsylvania State Lotto! He is extremely excited and looks forward to a happy rest of his life, as well as that of his children.
    a. Hector should move to California to ensure his happiness.
    b. Hector should get divorced and stay single if he wants to stay happy.
    c. Hector should stop going to church because religious people are less happy.
    d. Unfortunately, according to research evidence, Hector is unlikely to be happy for very long.

12. You've received a mailing announcing the local engagement of a world-renowned motivational speaker. Should you shell out the shekels to attend?
    a. No, you'll get more motivated watching an infomercial on TV.
    b. No, the research evidence shows only a small and temporary positive motivational effect.
    c. Yes, research evidence shows these speakers jump-start long-term changes in people's lives.
    d. Yes, the fact that the speaker sells out each time means he must be good at motivating others.

13. You've just written a new book and titled it *Homeostasis*. What would be a good subtitle for your book?
    a. *Maintaining of an Optimal Level of Equilibrium*
    b. *The Maximum Amount of Arousal Needed for Best Performance*
    c. *Engaging in an Act for Its Own Sake, Without Any External Reward*
    d. *A Positive Illusion in Which We Perceive Ourselves More Positively Than Others Do.*

14. An inverted-U function describes the relationship between
    a. drives and motives.
    b. approach and avoidance.
    c. arousal and performance.
    d. incentives and intrinsic motives.

15. Helga likes to paint for the fun of it; she has a(n) _____. Hans paints because he sells his paintings at high prices; he has a(n) _____.
    a. incentive; drive
    b. aesthetic reward; financial reward
    c. extrinsic motivation; intrinsic motivation
    d. intrinsic motivation; extrinsic motivation

16. Dr. Brown implanted an electrode in the hypothalamus of a rat. Then Dr. Brown electrically stimulated this area of the hypothalamus and the rat stopped eating. The electrode was probably implanted in the
    a. lateral hypothalamus.
    b. ventromedial hypothalamus.
    c. anterior hypothalamus.
    d. posterior hypothalamus.

17. An important source of energy for all parts of the body is
    a. insulin.
    b. sodium.
    c. glucose.
    d. serotonin.

18. Miranda will sometimes eat like there is no tomorrow and then feel guilty over her lack of control. She then forces herself to vomit and takes laxatives to avoid gaining weight. Miranda is probably suffering from what is called
    a. bulimia nervosa.
    b. anorexia nervosa.
    c. poor impulse control.
    d. irritable bowel syndrome.

19. A man who has a homosexual orientation is most likely to have a brother who is also homosexual if that brother is
    a. unfamiliar.
    b. an identical twin.
    c. a fraternal twin.
    d. adopted.

20. The variable that best predicts whether a relationship will develop between two individuals is
    a. proximity.
    b. reciprocity.
    c. serendipity.
    d. attractiveness.

After completing the test, calculate your percent correct
(/ 20 =   ) x 100 = _____.

How accurate were your expectations? Does your performance suggest the need for additional study?
For the items you missed, go back and identify why the "correct" answer is the best answer.

Before beginning this practice test, estimate the percent you expect to get correct.
Anticipated percent correct: _____

1. Evidence that emotions may be innate in all people includes which of the following?
   a. Newborn infants smile spontaneously while in REM sleep.
   b. Babies smile back at everyone who smiles at them.
   c. Babies smile when they have intestinal gas bubbles.
   d. Blind children smile when they want attention.

2. Which of the following is NOT generally considered to be one of the primary emotions?
   a. Envy
   b. Anger
   c. Disgust
   d. Contempt

3. Cross-cultural guidelines for how and when to express emotion are called
   a. motivational-structural rules.
   b. Duchenne guidelines.
   c. somatic markers.
   d. display rules.

4. According to the James-Lange theory, experiencing emotion starts with
   a. using "gut reactions" to determine our response to a specific situation.
   b. our labeling of our own body's arousal to external stimuli.
   c. our interpretation of pure autonomic failure.
   d. exhibiting the proper display rules.

5. Schachter's two-factor theory of emotion suggests that we distinguish between different emotions on the basis of
   a. different levels of arousal.
   b. whether we decide on fight or flight.
   c. our interpretation of an internal state or an external situation.
   d. whether the emotion was experienced in the presence or absence of arousal.

6. The idea that blood vessels in the face send information to the brain and that this affects the emotion we feel is known as the
   a. James-Lange theory.
   b. Ekman's Pan-Am theory.
   c. Schachter's cognitive theory.
   d. facial feedback hypothesis.

7. People sometimes misinterpret each others' statements in e-mail discussions because e-mail lacks
   a. proper use of grammar.
   b. adequate personal space.
   c. an emotional social intelligence prosthesis.
   d. nonverbal cues present in spoken language.

8. When a polygraph operator asks a subject, "Have you ever lied to your parents?" he or she is asking _____, which are designed to make almost anyone anxious.
   a. critical questions
   b. control questions
   c. irrelevant questions
   d. minor deception questions

9. Lie detection using brain scanning techniques
   a. suffers from many of the same problems as conventional lie detection.
   b. prove brain waves are more sensitive than blood pressure and heart rates at detecting lying.
   c. discriminate lying from thinking about lying.
   d. shows high reliability across brain areas.

10. In an effort to get at the truth of Ernest's past criminal history, investigators injected him with "truth serum." According to careful research studies,
    a. this might result in Ernest falsely owning up to crimes he didn't commit.
    b. this can force Ernest to own up to some of his crimes, but still omit others.
    c. this is unlikely to produce any more accurate information about Ernest's crimes.
    d. this will lower Ernest's inhibitions, allowing him to provide the information in his past history.

11. Carolina is an elementary school teacher who wants her students to excel. To this end, she spends a large part of each day working on self-esteem–boosting exercises with her students.
    a. You applaud her efforts because the research evidence suggests that people with high self-esteem are always less aggressive than those with low self-esteem.
    b. You caution her that the research evidence suggests that she should spend her class time on classwork, because high self-esteem does not automatically translate into better school performance.
    c. You point out to Carolina that this strategy is good because higher self-esteem alone is likely to boost her students' test scores significantly.
    d. You tell Carolina about the research evidence that this will also prevent her students from becoming self-centered, which will also benefit them in life.

12. A(n) _____ is an internal state of tension that motivates an organism to engage in activities that should reduce this aversive state.
    a. incentive
    b. emotion
    c. drive
    d. motive

13. Sue works on a factory line. Her tasks are simple, but because she wants a promotion, she needs to be productive and make few errors. The Yerkes-Dodson law would advise Sue to be
    a. unemotional in making decisions at work.
    b. moderately aroused for peak performance.
    c. in a very high state of arousal.
    d. in a low state of arousal.

14. Fernando loves to play baseball. Now that he is on a travel team, his dad has told Fernando he will pay him $1 for every hit he gets, and $5 for every home run. This new plan is likely to
    a. increase Fernando's internal motivation to play baseball.
    b. decrease Fernando's external motivation to play baseball.
    c. decrease Fernando's internal motivation to play baseball.
    d. undermine Fernando's external motivation to play baseball.

15. The start-eating center is located in the _____, and the stop eating center is located in the _____.
    a. amygdala; stomach
    b. lateral hypothalamus; ventromedial hypothalamus
    c. melanocortin receptor-4; leptin center
    d. homeostatic center, pleasure circuits

16. People tend to maintain a nearly constant body weight over the course of months, unless something unusual happens. That constant weight is referred to as
    a. a set point.
    b. homeostasis.
    c. healthy weight.
    d. the ideal weight.

17. The typical personality trait of people with bulimia nervosa is described as
    a. extroverted.
    b. unmotivated.
    c. perfectionist.
    d. introverted.

18. The typical order of human sexual response is
    a. excitement, desire, plateau, orgasm.
    b. pleasure, plateau, orgasm, relaxation.
    c. excitement, plateau, orgasm, resolution.
    d. excitement, euphoria, climax, relaxation.

19. Which of the following sayings best describes what research evidence tells us is true of long-term relationships?
    a. Opposites attract.
    b. Birds of a feather flock together.
    c. The enemy of my enemy is my friend.
    d. Absence makes the heart grow fonder.

20. Evolutionary models of attraction suggest that women place more emphasis than men on the _____ of a potential mate.
    a. height
    b. wealth
    c. youthfulness
    d. attractiveness

After completing the test, calculate your percent correct
(/ 20 =   ) x 100 = _____.

How accurate were your expectations? Does your performance suggest the need for additional study?
For the items you missed, go back and identify why the "correct" answer is the best answer.

AFTER YOU READ ... PRACTICE TEST ANSWER KEYS

Practice Test 1.

1. c (p. 406)
2. d (p. 408)
3. b (p. 408)
4. c (p. 409)
5. b (p. 411)
6. c (p. 412)
7. d (p. 414)
8. c (p. 419)
9. b (p. 419)
10. a (p. 421)
11. d (p. 424–425)
12. b (p. 429)
13. a (p. 429)
14. c (p. 429)
15. d (p. 431)
16. b (p. 433)
17. c (p. 433)
18. a (p. 436)
19. b (p. 441)
20. a (p. 444)

Practice Test 2.

1. a (p. 407)
2. a (p. 408)
3. d (p. 408-409)
4. b (p. 410)
5. c (p. 412)
6. d (p. 415)
7. d (p. 416)
8. b (p. 419)
9. a (p. 420-421)
10. a (p. 421)
11. b (p. 427–428)
12. c (p. 429)
13. b (p. 430)
14. c (p. 431)
15. b (p. 433)
16. a (p. 434)
17. c (p. 436)
18. c (p. 438-439)
19. b (p. 444)
20. b (p. 446)

AFTER YOU READ ... CONCEPT MAPPING ACTIVITY ANSWERS

ACTIVITY 1: Complete this concept map for the theories of emotion.

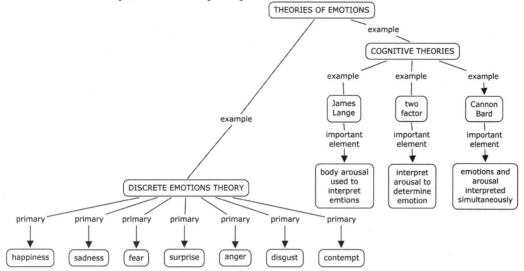

ACTIVITY 2: Complete this concept map for the variables associated with hunger.

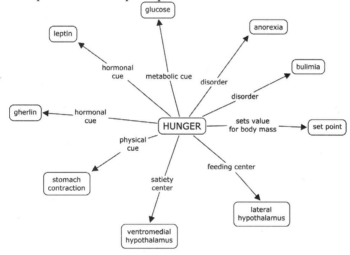

ACTIVITY 3: For this concept map, make your own, using terms for attraction and love. Here is a sample:

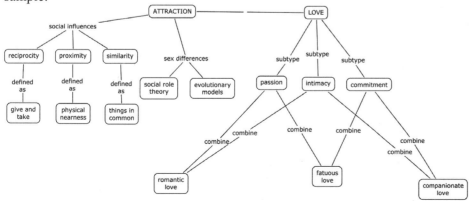

CHAPTER 12
STRESS, COPING, AND HEALTH
THE MIND-BODY INTERCONNECTION

BEFORE YOU READ ... CHAPTER PREVIEW

The terrorist attacks on September 11, 2001, provide insights into stress and coping. Most people (60%–90%) have experienced at least one traumatic event in their lifetimes, and surprisingly, most people successfully cope with these traumatic events. **Stress** consists of the tension, discomfort, or physical symptoms that arise when a *stressor* strains our ability to cope effectively. A *traumatic event* refers to a serious stressor. Researchers have examined stress from three perspectives. The *stressors as stimuli* approach identifies different events as being stressful. The *stressors as transactions* approach examines how people interpret and cope with stressors, with both a **primary appraisal** and a **secondary appraisal**. In **problem-focused coping,** we tackle challenges head on. In **emotion-focused coping,** we reinterpret events to perceive them as less stressful. Finally, the *stress as a response* approach examines the effects of stress, particular the actions of **corticosteroids**. Stress has been studied in terms of major life events and in terms of everyday **hassles**, or minor annoyances, which can have major long-term consequences.

In research studies of stress, Hans Selye proposed a **general adaptation syndrome** with three stages that are common across individuals: alarm, resistance, and exhaustion. During the *alarm reaction,* the autonomic nervous system is activated, adrenaline is released, the midbrain is excited, and people show a **fight-or-flight response**. Specifically, the limbic system, or *emotional brain* activates the *hypothalamus-pituitary-adrenal (HAP) axis*. During the *resistance stage,* people find ways to cope with the stress, which can vary across individuals. At the *exhaustion stage,* resistance breaks down; with prolonged stress, damage can occur to various organ systems or people may become depressed. Other researchers are finding differences in the effects of stress on people, especially among genders. Women are more likely than men to have a **tend and befriend** response to stress, turning to others for support. In addition, women secrete an additional hormone, oxytocin. With prolonged stress, some people develop *posttraumatic stress disorder (PTSD)*, accompanied by *flashbacks* during which they re-experience an extremely stressful event over a prolonged period of time. However, most people cope well, and are quite resilient.

Psychological stress has been shown to produce physical responses. Our **immune system**, which protects us from *pathogens* by producing *antigens*, suffers under stress. Normally we have specialized white blood cells called *phagocytes, lymphocytes (T-cells, B-cells),* and *macrophages* protecting us from bacteria and viruses. When the immune system fails, as in **acquired immune deficiency syndrome (AIDS),** then illness cannot be avoided. Conversely, when the immune system becomes overly active we can develop *autoimmune disorders,* in which the immune system mistakes healthy body tissues for unhealthy invaders, such as bacteria and viruses, and attacks healthy tissues. A new field of psychology, called **psychoneuroimmunology,** has developed to study these complex relationships between stress, the mind, and the body. This field has found clear research evidence that immunity is decreased during times of stress and that people are more prone, for example, to develop colds at such times. **Peptic ulcers** provide a model of the interaction of biological (bacterial) and psychological (stress) factors. Other disorders are also being linked to **psychophysiological** and **biopsychosocial** factors. In particular, **coronary heart disease** is being linked, via cholesterol levels and atherosclerosis, to stress levels. Several independent lines of research have shown a clear relationship between stress and coronary heart disease, with a mediating factor being personality type, especially **Type A**. Type A individuals are generally ambitious and goal-driven; but being high on the traits of anger and hostility best predicts coronary artery disease. Finally, illness can be the cause, rather than the result, of stress.

People show wide individual differences in the ways they cope with stress. Researchers have verified that **social support** and a perception of control over the stressful situation are important for successful coping. Behavior control is successful when it is *problem-focused*, and less so when it is *avoidance-oriented*. Cognitive control often takes the form of *emotion-focused coping* as people *restructure* or *think differently* about negative events. In decisional control, choices are made between different alternatives. In informational control, **proactive coping** allows people to anticipate negative events. Emotional control allows people to suppress or to express emotion. Although many people believe that *catharsis* is a good way to handle stress, research shows this is not the case. Furthermore, although *crisis debriefing* can help a few people, it may not only be ineffective, depending on the type of trauma and the individual, but might even increase PTSD. So what helps? Wide individual differences characterize successful coping. Attitudes, beliefs, and personality interact to produce **hardiness**: the ability to resist the negative effects of stress. Hardy individuals see stressors as a challenge rather than as a threat. Other individual difference variables that affect coping include being optimistic, having **spirituality,** and spending less time ruminating over negative events.

Psychologists and other health practitioners look to promote good health and reduce stress, because these factors go hand in hand. The fields of **behavioral medicine** and **health psychology** have been rapidly growing over the past decade, focusing on preventing both illness and stress. Here are four tips for promoting good health: stop smoking, reduce alcohol consumption, lose weight, and exercise. Of course, the problem with many of these tips is that they are difficult to put into practice. Because of the *availability heuristic,* people misestimate the risk of health problems, plus feeling powerless and personal inertia come into play. Prevention programs offer one approach to reducing bad health behaviors, but lessons learned from the failure of DARE programs need to be accounted for. Another approach for many people when it comes to poor health is to seek help from **complementary medicine** and alternative medicine (CAM). Americans spend $34 billion each year on unsupported vitamins, herbs, and food supplements. Other unsupported approaches include *chiropractic manipulation*, **acupuncture** (which involves the placement of needles along *meridians* that channel the flow of *qi*, or life force), and **homeopathic medicine**. Some positive results have been reported with **biofeedback** and **meditation**, both *concentrative meditation* and *awareness meditation*. It is quite likely that most CAM achieves its positive effects as a placebo effect. The bottom line is to always research the available literature for any scientific evidence for the effectiveness of these approaches.

BEFORE YOU READ ... LEARNING OBJECTIVES

After reading Chapter 12 you should be able to:

12.1	Explain how stress is defined and approached in different ways
12.2	Identify different approaches to measuring stress
12.3	Describe Selye's general adaptation syndrome
12.4	Describe the diversity of stress responses
12.5	Describe how the immune system functions
12.6	Identify how physical disorders such as ulcers are related to stress
12.7	Describe the role of personality in everyday experience, and socioeconomic factors in coronary heart disease
12.8	Describe the role of social support and different types of control in coping with stress
12.9	Explain how our attitudes, beliefs, and personality may influence responses to stress
12.10	Identify four behaviors that contribute to a healthy lifestyle
12.11	Identify reasons why it is difficult to change our lifestyles
12.12	Describe different alternative medicine from complementary medical approaches and compare their effectiveness with placebos

BEFORE YOU READ ... TERM IDENTIFICATION

acquired immune deficiency syndrome (AIDS) (p. 465)
acupuncture (p. 484)
aerobic exercise (p. 479)
alternative medicine (p. 481)
behavioral medicine (p. 475)
biofeedback (p. 483)
biopsychosocial perspective (p. 467)
complementary medicine (p. 481)
coronary heart disease (CHD) (p. 467)
corticosteroid (p. 458)
emotion-focused coping (p. 458)
fight-or-flight response (p. 462)
general adaptation syndrome (GAS) (p. 461)
hardiness (p. 472)
hassle (p. 460)
health psychology (p. 475)
homeopathic medicine (p. 487)

immune system (p. 465)
meditation (p. 483)
peptic ulcer (p. 467)
primary appraisal (p. 458)
proactive coping (p. 471)
problem-focused coping (p. 458)
psychoneuroimmunology (p. 465)
psychophysiological (p. 467)
secondary appraisal (p. 458)
social support (p. 470)
spirituality (p. 472)
stress (p. 457)
tend and befriend (p. 462)
Type A personality (p. 468)

As You Read ... Practice Activities

WHAT IS STRESS?

1. Differentiate between a stressor and a traumatic event. (LO 12.1)

2. Stress can be perceived in three ways: as a stimulus, as a transaction, or as a response. Summarize these three perspectives here. (LO 12.1)

3. Compare problem-focused and emotion-focused coping. Provide an original example of how each of these coping approaches might be implemented. (LO 12.1)

4. Score yourself on the Social Readjustment Rating Scale (p. 459). How did you score? What insights does this assessment provide into your own stress levels? What changes can you make in your life to reduce some of the major stressors that might later affect your health? (LO 12.2)

5. Go to http://www.drstephanie.org/dailyhassles.htm where you will find a "Hassles and Uplifts Scale." One of the things to note is that some things can be both a hassle *and* an uplift. Go over the list of events and note which ones are more often hassles for you, which are more often uplifts, and which are about half and half. What changes could you make in your life to maximize the uplifts and minimize the hassles? (LO 12.2)

HOW WE ADAPT TO STRESS: CHANGE AND CHALLENGE

1. Summarize, in your own words, the three stages of Selye's general adaptation syndrome (GAS). (LO 12.3)

2. Imagine yourself taking an extremely important exam (maybe the SATs, AP exam, or an important final exam) and you find yourself unable to answer item after item after item. Note the progression of activation through the hypothalamus-pituitary-adrenal (HPA) axis over the course of taking this exam. (LO 12.3)

3. Compare the fight-or-flight response with the tend-and-befriend reaction to stress. (LO 12.3, LO 12.4)

THE BRAIN-BODY REACTION TO STRESS

1. Ikema and Nakagawa (1962) elicited a poison-ivy type of rash. Describe their study here. (LO 12.5)

   Study:

   Results:

   Lesson learned:

2. Know the key terms related to the immune system, including antigen, pathogen, phagocyte, lymphocyte, macrophage, antibodies, T-cell, and B-cell. (LO 12.5)

3. Discuss the work of Cohen and colleagues, who examined the relationship between stress and colds. (LO 12.5)

   Study:

   Results:

   Lesson learned:

4. Peptic ulcers provide a good model of how physical and psychological factors interact in illness. Research asthma on your own and develop a similar model. (LO 12.6)

5. Several independent sources of correlational evidence link stress and coronary heart disease. Go over the evidence and determine whether the evidence is sufficient to convince you of a causal relationship. Are you convinced? Why or why not? (LO 12.7)

6. Recently, researchers have been considering the "Type D" personality. (LO12.7)
   You can read about Type D Personality at this website:
   http://www.hqlo.com/content/8/1/9

   Take the Type D Personality test at the following website:
   http://www.health.harvard.edu/newsweek/Type_D_for_distressed.htm

   How did you do? What changes can you make to your life right now and for the rest of your life to protect you from coronary heart disease, on the basis of this test?

COPING WITH STRESS

1. Describe the evidence that supports the following statement: "Social support is probably the single most important factor affecting successful coping with stress." (LO 12.8)

2. Think of a stressful situation in your life and develop a coping plan based on each of the five areas in which you can gain control: behavioral, cognitive, decision, informational, and emotional. (LO 12.8)

3. T or F: Catharsis is a good thing. What evidence supports your conclusion? (LO 12.8)

4. T or F: Crisis debriefing is always a good thing. What evidence supports your conclusion? (LO 12.8)

5. What are some of the characteristics of a "hardy" individual when it comes to coping with stress? Which of these characteristics do you possess? What personal characteristics should you try to develop to increase your hardiness? (LO 12.9)

PROMOTING GOOD HEALTH—AND LESS STRESS!

1. Working under the assumption that everyone could improve personal health habits to some extent, pick one of the four health tips elaborated in your text and set up a plan for yourself to enhance your adherence to that health tip. Work out that plan here. (LO 12.10)

2. Why do you think it is so difficult to make lifestyle changes, even if we know it is the best thing to do for ourselves? Think of some ideas on your own, then discuss some of the reasons suggested by the text. (LO 12.11)

3. Each year the government earmarks more than $6 million for DARE.
   T or F: DARE is an effective program. Evaluate the evidence based on carefully controlled research studies. (LO 12.11)

4. What is the difference between alternative medicine and complementary medicine? (LO 12.12)

5. T or F: The fact that many herbal supplements are "natural" makes them safe. Why? (LO 12.12)

6. Discuss why "sham" (fake) acupuncture treatments may still provide pain relief to patients. (LO 12.12)

AS YOU READ ... CONCEPT MAP ACTIVITIES

ACTIVITY 1: Complete this concept map for general concepts related to stress.

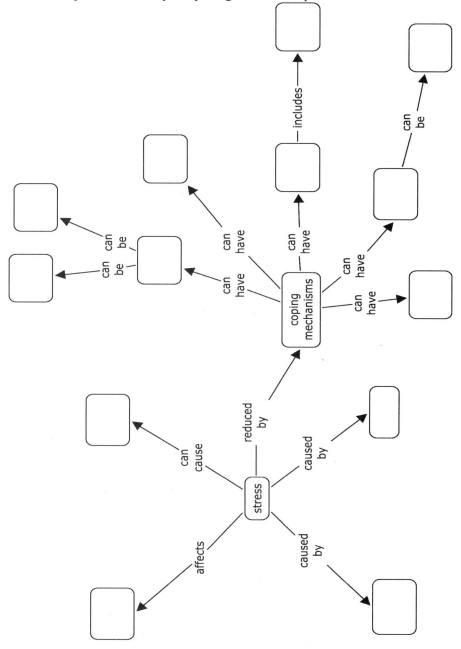

Author activity content supported by *IHMC Cmap Tools* Copyright ©1998-2007 Institute for Human & Machine Cognition

ACTIVITY 2: Create your own concept map for CAM. Here are some terms you might want to include:

acupuncture	chiropractic	meditation
awareness	complementary medicine	supplement
alternative medicine	concentrative	yoga
biofeedback	homeopathy	

AS YOU READ... MYTH OR REALITY?

Myth: Only negative events produce stress in our lives.
Reality: Even good things can cause stress in our lives.

1. Provide two examples of events that have occurred in your own life that were positive events, but that created "stress" for you.

2. Do you believe that this type of stress can be as damaging to your overall health as the stress created by negative life events? Why or why not?

Myth: By applying the principles of *The Secret,* your life can be stress- and illness-free.
Reality: There is no "quick fix" to stress and illness in our lives.

1. The secret is based on the "Law of Attraction" in which people's feelings and thoughts attract real events in the world into their lives. Thus, if you think good, positive thoughts, good and positive things will happen to you, and if you think bad, negative thoughts, bad and negative things will happen to you. Review the official website at http://www.thesecret.tv and provide a critique of the content.

> AS YOU READ ... PUT YOUR SCIENTIFIC THINKING SKILLS TO THE TEST

1. The Social Readjustment Rating Scale has been criticized as not being applicable to large segments of the population, such as younger adults, older adults, and many minority groups.

    a. Go through the items and evaluate the items individually to decide which items might not apply to all people across the board.

    b. Can you think of major life events that are more likely to involve these different subgroups of people? What are they?

2. Two problems with correlational evidence include the two-way nature of the relationship and the potential of a third variable responsible for both of the related variables.
    a. Point out the evidence that stress causes illness and then point out the evidence that illness causes stress. Which seems more convincing to you?

    b. Alternatively, consider some potential third variables that might be responsible for causing both stress and illness.

AS YOU READ... MYPSYCHLAB CONNECTION

What Is Stress?
Review how stress is measured with the **Simulation** *How Stressed Are You?* **Explore** *The Effect of Cognitive Appraisal on Responses to Stressors* to see how people appraise stress. To see examples of the effects of life stressors and traumatic events on stress, **Watch** *9/11 and Post Traumatic Stress Disorder*. **Explore** *Selye's General Adaptation Syndrome* and **Listen** to the corresponding podcast to review Selye's theory on the General Adaptation Syndrome (G.A.S.).

How We Adapt to Stress: Change and Challenge
Go to the **Simulation** *Stress and the Fight-or Flight Response* for more on how we adapt to stress and the effect of stress on health. Gender differences and stress are discussed in **Watch** *Gender Differences in Stress Vulnerability*.

The Brain-Body Reaction to Stress
Watch *Stress and Sleep* to see how specific stressors affect the body.

Coping with Stress
Explore *Coping Strategies and Their Effects* for an interesting activity illustrating how various coping strategies can affect how individuals can approach daily stressors. **Watch** *Coping with Stress*, *Socializing and Stress,* and *Optimism and Resilience* for more on understanding how individuals cope with stress. **Watch** *Emotion Regulation: James Coan* to see how social support affects our reactions to stress. To see how spirituality impacts coping with stress, **Watch** *Religion and Longevity.*

Promoting Good Health –and Less Stress!
How does your lifestyle affect your health? To find out, take the **Simulation** *How Healthy Are You?* The effects of stress on health can be experienced in the **Simulation** *Stress and Health.*

AFTER YOU READ... PRACTICE TEST #1

Before beginning this practice test, estimate the percent you expect to get correct.
Anticipated percent correct: _____

1. Research shows that, on average, approximately _____% of people experience a major traumatic event in their lifetime.
   a. 10–30
   b. 40–50
   c. 60–90
   d. 90–95

2. When asked about stress in his life, Josh sees it as coming from specific events. Josh sees stress
   a. as a transaction.
   b. as an appraisal.
   c. as a response.
   d. as a stimulus.

3. When we compare hassles to major life events,
   a. only hassles can predict subsequent health.
   b. hassles are a relatively better predictor of subsequent health.
   c. only major life events can predict subsequent health.
   d. major life events are a relatively better predictor of subsequent health.

4. Dat feels a sudden shaking throughout his house. At first he is alarmed, but then calmly gets under a sturdy table and waits to see whether it is a serious earthquake or just a little shaker. Dat is now in the _____ stage of the general adaptation syndrome.
   a. fight
   b. befriend
   c. resistance
   d. exhaustion

5. Men's and women's stress responses tend to differ because women are more likely to produce the hormone _____ during stress.
   a. oxytocin
   b. adrenaline
   c. cholesterol
   d. epinephrine

6. Soldiers who fought in wars such as Vietnam or Iraq may sometimes experience nightmares and anxiety, as well as fear and anger long after their military service is over. Such an experience reflects
   a. rumination.
   b. homeopathy.
   c. posttraumatic stress disorder.
   d. the exhaustion phase in Selye's general adaptation syndrome.

7. Rochelle is convinced that her pessimistic style of thinking has led to her development of cancer. You reassure her that
   a. no research evidence supports the idea that a pessimistic attitude "causes" cancer.
   b. research shows that she can protect herself from cancer with a positive attitude.
   c. research shows that she can reverse her cancer with a positive attitude from now on.
   d. although negative thinking can cause colds, it has been found to protect individuals from serious illnesses, such as cancer.

8. Psychoneuroimmunology examines the relationship between
    a. antigens and pathogens.
    b. nocebo effects and placebo effects.
    c. social support and the benefits of catharsis.
    d. the immune system and the central nervous system.

9. Jamal has a stomach ulcer. His grandmother makes milk-toast for him whenever he visits her, even though he is an adult. She also insists that he relax, believing that is all he needs to "cure" his ulcer. Unfortunately, this will not work because he needs to treat the trigger cause of his ulcer which is
    a. the *heliobacter pylori* bacterium.
    b. atherosclerosis.
    c. a hostile and angry attitude.
    d. corticosteroid deficiency.

10. The personality trait that best predicts coronary heart disease is
    a. perfectionism.
    b. irritability.
    c. ambition.
    d. hostility.

11. One of the most important factors for coping with stress is
    a. strong social support.
    b. the immediacy of crisis counseling.
    c. having a positive attitude.
    d. whether one responds with anxiety or with depression.

12. Behavioral control can be _____, whereas cognitive control can be _____.
    a. exercise-based; informational
    b. restructuring; avoidance-oriented
    c. problem-focused; emotion-focused
    d. proactive coping; retroactive coping

13. At Janet's school, a student died in a car accident. The next day crisis counselors went to all of Janet's classes, asking students to talk through their grief. Janet did not know this student, but felt a bit sad for her family. However, after the counseling sessions she felt guilty that her sadness was not deeper.
    a. This is surprising because crisis counseling reduces the effects of trauma.
    b. This is not surprising in that crisis counseling is not necessary for everyone.
    c. This is surprising in that Janet was allowed to disclose her emotions in a public forum.
    d. This is not surprising because Janet might have been withholding her emotions prior to the counseling session.

14. Viewing change as a challenge rather than a threat is called
    a. optimism.
    b. hardiness.
    c. rumination.
    d. self-enhancement.

15. Jerry is very religious. He is
    a. less likely to recover from a serious illness.
    b. less likely to have a strong immune system.
    c. more likely to have high blood pressure.
    d. more likely to have good health habits.

16. The specialty area of psychology that studies how to prevent illness and promote good health is called
    a. stress psychology.
    b. health psychology.
    c. behavioral psychology.
    d. psychoneuroimmunology.

17. The most serious consequences of binge drinking include
    a. a hangover the next day.
    b. a weakened immune system.
    c. an increase in certain types of cancer and even fatal liver problems.
    d. an inability to cope with stress, leading to increased autoimmune disorders.

18. All of the following are reasons for generalized weight gain in society EXCEPT
    a. a lack of sufficient sleep.
    b. Darwinian natural selection.
    c. having a comfortable indoor climate.
    d. mothers giving birth at a younger age.

19. Although acupuncture has been practiced for at least 2,000 years, doubt is cast on its validity because
    a. the realignment of qi (chi) as the source of relief has recently been falsified.
    b. studies show the needles can be placed incorrectly and still relieve migraines.
    c. the needles would need to be placed much deeper to produce the supposed effect.
    d. research studies have shown only symptom relief, but underlying causes of the illness remain.

20. Homeopathic treatments probably work so well because
    a. like-goes-with-like, the same as why vaccines work to prevent illness.
    b. symptom relief may simply occur because the illness, such as a cold, has run its course naturally.
    c. memory of the substance is just as effective as the substance itself, thereby eliminating all side-effects.
    d. the small dosages have fewer side effects than comparable medical prescription drugs that are usually given in higher dosage levels.

After completing the test, calculate your percent correct
(/ 20 =   ) x 100 = _____.

How accurate were your expectations? Does your performance suggest the need for additional study?
For the items you missed, go back and identify why the "correct" answer is the best answer.

AFTER YOU READ ... PRACTICE TEST #2

Before beginning this practice test, estimate the percent you expect to get correct.

Anticipated percent correct: _____

1. Following severely traumatic events, _____ turn out to be psychologically resilient.
    a. most people
    b. a few people
    c. about half of all people
    d. about 10% of all people

2. JoBeth finds that the loss of her home following a hurricane is a major loss to her; but she can rebuild, and is grateful to be alive to do so. JoBeth has engaged in looking at stress
    a. as a stimulus.
    b. as a response.
    c. as an appraisal.
    d. as a transaction.

3. Being late for an appointment because you couldn't find a parking space is an example of _____, but getting fired from your job is an example of _____.
    a. a stressor; a trauma
    b. a frustration; an irritation
    c. a hassle; a major life event
    d. a inconvenience; a pressure

4. People with higher scores on the Social Readjustment Rating Scale
    a. cope better with stress.
    b. can manage more hassles.
    c. are more vulnerable to illness.
    d. react more negatively to stress.

5. The three stages of the general adaptation syndrome (GAS) include
    a. alarm, resistance, and exhaustion.
    b. fight, flight, and tend-and-befriend.
    c. stimulus, response, and transactions.
    d. major life events, major daily pressures, and hassles.

6. Ulcers provide a nice example of
    a. how stress and personality type interact to cause a physical illness.
    b. how gender differences in stress and resilience act to produce illness.
    c. which alternative treatments are most effective in treating stress-related illnesses.
    d. the interaction of a physical cause with a psychological cause to result in illness.

7. The greatest health risk for coronary heart disease comes from
    a. smoking.
    b. a hostile attitude.
    c. being overweight.
    d. having high cholesterol.

8. We can gain control of stressors in our lives several ways, including
   a. through faith, religion, and spirituality.
   b. with crisis counseling, catharsis, and rumination.
   c. increasing behavioral, cognitive, and emotional control.
   d. using alternative, complementary, and homeopathic medicines.

9. Proactive coping helps people to cope with stress because they can
   a. anticipate problems and be prepared for them.
   b. forget earlier stressful events by focusing on later, happier events.
   c. automatically take part in crisis debriefing, which is always helpful.
   d. build up their immune system to better protect against any ill effects on body systems.

10. Jessica has always heard that it's best to get stress "out of her system," so whenever she feels stressed she throws things. Jessica's coping behavior is a _____ idea, because research evidence shows that _____.
    a. good; indeed, this is a surefire way to reduce overall internal stress
    b. bad; "getting things off one's chest" helps in the long run but not in the short run
    c. bad; "getting it [anger] out of your system" can actually increase anger and stress
    d. good ; catharsis is successful in psychoanalytic and humanistic therapy in reducing stress

11. People who "see the glass as half empty"
    a. are more optimistic.
    b. have a more difficult time handling frustration.
    c. show less commitment to their lives and work.
    d. relive the negative events in their lives, over and over again.

12. Clemente sees each of life's hassles as a challenge that he can master and overcome. Clemente is likely to have a strong sense of
    a. rumination.   c. religiosity.
    b. hardiness.   d. helplessness.

13. Which of the following statements is true regarding smoking?
    a. Each time people try to stop smoking, they smoke even more.
    b. Each time people try to stop smoking, their chances of succeeding improve.
    c. Approximately 50% of American men smoke.
    d. Smoking in both men and women is on the decline.

14. Binge (heavy episodic) drinking is, unfortunately, not rare among college students. According to your text, it is defined as
    a. drinking to the point of a blackout each time you drink.
    b. drinking to the point of intoxication, but only very infrequently.
    c. five or more drinks for men, four or more drinks for women, on a single occasion.
    d. drinking almost to the point of intoxication, waiting to sober up, and repeating this process in a single session of drinking.

15. Studies suggest that genetics play a role in weight control. In reality,
    a. prior beliefs have the most powerful effect on weight.
    b. about 50% of the predisposition to obesity appears to be genetic.
    c. environmental factors appear to play a larger role in weight control.
    d. most of the people who take off weight in a medically managed program keep it off.

16. Lupe wants to lose weight. She shows you the advertising slogans of several weight loss programs, all of which cost the same. Which would you advise her to pursue as potentially the best, based on its slogan?
    a. "We May Be Slow, But We Are Steady."
    b. "Lose All the Weight You Want in Less Than a Month."
    c. "Miracle Sleep: Take Our Sleeping Aid, and the More You Sleep, the More Comes Off."
    d. "No Special Foods, No Special Appliances, Just Pure, Clean Water from Our Private Glacier Flushes Away That Fat."

17. People often mistake the serious consequences of stress-related illnesses, thinking that other events, such as accidents or natural disasters, have higher mortality rates. This bias in thinking reflects
    a. the availability heuristic.
    b. the representativeness heuristic.
    c. self-fulfilling prophecies.
    d. feelings of powerlessness.

18. Chiropractic manipulation is most likely effective due to
    a. the realignment of spinal subluxations.
    b. the medications that the chiropractors prescribe.
    c. the nutritional advice the chiropractor provides.
    d. the attention, support, and advice the patient receives from the chiropractor.

19. Acupuncture has been scientifically demonstrated to relieve nausea after surgery as well as some pain-related conditions. This is probably because of the
    a. placement of needles along meridians.
    b. change in the flow of qi.
    c. caring nature of the CAM practitioners.
    d. placebo effect.

20. The bottom line on alternative treatments is
    a. none of them have been shown to be effective as of this time.
    b. some work, some don't; it's best to consult an authority and the scientific literature.
    c. small doses may not help at all, but they won't harm you, and they might actually help.
    d. many work; large pharmaceutical companies tell people they don't work for financial gain reasons.

After completing the test, calculate your percent correct
(/ 20 =   ) x 100 = _____.

How accurate were your expectations? Does your performance suggest the need for additional study? For the items you missed, go back and identify why the "correct" answer is the best answer.

AFTER YOU READ... PRACTICE TEST ANSWER KEYS

Practice Test 1.

1. c (p. 456)
2. d (p. 457)
3. b (p. 460)
4. c (p. 462)
5. a (p. 462)
6. c (p. 464)
7. a (p. 465)
8. d (p. 465)
9. a (p. 467)
10. d (p. 468)
11. a (p. 470)
12. c (p. 471)
13. b (p. 472)
14. b (p. 473)
15. d (p. 473-474)
16. b (p. 475)
17. c (p. 476)
18. d (p. 478)
19. b (p. 485)
20. b (p. 486)

Practice Test 2.

1. a (p. 457)
2. d (p. 458)
3. c (p. 459-460)
4. c (p. 460)
5. a (p. 461)
6. d (p. 467)
7. b (p. 468)
8. c (p. 471)
9. a (p. 471)
10. c (p. 472)
11. b (p. 473)
12. b (p. 473)
13. b (p. 476)
14. c (p. 476)
15. b (p. 478)
16. a (p. 478)
17. a (p. 481)
18. d (p. 483)
19. d (p. 485)
20. b (p. 487)

AFTER YOU READ ... CONCEPT MAPPING ACTIVITY ANSWERS

ACTIVITY 1: Complete this concept map for general concepts related to stress.

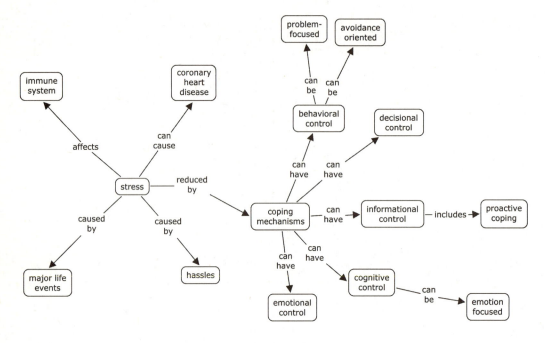

ACTIVITY 2: Here is a possible concept map for CAM.

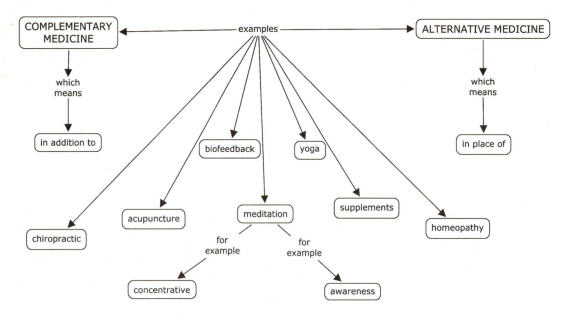

CHAPTER 13
SOCIAL PSYCHOLOGY
HOW OTHERS AFFECT US

BEFORE YOU READ...CHAPTER PREVIEW

Social psychology studies social influences on people's thoughts, feelings, and behaviors. Social influences are powerful and often qualified by individual characteristics and situational contexts. Humans are a social species who, according to *need to belong theory*, form social groups. **Social comparison** reflects the process of looking to others to help us interpret the meaning of a situation and how to behave in the situation. In *upward social comparison,* we compare ourselves to people who seem better than us; in *downward social comparison,* to those who seem inferior to us. There are advantages to each. However, this can lead to **mass hysteria** and *collective delusions* and can also become the source of urban legends. The presence of others can differentially lead to either **social facilitation** or *social disruption*. We often make **attributions** for other people's behaviors, looking for their causes. People often assume that *internal dispositions* play the major role in causing other people's behavior and fail to see the power of *situational influences* on behavior. This tendency is called the **fundamental attribution error**.

Conformity is the tendency for people to change their behavior as a result of group influence. When measured in laboratory situations with *confederates*, conformity is sensitive to social influences of group size, unanimity, and differences in wrong answers. **Deindividuation** occurs when people violate their normal behavior patterns in situations where they cannot be identified as individuals. The Stanford Prison study showed how easily the situation can affect social behavior. Crowds and mobs provide additional examples of changes in normal behavior. **Groupthink** occurs when a tightly knit group conforms to group pressure and avoids dissent. As with conformity, the presence of a deviant voice can be critical in avoiding groupthink. Similarly, with **group polarization** the more dominant voices influence the overall group attitude. This is highlighted in the behavior of **cults.** Resisting cult influence is difficult, but the **innoculation effect** offers promise that debunking the cult early on can be effective. Most cult members are neither mentally ill nor *brainwashed*. In **obedience**, pressure comes from a person in authority. In Milgram's study, over half of his participants followed orders to deliver what they believed were severe shocks to another person. The study is considered a classic because it resulted in surprising findings and because it created an ethical controversy surrounding the degree of stress experienced by the participants. Replication studies show that obedience may be influenced by the prestige of the authority, proximity to the authority or victim, and the presence of another who disobeys.

Research on **prosocial behavior** has also focused on bystander nonintervention and suggests that people are less likely to help when others are present. This lack of intervention may be due to **pluralistic ignorance** (an ambiguous situation is interpreted by social comparison – others are not intervening) and **diffusion of responsibility** (when there are many other people, each one feels less responsible for the consequences of not helping). **Social loafing** describes the phenomenon where people slack off in groups. **Altruism** focuses on helping behavior for unselfish reasons. Researchers have described an **enlightenment effect** in which knowledge of research findings alone can bring about more prosocial behaviors. Research on **aggression** suggests that many factors interact to affect aggression, including interpersonal provocation, frustration, media influences, aggressive cues, arousal, alcohol, drugs, and temperature. Males tend more to physical aggression and females tend more to **relational aggression**.

Attitudes are *beliefs* and often include an emotional component. Attitudes do not always predict behavior and are affected by each person's degree of **self-monitoring**. According to the *recognition* *heuristic,* we form attitudes based on how often we've heard something. Psychologists have explained attitude change in terms of **cognitive dissonance**. **Cognitive dissonance theory** proposes that inconsistencies in our cognitions produce a feeling of uneasiness that we are motivated to reduce. When we behave in a manner that is discrepant from our attitudes, one way to reduce dissonance is to change our attitude. According to **self-perception theory,** we acquire attitudes by observing others. Proponents of **impression management theory** suggest that attitudes actually don't change; people just claim they do to preserve appearances. People can be readily persuaded to engage in various behaviors. The *dual process model* suggests that persuasion can occur along a *central route*, in which we evaluate merits of an argument for its *informational content*; or a *peripheral route*, in which we make quick judgments based on *surface aspects* of arguments. Persuasion techniques include the **foot-in-the door**, the **door-in-the-face**, and the **low-ball techniques**. Characteristics of the messenger are important. We tend to gravitate toward people who resemble us, a phenomenon known as the *implicit egotism* effect. Interesting research shows that as part of this effect people tend toward those whose names begin with the same first letter as their own, called the *name-letter* effect. Pseudoscientific marketers often use persuasion techniques such as vivid testimonials, consensus heuristic, scarcity heuristic, and the manufacturing source heuristic, among others.

Stereotypes are mental shortcuts that stem from adaptive cognitive processes. Stereotypes, however, can mislead us when we cling to them too rigidly. **Prejudice** can result when selected information is used to heighten our perception that others are different from us and can also result in the **ultimate attribution error,** in which we assume that entire groups of people are influenced primarily by similar internal dispositions of individual members. According to **adaptive conservatism,** we are predisposed to distrust anything that is unfamiliar or different, which can lead to an **in-group bias**, and a concomitant belief in **out-group homogeneity**. **Discrimination** refers to negative behaviors toward others. It is very easy to create discrimination even for those who start out just like us, by using the *minimal intergroup paradigm*. Prejudice can lead to **scapegoating** and a belief in the **just-world** hypothesis. Prejudice can be **explicit** (we are consciously aware of the characteristics of an out-group) or **implicit** (we are not aware of our negative attitudes regarding characteristics of an out-group). We can combat prejudice by having groups work together, as in the **jigsaw classroom**.

BEFORE YOU READ... LEARNING OBJECTIVES

After reading Chapter 13 you should be able to:

13.1   Identify the ways in which social situations influence the behavior of individuals
13.2   Explain how the fundamental attribution error can cause us to misjudge others' behaviors
13.3   Determine the factors that influence when we conform to others
13.4   Recognize the dangers of group decision-making and identify ways to avoid mistakes common in group decisions
13.5   Identify the factors that maximize or minimize obedience to authority
13.6   Distinguish those aspects of a situation that increase or decrease the likelihood of bystander intervention
13.7   Describe the social and individual difference variables that contribute to human aggression
13.8   Describe how attitudes relate to behaviors
13.9   Evaluate theoretical accounts of how and when we alter our attitudes
13.10   Identify common and effective persuasion techniques and how they're exploited by pseudo-scientists
13.11   Distinguish prejudice and stereotypes as beliefs from discrimination as a behavior
13.12   Identify some of the causes of prejudice and describe methods for combating it

---

BEFORE YOU READ...TERM IDENTIFICATION

---

adaptive conservatism (p. 529)
aggression (p. 517)
altruism (p. 516)
attitude (p. 520)
attribution (p.499)
cognitive dissonance (p. 522)
conformity (p. 500)
cult (p. 507)
deindividuation (p. 502)
diffusion of responsibility (p. 515)
discrimination (p. 530)
door-in-the-face technique (p. 524)
enlightenment effect (p. 517)
explicit prejudice (p. 532)
foot-in-the door technique (p. 524)
fundamental attribution error (p. 499)
group polarization (p. 506)
groupthink (p. 505)
implicit prejudice (p. 532)
impression management theory (p. 524)
in-group bias (p. 529)

inoculation effect (p. 507)
jigsaw classroom (p. 533)
just-world hypothesis (p. 531)
low-ball technique (p. 524)
mass hysteria (p. 496)
obedience (p. 508)
out-group homogeneity (p. 529)
pluralistic ignorance (p. 515)
prejudice (p. 527)
prosocial behavior (p. 513)
relational aggression (p. 519)
scapegoat hypothesis (p. 531)
self-monitoring (p. 521)
self-perception theory (p. 523)
social comparison theory (p. 496)
social facilitation (p. 498)
social loafing (p. 515)
social psychology (p. 494)
stereotype (p. 527)
ultimate attribution error (p. 529)

AS YOU READ...PRACTICE ACTIVITIES

WHAT IS SOCIAL PSYCHOLOGY?

1. T or F: Social influence processes are adaptive under most circumstances. Explain your answer. (LO 13.1)

2. Demonstrating the phenomenon of social facilitation, Zajonc found that cockroaches run faster when

    _____. (LO 13.1)

3. How can social comparison theory be used to explain collective delusions? (LO 13.1)

4. Describe the fundamental attribution error and give an example from your own experience. (LO 13.2)

5. How do our attributions tend to differ when it comes to explaining our own behavior? (LO 13.2)

SOCIAL INFLUENCE: CONFORMITY AND OBEDIENCE

1. Describe Asch's study of conformity. (LO 13.3)

    Study:

    Results:

    Lesson learned:

2. John does not smoke but is offered a cigarette by a friend. He is with five other friends; all of these friends take a cigarette. Research suggests John's conformity to group pressure would be very likely because the group is unanimous in its behavior. If one of John's five friends *does not* take a cigarette, would John's own conformity be more or less likely? Why? (LO 13.3)

3. Describe the Stanford Prison Study. (LO 13.3)

    Study:

    Results:

    Lesson learned:

4. How can the lessons of this study help explain the behavior of prison guards at Abu Ghraib? (LO 13.3)

5. Differentiate between "groupthink" and "group polarization." (LO 13.4)

    Groupthink:

    Group polarization:

6. You are a member of a group charged with an important decision. What could you do to decrease the group's chances of falling prey to groupthink? (LO 13.4)

7. Explain how extreme forms of groupthink can lead to cults. How can one best resist cult influence? (LO 13.4)

8. Describe Milgram's study: (LO 13.5)

    Study:

    Results:

    Lesson learned:

9. The results of Milgram's study were "shocking" because… (LO 13.5)

   It created an ethical controversy because…

HELPING AND HARMING OTHERS: PROSOCIAL BEHAVIOR AND AGGRESSION

1. Everyone knows that there is safety in numbers. Or is there? What does the empirical evidence suggest about this common knowledge? (LO 13.6)

2. Draw lines linking each major influence on nonintervention with the appropriate question and example. (LO 13.6)

   "Am I the right person to provide help?"

   Pluralistic ignorance   "Is this situation an emergency?"

   Diffusion of responsibility   A person is lying on the sidewalk.

                                         A person is having a heart attack in a crowd.

3. List the factors that are likely to increase the probability of helping. (LO 13.6)
   Situational factors

   Individual factors

4. Social loafing: (LO 13.6)
   Is defined as…

   Is influenced by…

   Can be demonstrated using the example of…

   Can be remedied by…

5. For each of the situational influences on aggression below, provide a brief explanation and example. (LO 13.7)

Interpersonal provocation

Frustration

Media

Aggressive cues

Arousal

Drug/Alcohol

Temperature

6. Boys tend to be higher in physical aggression; girls tend to be higher in relational aggression. (LO 13.7)

What is relational aggression?

Have you ever been a victim of relational aggression?

ATTITUDES AND PERSUASION: CHANGING MINDS

1. T or F: Attitudes predict behaviors with a high level of certainty. Explain. (LO 13.8)

2. How can the recognition heuristic be used to help explain the acquisition of urban legends? (LO 13.1 and 13.8)

3. What are three ways we can reduce dissonance? Give an example of each. (LO 13.10)

    1)

    Example:

    2)

    Example:

    3)

    Example:

4. Briefly describe the Festinger & Carlsmith study. (LO 13.9)

    Study:

    Results:

    Lesson learned:

5. Match the following persuasion techniques with the appropriate example. (LO 13.10)

    a. Door-in-the face   _____ "Thank you for agreeing to stay at my
    house to take care of my cats while I'm
    gone. By the way, there are 7 of them."

    b. Low ball   _____ "Well if you can't help with our Beach
    Clean-up this weekend could you donate $10 to help
    others get there?"

    c. Foot-in-the door   _____ "Thank you for wearing our 'Save the
    trees' button. Could you help the trees
    by joining our organization at the $35 level?"

6. Match each of the following techniques used to market pseudoscience with the applicable principle of persuasion. (LO 13.10)

    a. Phantom goal   _____ "University researchers endorse the use of our subliminal tapes."

    b. Manufacture source credibility   _____ "Ours are the best selling subliminal tapes on the market."

    c. Scarcity heuristic   _____ "These subliminal tapes will only be offered for a limited time."

    d. Consensus heuristic   _____ "Our subliminal tapes can help you master psychology while you sleep!"

PREJUDICE AND DISCRIMINATION

1. Explain the two major biases that contribute to our tendency to ally with others. (LO 13.11)

    In-group bias

    Out-group homogeneity

2. T or F: Jane Elliot's study with brown-eyed and blue-eyed children found that it is hard to get children to discriminate against one another. Explain your answer. (LO 13.11)

3. Match the following contributors to the development of prejudice with its example. (LO 13.12)

    a. Scapegoating   _____New frat members are likely to express dislike of rival frat members.

    b. Just-world   _____The belief that times are bad because illegal aliens have taken away jobs.

    c. Social conformity   _____Rev. Jerry Falwell's statement after 9/11 that America brought this harsh punishment on itself because God was displeased with the country's godlessness.

4. Describe the Robber's Cave study. (LO 13.12)

    Study:

    Results:

    Lesson learned:

5. How did Aronson's Jigsaw Classroom incorporate lessons from the Robber's Cave study? (LO 13.12)

AS YOU READ... CONCEPT MAP ACTIVITIES

ACTIVITY 1:

As examples of social influence, conformity and obedience are similar concepts, yet they are also different. Complete the following concept map, indicating some basic differences. (LO 13.6)

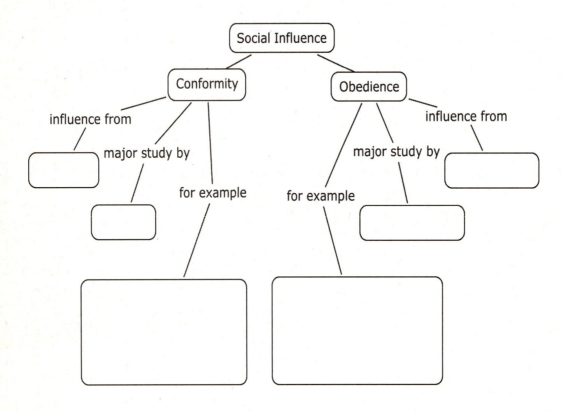

ACTIVITY 2:

The presence of others can have positive or negative effects, depending on the situation. Complete the concept map below, outlining these differences. (LO 13.1)

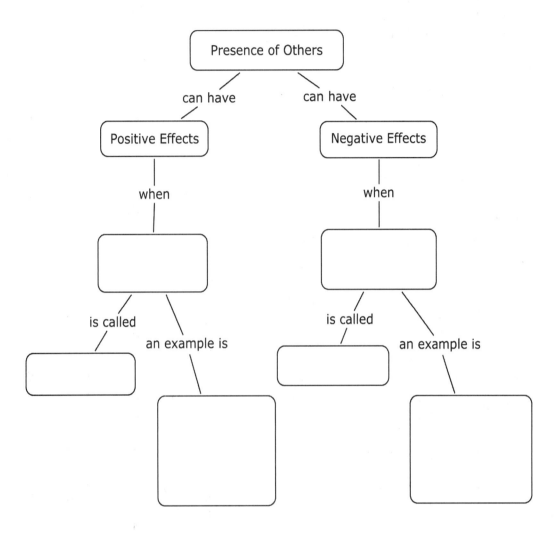

Author activity content supported by *IHMC Cmap Tools* Copyright ©1998-2007 Institute for Human & Machine Cognition

AS YOU READ... MYTH OR REALITY?

Myth: There's no adequate scientific explanation for UFO reports.
Reality: The overwhelming majority of UFO reports can be accounted for, with only 2% remaining truly unidentified.

1. Extraordinary claims require extraordinary evidence. What are some of the ordinary explanations for UFO sightings? How do these relate to the general principles of social psychology?

2. A hypothesis is scientific if it is falsifiable – evidence could be found to show the theory false. Why do the UFO believers' claims often fail to meet this criterion of falsifiability? Can you think of examples?

Myth: Women are yakkers, men are slackers.
Reality: There is greater variability among members of the same gender than between genders.

Claims that there are gender differences in chatter are countered by research suggesting that differences between men and women are not statistically significant.
> See: http://www.npr.org/templates/story/story.php?storyId=11762186&ft=1&f=1024

In addition, who talks more depends on the situation
> See: www.pbs.org/speak/speech/prejudice/women

1. How might the concepts discussed in this chapter on social influence help explain why we hold gender stereotypes?

2. Why might we hold on to our stereotypes despite disconfirming evidence?

1. An important characteristic of critical thinking is being able to see that the answer to many questions is, "It all depends." For example, although the chapter suggests brainstorming may not be all it's cracked up to be, there are situations where bringing groups of people together to work on a common task is effective. When is group work likely to be problematic? When can it be useful?

2. *Thinking critically about your own behavior...* According to a Pew Research Center survey, the number of things Americans say they can't live without has multiplied in the past decade: http://pewresearch.org/pubs/323/luxury-or-necessity

   To what extent do you think these perceptions reflect the processes of social comparison and conformity? Do you think these processes have affected your own perceptions of necessities?

3. How many of the urban legends in Figure 13.2 have you heard? Have you ever asked yourself why you believe these claims? What are some of the social influences that may have contributed to your belief?

What Is Social Psychology?

Explore *Fundamental Attribution Error* and engage in the **Simulation** *Social Facilitation*. Read more about urban legends and how you can use critical thinking skills to question such stories that circulate by choosing **Explore** *Urban Legends*. **Explore** *Internal & External Attributions* to learn more about causal attributions and how they differ cross-culturally.

Social Influence: Conformity and Obedience

To learn about the social influences on conformity, **Watch** *Conformity and Influence in Groups*. To learn more about the Stanford Prison Experiment, **Watch** *The Stanford Prison Experiment*. **Watch** the shocking re-creation of the *Milgram Obedience Study Today*.

Helping and Harming Others: Prosocial Behavior and Aggression

For more about how the presence of others affects our likelihood of providing assistance, **Explore** *Bystander Intervention*. Participate in the **Simulation** *Helping a Stranger* to gain a better understanding of why we don't always provide help.

Attitudes and Persuasion: Changing Minds

To learn more about how we modify our attitudes, **Explore** *Cognitive Dissonance & Attitude Change*. To experience how your own attitudes may not always be consistent with your actual behaviors, participate in a replication of a cognitive dissonance study with the **Simulation** *Cognitive Dissonance*. **Watch** the video *Attitudes and Attitude Change,* which illustrates how attitudes change. Persuasion techniques are demonstrated when you **Watch** the video *Car Salesman Example: Robert Cialdini.*

Prejudice and Discrimination

For a way to better understand that all individuals engage in implicit stereotyping, participate in the **Simulation** *Unconscious Stereotyping*. Then **Watch** the video *Prejudice*. To learn how children overcome prejudice in the classroom, **Listen** to the podcast *Jigsaw Technique*.

AFTER YOU READ… PRACTICE TEST #1

Before beginning this practice test estimate the percent you expect to get correct
Estimated percent correct: _____

1. Which of the following statements appears to be true on the basis of social psychological findings?
   a. There is safety in numbers.
   b. Social influences can be adaptive.
   c. Groups are superior to individuals at decision-making.
   d. Drinking can calm us down, lowering our risk for aggression.

2. When a situation is unclear, we often look to others for guidance about what to do and how to behave. This phenomenon is known as
   a. social comparison.
   b. cognitive dissonance.
   c. social loafing.
   d. groupthink.

3. Demonstrating the phenomenon of _____, Zajonc found that cockroaches will run faster when _____.
   a. conformity; running together.
   b. learning; reinforced
   c. social facilitation; other cockroaches are present
   d. social loafing; they are alone.

4. The effect of an audience on performance can be positive or negative depending on the situation. Social facilitation tends to occur when tasks are _____; social disruption tends to occur when tasks are _____.
   a. unmastered; well-learned
   b. meaningful; meaningless
   c. meaningless; meaningful
   d. well-learned; unmastered

5. When we try to figure out why others (or ourselves) are engaging in a behavior, we are trying to form _____ for the causes of the behavior.
   a. stereotypes
   b. cognitive categories
   c. attitudes
   d. attributions

6. "Sam and I had a big fight. He had been home all day but when I came home from work, the place was a disaster. I told him he was a lazy slob, and he had the nerve to tell me I was one, too. He said that I leave the bathroom a mess every morning. He's too stupid to see that I have to or I'd be late for work." In explaining the causes of the man's behavior, the woman in this example is demonstrating the social psychological principle of
   a. diffusion of responsibility.
   b. the fundamental attribution error.
   c. impression management.
   d. the scapegoat hypothesis.

7. _____ refers to the tendency for people to alter their behavior as a result of group pressure.
    a. In-group biasing
    b. Conformity
    c. The Fundamental Attribution Error
    d. Obedience

8. Keoki believes that global warming is a real threat. During a social gathering, however, most of the people discussing the issue appear to agree that the threat is greatly exaggerated. Keoki is most likely to express his opinion if
    a. all others in the group agree that the threat is exaggerated.
    b. the beliefs of the group are clearly wrong.
    c. there are five people in the group.
    d. one other person is expressing his belief that global warming is a real threat.

9. Which of the following characteristics tends to result in higher levels of conformity?
    a. being part of a collectivist culture
    b. high self-esteem
    c. observing non-conformists
    d. someone who self-identifies as an individualist

10. Which of the following statements is most likely to contribute to groupthink?
    a. "Let's hear some differing opinions."
    b. "What do you think?"
    c. "I'm sure we all agree on this."
    d. "We need to look at all of the evidence."

11. Julia, Annie, and Zora each think Dr. Strange can be a little rude to students at times. After discussing why each of them believes this to be so, they all conclude that Dr. Strange is a terrible teacher and start telling others. This episode provides an example of
    a. social facilitation.   c. group polarization.
    b. deindividuation.   d. the inoculation effect.

12. Cults seem to result when
    a. a group of emotionally unstable individuals come together.
    b. a group of individuals share unquestioning loyalty to a leader.
    c. people are brainwashed.
    d. group polarization becomes extreme.

13. Results of the Milgram study are "shocking" because
    a. psychologists surveyed before the study did not predict such a high level of obedience.
    b. Milgram gave electric shocks to human beings.
    c. Milgram showed that people have a need to harm others.
    d. the low level of compliance to shock another person was unexpected by Milgram.

14. Based on replications of Milgram's original study of obedience, which of the following soldiers would have the most difficulty following orders to injure another person?
    a. a soldier armed with a machine gun in a fortified bunker
    b. a soldier launching a missile
    c. a soldier armed only with a knife
    d. a bombardier releasing a load of bombs

15. Mike sees a man lying on a park bench. The man doesn't look well, but Mike notices that there are a lot of people passing by so he doesn't feel the need to stop. This is an example of
    a. pluralistic ignorance.
    b. groupthink.
    c. deindividuation.
    d. social loafing.

16. We come to believe strange things for no other reason than we've heard them from a lot of people. This phenomenon
    a. explains the enlightenment effect.
    b. reflects the recognition heuristic.
    c. reflects pluralistic ignorance.
    d. explains diffusion of responsibility.

17. "If you can't come to our $100-a-plate *Save the Trees* dinner, could you donate $5.00 to our campaign?" This statement reflects which of the following persuasive techniques?
    a. door-in-the face
    b. foot-in-the door
    c. low-ball
    d. the natural is commonplace

18. Prejudice is to discrimination as
    a. attitude is to behavior.
    b. cognition is to thought.
    c. action is to behavior.
    d. obedience is to conformity.

19. Which of the following is an example of discrimination?
    a. using judges who are blind to musician sex to evaluate musical performance
    b. believing that all teens are bad drivers
    c. denying housing to individuals because of their race
    d. thinking Asians are good students

20. The need to blame others for our own misfortune is
    a. the fundamental attribution error.
    b. the ultimate attribution error.
    c. an example of relational aggression.
    d. an example of the scapegoating hypothesis.

After completing the test, calculate your percent correct
(_____ / 20 = _____) x 100 = _____.

How accurate were your expectations? Does your performance suggest the need for additional study? For the items you missed, go back and identify why the "correct" answer is the best answer.

AFTER YOU READ... PRACTICE TEST #2

Before beginning this practice test, estimate the percent you expect to get correct.
Estimated percent correct _____.

1. During Orson Welles' *War of the Worlds* radio broadcast, tens of thousands of people came to believe that aliens had actually landed at Grover's Mill. Which of the following contributed to this phenomenon?
   a. People openly discussed alternative explanations.
   b. Social comparison processes drove people to look to others for what to think.
   c. Orson Wells did not tell people the radio show was fictitious.
   d. Other stations also covered the event.

2. We often assume that _____ play a major role in causing other people's behavior while we fail to see the power of _____.
   a. internal dispositions; situational influences
   b. pressures to conform; biological factors
   c. biological factors; internal dispositions
   d. situational influences; internal dispositions

3. In high school, Jesus wore his pants baggy, loose, and low—like the rest of the guys. When he got to college, he noticed a dramatic difference in pant wearing style. He are MOST likely to CHANGE his pant style if
   a. no one on campus wears their pants loose and low.
   b. his group of friends wears their pants low.
   c. others he know wears crazy clothes.
   d. his advisor tells him to buy some new pants.

4. Zimbardo's prison study and the Abu Ghraib situation are similar because both reflect
   a. groupthink.
   b. the influence of social roles.
   c. the strong link between attitudes and behavior.
   d. bystander apathy.

5. During the Vietnam War, Lt. William Calley ordered his men to shoot women and children in what came to be known as the My Lai massacre. This incident most closely reflects which of the following studies?
   a. Zajonc's study of social facilitation
   b. Solomon Asch's study of conformity
   c. Stanley Milgram's study of obedience
   d. Festinger & Carlsmith's study of cognitive dissonance

6. Which of the following accurately describes Milgram's study of obedience?
   a. The learners were given electric shocks.
   b. The "teachers" were stressed.
   c. Most participants refused to obey the authority figure.
   d. The experimenter lost objectivity.

7. Bystander non-intervention appears to result from
   a. bystander apathy and pluralistic ignorance.
   b. pluralistic ignorance and diffusion of responsibility.
   c. social debilitation and bystander apathy.
   d. conformity and obedience.

8. You have been assigned a psychology project in which six of you must write and present a group paper on an urban legend for only one group grade. Which of the following is likely to be true?
   a. The group paper will be better than any individual paper.
   b. Individuals are likely to work less hard than if they were working on individual papers.
   c. Students will feel personally responsible for group products.
   d. By brainstorming, the group will come up with twice as many creative ideas as group members would have come up with individually.

9. People are more likely to help another person if
   a. they are actually in a hurry.
   b. there are many people around.
   c. they are concerned about social approval.
   d. they are in a good mood.

10. Which of the following people would be most likely to come to the aid of another?
    a. someone who read about bystander intervention research
    b. a member of a crowd
    c. someone in a hurry
    d. someone concerned about social approval

11. Which of the following is a TRUE statement about aggression?
    a. Humans are the only species that wages all-out war against its own members.
    b. The presence of a gun can increase the chances one will act violently in response to provocation.
    c. The calming effects of alcohol reduce aggressive tendencies.
    d. There is little evidence that warmer temperatures are associated with higher rates of violence.

12. According to the research, which of the following is true?
    a. Compared with females, males tend to be more physically and relationally aggressive.
    b. Men tend to be more physically aggressive; females tend to be more relationally aggressive.
    c. Studies across the animal kingdom suggest there is no real difference between male and female aggression.
    d. Differences in aggression are biological, not cultural.

13. John smokes cigarettes despite warnings that smoking causes cancer. He justifies his smoking by saying he also exercises so smoking isn't that dangerous for him. His justification reduces
    a. insufficient obedience.   c. diffusion of responsibility.
    b. cognitive dissonance.   d. conformity.

14. Which of the following claims reflects the findings of social psychological research?
    a. Act as if you like someone and you soon will.
    b. Brainstorming is an effective way to come up with ideas.
    c. Brainwashing is a unique means of permanently changing behavior.
    d. The primary reason for bystander nonintervention is the apathy of the onlookers.

15. Which of the following describes a difference between the central and peripheral routes to persuasion?
    a. The central route involves reasoning; the peripheral route promotes snap judgments.
    b. The central route relies on techniques such as low-ball and door-in-the face.
    c. The central route is often relied upon by promoters of pseudoscience.
    d. The central route relies more heavily on the appearance and likeability of the communicator.

16. An ad for a new book claims it is an Oprah Book Club pick. This marketing technique relies on
    a. the consensus heuristic.
    b. the scarcity heuristic.
    c. manufactured source credibility.
    d. the goddess within.

17. During wartime, countries often emphasize the differences between their own culture and that of the enemy, pointing out differences such as race, language, religion, dietary habits, and fashion. This focus contributes to prejudice
    a. by emphasizing out-group homogeneity and in-group similarity.
    b. through implicit stereotyping.
    c. through social disruption.
    d. by increasing cultural knowledge.

18. The belief that times are bad because illegal aliens have taken away jobs is an example of
    a. the just-world hypothesis.
    b. social conformity.
    c. scapegoating.
    d. discrimination.

19. The just-world-hypothesis
    a. explains altruism.
    b. reflects the need to see the word just as it is.
    c. underlies why some believe cancer victims are responsible for their plight.
    d. avoids "blaming the victim."

20. Which of the following would be most effective in combating prejudice?
    a. allowing people to speak with a minority group member in a café setting
    b. providing information to groups about cultural differences
    c. creating a task in which the groups have to cooperate in order to succeed
    d. having groups compete against one another at a sporting event

After completing the test, calculate your percent correct
(/ 20 =   ) x 100 = _____.

How accurate were your expectations? Does your performance suggest the need for additional study? For the items you missed, go back and identify why the "correct" answer is the best answer.

AFTER YOU READ... PRACTICE TEST ANSWER KEYS

Practice Test 1.
1. b (p. 496)
2. a (p. 496)
3. c (p. 498)
4. d (p. 498)
5. d (p. 499)
6. b (p. 499)
7. b (p. 500)
8. d (p. 501)
9. a (p. 502)
10. c (p. 505)
11. c (p. 506)
12. b (p. 507)
13. a (p. 510)
14. c (p. 511)
15. a (p. 514)
16. b (p. 521)
17. a (p. 525)
18. a (p. 527, 530)
19. c (p. 530)
20. d (p. 531)

Practice Test 2.
1. b (p. 497)
2. a (p. 499)
3. a (p. 500)
4. b (p. 503)
5. c (p. 508)
6. b (p. 509)
7. b (p. 514)
8. b (p. 515)
9. d (p. 516)
10. a (p. 517)
11. b (p. 518)
12. b (p. 519)
13. b (p. 522-523)
14. a (p. 523)
15. a (p. 524)
16. c (p. 527)
17. a (p. 529)
18. c (p. 531)
19. c (p. 531)
20. c (p. 533)

AFTER YOU READ... SAMPLE CONCEPT MAPS

ACTIVITY 1:

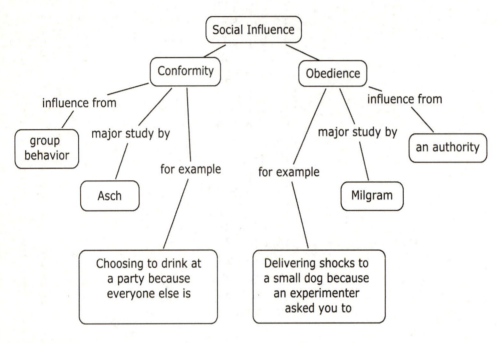

ACTIVITY 2:

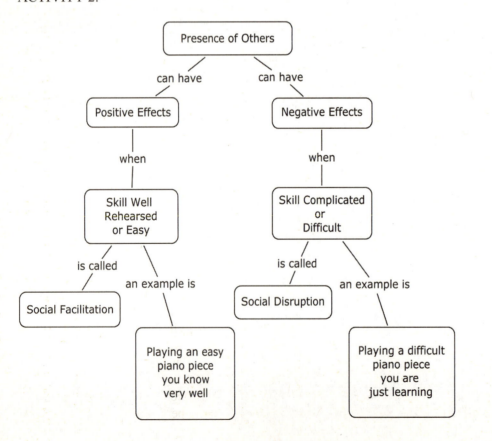

BEFORE YOU READ ... CHAPTER PREVIEW

Personality can be conceived of as composed of **traits**, which reflect typical ways in which people respond, think, behave, and feel. There are two approaches to studying personality. In the **nomothetic approach,** researchers examine general principles across individuals. The **idiographic approach** focuses on individual differences. Together, these approaches explain *both commonalities and differences* across people. The study of personality follows three broad influences on behavior: *genetic factors, shared environmental factors,* and *nonshared environmental factors.* Research studies show that the genetic component for many personality traits is strong in identical twins, even when reared apart. *Adoption studies* show that adopted children share more personality traits with their biological parents than with their adoptive parents. Nevertheless, the evidence for genetic factors is not perfect, demonstrating the influence of nonshared environmental factors. The bottom line: *shared environmental factors seem to play a small role* in adult personality. **Molecular genetic** studies seek to identify which genes are associated with specific traits.

Most psychologists approach the study of personality through several major frameworks, including the psychoanalytic, trait, behavioral, and humanistic approaches. *Psychoanalytic theory*, developed by Sigmund Freud, suggests that the mind and the body have distinct influences on behavior. Freud suggested three core assumptions for psychoanalytic theory: **psychic determinism**, *symbolic meaning*, and *unconscious motivation*. These three assumptions can then be seen within the interactions of the three parts of human personality: the **id**—which operates on the *pleasure principle*; the **ego**—which operates on the *reality principle;* and the **superego**. These three components are often in conflict. One of the coping mechanisms people use to reduce the anxiety caused by this conflict is the use of **defense mechanisms**. These include **repression** (*motivated forgetting*), which accounts for *infantile amnesia*, as well as **denial, regression, reaction-formation, displacement, projection, rationalization, identification with the aggressor** (the basis of the Stockholm syndrome), and **sublimation.** According to Freud's approach to personality, early *psychosexual development* is critical, proceeding through a series of stages, each of which focuses on different **erogenous zones.** Freud's stages of psychosexual development include an **oral stage**, an **anal stage**, a **phallic stage** (during which boys might develop an *Oedipus complex* and girls might develop an *Electra complex* and *penis envy*)**,** a **latency stage**, and a **genital stage.** Freud believed that if people get **fixated** in a particular stage, then they have difficulty passing through later stages. Although Freud's work has had a powerful impact on society, criticisms of his approach include an inability to falsify major features of his approach, a failure of predictions, a questionable conception of the unconscious, a reliance on a limited and unrepresentative sample, and flawed assumptions of shared environmental influence. Freud's students and followers developed **neo-Freudian theories,** which toned down the emphasis on sexuality and Freud's pessimistic view of our ability to change while retaining his focus on the unconscious and the importance of early life experiences in shaping personality. For example, Adler suggested that we are all **striving for superiority**, crafting our own **style of life** but are susceptible to an **inferiority complex**. In addition to a *personal unconscious*, Carl Jung argued for a **collective unconscious** that contains cross-cultural archetypes. Many of the approaches developed by Freud's followers suffer from the same criticisms as did Freud's approach, particularly an inability to falsify many of the central premises of their approaches.

Another approach to personality grew from the behaviorist's influence on psychology. This group of theorists rejected the influence of early childhood experiences in shaping personality and believed that *environmental contingencies* cause our behaviors. The two major assumptions underlying the behavioral view of personality include a focus on genetics and on reinforcers and punishers in the environment. A more moderate approach was proposed by **social learning theorists,** who emphasized the effect of **reciprocal determinism** on personality. Social learning approaches proposed *observational learning* as important to development. In addition, people's attributions were accounted for by an internal or external **locus of control**. Behavioral and social learning approaches are favored for their empirical attitude. However, strict behaviorist explanations of personality are criticized for excluding a causal role for thinking in shaping personality and because the predictions of observational learning have not panned out.

Humanistic approaches to personality provide a third view. Humanistic approaches emphasize free will and **self-actualization**, a desire to be the best that we can be, at the core of personality development. In contrast to a Freudian view of a pleasure-seeking id driving our behavior, the humanistic view sees human nature as constructive. Humanists see personality as made up of three components: *the organism, the self,* and **conditions of worth**. Incongruence between these various components leads to psychological disorders. Humanistic approaches have been criticized for being difficult to falsify and suffering from confirmation bias.

A final approach seeks to understand the *structure* of personality as a cluster of individual traits. This approach relies on **factor analysis** to define traits. The most scientifically supported model is called the **Big Five**. Taking a **lexical approach** based in language usage, according to this approach all people fall along a continuum in five dimensions of *extraversion, neuroticism, conscientiousness, agreeableness* and *openness to experience*. The Big Five provides evidence for people's *implicit personality theories*. A criticism of this approach is the finding of inconsistency of behaviors across situations. This criticism, however, has been countered by other research that shows that traits are good at predicting behavior on average, rather than in specific situations, therefore predicting behavioral trends, if not specific behaviors. Research evidence suggests that traits are stable across the lifespan, perhaps changing a little until age 30. Some of the Big Five traits are not found in all cultures, but different important traits emerge. *Individualism* versus *collectivism* may explain some cross-cultural differences. Thus, traits are useful in predicting long-term average behavior of individuals, and they describe individuals very well, but trait approaches *describe* but do not *explain* why people behave the way they do.

No discussion of personality is complete without an exploration of different approaches to personality assessment. Phrenology, one of the earliest attempts to assess personality based on the pattern of bumps on the skull, failed to withstand empirical testing. *Physiognomy*, based on facial types, also did not fare well. These days, assessments are evaluated for their *reliability* (consistency) and *validity* (the truthfulness of the measure). **Structured personality tests** are paper-and-pencil tests with fixed responses. The most widely used of these is the **MMPI-2,** popular because of its high validity and reliability. The MMPI-2 was developed by means of an **empirical** (data-based) **method of test construction.** Although low on **face validity,** it has three validity scales that detect *responses sets, impression management,* and *malingering*: the *L* scale, the *F* scale, and the *K* scale. Other structured tests have been developed using a rational/theoretical method of test construction. Although many structured tests have fair validity and reliability, such as the NEO-PI-R used to assess the Big Five, others, such as the Myers-Briggs Type Indicator (MBTI), have doubtful validity and reliability. In contrast to structured tests, **projective tests** require a person to interpret an ambiguous stimulus, such as the **Rorschach Inkblot Test** or the **Thematic Apperception Test**. Such tests are favored by the psychoanalytic approach because their underlying **projective hypothesis** is that the interpretation of a vague, ambiguous stimulus allows for a person to project their personality onto a stimulus and for unconscious motives to be revealed. Unfortunately, reliability and validity are both very poor. In particular, the Rorschach has been shown to have poor **incremental validity**. Other projective tests include *human figure drawing* tests and **graphology.** A final caution regarding all types of personality assessments involves the **P. T. Barnum**

effect: an interpretation that is sufficiently vague and general and could fit almost anybody and thereby provides personal validation.

BEFORE YOU READ ... LEARNING OBJECTIVES

After reading Chapter 14 you should be able to:
14.1   Describe how twin and adoption studies shed light on genetic and environmental influences on personality
14.2   Describe the core assumptions of psychoanalytic theory
14.3   Describe key criticisms of psychoanalytic theory and the central features of neo-Freudian theories
14.4   Identify the core assumptions of behavioral and social learning theories of personality
14.5   Describe key criticisms of behavioral and social learning approaches
14.6   Explain the concept of self-actualization and its role in humanistic models
14.7   Describe key criticisms of humanistic approaches
14.8   Describe trait models of personality, including the Big Five
14.9   Identify key criticisms of trait models
14.10 Describe structured personality tests, such as the MMPI-2, and their methods of construction
14.11 Describe projective tests, particularly the Rorschach, and their strengths and weaknesses
14.12 Identify common pitfalls in personality assessment

BEFORE YOU READ ... TERM IDENTIFICATION
---

anal stage (p. 551)
archetype (p. 554)
Big Five (p. 562)
collective unconscious (p. 554)
conditions of worth (p. 559)
defense mechanisms (p. 548)
denial (p. 548)
displacement (p. 551)
ego (p. 547)
Electra complex (p. 551)
empirical method of test construction (p. 568)
erogenous zone (p. 551)
face validity (p. 568)
factor analysis (p. 561)
genital stage (p. 551)
graphology (p. 572)
id (p. 547)
identification with the aggressor (p. 551)
idiographic approach (p. 541)
incongruence (p. 559)
incremental validity (p. 571)
inferiority complex (p. 554)
latency stage (p. 551)
lexical approach (p. 562)
locus of control (p. 557)
Minnesota Multiphasic Personality Inventory (MMPI) (p. 567)
molecular genetic study (p. 544)

neo-Freudian theories (p. 553)
nomothetic approach (p. 541)
Oedipus complex (p. 551)
oral stage (p. 551)
P. T. Barnum effect (p. 574)
peak experience (p. 560)
personality (p. 541)
phallic stage (p. 551)
pleasure principle (p. 547)
projection (p. 549)
projective hypothesis (p. 570)
projective test (p. 570)
psychic determinism (p. 547)
rational/theoretical method of test construction (p. 569)
rationalization (p. 551)
reaction-formation (p. 549)
reality principle (p. 547)
reciprocal determinism (p. 557)
regression (p. 549)
repression (p. 548)
Rorschach Inkblot Test (p. 570)
self-actualization (p. 559)
social learning theorists (p. 556)
structured personality tests (p. 567)
style of life (p. 553)
sublimation (p. 551)
superego (p. 547)

Thematic Apperception Test (TAT) (p. 571) | trait (p. 541)

AS YOU READ ... PRACTICE ACTIVITIES

PERSONALITY: WHAT IS IT AND HOW CAN WE STUDY IT?

1. Your text does not provide a definitive definition of "personality." Formulate a definition that takes into account your text's description of the factors that determine those behaviors we can call a person's "personality." (LO 14.1)

2. Review the logic of the evidence underlying the statement that shared environmental influences appear to have little effect on personality development. Write out at least two sources of converging evidence to support this conclusion. (LO 14.1)

3. Although the results of molecular genetics studies need to be interpreted with caution, a few studies have had more reliable findings. What seems to be the important underlying factor in these studies? (LO14.1)

PSYCHOANALYTIC THEORY: THE CONTROVERSIAL LEGACY OF SIGMUND FREUD AND HIS FOLLOWERS

1. Keep track of your "slips of the tongue" for the next several days. Then, look at the core assumptions of the psychoanalytic approach to personality (psychic determinism, symbolic meaning, and unconscious motivation). Do you believe that your "slips of the tongue" have provided an insight into your unconscious? If not, what do they tell you about your behavior? (LO 14.2)

2. Although the analogy between consciousness and an iceberg is intuitively appealing, and captures the static essence of the three components of personality, it fails to capture the dynamic interplay between the id, ego, and superego. Keeping in mind that the ego is constantly mediating between the desires of the id and the morality of the superego, suggest another analogy that would capture the essence of this active part of personality. (LO 14.2)

3. Go back to Chapter 10 on Human Development. Complete this table, mapping out the stages of psychosexual development in comparison to Piaget's stages of cognitive development based on age. Note the similarities and contrasts between these two descriptive approaches to development. (LO 14.2)

	birth -				
Piaget's Cognitive Development					
Freud's Psychosexual Development					

4. Match the defense mechanism to the example: (LO 14.2)

   a. Jamal, a professional golfer, missed an easy putt. Afterward, he banged his putter so hard into the ground that he bent the shaft.
   b. During her first semester away at college, Tanya called home every day to ask her mom how to do things around her dorm room.
   c. Maria can't understand why her neighbors gossip so much.
   d. Although Mike claims he was fired from his sales job because the boss's nephew was brought into the company, in reality his sales figures were very low.
   e. Sharona never really liked to be around children, but after having two of her own, she spends her days volunteering as room mother at her children's school.
   f. Bill is a successful basketball player, but as a child his parents had many phone calls from teachers about his aggressive nature on the playground.

   _____ displacement

   _____ regression

   _____ projection

   _____ rationalization

   _____ reaction- formation

   _____ sublimation

5. Your text provides five criticisms of Freud's psychoanalytic approach to personality. Go back to Chapter 1 and reread the section on ruling out rival hypotheses. Then suggest specific examples of ruling out rival hypotheses in Freud's approach. (LO 14.3)

6. Discuss the elements that neo-Freudians retained from the classic psychoanalytic approach, and those elements that they modified. Then note what each neo-Freudian did individually to advance studies of personality. (LO 14.3)

BEHAVIORAL AND SOCIAL LEARNING THEORIES OF PERSONALITY

1. Some aspects of behavioral and social learning approaches to personality are perhaps surprisingly similar to psychoanalytic approaches. Compare the two approaches. Note which aspects you found most surprising, and why. (LO 14.4)

2. How do you think that observational learning relates to the finding that social learning approaches were among the first to rely on "thinking" as important to personality development? (LO 14.4)

3. Go to http://www.similarminds.com/locus.html and take this test to determine whether you have an internal or external locus of control. Do you think the test results accurately reflect how you think about yourself when you think about locus of control? Did the items on this test reflect the tone of sample items in your text? (LO 14.4)

4. Go back to the first part of this chapter and reread the section on shared and unshared environments. Then develop the argument that observational learning and the findings on shared environments are in opposition to one another. (LO 14.5)

HUMANISTIC MODELS OF PERSONALITY: THE THIRD FORCE

1. Rogers's humanistic approach is often described in terms of conditional versus unconditional positive regard. In conditional positive regard, love and respect are given only when a person behaves in accordance with a significant other's wishes. However, in unconditional positive regard, a person is always valued, even if the person's actions are not. To quote another famous Mr. Rogers, "Sometimes, good people do bad things." Relate the notion of unconditional positive regard to the personality component, "conditions of worth." (LO 14.6)

2. How would a "whistle-blower" (a person who publicly discloses some negative aspect of a company's operations that the company prefers be kept secret) fit into Maslow's definition of a self-actualized person? (LO 14.6)

3. Some writers have provided evidence that Mother Theresa was no saint (c.f. see the review of Hitchens' scathingly negative view of Mother Theresa at http://www.population-security.org/swom-96-09.htm and http://www.slate.com/id/2090083).Given her need to seek funds for causes that most governments and organizations gave low priority to, and her strict religious beliefs, then her attitudes should not be surprising. With this new insight, do you still consider Mother Theresa to be a fully actualized person? Why or why not? Can your conclusion be falsified? How or why not? (LO 14.6)

4. Freud talked about many elements of human nature that appear to be innately negative, such as thanatos, a death drive inherent in all people, as well as the constant conflicts between various parts of our psyche. How can you resolve this general focus on negative aspects of human nature with the positive picture painted by humanists? (LO14.7)

TRAIT MODELS OF PERSONALITY: CONSISTENCIES IN OUR BEHAVIOR

1. Rank order where you might fall along the dimensions of the Big Five personality traits.

Agreeableness   LO|--|--|HI
Openness   LO|--|--|HI
Neuroticism   LO|--|--|HI
Conscientiousness LO|--|--|HI
Extraversion   LO|--|--|HI

Now go to http://www2.wmin.ac.uk/~buchant/wwwffi/ and complete the Big Five test.

How did your predictions compare to the test results? If your predictions were "off," what accounted for the differences? Is this type of test helpful in understanding your personality dynamics? Discuss the validity of your test results.

Now try this version: http://webspace.ship.edu/cgboer/bigfiveminitest.html.
Did you have trouble discriminating between some of the terms? Does this help you to better understand the criticism of the lexical approach? Why or why not?

You took two different tests that measured your five traits. Were your results consistent and reliable across both tests? What can you conclude about the reliability of Big Five testing? (LO 14.8)

2. Cosmetic psychopharmacology for one's personality is an interesting but controversial proposal, much like cosmetic surgery for the body. Do you believe it would be good for individuals and for society as a whole if we could take a pill to make our personalities more "attractive"? Why or why not? (LO 14.8)

3. The argument against trait approaches—that behaviors are inconsistent across situations—is tempered by the finding that traits do predict behavior averaged across many situations. Consider two traits of your own and note situations in which you behaved *in*consistently. Would you agree that on average, across a wide-range of situations, your behavior is consistent? Why or why not? (LO 14.9)

4. Consider the effects of caffeine on arousal. How might caffeine differentially affect introverts and extraverts? What about having a cup of coffee just before a crucial exam? Yes or no for introverts, extraverts, neither, or both? Make sure you understand Eysenck's argument in your text!(LO 14.9)

5. Complete the following table to help you summarize the key points of the four different approaches to personality (LO 14.2–LO 14.9)

	Psychoanalytic	Behavioristic	Humanistic	Trait
Importance of unconscious				
Behavior pre-determined or free will				
Personality structures				
Concept of conscience				
Principal motives				
View of human nature				

PERSONALITY ASSESSMENT: MEASURING AND MISMEASURING THE PSYCHE

1. Look in your text at Sheldon's body types in Figure 14.4. Based on the information provided in the text, which type are you? Do you believe the traits associated with this body type match you? Why or why not? Which ones match and which ones don't? (LO 14.10)

2. Imagine that you are ordered by a judge to have a psychological assessment. The court-appointed psychologist plans to base his entire assessment on the Rorschach Inkblot Test. What would you tell your attorney to convince him to ask the judge for a different psychologist? (LO 14.11)

3. Criminal profiling has been very popular on television shows and movies. Some studies, however, find that professional profilers are no more accurate than college chemistry majors in determining criminal profiles. Think of alternate hypotheses for this latter finding—and which might take us back to considering profiling as legitimate. (LO14.12)

As You Read ... Concept Map Activities

ACTIVITY 1: Of the four approaches to personality, the psychoanalytic is the most complicated. Complete this concept map to simplify this approach.

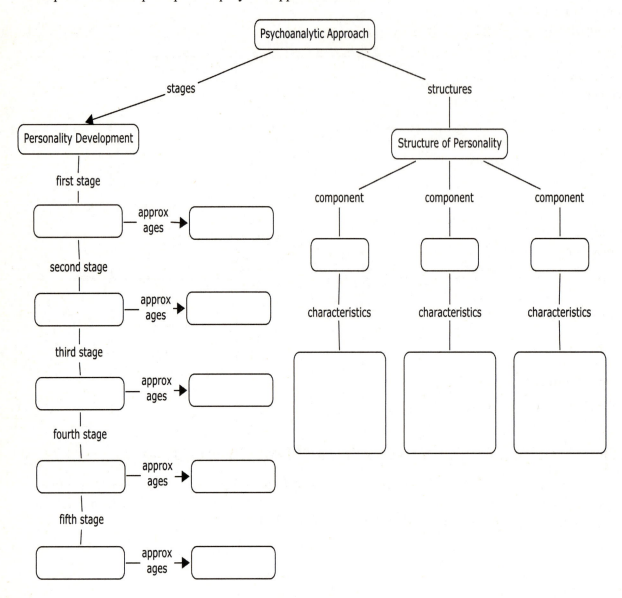

Author activity content supported by *IHMC Cmap Tools* Copyright ©1998-2007 Institute for Human & Machine Cognition

ACTIVITY 2: Complete this concept map for personality assessment.

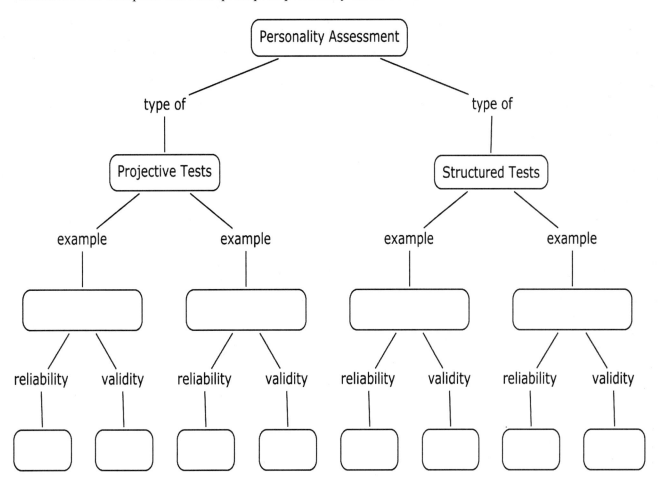

Author activity content supported by *IHMC Cmap Tools* Copyright ©1998-2007 Institute for Human & Machine Cognition

ACTIVITY 3: Take the information that you generated for the table for Practice Activity #5 at the end of the section evaluating Trait Models of Personality (where you summarize all four models), and "translate" that information from a table into a concept map that allows you to see a greater level of relationships by using one-way and two-way arrows.

As You Read... Myth or Reality?

Myth: Personality tests are good predictors of job performance.
Reality: Personality tests only work when they measure traits important to performing specific job tasks.

Personality testing in the workplace is becoming increasingly pervasive. Many employers are being sold by personality test salespeople's clever marketing that claims personality testing as the best way to assure the best employees. Some even go so far as to suggest that the resume or interview adds nothing that a quick computerized personality test can't detect.

1. Read about some of the critical reviews of personality testing in general and in the workplace at this website: http://www.enotalone.com/article/5584.html

2. Based on your readings of the text and this book excerpt, develop a rationale against the use of personality testing by potential employers.

Myth: Birth order affects personality development in life-long ways.
Reality: Personality is far too complex to be affected by birth order.

You can often hear people in conversations allude to one's successes and failures and then use birth order to explain these. You have certainly heard someone say something along the lines of, "Well, she's an only child, so that explains it." Or, "John was the first born and destined to be a leader."

1. Go to http://hmclarke12.tripod.com/id16.html and take the quiz.

2. At the end the authors make some comments on the validity and reliability of such quizzes, but what if your answers did fall in the predicted direction of birth order proponents? What alternative explanations could there be for this effect?

As You Read ... Put Your Scientific Thinking Skills to the Test

1. At http://www.myersbriggs.org/my%2Dmbti%2Dpersonality%2Dtype/mbti%2Dbasics/ you can read promotional information on the Myers-Briggs Type Indicator (MBTI). Then go to http://skepdic.com/myersb.html to read a critique of the MBTI. Take what you read there and in your text about the Jungian approach to personality, as well as the section in the chapter about personality assessment, develop an argument, and come to a conclusion with evidence for whether you believe the MBTI is a good measure of personality.

2. Go to http://www.wizardrealm.com/tests/index.html and pick any of the personality tests offered there. Take the test and read about your results. What elements of personality did this test measure? Was this a projective or structured test? How appropriate do you think that the test is for measuring the personality characteristics that were in your report? What do you think would be its validity and reliability? Compare the items in that test with the kinds of items that *should* be included in tests of personality that would correspond to the aspects of personality described in your textbook.

AS YOU READ... MYPSYCHLAB CONNECTION

Personality: What Is It and How Can We Study It?
What is personality? **Listen** to the *Personality* podcast to find out. To see the roles nature and nurture played in the development of their personalities, **Watch** *Twins Separated at Birth, Reunited.*

Psychoanalytic Theory: The Controversial Legacy of Sigmund Freud and His Followers
For a good review of Freud's theories on personality development, go to the following **Explore** modules: *Id, Ego, Superego, Freud's Five Psychosexual Stages of Personality Development*, and *Defense Mechanisms*. To learn more about Freud's followers, **Watch** *Carl Jung: Unconscious.*

Behavioral and Social Learning Theories of Personality
Compare behavioral and social learning theories of personality when you **Explore** *Behavioral Versus Social Learning Theories of Personality.*

Humanistic Models of Personality: The Third Force
To compare Humanistic Theories against other personality theories, go to **Explore** *Psychodynamic, Behavioral, Trait & Type, Humanistic and Cognitive Approaches to Personality.*

Trait Models of Personality: Consistencies in Our Behavior
For a review of Trait Models of personality, **Explore** *The Five Factor Model* and *Mischel's Theory of Personality.*

Personality Assessment: Measuring and Mismeasuring the Psyche
For more on how researchers and clinicians attempt to measure personality and diagnose personality disorders, **Explore** *Personality Assessment.*

AFTER YOU READ… PRACTICE TEST #1

Before beginning this practice test, estimate the percent you expect to get correct.
Anticipated percent correct: _____

1. Jane is listening to a radio talk show host and decides she is going to follow the advice given out to someone else. You tell Jane to follow this radio host's advice
   a. confidently, this radio host's training has prepared her to synthesize complicated constructs into simpler ones.
   b. confidently, because this host takes primarily a nomothetic approach to understanding the caller's problem.
   c. cautiously, because this host often takes a complicated, multifaceted construct, and provides single-cause explanations.
   d. confidently, this host tries to interpret problems based on wide-ranging influences such as genetic, familial, and social forces.

2. Personality is generally a function of three broad influences that include
   a. culture, family life, and school experiences.
   b. nomothetic factors, idiographic factors, and genetic factors.
   c. traits, early childhood experiences, and reward contingencies.
   d. genetics, shared environmental factors, and nonshared environmental factors.

3. A strong conclusion about personality development, based on various studies of identical twins raised both together and apart, is that
   a. genetic factors have, at best, only a small effect on adult personality.
   b. genetics and shared environmental factors together determine adult personality.
   c. shared environmental factors have, at best, only a small effect on adult personality.
   d. shared and nonshared environmental factors contribute equally to personality development.

4. Jermaine argues that psychic determinism, symbolic meaning, and unconscious motivations influence our personality. Jermaine believes in the _____ approach to personality.
   a. trait   c. behaviorist
   b. humanistic   d. psychoanalytic

5. In purely Freudian psychoanalytic terms, the core assumptions of determinism and unconscious psychic motivation suggest that
   a. people have little free will.
   b. free will is limited by the id's desires.
   c. we can choose our own actions, as long as the superego permits them.
   d. we have the power to control forces outside of our conscious awareness.

6. The pleasure principle drives the _____, whereas the reality principle drives the _____.
   a. ego; id   c. id; superego
   b. id; ego   d. ego; superego

7. In order, from birth onward, the stages of psychosexual development are
   a. oral, anal, penile, phallic, genital.
   b. oral, penile, anal, latency, phallic.
   c. oral, anal, phallic, latency, genital.
   d. oral, anal, genital, latency, phallic.

8. Compared to strict Freudian approaches, the neo-Freudians shared Freud's idea of _____, but differed in _____.
   a. cross-cultural archetypes; am emphasis on unconscious forces
   b. psychosexual development; an emphasis on a personal unconscious
   c. unconscious influences on behavior; placing less emphasis on the central role of sexuality
   d. optimism for personality change in adulthood; the importance of early experiences in shaping behavior

9. Because radical behaviorist views of personality focus on contingencies in the environment, they rely heavily on the principles of
   a. psychoanalysis.
   b. operant conditioning.
   c. classical conditioning.
   d. information-processing.

10. Justin always wears a helmet when riding a motorcycle. He knows that he can actively do something to keep himself safe. Justin must have a(n) _____ locus of control.
    a. primary
    b. internal
    c. external
    d. secondary

11. Which of the following individuals shows the greatest self-actualization?
    a. John. During the baseball season, he likes to take in a ballgame after work.
    b. Carmen. She was recently voted "most popular" by her many friends in her sorority.
    c. Mike. He regularly runs errands for his grandmother because he has no job and has the time to help her out.
    d. Tasha. After retiring from her teaching job, she spends six months out of each year working in a refugee camp in Darfur.

12. Which of the following is true of the Big Five traits?
    a. Tenacity is a sixth trait found among chimpanzees.
    b. The traits are found universally.
    c. Scores on the Big Five are correlated with intelligence.
    d. These traits show up most consistently in factor analyses.

13. Mamoru is taking the Big Five personality test, but he's stuck. One of the problems with trait approaches is that they do rely on a lexical approach to personality. Mamoru may be having a difficult time deciding if he is
    a. kind or rude.
    b. bashful or shy.
    c. jealous or creative.
    d. careless or thoughtful.

14. When a particular test is consistent in assessing some characteristic, this is known as
    a. validity.
    b. reliability.
    c. standardization.
    d. truthfulness of the measure.

15. Personality tests can be divided into two broad categories. These include
    a. implicit and explicit.
    b. intrinsic and extrinsic.
    c. structured and projective.
    d. conscious and subconscious.

16. Lukasz has been asked by a potential new employer to complete the MBTI as part of his job application process. Lukasz should
    a. complete the test because knowing his "type" will provide useful information both for his new employer and for himself.
    b. walk out the door, because any potential employer who uses such a poor test is not worth working for, no matter the quality of the position.
    c. refuse to complete the test because he knows it will reveal his weaknesses, which may lead the new employer to not hire him.
    d. complete the test, then tactfully provide scientific references to the personnel director, noting that the validity and reliability of this measure are questionable.

17. The Rorschach and the TAT are considered
    a. honest tests.
    b. projective techniques.
    c. unstructured interviews.
    d. personality questionnaires.

18. Janet is taking the TAT. She is looking at a series of
    a. inkblots.
    b. genetic tests.
    c. observations of others.
    d. ambiguous-situation drawings.

19. Graphology, the psychological interpretation of handwriting,
    a. is among the lowest in validity and reliability of all projective measures.
    b. has successfully helped people change their personalities, by changing their handwriting.
    c. shows high reliability when the content of what is written is neutral, so that the handwriting sample is pure.
    d. should be used by employers who hire people to handle money, because of how well it predicts dishonest behavior.

20. You are writing a review article that evaluates a new personality inventory. Based on a potential problem with all personality tests, you title your paper
    a. "Beware of the Dog."
    b. "Beware the Ides of March."
    c. "Beware of Cheap Imitations."
    d. "Beware the P. T. Barnum Effect."

After completing the test, calculate your percent correct
(/ 20 =   ) x 100 = _____ .

How accurate were your expectations? Does your performance suggest the need for additional study? For the items you missed, go back and identify why the "correct" answer is the best answer.

AFTER YOU READ ... PRACTICE TEST #2

Before beginning this practice test, estimate the percent you expect to get correct.
Anticipated percent correct: _____

1. The idiographic approach to personality examines a person's _____, whereas a nomothetic approach to personality examines a person's _____.
   a. early history; sexual orientation
   b. common aspects; unique aspects
   c. global traits; individualistic traits
   d. idiosyncrasies; degree of being average

2. In terms of identical twins,
   a. a correlation of sharing a given trait that is lower than for fraternal twins indicates the influence of genetics on personality development.
   b. a correlation of sharing a given trait that is higher than for fraternal twins specifically indicates the influence of unshared environmental factors on personality development.
   c. a strong correlation for both twins possessing the same trait, even if they are raised apart, provides evidence for the influence of genetics on personality development.
   d. studies show high correlations for some traits, which points to the importance of shared environmental factors in personality development.

3. Except for minimal exceptions, molecular genetic studies find
   a. little consistency between specific genes and personality traits.
   b. great consistency between specific genes and personality traits.
   c. consistent results and so no further studies are currently underway.
   d. little consistency for half of all personality traits, and good consistency for the other half.

4. Your friend, Thasnim, is getting divorced for the third time, just like her mother did. She laughs about inheriting the "divorce gene." You respond by saying,
   a. "Yes, you must be right, especially if your dad and siblings also have high divorce rates."
   b. "No, you only had a 25% chance of inheriting that gene, unless your dad also had many divorces."
   c. "Well, I suppose it's possible for a single gene to control such complex behavior, but it would probably be numbered, and not named."
   d. "There is no such thing as a 'divorce gene,' although you might have inherited other genes that predispose you to make poor decisions in picking partners."

5. Your "id" is talking to you. It is telling you to
   a. apply moral values in satisfying wishes.
   b. pursue pleasure and satisfy biological drives.
   c. satisfy wishes through socially acceptable methods.
   d. push unacceptable biological drives into the unconscious.

6. According to Freud, any serious threat to the ego results in a state of
   a. anxiety.   c. misalignment.
   b. depression.   d. defensiveness.

7. Tanikwa is a 21-year-old who smokes two packs of cigarettes a day. According to psychodynamic approaches to personality, she
   a. has an external locus of control.
   b. may be fixated in the oral stage.
   c. may be sublimating an Electra complex.
   d. is exhibiting signals from her collective unconscious.

8. Perhaps the greatest difference between psychoanalytic and strict behaviorist conceptions of personality is that behaviorists, relative to Freudians, minimize
   a. their views of determinism.
   b. the importance of early childhood experience.
   c. our unconscious awareness underlying our own behaviors.
   d. explanations of behavior as a result of processing certain personality traits.

9. When a parent tells a child, "Do as I say, and not as I do," the parent is ignoring the principles of
   a. unconscious forces.
   b. observational learning.
   c. an external locus of control.
   d. our free will to depart from behavioral contingencies.

10. Behaviorists focus on external contingencies, whereas humanists focus on
    a. ego strength.
    b. trait analysis.
    c. personal growth.
    d. observational learning.

11. The lifelong process of striving to realize one's potential is known as
    a. self-promotion.
    b. self-actualization.
    c. ego enhancement.
    d. psychological narcissism.

12. Three important components of Rogers's humanistic approach to personality development are
    a. id, ego, and superego.
    b. the organism, traits, and collective unconscious.
    c. external contingencies, rewards, and punishments.
    d. genetic makeup, sense of self, and sense of worth.

13. Carlos is friendly, sociable, lively, and easy to get along with. Based only on this description, Carlos is probably high on the Big Five traits of
    a. openness and neuroticism.
    b. openness and agreeableness.
    c. agreeableness and extraversion.
    d. extraversion and conscientiousness.

14. After completing the Big Five personality test, which of these people's behavior will be most difficult to predict based on an interaction of culture and test results?
    a. Akina, who lives in a collectivistic culture. Her behavior will be modified by social norms.
    b. Indira, who lives in a collectivistic culture. Her behavior will reflect her personal goals.
    c. Amy, who lives in an individualistic culture. Her behavior will be modified by social norms.
    d. Chantal, who lives in an individualistic culture. Her behavior will reflect her personal goals.

15. One of the main arguments Walter Mischel levied against trait approaches to personality is that
    a. specific situations appear to be subject to behavioral inconsistencies.
    b. the roots of trait development in early childhood are overemphasized.
    c. the effects of culture are greater than traits could ever be.
    d. unconscious forces affect trait expression in ways that cannot be scientifically determined.

16. Phuong is taking a personality test with good reliability and validity. She must complete nearly 600 true-false items as they best describe her. She is probably taking the
    a. MBTI.   c. Rorschach Test.
    b. MMPI-2.   d. Thematic Apperception Test.

17. Projective tests
    a. are favored by trait psychologists because people with certain traits consistently interpret the images in similar ways.
    b. are favored by psychoanalytic psychologists because they assume test-takers project their personalities onto the stimuli.
    c. are favored by humanistic psychologists because the interpretation of ambiguous stimuli allows a clear picture of the "true self" to emerge.
    d. are favored by behaviorists because the images provide a direct stimulus for eliciting a clear response related to environmental contingencies.

18. A critique of the Rorschach shows that it
    a. has both high test-retest reliability and interrater reliability
    b. has little relationship between interpretations and actual disorders.
    c. contributes little additional information above and beyond more efficient measures.
    d. can detect faking by respondents, including particular disorders.

19. Juanita went to a fortune-teller at the county fair and was amazed at how accurate the fortune-teller was in describing her personality. It is likely that the fortune-teller's accuracy was due to
    a. ESP.   c. the Barnum principle.
    b. inside information.   d. projective techniques.

20. A tragic event in Sharon's life was the murder of her uncle. Because the police were making little progress in their investigation, Sharon's family wanted to hire a high-priced criminal profiler. You advise Sharon to
    a. save her money and watch all three *CSI* shows on TV—they use all of the same principles.
    b. go ahead with the plan; research evidence reliably confirms the success of trained profilers.
    c. save her money and call in the FBI. Their track record of solving crimes using profiles is excellent.
    d. save her family's money! Even chemistry majors with no training in criminology have been shown to provide more accurate profiles than professional profilers.

After completing the test, calculate your percent correct
(/ 20 =   ) x 100 = _____.

How accurate were your expectations? Does your performance suggest the need for additional study? For the items you missed, go back and identify why the "correct" answer is the best answer.

AFTER YOU READ ... PRACTICE TEST ANSWER KEYS

Practice Test 1.

1. c (p. 540)
2. d (p. 541)
3. c (p. 543)
4. d (p. 546)
5. a (p. 546)
6. b (p. 547)
7. c (p. 550)
8. c (p. 553)
9. b (p. 556)
10. b (p. 557)
11. d (p. 559)
12. d (p. 561)
13. b (p. 562)
14. b (p. 567)
15. c (p. 567, 570)
16. d (p. 570)
17. b (p. 571)
18. d (p. 571)
19. a (p. 572)
20. d (p. 574)

Practice Test 2.

1. d (p. 541)
2. c (p. 543)
3. a (p. 544)
4. d (p. 544)
5. b (p. 547)
6. a (p. 548)
7. b (p. 550-551)
8. b (p. 556)
9. b (p. 557)
10. c (p. 559)
11. b (p. 559)
12. d (p. 559)
13. c (p. 562)
14. a (p. 563)
15. a (p. 565)
16. b (p. 567-568)
17. b (p. 570)
18. c (p. 571)
19. c (p. 574)
20. d (p. 575)

AFTER YOU READ ... CONCEPT MAPPING ACTIVITY ANSWERS

ACTIVITY 1:
Of the four approaches to personality, the psychoanalytic is the most complicated. Complete this concept map to simplify this approach.

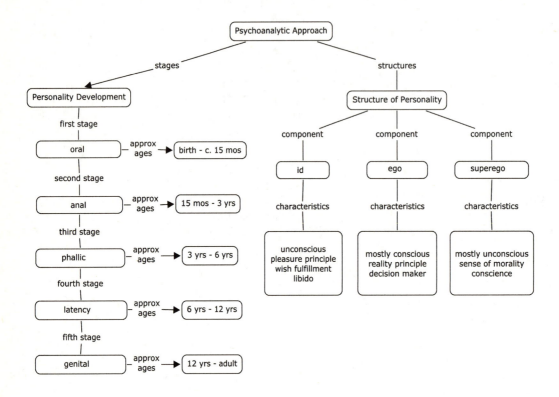

ACTIVITY 2:
Complete this concept map for personality assessment.

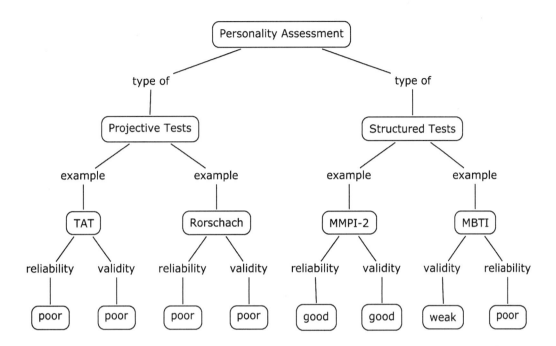

CHAPTER 15
PSYCHOLOGICAL DISORDERS
WHEN ADAPTATION BREAKS DOWN

BEFORE YOU READ ... CHAPTER PREVIEW

The most important issue in examining mental disorders is determining what distinguishes abnormality from normality. *Psychopathology*, or mental illness, covers a broad range of disorders and many researchers take a *failure analysis approach* to understanding its mechanisms. Five criteria define mental disorders, include statistical rarity, subjective distress, impairment, societal disapproval, and biological dysfunction. Because mental disorders share a cluster of features, many researchers argue for a *family resemblance view* of mental disorders. Throughout history, people have suffered with "demons," and early **demonic models** assumed demonic possession. After the Middle Ages, a **medical model** dominated. The mentally ill were seen as in need of medical treatment. Treatments included placement in **asylums**, bloodletting, or being tossed into a *snake pit*. In the 1800s, the **moral treatment** movement led to improved care. In the modern era of treatment, medication-based treatment has increased, especially *chlorpromazine*. Many mentally ill patients are doing better and have been **deinstitutionalized**, with *community mental health centers* and *halfway houses* used to care for them. Although some patients might lead normal lives, many cannot sustain a normal life because of their illnesses. Some psychopathologies are culture-bound, such as *koro* or *taijin kyofushu*; other pathologies appear worldwide, even if named differently, including schizophrenia, alcoholism, and psychopathic personality disorder. The general public has many misconceptions about psychiatric diagnosis, including that it just sorts people into categories, is unreliable, is invalid, and according to **labeling theorists**, stigmatizes people. In reality, diagnosis helps pinpoint problems and makes it easier for professionals to communicate. Diagnoses follow an official system based on the ***Diagnostic and Statistical Manual of Mental Disorders*** (DSM), in which the number of symptoms, their frequency, and duration are all considered. The **prevalence** (percentage of people in a population who have a disorder) is important. The DSM assesses people along several **axes** or dimensions of functioning, reflecting a *biopsychosocial* approach. Criticisms of the DSM include problems of **comorbidity** (some disorders tend to co-occur) and a reliance on a **categorical model**: you have the disorder or you don't. In reality, most disorders reflect a **dimensional model**. Except for a small subset of disorders, the mentally ill are NOT more violent. Also, many people don't understand that "insanity" is a purely legal definition and that the **insanity defense** is rare; even when it is used, it is rarely successful. Nevertheless, some people do need to be committed against their will; this controversial practice is called **involuntary commitment** or *civil commitment* (to contrast from *criminal commitment*).

The most common disorders are anxiety-based. Some, such as **somatoform disorders**, manifest themselves physically; others are mental disorders such as *hypochondriasis*. **Generalized anxiety disorders** are characterized by an almost constant sense of worry. In **panic disorders,** extreme anxiety comes on suddenly and for no apparent reason in the form of a *panic attack*. Many different types of **phobias**, including **agoraphobia, specific phobias,** and **social phobia**, are common. In **posttraumatic stress disorder**, a precipitating event results in persistent anxiety. In **obsessive-compulsive disorder (OCD),** a person has repetitive thoughts (**obsessions**) resulting in repetitive, unnecessary behaviors (**compulsions**). The explanations for anxiety disorders vary, including classical and operant conditioning models, *catastrophizing*, individual differences in **anxiety sensitivity**, and genetic and biological influences.

The second most common category of disorders are *mood disorders*, including **major depressive episodes**. Explanations for depression are complicated by biological, psychological, and social factors. Stressful life events can trigger depression. *Behavioral models* suggest that depression results from low rates of positive reinforcement. According to Beck's **cognitive model,** negative beliefs and expectations (a *cognitive triad* of *negative schemas*, as well as *cognitive distortions*) can bring on and maintain depression. Most nondepressed people have some *illusory control* over their environments, but depressed individuals exhibit *depressive realism*. Seligman proposed that a prior inability to control events in one's life leads to **learned helplessness**, accompanied by depressive symptoms. Twin studies provide evidence for a genetic component, and other evidence points to problems with neurotransmitters. When depression alternates with extreme elation and **manic episodes, bipolar disorder** is diagnosed, with high heritability. A serious consequence of depression is suicide. Suicide rates are highest in bipolar disorder.

Another category of mental disorders includes **personality disorders**, characterized by inflexible, maladaptive traits. **Borderline personality disorder** is characterized by instability in mood and impulse control. **Psychopathic personality,** which overlaps with **antisocial personality disorder** is characterized by superficial charm, self-centeredness, guiltlessness, risk-taking, and irresponsible actions. Some people with this disorder are not violent, although about 25% of prison inmates meet the criteria for this disorder. Explanations for psychopathic personality disorder show an inability to develop classical conditioning to painful stimuli and a general underarousal of the nervous system. The **dissociative disorders** are controversial. In **depersonalization disorder**, along with *derealization*, a person feels detached from the self. **Dissociative amnesia**, in which a person forgets important autobiographical details, is more severe, but not as severe as **dissociative fugue,** in which a person not only forgets important details of his or her life, but often ends up lost in a strange city or country. Finally, the most controversial disorder is **dissociative identity disorder (DID),** characterized by the presence of two or more distinct identities within a single person. Some people attribute this compartmentalization of different personalities to severe early trauma, but other evidence fails to support this explanation. Many cases of DID may be incorrectly diagnosed cases of other disorders. The number of documented cases of DID has mushroomed since a much-publicized case in the 1970s, which might have been a misdiagnosed case of schizophrenia.

The most serious disorder of all is **schizophrenia**. The term literally means "split mind" and many people confuse it with having multiple personalities within a single person. More accurately, it refers to a disordered single personality. Most schizophrenics cannot function on their own without both social support and medication. However, many of them can become functional with such support. Schizophrenia is characterized by **psychotic symptoms** which include **delusions**, which are strongly held beliefs that have no basis in reality. Auditory **hallucinations** are common, as are *command hallucinations*, although vivid visual hallucinations are rare. Speech can become highly disorganized, with thoughts rapidly jumping in the person's mind so that others just hear a jumbled *word salad*. In more severe cases, people might become **catatonic**, alternating between extreme bodily rigidity to constant, aimless movement. Researchers have examined the causes of schizophrenia and rejected parents and family members as "causing" this disorder (*schizophrenogenic*). Instead, researchers have found that the brains of schizophrenics show distinct differences, including enlarged *ventricles, hypofrontality*, and a disorder of the neurotransmitter *dopamine* . Finally, a strong heritability factor is also evidenced by family studies and twin studies. Currently, the dominant model is the **diathesis-stress model**, which focuses on the interaction between a genetic predisposition that is triggered by environmental factors. Only a fraction of the people with the genetic predisposition develop the disorder, although some develop a *schizotypal personality disorder*, in which symptoms are much reduced and everyday functioning is intact.

Childhood disorders have recently created much controversy in the general public, especially as regards **autistic disorder**, characterized along a continuum of language deficits and sometimes accompanied by mental retardation. Although the precise cause is unknown, recent hype about a discredited and debunked vaccine link was popular in the press, bringing this disorder to public attention. This link probably resulted from *an illusory correlation* between normal ages for development of language and receiving vaccinations. A milder form of this disorder is called *Asperger's Syndrome*. Another well-popularized childhood disorder is **attention deficit/hyperactivity disorder (ADHD),** which is characterized by high levels of activity in childhood, but which gradually decreases in adulthood. There are strong genetic markers for ADHD with serotonin, dopamine, and norepinephrine systems implicated. Finally, childhood onset bipolar disorder has been diagnosed more frequently in recent years, but this may be a result of inaccurate diagnosis.

BEFORE YOU READ ... LEARNING OBJECTIVES

After reading Chapter 15 you should be able to:

15.1   Identify criteria for defining mental disorders

15.2   Describe conceptions of diagnoses across history and cultures

15.3   Identify common misconceptions about psychiatric diagnoses, and the strengths and limitations of the current diagnostic system

15.4   Describe the many ways people experience anxiety

15.5   Identify the characteristics of different mood disorders

15.6   Describe how life events can interact with characteristics of the individual to produce depression symptoms

15.7   Identify common myths and misconceptions about suicide

15.8   Identify the characteristics of borderline and psychopathic personality disorders

15.9   Explain the controversies surrounding dissociative disorders, especially dissociative identity disorder

15.10   Recognize the characteristic symptoms of schizophrenia

15.11   Explain how psychosocial, neural, biochemical, and genetic influences create the vulnerability to schizophrenia

15.12   Describe the symptoms and debate surrounding disorders diagnosed in childhood

BEFORE YOU READ ... TERM IDENTIFICATION

agoraphobia (p. 599)

antisocial personality disorder (p. 612)

anxiety sensitivity (p. 601)

asylum (p. 586)

attention-deficit/hyperactivity disorder (ADHD (p. 591)

autistic disorder (p. 623)

axis (p. 592)

bipolar disorder (p. 609)

borderline personality disorder (p. 612)

catatonic symptoms (p. 619)

categorical model (p. 593)

cognitive model of depression (p. 606)

comorbidity (p. 593)

compulsion (p. 600)

deinstitutionalization (p. 587)

delusion (p. 617)

demonic model (p. 586)

depersonalization disorder (p. 614)

Diagnostic and Statistical Manual of Mental Disorders (DSM) (p. 591)

diathesis-stress model (p. 622)

dimensional model (p. 593)

dissociative amnesia (p. 614)

dissociative disorder (p. 614)

dissociative fugue (p. 614)

dissociative identity disorder (DID) (p. 614)

generalized anxiety disorder (p. 598)

hallucination (p. 618)

hypocondriasis (p. 598)

insanity defense (p. 595)

involuntary commitment (p. 596)

labeling theorists (p. 591)

learned helplessness (p. 607)

major depressive episode (p. 603)

manic episode (p. 608)

medical model (p. 586)

moral treatment (p. 587)

obsession (p. 600)

obsessive-compulsive disorder (OCD) (p. 600)

panic attack (p. 598)

panic disorder (p. 598)

personality disorder (p. 611)

phobia (p. 598)

posttraumatic stress disorder (PTSD) (p. 599)

prevalence (p. 592)

psychopathic personality (p. 612)

psychotic symptom (p. 617)

schizophrenia (p. 616)

social phobia (p. 599)

somatoform disorder (p. 596)

specific phobia (p. 599)

AS YOU READ ... PRACTICE ACTIVITIES

CONCEPTIONS OF MENTAL ILLNESS: YESTERDAY AND TODAY

1. Your text provides five guidelines for determining whether a behavior should be considered to be "abnormal." Briefly describe each of the five guidelines here, in your own words. Which one do you think is the most important? Why? (LO 15.1)

2. Consider a disorder such as anorexia, with which most people are at least somewhat familiar. Which of the five criteria for a mental disorder best describes anorexia? Do you believe that more than one criterion should be used? Which ones should be used? (LO 15.1)

3. Deinstitutionalization has led to both positive and negative effects. Outline several of each of the positive and negative effects. (LO 15.2)

4. T or F: Psychiatric diagnoses can truly be culture-bound. Explain your answer and provide examples as appropriate. (LO 15.2)

5. Psychiatric diagnosis is frequently made by assessing symptoms as well as their frequency and duration. How might this approach lead to the creation of diagnostic labels for behaviors that together describe problem behaviors? Be sure to consider how "labels" differ from "diagnoses." (LO 15.3)

6. Write out the four misconceptions about psychiatric diagnosis, leaving some space between them. Next, in the space you left, go back and briefly state the correct information about each misconception. (LO 15.3)

ANXIETY DISORDERS: THE MANY FACES OF WORRY AND FEAR

1. Match the symptom complex to the diagnosis for that disorder. (LO 15.4- 15.11)

a. Agoraphobia	1. Constant, underlying, worry and anxiety
b. Attention deficit hyperactivity disorder	2. Inattention, impulsivity, and overactivity
	3. Fear of being in open places and spaces
c. Bipolar disorder	4. Increased sensitivity to anxiety-provoking symptoms following a severe trauma
d. Generalized anxiety disorder	5. Unpredictable, sudden terror with racing heart rate and light-headedness
e. Hypochondriasis	6. Repeated thoughts to perform unnecessary actions on a repetitive basis
f. Major depression	7. A longtime lingering depressed mood that prevents normal everyday functioning
g. Obsessive-compulsive disorder	8. Having periods of deep depression followed by periods of manic hyperactivity
h. Panic disorder	9. Having disordered thought patterns, hallucinations, and delusions
i. Posttraumatic stress disorder	10. Continuous preoccupation of suffering from a physical disorder
j. Psychopathic personality disorder	11. Showing no sense of remorse or guilt for harmful behaviors
k. Schizophrenia	

2. Have you ever experienced an "earworm"? If you have, then you must certainly remember what it was. What was it? Were there particular times you seemed to experience it? Can you remember what you had to do to get it out of your mind? (LO 15.4)

3. Learning models of anxiety and explanations based on genetic and biological influences suggest an interplay between nature and nurture in anxiety. Based on the readings in the chapter, discuss how these two influences (learning and genetics) might interact to produce an anxiety disorder in an individual. (LO 15.4)

4. People who have been in therapy for anxiety and have seen a successful decrease in their symptoms often see them recur. How might anxiety sensitivity act to increase this vulnerability to relapse? (LO 15.4)

5. As you consider all of the major anxiety disorders, how could you tell whether a new college roommate might suffer from a specific anxiety disorder? (LO 15.4)

MOOD DISORDERS AND SUICIDE

1. A frequent analogy is made between depression as the mental health equivalent of the common cold. The authors of your text, however, argue that this analogy is not a particularly good one. Compare the two conditions: depression and the common cold. In the end, do you agree or disagree with your text's authors? Why? (LO 15.5)

2. Depression appears to beget depression: Most people do not really like to interact with depressed individuals. How might this lead to a vicious cycle that maintains depression? (LO 15.6)

3. If the interplay between nature and nurture is complicated for the anxiety disorders, it seems even more so for the mood disorders. Describe some of the complicated interactions of the contributions of nature and nurture to depression. (15.6)

4. Describe Seligman's (1975) study of leaned helplessness. (LO 15.6)

   Design:

   Results:

   Lesson learned:

5. How does bipolar disorder differ from major depression? What are some of the objective biological findings that discriminate between these two disorders? (LO 15.6)

6. Your new roommate seems sad, isn't eating, and cries much of the time. Describe specific behaviors and risk factors that would lead you to believe that she might consider attempting suicide, and might need intervention. You can see more risk factors for younger adults at http://www.yellowribbon.org/WarningSigns.html. (LO 15.7)

PERSONALITY AND DISSOCIATIVE DISORDERS: THE DISRUPTED AND DIVIDED SELF

1. In everyday life, we talk about people with a "bad" personality. Compare this everyday way of talking about personality to the way that psychologists talk about personality disorders. (LO 15.8)

2. T or F: Personality disorders are every bit as debilitating as schizophrenia or major depressive disorders. Provide evidence to support your answer. (LO 15.8)

3. A person is arrested for theft. He says he is sorry and will never steal again. How can you tell whether he is sincere or has a sociopathic personality disorder? (LO 15.8)

4. If extraordinary claims require extraordinary evidence, just what would it take to convince you that a person has more than 100 distinct personalities? Would you need to meet each one on a one-to-one basis? At which point would you be convinced that each one is truly unique and distinct? (LO 15.9)

5. Because many people have experienced either derealization or depersonalization, it shouldn't be too hard for you to find someone among your friends who has. Describe one of their experiences and why you think it would fit the definition of either experience, based on your text's description. (LO 15.9)

6. Differentiate between a dissociative fugue and dissociative amnesia. (LO 15.9)

THE ENIGMA OF SCHIZOPHRENIA

1. Although schizophrenia is the least diagnosed mental disorder, with less than 1% of the population suffering from schizophrenia, people with this diagnosis account for the largest percentage of patients hospitalized with any mental disorder. Why might this contradictory set of findings make sense? (LO 15.10)

2. Rather than think of schizophrenia as a single disorder, it might be better to think of it as a family or range of disorders. Which aspects of this disorder, as described in your text, would lead to this conclusion? (LO 15.10)

3. Your text describes schizophrenics as having a "flat affect." What does this mean? You may have to go to the web to find a satisfactory definition. (LO 15.10)

4. Differentiate between the various subtypes of schizophrenia. (LO 15.10)

5. Show how the diathesis-stress model of vulnerability to schizophrenia is a good example of the interaction of nature and nurture. (LO 15.11)

CHILDHOOD DISORDERS: RECENT CONTROVERSIES

1. How might confirmation bias lead a person to not only believe that vaccinations "cause" autism, but to actually strengthen that belief over time? (LO 15.12)

2. Compare autism to Asperger's Syndrome. If Asperger's Syndrome were considered to be part of a continuum of disorders related to autism, how might this affect the prevalence of autism? (LO 15.12)

3. One subgroup of individuals diagnosed with autism are considered "savants." Search the web for information on the prevalence of savants among those who are diagnosed with autism. How might the representative heuristic lead people to over-estimate this prevalence? (LO 15.12)

4. Attention deficit hyperactivity disorder is characterized by an inability to focus attention. However, there are instances where children who exhibit symptoms of ADHD in one situation do not exhibit those symptoms in other situations. What are the environmental effects that might make a definite diagnosis difficult to make? (LO 15.12)

AS YOU READ ... CONCEPT MAP ACTIVITIES

ACTIVITY 1: Complete this concept map for personality disorders, then read the assignment for Activity 2 and follow this model.

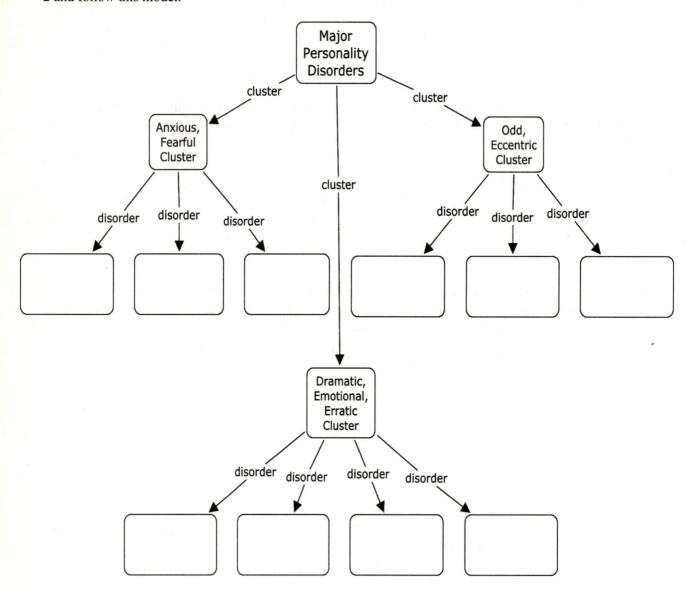

Author activity content supported by *IHMC Cmap Tools* Copyright ©1998-2007 Institute for Human & Machine Cognition

ACTIVITY 2: Make your own concept map for disorders. Be sure to include the major categories of disorders, such as anxiety disorders, mood disorders, personality disorders, schizophrenia, and dissociative identity disorder. Then include subtypes of each. You could connect these to nodes containing symptoms that distinguish each disorder. You can also connect them to related explanations via connections from multiple disorders to particular explanations, such as shared genetic components.

As You Read ... Myth or Reality?

Myth: Homeless people are too lazy to get a job.
Reality: Many homeless people are not able to maintain an independent lifestyle. In the past they might have been institutionalized, but following deinstitutionalization, many of these people who are unable to take care of themselves find themselves homeless.

1. Read about deinstitutionalization and its effects on increasing the population of homeless people at:
    http://www.pbs.org/wgbh/pages/frontline/shows/asylums/special/excerpt.html
    http://www.psychservices.psychiatryonline.org/cgi/content/full/55/10/1112

2. Has this information changed your perception of homeless people? How could you tell whether someone is "lazy" or is unable to maintain an independent lifestyle? Make a list of all the tasks it takes to live independently. Do you take for granted your ability to do these things on a daily basis?

3. What can you, as an individual in society, do to help the homelessness problem?

Myth: People who suffer from schizophrenia have a "split personality."
Reality: Schizophrenia is really the fracturing of a single personality. The more commonly accepted terminology of a "split personality" refers to the type of multiple personality disorder seen in dissociative identity disorder (DID).

1. You should be clear about the distinction between schizophrenia and DID. They are distinct disorders, one of which has been around perhaps as long as recorded history, and the other a newcomer to mental disorder diagnoses.

2. Review the two disorders and map out the differences between them, making note of the more prominent and less prominent symptoms that would lead to a diagnosis.

Myth: Most suicides are committed by 15- to 24-year-olds.
Reality: Most suicides are committed by males over the age of 65.

1. You can download suicide facts for the most recent year for which they are available at this website:
    http://www.suicidology.org/c/document_library/get_file?folderId=232&name=DLFE-242.pdf

2. Examine Table 15.10 in your text, which lists major suicide risk factors. Additional risk factors are available at http://www.cdc.gov/ncipc/dvp/Suicide/Suicide-risk-p-factors.htm. Evaluate how each of these might differentially impact 15- to 24-year-olds and those over age 65. Also, older white males in particular are more vulnerable to suicide. Why do you think this might be?

AS YOU READ... PUT YOUR CRITICAL THINKING SKILLS TO THE TEST

---

1. One of the biggest critics of the entire concept of mental disorders is Thomas Szasz. To quote Szasz from his book, *The Second Sin* (1973): "If you talk to God, you are praying; if God talks to you, you have schizophrenia. While people behave and think in ways that are very disturbing, this does not mean they have a disease." To Szasz, mental illness is simply another way of talking about behaviors we do not approve of, such as talking to one's self, going on spending binges, or taking another person's life.

   a. Consider the implications of this idea, that psychopathology is a myth, an epiphenomenon—a consequence of some other event, but not a real part of that event. Do you agree or disagree? Why?

2. Some people consider schizophrenia to be the ultimate attention deficit disorder. At times, people with schizophrenia cannot focus on any one relevant stimulus; at other times, they cannot disengage their attention from an irrelevant stimulus.

   a. For example, you can read abstracts of some of the work by Michael Posner and his collaborators at http://stinet.dtic.mil/oai/oai?verb=getRecord&metadataPrefix=html&identifier=ADA184483 http://www.blackwell-synergy.com/doi/abs/10.1046/j.1440-1819.2003.01150.x?journalCode=pcn

   b. In reading through your text, find examples of typical indicators or symptoms of schizophrenia that fit this idea of a disorder of the attentional system.

AS YOU READ... MYPSYCHLAB CONNECTION

Conceptions of Mental Illness: Yesterday and Today
What is mental illness? To learn answers to this question, **Watch** *Current Diagnostic Models: Sue Mineka.* Is escaping from slavery a mental illness? **Watch** *Drapetomania: Robert Guthrie.* For more on mental illness, complete the **Simulations** *Psychological Disorders, Overview of Clinical Assessment Methods,* and *Overview of Clinical Assessment Tools.* When reviewing the DSM-IV, **Explore** *The Axes of the DSM.*

Anxiety Disorders: The Many Faces of Worry and Fear
When reviewing anxiety disorders, complete the **Simulation** *Obsessive Compulsive Test* and **Watch** *Anxiety Disorders* and *When Does a Fear Become a Phobia: Sue Mineka.* **Listen** to a *Generalized Anxiety* podcast.

Mood Disorders and Suicide
Explore *Bipolar Disorder* for information on the seriousness of this disorder with regard to suicidal ideation. **Watch** *Nathan: Bipolar Disorder* and *Helen: Major Depression* to learn more about mood disorders and how they affect patients. For more on emotion and cognition, **Watch** *Interaction of Cognition and Emotion: Jutta Joormann.* For more information on suicide, **Listen** to the *Suicide* audio file.

Personality and Dissociative Disorders: The Disrupted and Divided Self
Watch *Janna: Borderline Personality Disorder* to view a real case study of an individual with this disorder. **Explore** *Dissociative Identity Disorder* to learn more about the clinical presentation of an individual with DID.

The Enigma of Schizophrenia
To review the different subtypes of schizophrenia, use the **Simulation** *Schizophrenia Overview.* **Watch** *Rodney: Schizophrenia* and *Genetic Schizophrenia* to learn more about the etiology, symptoms, and clinical presentation of the disorder.

Childhood Disorders: Recent Controversies
To learn more about autistic disorders, **Watch** *Autistic Children.*

AFTER YOU READ ... PRACTICE TEST #1

Before beginning this practice test, estimate the percent you expect to get correct.
Anticipated percent correct: _____

1. Lorena likes to put Tabasco sauce on her ice cream. Her favorite dessert is vanilla ice cream with strawberries, smothered in hot sauce. Most people might consider Lorena's taste in desserts "abnormal" based on which criterion of abnormality?
   a. Impairment
   b. Statistical rarity
   c. Subjective distress
   d. Biological dysfunction

2. Which of the following was NOT an early treatment for mental illness?
   a. Blood-letting
   b. Use of chlorpromazine
   c. Exorcism
   d. Placement in a pit with snakes

3. In terms of the modern treatment of mental illness,
   a. most of today's modern medications now offer a lifelong "cure" for most disorders.
   b. deinstitutionalization has lead to a large upswing in the number of people in mental hospitals.
   c. few if any of today's treatments offer a genuine "cure."
   d. the number of homeless people is now limited to those who are lazy and/or jobless.

4. In the United States, one is more likely to experience _____, whereas in China one would be more likely to experience _____.
   a. eating disorders; koro
   b. koro; eating disorders
   c. amok; windigo
   d. brain fog; amok

5. The criteria for validity of psychiatric diagnoses suggest that the diagnosis
   a. is more descriptive than predictive.
   b. can fully explain the person's behavior.
   c. provides the proper label for the individual.
   d. predicts a person's performance on various assessments.

6. DSM-IV
   a. refers to a book that lists the drugs that are used in psychiatry and their side effects.
   b. is a system of classifying psychological disorders.
   c. specifies ethical standards for the treatment of patients with psychological disorders.
   d. lists the diagnostic schizophrenic methods.

7. Comorbidity means that
   a. obese people tend to have more problems than thin ones.
   b. some problems are more life-threatening than are others.
   c. individuals with one diagnosis often shows signs of a specific other disorder, as well.
   d. some disorders fit better along a continuum, rather than being considered all-or-none.

8. Insanity
   a. can easily be faked.
   b. is a legal definition of responsibility for a crime.
   c. refers to a severe psychopathology, such as schizophrenia.
   d. is a successful defense in many criminal trials, as seen in the case of Andrea Yates.

9. _____ disorders are more prevalent than _____ disorders, which are more prevalent than _____ disorders.
   a. Phobia; mood; alcoholism
   b. Dissociative identity; anxiety; mood
   c. Mood; anxiety; dissociative
   d. Anxiety; mood; dissociative

10. Abdallah was sitting in class, when suddenly he started to sweat, his heart raced, he felt he was going to pass out and had to get out of the room, but could not move. Abdallah showed symptoms of
    a. panic disorder.
    b. a manic episode.
    c. schizophrenia.
    d. social phobia.

11. Studies of biological influences on anxiety show that people with obsessive-compulsive disorder seem to have a particular problem with the neurotransmitter
    a. serotonin.
    b. dopamine.
    c. adrenaline.
    d. acetylcholine.

12. Approximately _____ of people are likely to develop a mood disorder in their lifetime.
    a. 20%
    b. 40%
    c. 60%
    d. 80%

13. Jamal is depressed. To make it worse, he has isolated himself from his friends because he doesn't find any rewards in interacting with them. This isolation actually prolongs his depression. Jamal's situation illustrates the _____ model of depression.
    a. cognitive
    b. biological
    c. behavioral
    d. interpersonal

14. According to learned helplessness as described by Seligman, after several uncontrollable events in their life, people
    a. expend excessive effort to control their lives, resulting in exhaustion.
    b. attribute negative events to external factors and positive events to internal factors.
    c. just stop trying to effect changes and later fail to change controllable circumstances for the better.
    d. spend more time trying to escape from all circumstances in their lives, even the ones they can control.

15. Sophie has fluctuated between episodes of feeling sad and depressed, and at other times feeling energized and as if she can do anything. Sophie probably suffers from
    a. histrionic personality disorder .
    b. bipolar disorder.
    c. major depression.
    d. dysthymia.

16. Pam has been severely depressed for several weeks, to the point of not getting out of bed for several days at a time. With psychotherapy and medications, her depression is lifting. This could be a warning sign that
    a. her risk of suicide is actually rising.
    b. she is leaving a prolonged period of susceptibility to suicide.
    c. you should avoid talking to her about suicide because it will reverse her progress.
    d. she might relapse as she considers the time she wasted by being depressed, creating a vicious cycle.

17. In the movie *Girl, Interrupted*, the main character's behaviors showed an instability in mood, impulsivity, sexual promiscuity, and difficulty in controlling her emotions. She was (probably correctly) diagnosed with _____ personality disorder.
    a. avoidant
    b. borderline
    c. schizotypal
    d. psychopathic

18. As long as Ernie lines his underwear with aluminum foil so that "rays" cannot penetrate to his skin, he is able to function fairly normally on a day-to-day basis. He does, however, need to wear long sleeves and pants and keep everything lined. His fear of "rays" reflects a
    a. shadow.
    b. delusion.
    c. diathesis.
    d. hallucination.

19. Lottie has completely stopped bathing or taking care of herself. She was diagnosed with schizophrenia after a prolonged period of immobility. Although her doctor could freely move her limbs, she could not respond to his commands to move her limbs by herself. Lottie probably has the _____ type of schizophrenia.
    a. residual
    b. catatonic
    c. disorganized
    d. undifferentiated

20. The recent increase in diagnoses of early onset (childhood) bipolar disorder suggests that
    a. the increased number of childhood immunizations may be triggering the disorder.
    b. greater specificity in diagnostic signs have made it easier to diagnose correctly.
    c. if both parents have a strong family history of bipolar disorder, they should consider not having children.
    d. it may be overdiagnosed and requires more prospective studies.

After completing the test, calculate your percent correct
(/ 20 =   ) x 100 = _____.

How accurate were your expectations? Does your performance suggest the need for additional study? For the items you missed, go back and identify why the "correct" answer is the best answer.

AFTER YOU READ ... PRACTICE TEST #2

Before beginning this practice test, estimate the percent you expect to get correct.
Anticipated percent correct: _____

1. The oldest notions about mental illness reflected a belief that people
   a. had a physical disorder.
   b. were possessed by the devil.
   c. could best be cured with blood-letting.
   d. could best be cured with placebo drugs.

2. Chlorpromazine was developed to particularly treat
   a. bedlam.
   b. bulimia.
   c. drapetomania.
   d. schizophrenia.

3. Evidence for the reliability of psychiatric disorders comes from
   a. studies that show that they are valid.
   b. high agreement between different diagnosticians.
   c. different expert witnesses coming to different conclusions.
   d. predictions of how well people with a particular diagnosis respond to treatment.

4. DSM-IV
   a. lists more than 350 classes of disorders.
   b. provides labels everyone can easily understand.
   c. provides therapists with definitive diagnoses of their clients' disorders.
   d. includes diagnostic criteria for medically related problems, such as hypothyroidism.

5. Calvin has always been happy and healthy. Recently, while reading the chapter on psychopathology for his psychology class, he started to notice how often his heart races for no reason, and then he started feeling light-headed and broke out into a sweat. Most likely Calvin is now suffering from
   a. medical students' syndrome.
   b. generalized anxiety disorder.
   c. anxious personality disorder.
   d. panic attack syndrome.

6. The lifetime prevalence of developing any mental disorder is approximately
   a. 10%.
   b. 20%.
   c. 25%.
   d. 50%.

7. Natsumi is afraid to leave her home. She worries she will do something embarrassing and shame herself and her family. She is completing her college degree online, calls for home delivery of groceries to her home, and buys everything else at Costco.com. Natsumi has many of the symptoms of
   a. PTSD.
   b. agoraphobia.
   c. claustrophobia.
   d. social inhibition.

8. Howie is concerned about catching an illness. He avoids touching things in public and doesn't allow other people to shake his hand or hug him in greeting. Howie probably suffers from
   a. bipolar disorder.
   b. hypochondriasis.
   c. histrionic personality disorder.
   d. obsessive-compulsive disorder.

9. Studies of gender show that in terms of mood disorders
    a. no differences are evident between men and women.
    b. generally more men than women develop mood disorders.
    c. generally more women than men develop mood disorders.
    d. across cultures sometimes many more men and sometimes many more women are affected.

10. In which of these ways is depression MOST like the common cold?
    a. Both tend to occur more often in women.
    b. Major depression, like a cold, produces severe impairment.
    c. The symptoms can develop gradually over days and weeks.
    d. People can experience several episodes over their lifetimes.

11. According to Beck's cognitive model,
    a. depressed individuals have negative schemas and cognitive distortions.
    b. genetic factors dominate all other factors that might contribute to depression.
    c. early life events set the stage for later responses to stressful situations with depression.
    d. a low rate of response-contingent positive reinforcement is instrumental in the development of depression.

12. The mental disorder with the highest rate of heritability is
    a. bipolar disorder.
    b. major depression.
    c. panic attack syndrome.
    d. obsessive-compulsive disorder.

13. Personality disorders
    a. consist of a wide range of disorders that cluster along three main subtypes.
    b. are just a mild form of serious disorders.
    c. provide support for Freud's psychodynamic approach to personality.
    d. are coded on Axis I of the DSM-IV.

14. Hilda remembers going to summer camp when she was 10 years old. She remembers the beach, camp fires, and hikes, but she cannot remember any of the children or leaders. It is likely that
    a. she is repressing a traumatic experience from camp.
    b. a good hypnotherapist can help Hilda recover her memories of the other people.
    c. this is a perfectly normal example of forgetting something she hasn't thought about in a while.
    d. she has a dissociative identity disorder, and only one of her alters remembers the other people.

15. As a child Yumi's parents sent her for figure skating lessons. She is 18 now and never really developed into a very good skater. Nevertheless, she believes that she is Olympic gold medalist Kristi Yamaguchi, hiding from people who want to steal her gold medals. She spends all her time at the skating rink and does not work or go to school. She just skates around the rink whispering that she is Kristi Yamaguchi. Yumi probably suffers from
    a. a temporary manic episode associated with bipolar disorder.
    b. a delusion associated with schizophrenia.
    c. a narcissistic personality disorder.
    d. a histrionic personality disorder.

16. Which of the following is NOT a brain abnormality found among schizophrenia patients?
    a. The sulci are larger, resulting in less brain tissue in surrounding areas.
    b. The ventricles are enlarged, resulting in shrinkage of other brain areas.
    c. The frontal lobes are less active, possibly resulting in reduced ability to concentrate.
    d. The temporal lobes, responsible for auditory processing, are enlarged..

17. Studies of identical twins raised apart show
    a. a strong genetic component to schizophrenia.
    b. no evidence for a genetic component to schizophrenia.
    c. that the environment plays a role only if a history of schizophrenia is present in the adoptive family.
    d. a powerful effect of shared environmental factors, especially mothers, on the development of schizophrenia.

18. The finding that more people who develop schizophrenia are born in the winter and spring suggests
    a. support for a diathesis-stress model: viral infections that are more common in fall and winter might be a trigger for fetuses with a genetic predisposition.
    b. support for a family model: mothers who are vulnerable to certain virus infections carry the genetic predisposition to schizophrenia.
    c. support for a biological model: the prevalence of schizophrenia is very high in people with a genetic predisposition, if their mothers were drug abusers.
    d. support for an biochemical model: the preservatives in drugs used to treat viral infections appear to be a direct cause for schizophrenia.

19. The number of children diagnosed with autism is on the rise, which can most likely be attributed to
    a. the increase in the number of children getting vaccinated.
    b. the increase in the number of vaccinations each child is required to get.
    c. looser diagnostic criteria, so more children meet the minimum definition.
    d. the increased use of thimerosol as a preservative in children's vaccinations.

20. Children diagnosed with attention-deficit hyperactivity disorder typically
    a. show persistence of high physical activity levels well into adulthood.
    b. are easily diagnosed because their activity levels are so markedly different from those of normally active children.
    c. can concentrate for prolonged periods of time if something has a personal interest for them.
    d. often require tranquilizers to slow them down.

After completing the test, calculate your percent correct
(/ 20 =   ) x 100 = _____ .

How accurate were your expectations? Does your performance suggest the need for additional study? For the items you missed, go back and identify why the "correct" answer is the best answer.

AFTER YOU READ ... PRACTICE TEST ANSWER KEYS

Practice Test 1.

1. b (p. 585)
2. b (p. 586)
3. c (p. 587)
4. a (p. 588–589)
5. d (p. 590)
6. b (p. 591)
7. c (p. 593)
8. b (p. 595)
9. d (p. 597, 604, 614)
10. a (p. 598)
11. a (p. 602)
12. a (p. 604)
13. c (p. 605)
14. c (p. 607)
15. b (p. 608)
16. a (p. 609)
17. b (p. 612)
18. b (p. 617)
19. b (p. 619)
20. d (p. 625)

Practice Test 2.

1. b (p. 586)
2. d (p. 587)
3. b (p. 589)
4. d (p. 592)
5. a (p. 594)
6. d (p. 597)
7. b (p. 599)
8. d (p. 600)
9. c (p. 604)
10. d (p. 604)
11. a (p. 606)
12. a (p. 608)
13. a (p. 611)
14. c (p. 614)
15. b (p. 618)
16. d (p. 620)
17. a (p. 621)
18. a (p. 622)
19. c (p. 624)
20. c (p. 625)

AFTER YOU READ ... CONCEPT MAPPING ACTIVITY ANSWERS

ACTIVITY 1: Complete this concept map for personality disorders, then read the assignment for Activity 2 and follow this model.

The answers you should have properly placed in the diagram are:

Odd, eccentric: paranoid personality disorder, schizotypal personality disorder, and schizoid personality disorder

Dramatic, emotional, erratic: antisocial personality disorder, borderline personality disorder, histrionic personality disorder, and narcissistic personality disorder

Anxious, fearful: avoidant personality disorder, dependent personality disorder, and obsessive-compulsive personality disorder

ACTIVITY 2: There is no "right" answer to this one; a reasonable diagram of the interrelationships between concepts should be most helpful to you.

CHAPTER 16
PSYCHOLOGICAL AND BIOLOGICAL TREATMENTS
HELPING PEOPLE CHANGE

BEFORE YOU READ ... CHAPTER PREVIEW

Psychotherapy refers to a psychological intervention that helps people resolve problems and increase their quality of life. About 20% of Americans of all ages and backgrounds will receive some form of therapy. The probability of seeking therapy varies by gender and ethnicity. Patients who are better adjusted to begin with benefit the most. Therapy can be provided by a variety of individuals with a variety of backgrounds. Professional degrees include clinical psychology (PhD/PsyD), psychiatry (MD), and social work (MSW/LCSW). **Paraprofessionals** may have little formal training. Although consulting with professionals provides certain advantages, paraprofessionals may be able to provide needed hope, support, and advice. A word of caution: The term "*therapist*" is not legally protected or defined.

The image of the couch originates with the first of the psychotherapies, Freud's *psychodynamic* approach. According to psychoanalytic theory, therapy can help uncover the unconscious motives underlying behavior by *interpreting* childhood memories with dream analysis and **free association**, and by behaviors that occur during therapy, such as **resistance** and **transference**. Psychoanalytic therapists believe *insight* into the meaning of behaviors reduces guilt and distress, but that such *working through* is difficult. *Neo-Freudian* therapists are more optimistic about change and consider a broader range of influences on personality, including culture. **Interpersonal psychotherapists** attempt to discover unrealistic attitudes and work on developing social skills. Psychoanalytic theory can be criticized for its lack of scientific rigor and is based on anecdotal evidence from biased samples, makes unfalsifiable claims, and the claims that can be tested tend not to be supported. For example, research suggests that insight is not required in the relief of distress and few traumatic memories are repressed.

Humanistic psychotherapies are another type of **insight therapy** and share the belief that human nature is basically positive. The goal of humanistic therapy is to help people overcome their sense of alienation and actualize their potential. **Person-centered therapies** provide a warm, nonjudgmental setting that is at the heart of *motivational interviewing*, and in which the client can accept him- or herself and think more realistically about his or her situation. **Gestalt therapy** often uses the *two-chair technique* to integrate opposing aspects of personality into a unified whole. A scientific evaluation of humanistic therapies is difficult because the concepts are difficult to define and to falsify. Elements of person-centered therapy have been shown to be effective, but overall the results are inconsistent.

Group therapy is an efficient way of providing therapy. Group therapies offer the advantage of the group setting for individuals to practice developing skills. The best known of the group therapies is the *self-help group* **Alcoholics Anonymous**. Because only some people choose to participate in AA and a large percentage drop out, research is needed to clarify which alcoholics are best served by AA. Another form of group therapy, *family therapy*, views psychological problems as rooted in the family. Its goal is to improve communication and relationships in the family by using either **strategic family interventions** or **structured family therapy**.

Behavior therapies focus on change rather than insight. These therapies are based on the principles of conditioning. In **exposure therapy**, individuals confront fear-producing stimuli with the goal of reducing the fear through extinction. In **systematic desensitization**, clients learn to relax while being exposed to fear-producing stimuli in gradual steps. *Reciprocal inhibition* and *counter-conditioning* are used. **Dismantling** studies show that any single element might be effective either alone or in combination with other elements. In contrast to systematic desensitization, flooding therapies start with the most feared stimulus, followed by **response prevention**. Newer approaches use *virtual reality exposure*. Another form of behavior therapy involves **participant modeling**, a form of *observational* or *vicarious learning*, and includes assertion training and behavioral rehearsal. Finally, **token economies** and **aversion therapies** focus on the consequences of behavior. On the fringes, and thought to be ineffective, are *thought field therapy (TFT)* and *eye movement desensitization and reprogramming (EMDR)*. Behavior therapies are effective for a variety of disorders. An unsupported criticism concerns *symptom substitution*.

Cognitive therapies, such as *rational emotive behavior therapy*, suggest that irrational thoughts underlie psychological disorders. The goal of therapy is to identify and replace the irrational thoughts with more rational cognitions. Therapists play an active role, encouraging clients to rethink their assumptions. *Stress inoculation therapies* help clients prepare for stress by developing cognitive skills to minimize its harm. **Cognitive behavior therapy (CBT)** combines elements of cognitive therapy with purely behavioral approaches. These are called *third-wave therapies*. *Dialectical* behavior therapy addresses contradictions between opposing beliefs and behaviors. Others use an *eclectic* approach: drawing from all approaches to meet each client's needs. CBT has the strongest scientific support.

Meta-analyses show that although most therapies are more effective than no therapy and many are about equal in effectiveness, some exceptions exist. Cognitive therapy is more effective for depression; behavioral therapy is more effective for phobias. Some forms of psychotherapy can actually make clients worse, including facilitated communication, recovered memories, critical incident debriefing, and coercive restraint. Effective therapies share *common factors,* including empathic listening, hope that things will improve, and a new way of thinking. Some therapies challenge thoughts and teach skills. *Specific factors* of specific approaches offer mixed research evidence for their effectiveness. Advocates of **empirically supported therapies (ESTs)** point out that clarifying which therapies have demonstrated effectiveness with specific disorders is an important guide for therapists. Unfortunately, some therapies that lack empirical support nevertheless appear to be effective for various reasons. For example, individuals may feel better because of the effect of spontaneous remission, placebo effects, self-serving bias, retrospective rewriting of the past, or regression to the mean. Self-help books can help when the book is based on research and used by individuals who are motivated to read the book and whose problems are relatively minor.

Biological treatments are those that alter brain chemistry or physiology. Although many psychological disorders appear to be associated with chemical imbalances, biological treatments have been criticized for a variety of reasons. **Psychopharmacotherapy**, the use of drugs to treat psychological problems, began with Thorazine in the 1950s, and the number of medical treatments for psychological disorders continues to proliferate; we don't know how many of these medications work, and all of them have side effects—many of them serious. Although in most states only psychiatrists (MDs) can prescribe medications, a movement is growing that would allow psychologists, who lack specific medical training, to have prescription privileges. Other controversies include the overprescribing of medications to populations for whom the medication's effectiveness is not demonstrated. Critics of medication also point out that some therapies, like CBT for depression, have been shown to be as effective as medication with less likelihood of relapse. Most admit that medication should be at least combined with other forms of therapy.

Electroconvulsive therapy (ECT), another controversial treatment, involves brief electrical pulses to the brain to produce a seizure. It may be used to treat disorders, such a severe depression, that fail to respond to other treatments. It is a misconception that ECT results in drastic personality change or brain damage. **Psychosurgery**, at least as performed during the mid-1900s, did produce dramatic personality change. Today it is used only as a last resort in only a few cases.

BEFORE YOU READ ... LEARNING OBJECTIVES

After reading Chapter 16 you should be able to:

16.1   Describe who seeks treatment, who benefits from psychotherapy, and who practices psychotherapy

16.2   Distinguish between professionals and paraprofessionals and describe what it takes to be an effective therapist

16.3   Describe the core beliefs and criticisms of psychodynamic therapists

16.4   Describe and evaluate the effectiveness of humanistic therapies.

16.5   List the advantages of group methods and describe the research evidence concerning the effectiveness of Alcoholics Anonymous

16.6   Identify different approaches to treating the dysfunctional family system

16.7   Describe the characteristics of behavior therapy and identify different behavioral approaches

16.8   Describe the features of cognitive-behavioral therapies (CBT)

16.9   Evaluate the claim that all psychotherapies are equally effective

16.10   Explain how ineffective therapies can sometimes appear to be effective

16.11   Recognize different types of drugs and cautions associated with drug treatment

16.12   Outline key considerations in drug treatment

16.13   Identify misconceptions about biomedical treatments

BEFORE YOU READ ... TERM IDENTIFICATION

Alcoholics Anonymous (p. 641)
aversion therapy (p. 647)
behavior therapist (p. 643)
cognitive-behavior therapy (p. 647)
dismantling (p. 644)
electroconvulsive therapy (ECT) (p. 662)
empirically supported treatment (EST) (p. 653)
exposure therapy (p. 643)
free association (p. 637)
Gestalt therapy (p. 640)
group therapy (p. 641)
humanistic psychotherapy (p. 638)
insight therapies (p. 635)
interpersonal therapy (p. 637)

meta-analysis (p. 651)
paraprofessional (p. 634)
participant modeling (p. 646)
person-centered therapy (p. 639)
psychopharmacotherapy (p. 658)
psychosurgery (p. 664)
psychotherapy (p. 632)
resistance (p. 637)
response prevention (p. 645)
strategic family intervention (p. 642)
structural family therapy (p. 642)
systematic desensitization (p. 643)
token economy (p. 647)
transference (p. 637)

AS YOU READ ... PRACTICE ACTIVITIES

PSYCHOTHERAPY: CLIENTS AND PRACTITIONERS

1. How does the common image of psychotherapy differ from the reality? (LO 16.1)

2. T or F: There is no difference between psychologists and psychiatrists. Explain your answer. (LO 16.1)

3. Therapists don't necessarily need to be professionally trained to be effective. Based on the discussion of the characteristics of effective therapists and therapies, explain why this is true. (LO 16.2)

4. Review the characteristics to look for in a therapist in Table 16.2. How does characteristic #6 "My therapist uses scientifically based approaches and discusses the pros and cons of other approaches," reflect the characteristics of critical thinking discussed in this text? (LO 16.2)

INSIGHT THERAPIES: ACQUIRING UNDERSTANDING

1. The Skeptic's Dictionary notes that New Age therapies share an emphasis on past trauma, a determination to uncover the cause of the disorder, and a lack of interest in objective evidence. How does this description parallel the first therapy, psychoanalysis? (LO 16.3)

2. The Skeptic's Dictionary also describes psychoanalytic therapy as a search for what probably does not exist (repressed childhood memories), on an assumption that is probably false (childhood experiences cause problems), and therapeutic theory with little probability of being correct (bringing repressed memories to consciousness is essential to cure). Describe the research evidence that supports the idea that psychoanalysis is based on illusion. (LO 16.3)

3. Although both humanistic therapies and psychoanalytic therapies are interested in their clients' gaining insight into their disorders, they differ in a number of ways. Complete this table differentiating these therapies along the following dimensions. (LO 16.3, 16.4)

	Psychoanalytic	Humanistic
View of human nature		
Potential for change		
Therapeutic techniques		
Who interprets information		
Focus on the past		

4. Which of the insight therapies is based on a philosophical perspective? What is this perspective and how does it influence the goals of therapy? (LO 16.4)

5. AA studies are affected by self-selection and dropout. What characteristics would a study need to provide clear evidence for the effectiveness of AA? (LO 16.5)

6. What are the advantages of group therapy? Of family therapy? (LO 16.5, L0 16.6)

BEHAVIORAL APPROACHES: CHANGING MALADAPTIVE ACTIONS

1. Review the principles of conditioning discussed in Chapter 6. Show how the behavior therapies listed here are based on learning principles. (LO 16.7)

Exposure

Systematic desensitization

Participant modeling

Token economies

Aversion therapies

2. Sophia is a college freshman. She is so terrified of speaking in public it makes her sick to her stomach just to think about it. She just found out that one of her classes will require a presentation to the class for the final project. She cannot sleep or concentrate and has come to you, a counselor, for help. How would you help Sophia as a behavioral therapist? How would you help if you were a cognitive therapist? (LO 16.7, LO 16.8)

3. Compare the chapter's coverage on Thought Field Therapy (TFT) with the information provided at www.tftrx.com. What do you conclude about the effectiveness of TFT? Why do you think so many therapists (and patients) believe in it? (LO 16.7)

4. Cognitive therapy attempts to replace irrational with rational thoughts. Complete this table. (LO 16.8)

Event	Irrational Thought	Rational Alternative
Getting an "F" on a test		
A relationship breaking up		
Being let go from a job		

5. Cognitive-behavioral therapies will often help individuals identify irrational thought by recommending they keep a journal. Once thoughts are identified, the therapist might give the client homework assignments designed to test out their beliefs. We all think irrationally, at least occasionally. Such thoughts can lead to stress. Keep a journal for a week. Note the thoughts you have following events. At the end of the week, review the thoughts. How "rational" are your thoughts? How can you think differently about the events you experienced? (LO 16.8)

6. If therapies are based on views of what underlies psychological disorders, what beliefs would contribute to a therapist being eclectic? (LO 16.9)

7. Which type of therapist would say the following: (LO 16.3, LO 16.4, LO 16.7, LO 16.8)

"So tell me about your dream."_____

"It sounds like you may be feeling angry about that test grade."_____

"So we are going to start with a picture of the spider." _____

"You're saying you will never be happy without this person. Let's think about that." _____

IS PSYCHOTHERAPY EFFECTIVE?

1. Look carefully at the graph in Figure 16.4. Describe the effectiveness of therapy in your own words. (LO 16.9)

2. Which therapies are clearly helpful for which disorders? Why should therapists be aware of these relations? (LO 16.9)

3. Therapies with no demonstrated effectiveness can appear to be effective. Describe how each of the following might give the illusion of effectiveness: (LO 16.10)

    Spontaneous remission

    Placebo effect

    Self-serving bias

    Regression to the mean

    Rewriting the past

4. Self-help books can be beneficial in certain situations. What are the characteristics of such books? Have you ever read a self-help book? Do you think its success (or failure) was influenced by its meeting the criteria listed? (LO 16.10)

BIOMEDICAL TREATMENTS: MEDICATIONS, ELECTRICAL STIMULATION, AND SURGERY

1. What are the pros and cons of drug therapy? (LO 16.11)

2. Compete this table. (LO 16.11)

Type of Drug	Example	Disorder for Which It Might Be Prescribed
Anti-anxiety		
Antidepressants	Prozac	
Mood stablizers	Lithium	
Antipsychotics		

3. Just for fun … check out this flash parody
   http://www.astonishedhead.com/images/OVOID_123.swf.

4. Review the discussion of neurotransmission in Chapter 3. Describe how researchers think Prozac works. (LO 16.11)

5. A close family member has been diagnosed with a psychological disorder. Based on the research evidence, what would tell your family member about taking medication for treatment? (LO16.12)

6. What are the myths and realities concerning electroconvulsive therapy? (LO 16.13)

AS YOU READ ... COGNITIVE MAP ACTIVITIES

ACTIVITY 1: The chapter suggests that many forms of therapy are available. Many of these therapies are based on theories of personality or learning described in the text. Creating a map of the various forms of therapy (e.g., psychodynamic, behavior), their theoretical basis (e.g., unconscious conflict), and features of therapy will help you organize and remember the relations.

ACTIVITY 2: This alternative to Practice Activity 1 under Behavioral Approaches should provide you with a representation of the links between learning principles and therapeutic techniques.

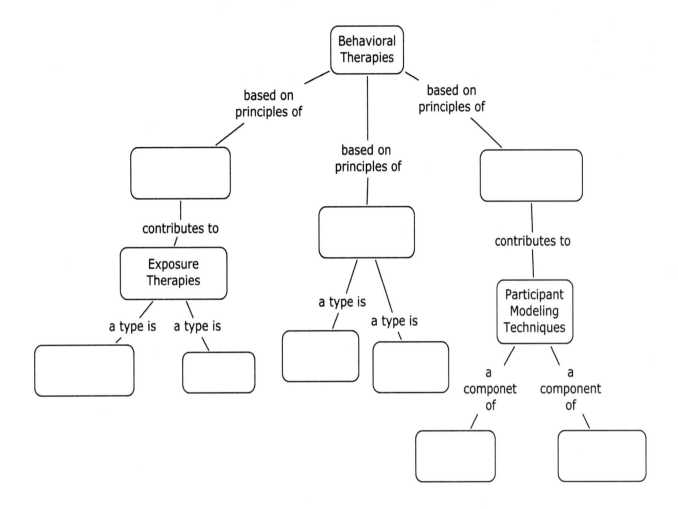

AS YOU READ... MYTH OR REALITY?

Myth: Psychologists psychoanalyze people.
Reality: Traditional psychoanalysis is rarely used today. Most therapists are eclectic in their practice, selecting from cognitive-behavioral and interpersonal forms of therapy.

1. Why do you think most people think of Freud and psychoanalysis as representing psychology?

2. Do you think telling them that psychology is more than Freud would convince them?

3. Look at some of these articles for a discussion of how difficult it is to change misconceptions.
   http://www.encyclopedia.com/doc/1G1-126582634.html
   http://teachpsych.org/resources/e-books/eit2004/eit04-03.rtf

Myth: Insight into the cause of one's disorder will result in dramatic improvement.
Reality: Insight is not required for success in therapy. Some individuals who improve do not gain "insight"; some who gain insight do not improve. In addition, it is not possible to know whether what is perceived to be "insight" reflects reality.

1. How is this insight myth perpetuated by film? Describe a film you have seen that perpetuates this myth.

AS YOU READ … PUT YOUR SCIENTIFIC THINKING SKILLS TO THE TEST

1. Despite some evidence that type of training makes little difference, some characteristics of therapists do make a difference. One of these is whether the individual responds to scientific literature. Read Tavris's discussion of the mind games. Why is scientific literacy a concern? http://chronicle.com/free/v49/i25/25b00701.htm

2. Searching for a therapy? Among the hundreds of "therapies" being practiced today, many New Age therapies are mixes of metaphysics and pseudoscience. Angel therapy, for example, works with your guardian angel to heal and harmonize every aspect of your life. http://www.angeltherapy.com/about_at.php

   The Skeptic's Dictionary suggests that the popularity of New Age therapies reflect a rise in irrationality as well as a demand created by talk shows and book circuits. Take a look at angel therapy or search for other therapies on the web. On what claims are the therapies based? For example, some New Age therapies believe children who demonstrate symptoms labeled ADHD are really examples of a newly evolved human species, the Indigo children (www.indigochild.com; http://skepdic.com/indigo.html). How do the underlying assumptions for these therapies and the support for these therapies differ from the EST discussed in the text?

3. In medical studies of antidepressants, "active placebos" (i.e., drugs that are not antidepressants but do have noticeable subjective or physiological effects) can produce substantial changes on measures of depression. http://www.biopsychiatry.com/placebo.htm
   Why might individuals respond more to "active placebos" compared with placebos without noticeable effects?

AS YOU READ ... MYPSYCHLAB CONNECTION

Psychotherapy: Clients and Practitioners
Explore *Psychotherapy Practitioners and Their Activities* to learn about the different career fields and professional training requirements. How do psychologists treat disorders? **Watch** the video titled *"Recent Trends in Treatments: Sue Mineka."*

Insight Therapies: Acquiring Understanding
For review on insights therapies, **Explore** *Key Components in Psychoanalytic, Humanistic, Behavior, and Cognitive Therapies,* where you can summarize and compare psychotherapeutic approaches. **Watch** *Carl Rogers: Role of a Therapist* to learn more about person-centered therapies. **Listen** as two psychologists discuss different psychological approaches to therapy and how they are applied in *Psychological Therapies*. **Listen** to the audio file *e-Therapy*. **Watch** the *Family Therapist* interview as she discusses the challenges and rewards of being a family crisis counselor.

Behavioral Approaches: Changing Maladaptive Actions
For more on evidence-based therapeutic approaches, **Watch** *Cognitive-Behavioral Therapy*.

Is Psychotherapy Effective?
Watch *The Secret* to learn more about this self-help book and how students should apply their critical thinking skills to the claims. How do you know it is your therapeutic treatment that resulted in a patient feeling better? Participate in the **Simulation** *Ineffective Therapies*.

Biomedical Treatments: Medications, Electrical Stimulation, and Surgery
Explore *Drugs Commonly Used to Treat Psychiatric Disorders* to learn about the different psychotropic medications that are used to treat psychiatric disorders. **Listen** to the podcast on *Antidepressant Warning Labels*.

AFTER YOU READ ... PRACTICE TEST #1

Before beginning this practice test, estimate the percent you expect to get correct.
Anticipated percent correct: _____

1. Joanna is having increasing interpersonal problems in her life. She is most likely to benefit from psychotherapy if she is
   a. Asian-American.
   b. Hispanic–American.
   c. experiencing depression symptoms.
   d. experiencing anxiety symptoms.

2. In some ways, Harry Stack Sullivan's neo-Freudian interpersonal therapy resembles
   a. behavior therapy because both emphasize classical conditioning principles.
   b. cognitive therapy because both emphasize stress inoculation.
   c. cognitive-behavioral therapy because both emphasize communicating to clients their unrealistic beliefs.
   d. humanistic therapy because both emphasize long-term talk and insight aspects of therapy.

3. Which of the following statements regarding psychoanalytic theory is TRUE?
   a. Freud is the founding father of modern psychological science.
   b. Freud's theory of catharsis that releasing aggressive energy relieves aggressive urges, has been supported by empirical research.
   c. By ignoring the falsifiabilty criterion, psychoanalytic theorizing contributes to an illusion of understanding.
   d. Psychoanalysis is the dominant form of therapy practiced today.

4. Which of the following psychotherapies emphasizes the individual's inherent potential for self-actualization?
   a. Behavior therapy
   b. Humanistic therapy
   c. Psychoanalytic therapy
   d. Cognitive-behavioral

5. Which of the following claims is TRUE?
   a. Most people's difficulties stem from the repression of traumatic events.
   b. Insight into the origin of one's problem is always a crucial ingredient in therapeutic change.
   c. Dreams are important in expressing unconscious content or foretelling the future.
   d. Psychodynamic and humanistic therapies all share a goal of expanding awareness and insight.

6. Which of the following statements about group therapy is TRUE?
   a. The self-help group, AA, has been proven more effective for alcoholics than other forms of therapy.
   b. In family therapy, usually one targeted family member is treated in therapy.
   c. Group therapy is more costly and time consuming than individual therapy.
   d. Groups provide opportunities for individuals to practice new skills.

7. Which of the following best describes the principle assumption of behavior therapy?
   a. All types of therapy are based on classical conditioning.
   b. Unconscious conflicts can be uncovered and eliminated.
   c. Problems in behavior are learned and can be changed.
   d. Symptoms cannot be alleviated until the causes are diagnosed.

8. Mike is a 19-year-old with a fear of bees. Whenever he sees a bee, even at a distance, he gets so anxious and afraid that he runs the other way. A therapist who sees Mike's problem as the result of learning
   a. is likely to investigate his childhood experiences.
   b. is a psychoanalytic therapist.
   c. is a behavior therapist.
   d. is likely to promote a biomedical treatment.

9. Ron has a great fear of final exams. Using systematic desensitization, his therapist first teaches him to relax. The next step in Ron's therapy will be
   a. to think about taking a major final exam.
   b. to make a list of his exam-related fears from lowest to highest
   c. to complete a homework assignment (e.g., take an exam and report back to the therapist).
   d. to question how rational his fears really are.

10. Research studies dismantling the components of EMDR suggest its effectiveness is likely due to
    a. exposure techniques.
    b. highly trained therapists.
    c. the brain alignment.
    d. eye movement.

11. Which of the following best represents the perceived cause of psychological disorders according to cognitive therapists?
    a. Problems are rooted in unconscious conflicts left over from childhood.
    b. Problems are rooted in negative thoughts and errors in thinking.
    c. Problems are rooted in biochemical malfunctions.
    d. Problems are rooted in conditioned behaviors.

12. An eclectic therapist
    a. bases treatment on the existential search for meaning in life.
    b. may use any of a variety of techniques, depending on the client and the problem.
    c. emphasizes achieving insight into the root causes of the problem.
    d. views maladaptive behaviors as expressions of unfulfilled wishes.

13. Psychotherapy outcome studies suggest that
    a. therapy is no more effective than a good friend and a bottle of Scotch.
    b. it is not possible to measure therapeutic effectiveness.
    c. therapy is indeed effective.
    d. therapy harms as many people as it helps.

14. Which of the following is NOT listed in your text among the key ingredients of effective psychotherapy?
    a. Insight into the cause of one's problems
    b. A new perspective
    c. A supportive relationship
    d. A sense of hope

15. Which statement about psychotherapy is FALSE?
    a. Therapy's major benefit is that it provides comfort, support, and a way to make positive changes.
    b. Therapy usually brings about a dramatic end to a person's suffering.
    c. Effective therapies provide hope and new perspectives.
    d. Spontaneous remission refers to improvement in symptoms with the passage of time.

16. Alicia was having problems in relationships so she bought the self-help book, *Change Your Life!* The book claimed its techniques would change your life and encouraged readers to attend the seminar offered by the authors. Alicia has now attended several seminars and bought every book and DVD available from the authors. Now despite the fact that Alicia is still having relationship problems, she is convinced that the Change Your Life program is effective. What might explain Alicia's thinking?
    a. Her investment in time and money has resulted in her convincing herself it has worked.
    b. Self-help books and seminars are effective in most cases.
    c. When we expect to change, we may adjust our memories of the past.
    d. The seriousness of her problems predicted this outcome.

17. Of the following individuals, who would be most likely to benefit from Prozac?
    a. Sharena is too afraid to go out with her friends to parties or other social events.
    b. Billie hears voices that he believes come from outer space.
    c. John experiences episodes of such incredible energy he doesn't sleep for days.
    d. Rhonda is feeling sad that her best friend just moved away.

18. Antipsychotic drugs appear to have their effect by blocking receptor sites for the neurotransmitter
    a. dopamine.
    b. GABA.
    c. norepinephrine.
    d. acetylcholine.

19. Which of the following statements about drug therapy is TRUE?
    a. Most medications improve behavior, while producing very few negative side effects.
    b. The use of Thorazine in the 1950s resulted in scores of "dehumanized zombies."
    c. Medication without additional support and psychotherapy is likely to result in relapse.
    d. Studies of children diagnosed with ADHD show that dietary restrictions are more effective than pharmacotherapy

20. Which of the following statements regarding electroconvulsive therapy is TRUE?
    a. ECT is painful.
    b. ECT invariably produces memory loss.
    c. ECT invariably produces personality changes.
    d. ECT is used in cases of very severe depression.

After completing the test, calculate your percent correct
(/ 20 =) x 100 = _____.

How accurate were your expectations? Does your performance suggest the need for additional study? For the items you missed, go back and identify why the "correct" answer is the best answer.

AFTER YOU READ... PRACTICE TEST #2

Before beginning this practice test, estimate the percent you expect to get correct.
Anticipated percent correct: _____

1. In which of the following ways are clinical psychologists and psychiatrists similar?
   a. They are similar in education and training.
   b. They are likely to work primarily in research settings.
   c. They are both authorized to prescribe medication.
   d. They are both trained in providing psychotherapy.

2. When it comes to paraprofessionals
   a. you might as well save your money and see a professional.
   b. there are rigorous standards in the United States governing their licensure.
   c. they lack professional training but fill an important gap in service provision.
   d. their background in parapsychology leads them to promote questionable practices.

3. Which of the following therapists would you want to see for therapy?
   a. Dr. Who is quite friendly and likes to chat about his family and personal life.
   b. Ms. Donno listens carefully to what is said and provides useful feedback.
   c. Dr. Sure is confident in his techniques because he has seen them help many people.
   d. Pastor Oneway sees prayer as the universal answer to problems.

4. Jeremy's therapist has asked him to recount his dreams and has interpreted the dream's content. It is likely the therapist has a _____ orientation toward therapy.
   a. humanistic
   b. cognitive
   c. psychoanalytic
   d. behavioral

5. The scientific evidence concerning "insight" in therapy suggest that insight
   a. by itself is not sufficient to relieve psychological distress.
   b. by itself frequently brings about relief of psychological distress.
   c. can help uncover repressed memories, therapy proving relief for psychological distress.
   d. must precede behavioral interventions for those interventions to succeed in relieving psychological distress.

6. Yolanda went to a therapist hoping he'd tell her what was "wrong" with her and how to fix it. Instead, she found that the therapist was expecting her to discover ways of dealing with her problems. It is likely that Yolanda's therapist is a
   a. humanistic therapist.
   b. behavioral therapist.
   c. psychoanalytic therapist.
   d. family therapist.

7. Which type of therapist would say "It sounds like you're feeling really angry right now"?
   a. A cognitive therapist
   b. A person-centered therapist
   c. A psychoanalytic therapist
   d. A behavioral therapist

8. Humanistic and psychoanalytic therapies differ in that
   a. humanistic therapies highlight sexual motivations.
   b. humanistic therapies are more positive about human nature.
   c. humanistic therapies focus more on unconscious motivations.
   d. humanistic therapies place greater emphasis on present relationships.

9. Lenita is afraid of flying. Her therapist taught her to relax and then asked her to create a hierarchy of stimuli related to flying that produce anxiety for her. The form of therapy Lenita is in is probably
   a. existential therapy.
   b. person-centered therapy.
   c. systematic desensitization.
   d. aversive conditioning.

10. Manny has been diagnosed as experiencing severe attention-deficit-hyperactivity disorder. He attends a school in which his teacher gives him poker chips following specific desired behaviors such as raising his hand to speak. It's likely this school is trying to modify Manny's behavior by using
    a. systematic desensitization.
    b. a token economy.
    c. exposure.
    d. aversive conditioning.

11. The meta-analysis described in your text evaluated nearly 500 studies of the effectiveness of psychotherapy. What were the conclusions of this meta-analysis?
    a. Behavioral therapy is more effective than psychodynamic therapy, which is more effective than person-centered therapy.
    b. Therapy primarily helps weak people; strong people do just as well without it.
    c. Overall, paraprofessionals and professionals are about equal in effectiveness in providing therapy.
    d. Therapy is effective in 80% of the cases, compared to no therapy.

12. The "Dodo bird verdict" refers to the finding that
    a. many therapies should become extinct.
    b. most therapies are equivalent in terms of their therapeutic outcomes.
    c. most therapies are for the birds.
    d. therapies that appear odd are often the most effective therapies.

13. Which of the following has been shown to be a potentially harmful therapy?
    a. DARE   c. EMDR
    b. Thought field therapy   d. Psychoanalysis

14. Which of the following is TRUE?
    a. Extensive professional training is necessary to produce good therapeutic outcomes.
    b. Behavioral therapies place a great deal of importance on insight.
    c. AA is more effective than other alcohol abuse treatments.
    d. Common factors may help explain why many different therapies are equally effective.

15. _____ is an empirically supported therapy for _____.
    a. Dolphin therapy; autism
    b. Laughter therapy; depression
    c. Interpersonal therapy; bulimia
    d. Critical incident debriefing; post-traumatic stress disorder

16. Tabitha had been feeling quite anxious, but since seeing her alien abduction therapist she now reports feeling much better. What might explain Tabitha's improvement?
    a. Spontaneous remission
    b. The Dodo bird effect
    c. Insight
    d. Removal of implanted probes

17. Your roommate is having problems with her boyfriend and has decided to go to the bookstore and check out the books about relationships. You recommend she look for a book
    a. based on published research that supports its claims.
    b. based on many years of observations of improvement in therapy.
    c. that promises positive results will be achieved for everyone, not just a few people.
    d. that simplifies concepts so they are easy to understand, like *Men are from Mars.*

18. Selective serotonin reuptake inhibitors (SSRI) are prescribed
    a. to help lessen the manic episodes in bipolar disorder.
    b. to eliminate hallucinations in schizophrenic individuals.
    c. to lessen symptoms of depression.
    d. to increase focus and attention in individuals with ADHD.

19. Elgin suffers from auditory hallucinations and believes that the people on TV can see him. Elgin's symptoms may be relieved by
    a. antipsychotic drugs.
    b. psychoanalytic psychotherapy.
    c. counterconditioning.
    d. psychosurgery.

20. Which of the following statements regarding drug therapy is TRUE?
    a. Medications today have few side effects.
    b. Changes in brain chemistry can only be produced with medications.
    c. Drugs are being prescribed for individuals whose behavior could be treated with other methods.
    d. The effectiveness of a drug in curing a disorder proves the cause of the disorder is biological.

After completing the test, calculate your percent correct
(____ / 20 =) x 100 = _____ .

How accurate were your expectations? Does your performance suggest the need for additional study? For the items you missed, go back and identify why the "correct" answer is the best answer.

AFTER YOU READ ... PRACTICE TEST ANSWER KEYS

Practice Test 1.

1. d (p. 633)
2. c (p. 637, 647)
3. c (p. 638)
4. b (p. 638)
5. d (p. 640)
6. d (p. 641)
7. c (p. 643)
8. c (p. 643)
9. b (p. 644)
10. a (p. 646)
11. b (p. 648-649)
12. b (p. 650)
13. c (p. 651)
14. a (p. 653)
15. b (p. 653-655)
16. c (p. 656)
17. a (p. 659)
18. a (p. 659)
19. c (p. 661-662)
20. d (p. 663)

Practice Test 2.

1. d (p. 633)
2. c (p. 634)
3. b (p. 635)
4. c (p. 636)
5. a (p. 638)
6. a (p. 639)
7. b (p. 639)
8. b (p. 640)
9. c (p. 644)
10. b (p. 647)
11. d (p. 651)
12. b (p. 651)
13. a (p. 652)
14. d (p. 653)
15. c (p. 654)
16. a (p. 655)
17. a (p. 657)
18. c (p. 659)
19. a (p. 659)
20. c (p. 661)

AFTER YOU READ ... COGNITIVE MAP ACTIVITIES ANSWERS

ACTIVITY 1:
The chapter suggests that many forms of therapy are available. A map of the various forms of therapy, their theoretical basis, and features of therapy is likely to be complicated and could take different forms. However, your map should at least include the following:

psychoanalytic therapy, humanistic therapy, behavioral therapy, cognitive therapy, unconscious conflict, alienation, maladaptive learning, irrational thoughts, free association, unconditional regard, operant and classical conditioning, challenging thoughts

ACTIVITY 2: This alternative to Practice Activity 1 under Behavioral Approaches should provide you with a representation of the links between learning principles and therapeutic techniques.

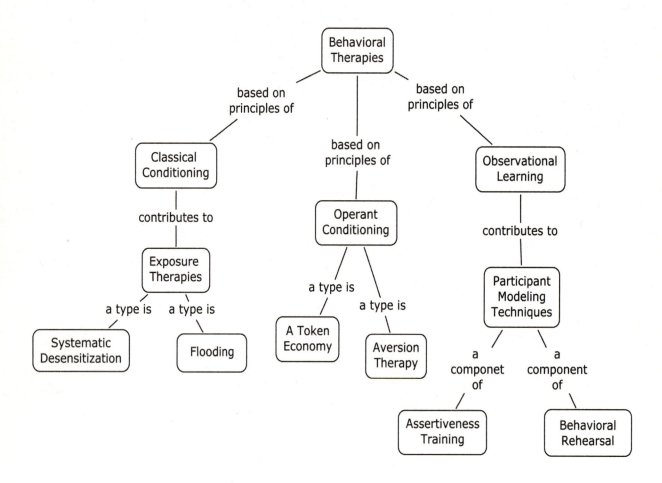